The Cybersleuth's Guide to the Internet

Conducting Effective Free Investigative & Legal Research on the Web

by
Carole A. Levitt, J.D., M.L.S.
&
Mark E. Rosch

I F L
PRESS
www.netforlawyers.com

©2011 Eleventh Edition
Carole A. Levitt, J.D., M.L.S.
Mark E. Rosch
Internet For Lawyers, Inc.
7820 Enchanted Hills Dr.
Suite A-215
Rio Rancho, NM 87144
info@netforlawyers.com
www.netforlawyers.com

Previous editions published under the title "Internet For Lawyers: How to Use the Internet for Legal & Investigative Research – A Guide for Legal Professionals."

Commitment to our readers: Internet For Lawyers is committed to providing the most credible and up-to-date information about the free and low-cost resources on the Internet that are useful for investigative and legal research. Because we are committed to serving our readers' needs, we welcome your feedback. We invite your comments about this book to iflpress@netforlawyers.com.

Since 1999, Internet For Lawyers has provided local and state Bar Associations around the country with professional and entertaining turn-key CLE programs for their members. Our seminars are popular with attendees and the substantial revenue those seminars generate is popular with our Bar partners. We also provide in-house training seminars for law firms and companies, as well as working with selected training companies.

Our programs focus on teaching legal professionals how to use the Internet and technology to practice law and research more efficiently and cost effectively.

We primarily offer all-day seminars, but can also create half-day seminars upon request. Some Bar associations choose to market two separate half-day seminars to offer their members maximum flexibility, while others have invited us to present multiple one-hour programs as part of an annual meeting or retreat.

The information contained in this book is useful to any individual who needs to locate investigative or legal information on the Internet – not just attorneys. It is provided as a service to the community. While we try to provide the highest quality information, we make no claims, promises, warranties or guarantees about the accuracy, completeness, or adequacy of any of the resources discussed in this book. Readers should not rely solely on the content of this book as the basis of their online research efforts. The sites discussed in this book are meant to be descriptive as a starting point for readers' research efforts.

This information does not constitute legal advice.

Because legal advice must be tailored to the specific circumstances of each case, and because we do not solicit or accept any legal questions, queries, or requests for advice, nothing provided herein entails, should be construed as, or should be used as a substitute for the advice of competent counsel.

If you are in need of legal assistance, contact the State Bar Association of your state and ask if they have a lawyer referral program. The American Bar Association has compiled a list of links to State Bar Association Web sites at bit.ly/6i8wP.

Cataloging-in-Publication Information
Levitt, Carole A.
The cybersleuth's guide to the internet / Carole A. Levitt, Mark E. Rosch – 11th ed.
476 p. cm.
Includes index.
ISBN 978-0-9713257-5-3
1. Legal research--United States--Computer network resources.
2. Legal research--Computer network resources.
3. Internet research
4. Internet searching—I. Rosch, Mark E. II. Title
KF242.A1L481 2010

Discounts are available for books ordered in bulk.
Special consideration is given to state bar associations, CLE programs and, other bar-related organizations.
Contact us at: IFL Press, 7820 Enchanted Hills Dr., Suite A-215, Rio Rancho, NM 87144; iflpress@netforlawyers.com, 888/393-6181.

ABOUT THE AUTHORS
Carole A. Levitt, JD, MLS

Carole Levitt is a nationally recognized author and speaker on Internet research. She has over twenty years of experience in the legal field as a Law Librarian, Legal Research and Writing Professor, California Attorney, and Internet Trainer. She is a skilled online searcher, focusing on legal, public record, investigative, and business research. With Mark Rosch, Carole co-authored three A.B.A. Law Practice Management (LPM) Section books: *Find Info Like a Pro, Volume 1: Mining the Internet's Publicly Available Resources for Investigative Research* (http://bit.ly/aoyj5D), *Google For Lawyers* (http://linkon.in/ayTg6U), and *The Lawyer's Guide to Fact Finding on the Internet*.

As President and founder of Internet For Lawyers (www.netforlawyers.com), she provides customized Internet research training to legal professionals (with continuing legal education credit). Ms. Levitt has presented at the A.B.A. TechShow; LegalWorks; LegalTech; the annual meetings of the A.B.A., The National Association of Bar Executives, the Association of Continuing Legal Education, and the California State Bar Association; the worldwide Gibson, Dunn & Crutcher corporate attorney retreat; law firms, bar associations; and library associations throughout the country. Ms. Levitt serves on the Executive Council and also on the Publishing Board of the A.B.A.'s Law Practice Management (LPM) Section. Previously, she was Chair of the California State Bar's Law Practice Management & Technology Section and served on the Executive Board of the Los Angeles County Bar Law Practice Management Section, among various other professional association activities.

She was a regular contributor to the *Los Angeles Lawyer* magazine's "Computer Counselor" column for eight years and has also written for numerous magazines, newsletters, and web sites such as *California Lawyer, Trial, The Internet Lawyer, Computer and Internet Lawyer, Research Advisor, Nashville Lawyer, FindLaw, CEB Case N Point,* and *LLRX.*

Ms. Levitt received her Juris Doctorate from The John Marshall Law School, where she graduated with distinction and was a member of the school's law review. She earned her Bachelors in Political Science and her Masters in Library Science at the University of Illinois. Ms. Levitt can be contacted at clevitt@netforlawyers.com.

Mark E. Rosch

As Vice President of Internet For Lawyers (IFL), Rosch is the developer and manager of the Internet For Lawyers Web site. He writes and speaks about how to use the Internet for research and on technology implementation for the legal community. With Carole Levitt, Mark co-authored three A.B.A. LPM Section books (see Carole's bio above). Mr. Rosch has also written about the application of computer technology in the law office for *California Lawyer, Law Technology News, Law Office Computing, Los Angeles Lawyer,* and the *Los Angeles Daily Journal* among other publications.

Additionally, he has presented at the Annual meetings of the A.B.A., the National Association of Bar Executives, the Association of Continuing Legal Education, the California State Bar, and in-house at various firms.

Mr. Rosch is a member of the A.B.A. and served on its LPM Section Education Board. He is also a member of the Association of Continuing Legal Education (ACLEA) and served as Chair of ACLEA's Entrepreneur's section. He has also served as a member of the Academy of Television Arts & Sciences' Public Relations steering committee, the Television Publicity Executives Committee, and the American Film Institute.

During his nearly 20 years of marketing experience, Mr. Rosch has developed and supervised the publicity, promotions, and marketing campaigns for numerous and varied clients, from legal portals to new media developers. He has also provided web management consulting to the State Bar of California Law Practice Management & Technology section's Web site and various law firms and solo practitioners.

He was graduated from Tulane University, in New Orleans, with a B.A. degree in Sociology. Mr. Rosch can be reached at mrosch@netforlawyers.com.

Stop Searching for information on the Internet...and Start Finding it Instead
Books by Carole A. Levitt and Mark E. Rosch

The Cybersleuth's Guide to the Internet
By Carole A. Levitt and Mark E. Rosch

The all new expanded 11th edition of the *Cybersleuth's Guide to the Internet* features Internet investigative search strategies and tips, the best federal legal research resources, as well as extensive information for locating state and local resources for all 50 states. This new edition also includes detailed reviews of the newest Internet resources such as Social Networking sites. It also includes detailed recommendations for free public records, investigative and people finder resources available for free on the Internet, as well as low-cost pay services, such as Merlin and Accurint and free sources for case law such as Justia and PLoL and low-cost case law sources like FastCase and CaseMaker.
2010 8.5x11 420 pages   Paperback **$64.95**

Google for Lawyers: Essential Search Tips and Productivity Tools
By Carole A. Levitt and Mark E. Rosch

Designed to help lawyers learn how they can put all of Google's power to work in their practices, this guide will unlock access to various free Google services. From the lesser-known Google Voice, Google Scholar, and Google Translate to the better-known office applications such as Gmail, Google Docs, and Google Calendar, these services can make novice, intermediate, and advanced users alike, more productive attorneys. The book's tips, tactics, strategies and free office applications will make it one of the most powerful weapons in your arsenal.
2010 7x10 544 pages   Paperback **$79.95**

Find Info Like a Pro, Volume 1: Mining the Internet's Publicly Available Resources for Investigative Research
By Carole A. Levitt and Mark E. Rosch

This complete hands-on guide shares the secrets, shortcuts, and realities of conducting investigative and background research using the sources of publicly available information searchable on the Internet. The guide lists, categorizes, and describes hundreds of free and fee-based Internet sites which are useful for investigations, depositions, locating missing witnesses, clients, or heirs, trial preparation, and much more. In addition, a CD-ROM is included which features clickable links to all of the sites contained in the book.
2010 7x10 408 pages   Paperback + CD-ROM **$79.95**

YES! I want to order _____ copy/copies) of **Cybersleuth's Guide to the Internet** for $_____
Find Info Like a Pro, Volume 1 for $_____ and/or _____ copy/copies) of **Google for Lawyers** for $ _____
+ $6.25 (shipping) = $ _____ TOTAL

Payment: ☐ Check enclosed payable to Internet For Lawyers   ☐ VISA   ☐ MasterCard   ☐ American Express

Acct.#_____Exp. Date_____Signature _____

Name: _____   V Code: _____

Firm/Org: _____

Address: _____

_____

City, State & Zip: _____

Phone: _____   E-mail: _____

Mail to:
Internet For Lawyers
7820 Enchanted Hills Bl
Suite A-215
Rio Rancho, NM 87144

Internet For Lawyers • Phone: **888-393-6181**• Fax: **678-550-1632**

Who Should Use This Book

The Cybersleuth's Guide to the Internet is meant to be a guide to free and low cost resources for any one who needs to conduct investigative and legal research on the Internet. The book starts off at the "beginning" laying out Web browser functions some Web users might be less familiar with. It then lays the groundwork of how search engines locate and retrieve the information we're searching for before it moves on to discuss more sophisticated search techniques and then how to apply those techniques to other Web sites to locate the information you're looking for.

Because the vast majority of sites discussed in this book are freely available on the Internet many of these resources could be located through Web searches – if you had the time to conduct those searches, sift through all of the results, and test out the sites until you'd culled down the millions of potential sites to a list of the most credible, relevant, and useful.

How to Use This Book

The Cybersleuth's Guide to the Internet is a reference book; it is not meant to be read cover to cover. We have tried to organize this book the way researchers think – by keeping like topics together. There are a number of concepts and search strategies that are applicable to types of research we discuss in different chapters. Therefore, some strategies appear in more than one place in the book to keep the back and forth page flipping to a minimum.

Throughout the book we have adopted a number of conventions to distinguish different types of information.

- Web site names are **boldfaced** to make them stand out on the page when you're scanning for them.
- Text that appears on Web pages like the labels on pull-down menus or search fields (e.g., *Search* or *Last Name*) are *italicized* to make them unique from the site descriptions.
- In our sample searches, the *search terms*, *keywords*, or *phrases* that we enter into search boxes are *italicized* to make them unique from the site descriptions.

We've made locating all of the Web sites in the book easy by creating a full index of more than 1,200 entries. Sites are indexed by site name (e.g., Google), type of site (e.g., Search Engine: Google), and type of information they contain (e.g., Bankruptcy Dockets: PACER).

What's New in the 11ᵗʰ Edition – 100 Pages of New Information!

The three things we can count on when it's time to revise *The Cybersleuth's Guide to the Internet* are:

- many of the sites in the book have changed some features or functions
- there are a number of new useful Web sites to add
- some Web sites no longer exist

The 11ᵗʰ edition is no exception. The function of every Web site discussed in the previous edition has been verified and updated for this edition. Many sites have added (or taken away) functions and features – and those changes have been noted in the sites' descriptions in this new edition. To illustrate those changes, we captured hundreds of new screenshots. In addition to all of those changes, the following is just some of the new information covered in this edition:

- Adobe Acrobat Pro Extended 9 – More features highlighted and added more screenshots
- AltLaw.org – No longer online (Free case law database)
- BlogPulse
- Casemaker – New interface and features (Free "member benefit" case law database)
- Cornell LII – New design/interface
- Facebook – Expanded discussion and added screen shots
- Fastcase – New features (Free "member benefit" case law database)
- FDsys – More "collections" added to new GPO search interface
- Google – New search feature (Google Instant)
- Google – New display of search results (Search Tools, Updates, Timeline, Wonder Wheel, etc.)
- Google Scholar – New free databases: case law, articles, and patents
- Google Patent Search
- ImageToss – Image search engine
- InCite (Free "member benefit" case law database)

- Law.gov – Free access to legal materials initiative
- MySpace – Expanded discussion and added screen shots
- PACER – New Features (Case Locator, etc.) and new pricing
- PicSearch – Image search engine
- PreCYdent – No longer online (Free case law database)
- RECAP – New free docket database
- Search Engine Features Comparison Chart – Updated
- Search Systems – New interface
- Social Networking – Expanded discussion and added screen shots
- Twitter – Expanded discussion and added screen shots
- U.S. Supreme Court of the United States – New interface
- U.S. Territorial Resources added
- U.S. Tribal Resources added
- USA.gov – New design/interface
- Yippy.com (Formerly Clusty)

TABLE OF CONTENTS

Chapter One

INTRODUCTION TO THE INTERNET AND WEB BROWSERS

STARTING AT THE BEGINNING

This is a book about using the Internet for free (and low cost) investigative and legal research. The information in this book can be useful to Internet searchers of all comfort and skill levels.

For those of you who are regular Internet searchers, and are comfortable with the functions of your Web browser, you can probably skip *Chapter One*.

For those less comfortable with searching on the Internet, *Chapter One* should not be skipped.

WHAT IS THE INTERNET?

The Internet is a worldwide group of public and private computers linked together in a network to share information. It is not owned or regulated by anyone, but is a free, universal, shared resource. The Internet began as a Department of Defense project in the 1960s to create a communications network that could survive a nuclear attack. For the first twenty years, only the government, universities, and large corporations used the Internet. Beginning in approximately 1993, it became more available to the public at large. Now there are numerous consumer uses of the Internet, including communicating via e-mail, accessing shared information (news, research, stock quotes, etc.), participating in discussion groups, joining social networks, listening to music, and purchasing products (e-commerce), to name just a few.

WEB BROWSERS

The most common use of the Internet is to locate information by accessing the World Wide Web (WWW). The Web, as it is often referred to for short, is a collection of electronically linked files (Web pages) stored on millions of individual computers around the world. A Web site is an inter-connected collection of these Web pages, usually created by the same individual or organization. A home page is the first page of the site. Web sites can range from plain text, graphics, and animation, to specialized formats used primarily to display highly formatted documents such as forms (PDF), full-motion video, or animation. A Web browser, such as Microsoft Internet Explorer® (IE) or Firefox, is the software that permits you to locate and view these Web pages.

Initially, Netscape Communicator/Navigator was the most popular browser among Web users. Over time, however, Internet Explorer became the dominant browser with more than 90 percent of those on the Web using it to access sites. More recently, Firefox has gained in popularity as an alternative to Internet Explorer, with approximately 25 percent of those on the Web using it to access sites in June 2010. In September 2008, Google launched its Chrome browser. By June 2010, its market share was reportedly still in the single digits – between three and seven percent, depending on the report. Still, as of June 2010, nearly 60 percent of computer users access Web pages with Internet Explorer.

Because of its popularity, the following pages will illustrate the anatomy and functions of Version 8 of this most-often-used browser.

Microsoft Internet Explorer® is a registered trademark of Microsoft Corporation.

Note that as of this writing, a Version 9 of Internet Explorer is in development, but not yet available for review.

Title Bar

The dark blue strip across the top of the screen (see the illustration on the next page) is the "Title Bar." It displays the title of the current Web page (e.g., *The Blogs of Law | A Blawg Directory*) that you are viewing and the name of the browser.

Address Bar

The long white box near the top of the browser window is the "Address Bar." To reach a Web site using a browser, you need to type the site's address into the Address Bar. The technical name for the "address" which consists of the entire *http* string, is "URL" (Uniform Resource Locator). The part after the *www* (e.g., "theblogsoflaw.com") is known as the "domain" name.

Menu Bar

The next bar down (that begins with the word *File*) is the "Menu Bar" (see screenshot above). The Menu Bar is similar to the menu bar of any Windows program such as Word or WordPerfect. The *File* pull-down menu permits you to open, close, save, print, and send. The *Send* option allows you to send, via e-mail, the page or link you are viewing. You can also create a "shortcut" to the page you are viewing and put it on your computer desktop. A single click on this shortcut will take you directly back to that Web page. (See page 15 for information about saving pages as "Favorites.")

Internet Explorer allows you to save a Web page (such as the one below) to your own computer's hard drive. To do so, go to *File* and choose *Save as* from the menu (*Steps 1* and *2* below).

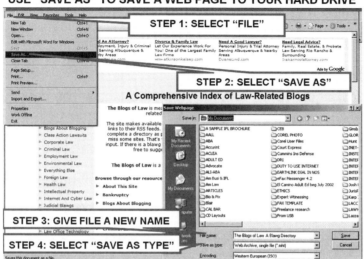

In the *Save in* box, browse through the folders on your hard drive to choose the folder where you want to save the file (*The Blogs of Law*). In the *File name* box (*Step 3* above), you can type a new file name ("TheBlogsofLaw.com"). In the *Save as type* box (*Step 4* above), you can choose from four different ways to save the page:

- *Webpage HTML Only* — saves just the HTML code (the programming language used to create most Web pages), but not graphics, audio, or other files; most of the Web page's original formatting will be lost

- *Webpage, complete* — saves the HTML code and the individual components (the graphics, audio, and other files) stored in their own folder on your hard drive and preserves the original formatting

- *Web Archive, single file* — saves all of the same information as a *Webpage, Complete*, but saves it into a single file

- *Text File* — saves only the visible text of the Web page you're viewing This allows you to easily open the file as a word processing document at a later date if you want to copy and paste portions of the Web page into a document you're writing.

Clicking the *Save* button in this dialog box adds the file to your computer's hard drive.

Saving a page in either of the first two formats allows you to later open the document in your Web browser. Both will retain the layout and formatting of the original Web page as it was first viewed. However, the third option (*Web Archive, single file*) will not only provide the most faithful recreation of the page as it appeared when it was viewed on the Web, it will also give you a copy of the graphic or audio files that could be taken down by the site's owner and no longer available to you on a subsequent visit to the Web page.

It's important to note that once you've saved a Web page in any of these formats to your own computer, with the right know-how you could alter the text, graphics, audio, or any content of the Web page (stored on your own computer) to say whatever you'd like. So, if you'll need to use your copy later as proof of something that was posted on the Web page that might have been changed, it is important that you document the date and time you saved the page, what its contents were at that time, etc. Also, burning a copy of the saved file(s) to a CD-ROM (where they cannot be easily changed) that shows the date on which you captured your copy of the page could be useful.

Downloading Information from Web Pages

Some Web sites offer you the choice of downloading (saving) documents found on the Internet as *Text* or *PDF* (another program format used to create Web-accessible documents). Choose *Text* if you want to download the material in a format easily accessible to your word processing software (and you want to be able to later manipulate the text; e.g., copy and paste it into one of your documents) or choose *PDF* to download what is essentially a "picture" of the document you're looking at (if you do not need to later manipulate the text). This version of the document would retain all of the formatting, fonts, colors, columns, tables, etc., of the original document—the same as if someone faxed you a copy. The PDF file format is often used for forms.

To view PDF files, you must have the Adobe's Reader program loaded onto your computer. The Adobe Reader is available for free on the Internet at http://get.adobe.com/reader/. The free Adobe Reader does not allow you to edit the PDF files. To edit them, you will need to buy the full version of the Adobe Acrobat software (http://store.adobe.com/store/main.jhtml) or a similar program.

Printing Web Pages

Printing pages from the Internet is not very different from printing a word processing document. Like word processing documents, you have a choice of how to initiate the printing process. Clicking on the "printer" icon sends all of the content of the Web page you're viewing to your connected printer. One important thing to note is that a Web "page" can be much longer than just one printed page or one screen. Clicking that "printer" icon can therefore deliver an untold number of printed pages if the page you are viewing is actually a long article or SEC filing.

PRINT A WEB PAGE YOU'RE VIEWING

STEP 1: SELECT "PRINTER" ICON HERE...

OR STEP 1: SELECT "PRINT HERE"

STEP 3: INDICATE SPECIFIC PAGES TO PRINT USING THE "PAGE RANGE" FUNCTION

To have more control over the number of pages you send to the printer, select *File* and *Print* (on the Menu Bar). This will pop up a *Print* dialog box. To print specific pages, click *Pages* in the *Print range* box and type in the page numbers (*Step 3* above). You can use the *Print Preview* function to see what content will appear on which printed page.

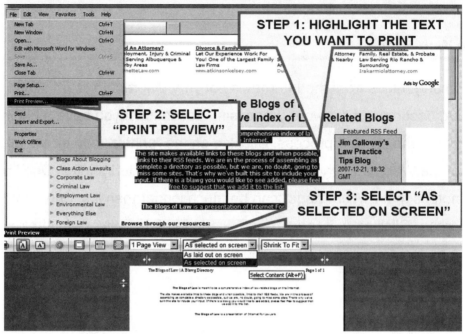

PRINT A PORTION OF THE WEB PAGE YOU'RE VIEWING

You can opt to print a portion of a page or a frame by highlighting the portion first and then selecting the *Print Preview* function (*Step 2* above). The *Print Preview* screen has a drop-down menu from which you can select *As Selected on Screen* to print only the area you've highlighted (*Step 3* above). You can also *Print to File*, which saves the page as a specially formatted printer file on your computer hard drive. (If you want to save an electronic version of the Web page to your computer's hard drive to access or manipulate later, see also the "Save" section earlier in this chapter.)

Additional options are available by clicking the *Options* tab in the *Print* dialog box. Clicking the *Options* tab gives you the ability to *Print all linked documents* which, as the name implies, prints the entire page you're viewing AND any pages that are linked to it. (BEWARE: That could be A LOT of pages.) You can also choose to print the specific page you're viewing and a *Table of links* that shows a list of other Web pages linked to the one you are viewing.

The most useful selection in the *Edit* pull-down menu is *Find on this Page*, which takes you directly to any search term you choose. Choosing the *Find on this Page* option opens a dialog box that allows you to type in any word or phrase you're looking for on the Web page you're viewing (*Step 3* below). Clicking the *Next* button takes you directly to your search term and highlights it. Clicking the *Next* button again takes you to the next instance of your search term on the Web page you're viewing (*Step 4* below). Version 8 of Internet Explorer also displays the number of times your search term appears on the page and highlights each occurrence on the page.

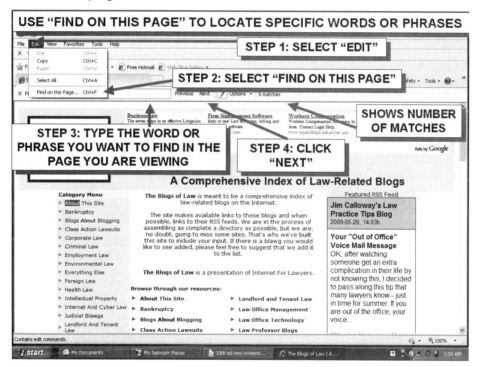

The *Edit* pull-down menu (on the browser's "Menu Bar") also permits you to copy text from most Web pages and paste it into your own e-mail or word processing document. The browser's *Copy* and *Paste* functions work the same way as the corresponding functions in Word or WordPerfect.

View Function

The *View* pull-down menu allows you to change the look of your browser window and the Web pages that appear in it. To make pages easier to read, you can increase or decrease the size of the Web page's text using the *Text Size* or *Zoom* features. (Those who prefer keyboard shortcuts, can press *Ctrl +* or *Ctrl -* to *Zoom* in or out of the Web page you're viewing.)

You can also hide the Menu Bar, Address Bar, etc., to increase the area of your browser window.

Tools

By clicking on *Internet Options* under *Tools* (located on the Menu Bar — see below), you can further customize your browser. For example, you can select your "home page" (the Web page that pops up when you first open the browser).

Version 8 of Internet Explorer also makes it easy for you to clear your computer of any temporary files your browser has saved on your hard drive. Over time, these temporary files can take up a substantial amount of disk space. These temporary files also provide a "Hansel-and-Gretel-like" trail of your Internet activity. Knowledgeable individuals could follow that trail if they gain access to your computer remotely (by hacking) or by using your computer when you're not around. For these, and other reasons, it's a good idea to delete this information regularly. Three of the most common of these temporary files are "Cookies," "Cache," and "History."

Cookies are small pieces of information that (some) Web sites you have visited write to your hard drive. Usually, these cookies are used by the site to recognize you on a return visit. Some advertising banners can also write a cookie to your hard drive to track the effectiveness of a particular ad, while at the same time, that cookie could be used to track your movement around the Internet. Click the *Delete* button in *the Browsing history* section of the *General* tab on the *Internet Options* pop-up box (see below) to remove this information.

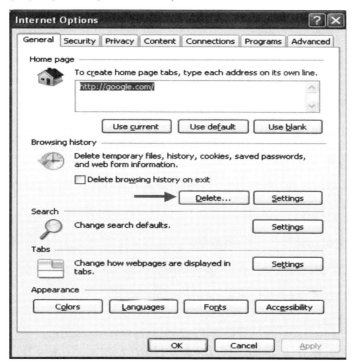

As you visit various Web sites, Explorer saves portions of the pages you visit in its cache files for future reference. On return trips to pages you've previously visited, Explorer checks its cache and compares the version found on the Web to the version stored in the cache. If there is no difference in the two versions, Explorer will display the copy stored on your computer, allowing the page to open faster. These files are also deleted by clicking this *Delete* button (shown above).

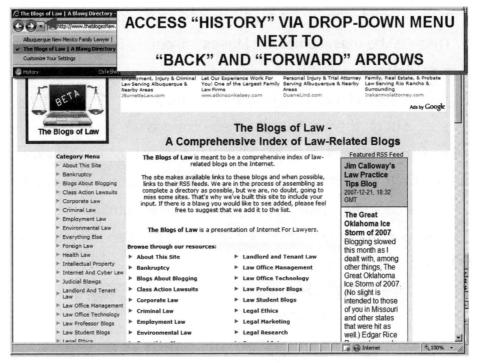

To help you find your way back to sites you've previously visited, Explorer keeps a running list in a history file. The list is maintained for a pre-set number of days before older entries are automatically removed. Clicking the *Delete* button on the *Internet Options* pop-up box (mentioned above) also clears out this information.

Version 8 has added a check box on the *General* tab of the *Internet Options* dialog box that allows you to *Delete browsing history on exit*—clearing the history every time you close your Web browser.

Toolbar (*Back, Forward, Stop, Refresh, Home*, and *Search*)

Also integrated into the Address Bar is the Toolbar that assists you in moving around the Internet (see illustration on next page). The *Back* button permits you to back up, one page at a time to earlier pages (or Web sites) that you have visited, while the *Forward* button does the opposite. The *Stop* button lets you stop loading the current page if it is either taking too long to load or if you have changed your mind about visiting that site.

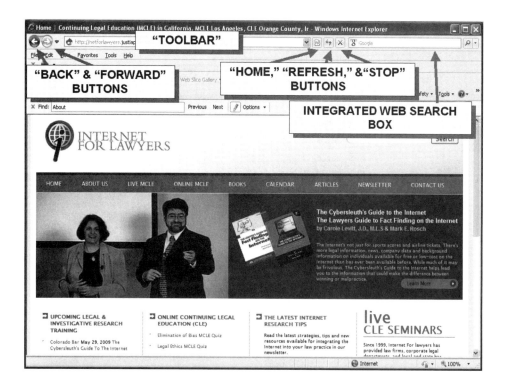

Use the *Refresh* button when you are visiting sites where the data change
continuously, such as stock quotes and sports scores, to be sure you are viewing
the most current data. The *Home* button brings you to the home page that you
have set to be the first page viewed whenever you open your browser. The
integrated *Search* box in the upper right-hand corner of the browser lets you
search the Web without having to visit a search engine. The default search
engine used is **Google**. However, you can use the drop-down menu next to the
search box to switch to Microsoft's search engine **Bing** (the service may still be
listed by its previous name **Live Search** in early releases of version 8), or to *Find
More Providers* and switch to **Yahoo!** or **Ask.com**.

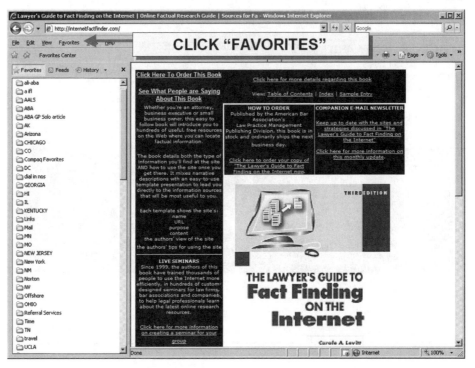

Also on the Menu Bar is the *Favorites* feature. It is perhaps one of the most useful features, aside from the *Find* function. Once you locate relevant Web sites to which you plan to return, you can save them as "Favorites" in your Web browser, so returning to them is a simple task. Adding *Favorites* is like creating a Web site address book—with speed dial. With just one click on the Web site name on your *Favorites* list, you will directly link to that site without needing to remember to type in the URL. You can add any page of a Web site as a *Favorite*. You could link to either the main home page of a Web site (such as the Supreme Court's home page) or a specific document that you use often at that Web site (such as a specific Supreme Court order) or both. (NOTE: Over time, documents might be removed from the Web, or Webmasters could change the location of a document on their Web site. In those cases, your Favorite would point to the old location, which may not hold the information it once did, or may no longer exist at all.)

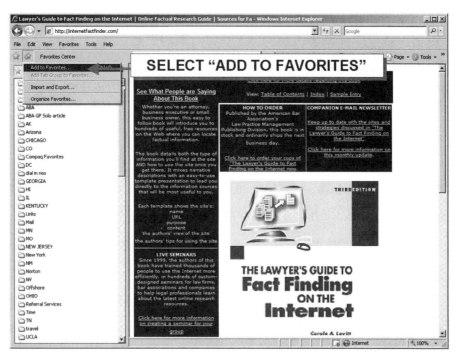

To add a Favorite, click on the *Favorites* button while you are viewing a site to which you want to return. Then select *Add to Favorites* from the drop-down menu to open the *Add a Favorite* dialog box.

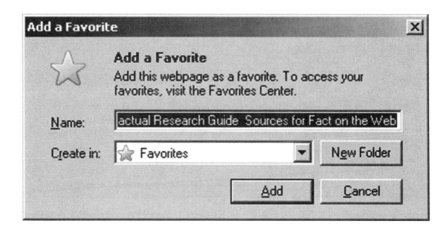

In this *Add a Favorite* dialog box, you have the option of giving your new Favorite a descriptive name or accepting the name of the Web page as assigned by its designer. You can also use the *Create In* drop-down menu to put your new Favorite into a pre-existing folder with other related Favorites. Clicking the *Add* button saves your new Favorite. If you don't use the *Create In* drop-down menu to organize your Favorite, it is saved at the end of your list of existing Favorites.

You can use the *Organize Favorites* option on the drop-down menu to arrange your Favorites into folders at a later time. This makes them easier to find as you build your collection of Favorites (see next page).

Saving Web Pages and Working Off-line

If you are using an earlier version of Internet Explorer, the *Add Favorite* dialog box also gives you the option of saving sites you have added to your Favorites offline, so you can view the site when you are not connected to the Internet. To do this, check off the *Make available offline* box before you click *OK* to save the Favorite. If you want to have the site automatically updated and placed in your *Work Offline* file, click on *Customize* and a "Wizard" will walk you through the steps. (Note: this *Work Offline* option is not available in version 8 of Internet Explorer.)

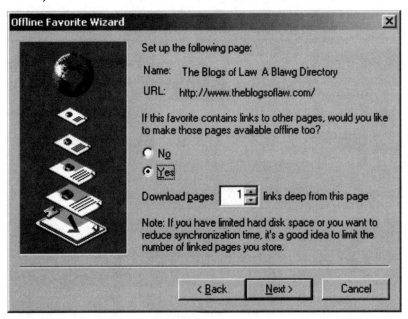

To view sites "offline," open Internet Explorer, but do not open your connection to the Internet. A dialog box will pop up and ask you if you want to work offline. After clicking *yes*, click the *Favorites* button and select the site that you have previously saved for viewing "offline" to view the version of the site you have saved. For whatever reason, Microsoft has chosen to eliminate this ability to save sites offline after version 6 of Internet Explorer.

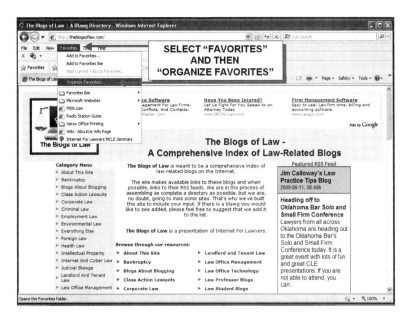

After adding Favorites, you can later organize them into folders by clicking on *Favorites* on the Menu Bar and then selecting *Organize Favorites* from the subsequent drop-down menu.

Using the *Organize Favorites* dialog box, you can move a Favorite you have saved into an existing Favorites Folder or move it into a newly created Favorites Folder. You can also rename a Favorite or a Favorites Folder, or delete a Favorites Folder or an individual Favorite. You can organize your Favorites

Folders by jurisdiction (e.g., *New Jersey*), by subject (e.g., *Medical*), by types of materials (e.g., *Public Records* or *Forms*) by a combination of a jurisdiction and a subject (e.g., *California Statistics*), or by any other system that is useful to you.

Creating Favorites Folders

Click on the *New Folder* button to create one or more new folders for organizing your Favorites.

A *New Folder* is added to the bottom of your list of Favorites. Clicking onto the *New Folder* gives you the ability to type in a new, more descriptive name for that folder (such as a folder titled *Forms* in the example above). Then hitting *return* or *enter* on your keyboard saves your newly created Favorites Folder.

To move individual Favorites to their new Folders, click *Favorites* on the Menu Bar and *Organize Favorites* from the subsequent drop-down menu. Then highlight the Favorite you wish to move (e.g., *Lawyer's Guide to Fact Finding on the Internet* as seen in *Step 1* below).

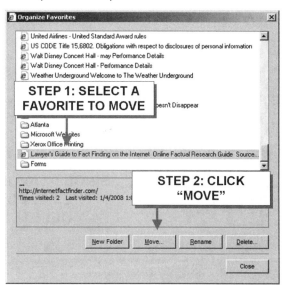

Next, click on *Move* (see *Step 2* above) to bring up the *Browse for Folder* box (see below left). Click on the chosen Folder (*Metasites* in *Step 3* below left) and click *OK*. The Favorite *Internet For Lawyers* will now be placed in the *Metasites* Folder (*Step 4*, below right).

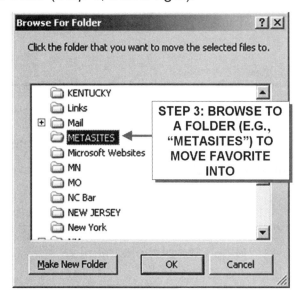

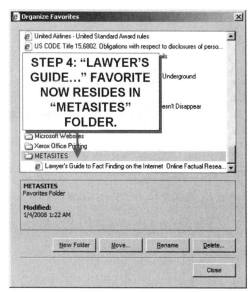

Deleting Favorites

To delete a Favorite, click on *Favorites* on the Menu Bar and then *Organize Favorites* from the subsequent drop-down menu. Click on an entire folder (e.g., *Public Records* in *Step 1* below) or on just one Favorite in the Folder (e.g., *LLRX* in *Step 1* below) that you would like to delete. Click the *Delete* button (*Step 2*) and then confirm the deletion by clicking *Yes* on the subsequent confirmation screen.

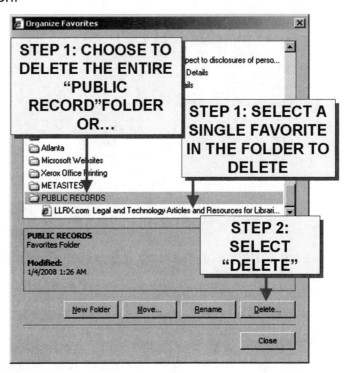

Viewing, Launching, and Closing Favorites

To view and launch (open in your Web browser) a favorite Web site, click *Favorites* on the Menu Bar and select the desired Favorite by scrolling down the drop-down list of folders and individual Favorites. Clicking once on the Favorite you've selected opens that site in your Web browser.

To view the individual Favorites stored in a Favotites Folder, click on the selected folder once (e.g., the *Georgia* folder below). All of the contents

(Favorites) in the *Georgia* folder, from *Georgia ICLE* through *State Bar of Georgia* will then appear in an expanded menu. Clicking once on the Favorite you've selected opens that site in your Web browser.

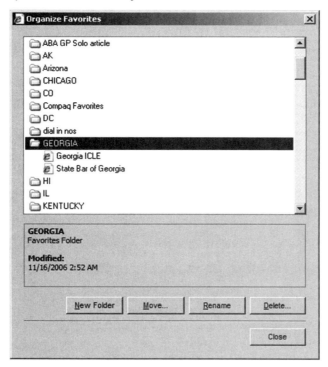

To close the *Organize Favorites* dialog box, click on the *X* in the upper right-hand corner or select the *Favorites* again from the Menu Bar.

To avoid losing those Favorites that you've painstakingly saved and organized, it is advisable to save those Favorites on a removable disk (e.g., external hard drive, flash drive, CD- or DVD-ROM, floppy or Zip disk) as a backup in case your hard drive crashes. You can also transfer them to another Web browser when you install a newer version of Explorer (or in some instances if you switch to another browser like Firefox, Safari, or Opera) by using the Import/Export Wizard. In Internet Explorer, click *File* on the Menu Bar, and then *Import and Export*.

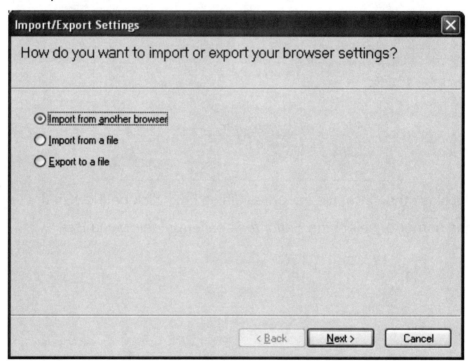

When the *Import/Export Wizard* appears, select one of the actions from the list and the click *Next* to begin (see above). The Wizard will walk you through the steps necessary to import or export your Favorites from one Web browser to another.

History

Sometimes you've visited so many sites — clicking from one to the next — that you lose track of where it all began. If you click the drop-down arrow next to the Back and Forward arrows (next to the Address Bar), you will find a list of all the prior sites that you have visited during an Internet session (or sessions). You can then return to them by clicking on the URL listed in the history list. See the "Tools" section earlier in this chapter for information on why you might want to clear this history.

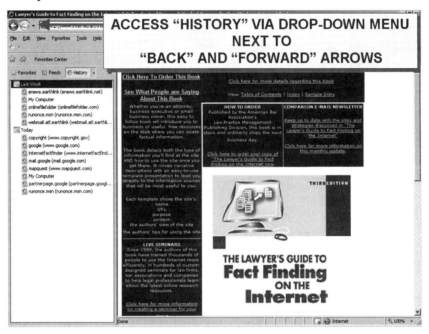

E-Mailing Internet Data

You can share information you find on the Internet by e-mailing it to others. One way is to simply "copy and paste" the text of the Web page into the body of an e-mail message. Another way is to e-mail just the link to the URL to the recipient so he or she can connect to the site with just one click on the URL noted in the e-mail. Finally, a Web page can be added to the e-mail as an attachment.

To illustrate these last two options, we will again focus on the most-used browser, Internet Explorer, and e-mail application — Microsoft's Outlook.

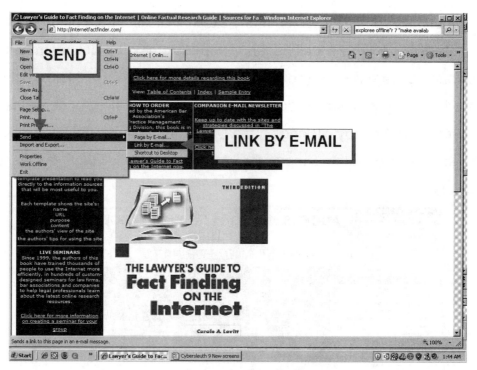

To send someone a link to a Web site, open a Web page in your browser and click *File* from the Menu Bar, then *Send*, and then *Link by E-mail* from the subsequent drop-down menus (see above). This opens a new e-mail message in your default e-mail program. Before you even begin typing your e-mail, the link should automatically appear in the body of your message and the Web site's name should already be in the subject line. Address the e-mail to your intended recipient(s), type in any additional message you desire, and then click *Send*. Once he or she receives the message, the recipient simply clicks on the link in the e-mail message to open the Web site.

To e-mail an entire Web page to someone, open a Web site and click *File* on the Menu Bar, then *Send*, and then *Page by E-mail* from the subsequent drop-down menus (see below) to send the page as an attachment to an e-mail message.

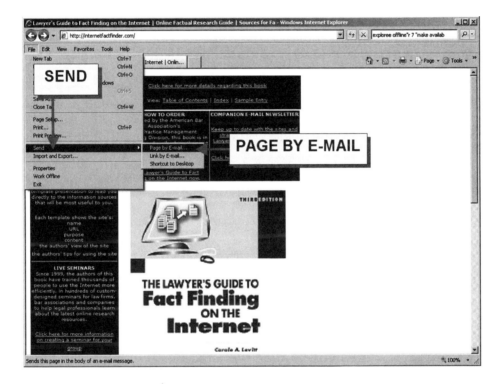

As in the earlier E-mailing a Link example, a new e-mail message will automatically open with the name of the Web page you're sending already in the Subject line. Rather than just a link to the site though, the content of the page will be appended to your message as an attachment. It is important to note, however, that depending on how the page has been built by its owner, there is a possibility that the recipient of your e-mail message will not receive all of the graphics included on the page you send.

WHAT EXACTLY IS A LINK?

A "link" is a pre-programmed Internet connection that either takes (links) you to (1) a completely different Web site from the one you are viewing; (2) other pages within the same Web site that you are viewing; or (3) other documents (e.g., word processing documents, forms, or other non-HTML documents) found either within the same site that you are viewing or elsewhere. There is no need to type in a URL (Web page address) or to even know the URL to access the desired page—it is only necessary to click on the link. Links are also sometimes called "hyper-links" or "hyper-text" or "hyper-media."

When your Web browser's cursor arrow turns into a hand with a pointing finger, you can click to begin the linking process. You activate a link by clicking once on any word, phrase, or URL that is underlined or appears in a different color (usually blue) or by clicking on an icon on the Web page that you are viewing (when the cursor turns into that hand with the pointing finger).

The links never end, unless they've gone "bad" (or "dead" or "missing"). This is the bane of any Internet researcher's life. If you receive a *HTTP Error 404* or *Not Found* message after clicking a link, this tells you that the Web server cannot find the site to which you attempted to link. Some 10 percent of links go bad every month. Why does this happen? It could mean that the site has (1) moved (missing); (2) ceased existing (dead); (3) been re-designed, with the location of the specific documents contained within the site now placed in different locations within the Web site, with a different URL; or (4) gone down temporarily. Generally, there won't be a forwarding address, a death notice, or any other information regarding a site if it has disappeared. It's therefore up to you to locate it.

To find a new URL for a site that has moved or been redesigned, type the Web site name into a search engine to see if the search engine spider has located the new URL. You can also visit a legal portal or legal directory in case their editors have located the new URL (if it is a law-related site you're looking for). If neither of the above options works, e-mail us at authors@netforlawyers.com and we will try to locate the new URL for you.

Chapter Two

RELIABILITY AND ADMISSIBILITY OF INFORMATION FROM THE INTERNET

In 1999, it might have been understandable that a district court cautioned against relying on data from the Internet as "voodoo information." *St. Clair v. Johnny's Oyster & Shrimp*, 76 F. Supp. 2d 773, 775 (S.D. TX. 1999). Today, fortunately, many judges are not only admitting information from the Internet into evidence, but they're also the ones conducting the Internet research to help make judicial decisions, as indicated by the following cases:

- In *Munster v. Groce*, 829 N.E.2d 52 (Ind. App. 2005) *available at* http://caselaw.lp.findlaw.com/data2/indianastatecases/app/0608050 1mpb.pdf, the court was incredulous that the plaintiff failed to "Google" the missing defendant (Joe Groce) as part of his due diligence process. The court stated, "We do note that there is no evidence in this case of a public records or Internet search for Groce…to find him. In fact, we [the judge] discovered, upon entering 'Joe Groce Indiana' into the Google™ search engine, an address for Groce that differed from either address used in this case, as well as an apparent obituary for Groce's mother that listed numerous surviving relatives who might have known his whereabouts." The court upheld the defendant's claim of insufficient service of process and affirmed the dismissal of the case.

- In a similar case the court noted that with ready access to the Internet, the investigative technique of merely calling directory assistance to find a missing defendant has gone "the way of the horse and buggy and the eight-track stereo." *Dubois v. Butler*, 901 So. 2d 1029 (FL App 2005) *available at* http://www.4dca.org/May2005/05-25-05/4D04-3559.pdf.

- In another tax sale case, this time in Louisiana, an appellate judge upheld the trial court's nullification of the government tax sale where the trial court judge conducted an Internet search and determined that the tax-delinquent owner was "reasonably identifiable" and would have been locatable if the government had run a simple "Internet search" to locate the named mortgagee. (The government claimed to have conducted a public records search and a **Lexis-Nexis** search.) Part of the basis of the appeal was whether it was appropriate for the trial court judge to have conducted an Internet search of his own. The Appeals court stated, "Nevertheless, we find any error the trial court may have committed by conducting the Internet search is harmless, because the trial court's ultimate conclusion that the tax sale violated Dr. Weatherly's due process rights is legally correct." *Weatherly v. Optimum Asset Management*, 928 So.2d 118 (La. App. 2005), *available at* http://www.la-fcca.org/Opinions/PUB2005/2005-12/2004CA2734Dec2005.Pub.10.pdf.

Yet, in a more recent Pennsylvania case, the court took the opposite view from the above cases (which had basically held that using the Internet and "Googling" were now considered part of an attorney's due diligence process). *Fernandez* v. *Tax Claim Bureau of Northampton County*, No. 1600 C.D. 2006 (Penn. Comm. Ct. 5/30/07) *available at* http://www.courts.state.pa.us/OpPosting/CWealth/out/1600CD06_5-31-07.pdf. The *Fernandez* court ruled that a Google search, which a county performed to locate someone who owed back taxes on a property, was insufficient and instead they should have used the telephone book. The court noted that if the county tax collectors had looked up the missing defendant's name in the telephone book, they might have been able to reach him because the telephone number in the telephone book was correct while the telephone number found using Google had been disconnected. The court, taking a very literal approach, concluded that the county's service by publication was insufficient because, by law, it was required to search the countywide telephone book to find an address to mail notice of a tax sale to a delinquent owner.

Beyond *Fernandez*, there are still some judges who will not allow information located on the Internet into evidence because they believe it to be inherently unreliable. Information found on **Wikipedia** (http://en.wikipedia.org/wiki/Main_Page) falls into this category. For example, in some cases, such as *Palisades Collection* v. *Graubard,* Docket No. A-1338-07T3 (NJ Superior Court April 17, 2009), *available at* http://linkon.in/aRzNOL, the judge did not allow information found at **Wikipedia** into evidence, while in other cases, such as *Allegheny Defense Project* v. *United States Forest Service*, 423 F.3d 215, (W.D. PA 2005), *available at* http://linkon.in/dkG8JW, the judge allowed into evidence information found at **Wikipedia**.

We do not recommend taking information found at **Wikipedia** ("the free encyclopedia that anyone can edit") as absolute fact because anyone can create or edit entries on **Wikipedia** on any given topic. On the other hand, if someone uploads something that is incorrect, it's often the case that someone else will correct it. Therefore, some people find **Wikipedia** to be reliable. It's best to cross-check your facts by using at least two different sources.

Getting information admitted into evidence that has been retrieved from the **Internet Archive** (http://www.archive.org; see page 110) is a completely different story. To quote the Judge in *Telewizja Polska USA.* v. *Echostar Satellite*, Case No. 02C3293 (N.D. Ill. Oct. 15, 2004), "Admittedly, the Internet Archive does not fit neatly into any of the non-exhaustive examples listed in Rule 901; the Internet Archive is a relatively new source for archiving Web sites. Nevertheless, Plaintiff has presented no evidence that the Internet Archive is unreliable or biased." (See pages 112-113 for a full discussion of this case and why the **Internet Archive** was ultimately not allowed into evidence.)

Chapter Three

HOW TO SEARCH THE WEB: SEARCH ENGINES AND DIRECTORIES

NAVIGATING TO INFORMATION ON THE INTERNET

Searchers use one of the following options to locate information on the Internet:

- a Web browser (e.g., Internet Explorer, Firefox, or Google Chrome), to type a known Web site address (URL) into the browser's Address Bar

- a search engine (e.g., Google, Bing, or Yahoo!), to type one or more words or phrases into the search engine's query box

- a directory, to click through the directory's topics and sub-topics until a relevant topic is found (or to type a keyword into the directory's internal search engine) and then click on the chosen topic for a list of Web sites

DIFFERENCES BETWEEN SEARCH ENGINES AND DIRECTORIES

As part of the discussion about locating information on the Internet, the terms "search engine" and "directory" have come to be used interchangeably. While both types of Web sites will help us locate information on specific topics from other Web sites, they do it in very different ways.

Generally, search engines do not reach out and search live pages on the Internet for every search conducted. To return the majority of its results, a search engine automatically crawls the Internet, sending out "spiders" or "robots" (software programs) that capture the content of a particular site at a particular point in time. It then builds an index of the content of those Web pages. When you conduct a search using a search engine, that search engine looks through its index for the word or phrase that you type into the query box.

If something new has been added to a particular site since the robot's last visit, it will not be reflected in your search results. That new information will only show up in search results after the search engine's spider visits the site again and the search engine adds this new information to its index. (In the Summer of 2010, **Google** made a step toward "real-time" search, with the introduction of a new category of "Updates" results. See page 55 for a more detailed description of these continuously-updated results.)

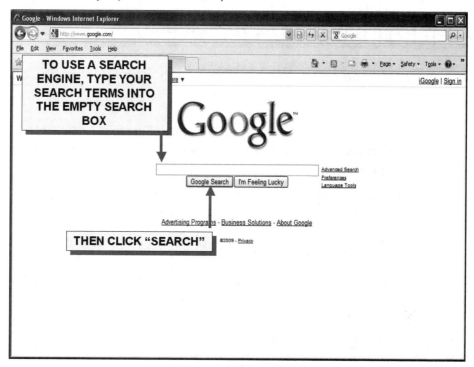

After completing your search, the Web pages that the search engine "thinks" are relevant to your search are then displayed as a list. This is a list of your "results" or "hits." Sometimes search engine results will be right on target and other times completely irrelevant, even though they contain your exact search terms.

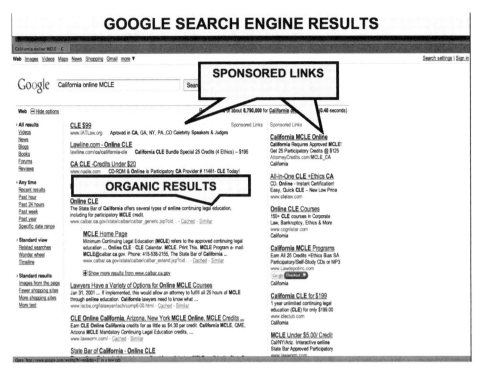

Search results may be divided into two categories: "Organic Results" and "Sponsored Links." As the names imply, the Organic Results are determined automatically by the robot, while positions in the Sponsored Links are for sale to the highest bidder. All of the major search engines offer the ability to purchase Sponsored Links.

Search engines are useful for general Web searching (when you do not have familiarity with a specific Web site or a subject-specific portal or directory) or when you truly want to cast a wide net and not use a selective group of Web sites found at a portal or directory. But not every Web page is searchable by a search engine — those that are not are said to be "invisible."

33

The earliest search engines were not as powerful as the ones we are using today. Those early search engines could only recognize and index a small range of document types — mainly those coded in the Hypertext Markup Language (HTML). Documents posted on the Web in any other file format, such as PowerPoint, Excel, Word, or the Portable Document Format (PDF), were not indexed, and therefore invisible to people using search engines to locate information on the Internet. Because these files were "invisible" to search engines, they (and other non-indexed material) were referred to as residing on the "Invisible Web" — documents that were freely available on the Internet, but only if you knew the exact URL to locate them. The documents that were readily retrievable via search engines were, conversely, referred to as residing on the "Visible Web." Documents that were once invisible to all search engines are now visible to many and will be discussed later in *Chatper Four*.

Despite the increased function and power of contemporary search engines, there are still many types of documents that are posted on the Internet that remain un-retrievable (invisible) via search engines. Some may be un-retrievable because the search engines do not (yet) know how to access or process the information found on a publicly available source, or the search engines may not know the pages exist because:

- the information is created dynamically, such as information contained in a database (see page 88 for information on how to find databases);
- they were not submitted to search engines for indexing;
- no other sites link to them;
- the pages are too current to have been indexed yet.

Additionally, some Web sites may prefer to make their content available only to registered users (e.g., members of a particular association) or paid subscribers. These resources, being protected by a firewall or otherwise password protected, would never be accessible to a search engine or its robot.

As a side note, if you own a Web site that is not included in the major search engines' search results, and you want it to be, then you should submit your site to be crawled by each search engine's spider. All of the major search engines provide a form on which you can submit your site's URL. Submitting your site adds it to the list of sites the search engine will crawl for addition to their indices: **Google** (http://www.google.com/submityourcontent/index.html), **Yahoo!** (http://search.yahoo.com/info/submit.html), and **Bing** (http://www.bing.com/docs/submit.aspx).

DIRECTORIES

Directories are comprised of links that are hand-selected by people who are (usually) subject specialists. They test and evaluate the sites before adding them to the directory. Therefore, the sites found on a directory might be more reliable (or at least more selective) than ones found using a search engine. Directories also generally contain fewer sites than search engines.

Some directories only allow users to click through categories until they come to the level that holds the information they're looking for (e.g., *Government> Law> Legal Research> Libraries*). This practice is often referred to as "drilling down." Other directories add the ability to search through their collection of links with an internal search engine to point the user to the category (or a specific site) where they'll find the information they need. This is where some confusion between search engines and directories comes in. The internal search engine of the directory is searching only through the collection of links assembled by the human editors of the directory, and not an index assembled automatically by robots or spiders the way a Web search engine does.

GOOGLE'S DIRECTORY

The **Google Directory** above (http://directory.google.com/) functions like a traditional directory. Click on topics or sub-topics until you find the information you need (drilling down), or use the internal search engine to conduct a keyword or phrase search through the list of sites the directory's editors have compiled. (Note that this is a smaller number of sites than contained in the Google search engines index of sites compiled automatically by its spider.)

DIFFERENCES BETWEEN VARIOUS SEARCH ENGINES

You will often retrieve different results if you conduct the same search using different search engines — because no two search engines work exactly alike. Every search engine has its own spider that it sends out to retrieve information, and every spider treats the information it finds differently when building its respective index. Most general search engines allow users to retrieve information using:

- keyword searching (e.g., *negligent*)
- phrase searching (e.g., *negligence per se*)
- Boolean connectors such as *AND, OR, NOT* (e.g., *negligent **OR** intentional **AND NOT** criminal*) between search words and phrases

Many pay databases (and some free Web sites that have internal search engines) allow more flexibility in creating searches, including allowing the use of:

- proximity connectors, such as *near* or *adjacent,* inserted in between search words and phrases (e.g., *carole **NEAR** levitt*)
- field searching, such as entering keywords or dates into *Title* or *Date* fields (e.g., *negligence **AND** date 1999*)
- natural language searching (e.g., *what is negligence?*)

Boolean Logic: How to Connect Search Words and Phrases

Boolean logic refers to the concept of connecting keywords and phrases together to construct an effective and logical search.

The following words are Boolean connectors:

- *AND*
- *OR*
- *NOT* (or *AND NOT*, or *BUT NOT*, or the minus sign (-) adjacent to the word you want to exclude)

You will get vastly different results if you use the *AND* Boolean connector instead of the *OR*, or if you use the *NOT* connector instead of the *AND* connector, so be sure you understand the differences before you begin constructing your search.

Differences Between Boolean Connectors

- *AND* — A search using the *AND* connector will result in all of the keywords or phrases showing up in the results list.

- *OR* — A search using the *OR* connector will result in either one or more (or all) of the keywords or phrases showing up in the results list.

- *AND NOT* — A search using the *AND NOT* connector excludes words or phrases from the search results.

Most major search engines support these three Boolean connectors. However, they may have different requirements for how you conduct an *AND*, an *OR,* and an *AND NOT* search. For example, to conduct an *OR* search at **Google**, you must type *OR* (in capital letters) between your keywords (or phrases), but to conduct an *AND NOT* search, you must type a minus sign next to the word or phrase you want to exclude.

For more details on which search engines employ which Boolean connectors, see the comparison chart discussed on page 45 and enlarged on the last page of this book.

Boolean Connector "Defaults"

Each search engine has a "default" Boolean connector so if you type more than one word (or phrase) into a search engine's query box and do not add a Boolean connector between each keyword or phrase, the search engine will add its default Boolean connector (behind the scenes) in between your keywords or phrases. Most search engines automatically default to *AND*. However, some do default to *OR*. Additionally, some Web sites' internal search engines default to OR. You can override a default by simply typing in the Boolean connector that you want to use in between each keyword or phrase.

A Search Engine's Default Boolean Connector Can Greatly Effect the Results that Search Engine Returns

Google and most other general search engines use the *AND* Boolean connector as its default connector. Prior to July 2002, **AltaVista**

(http://www.altavista.com) used the *OR* Boolean default so running the same search (*dog law*) at **AltaVista** and **Google** for instance (prior to July 2002), produced different results because **AltaVista** looked for all documents with just the word *dog **OR*** just the word *law* or both words together while **Google** only looked for documents with both the word *dog **AND*** the word *law* together.

In July 2002, **AltaVista** began using *AND* as its default Boolean connector.

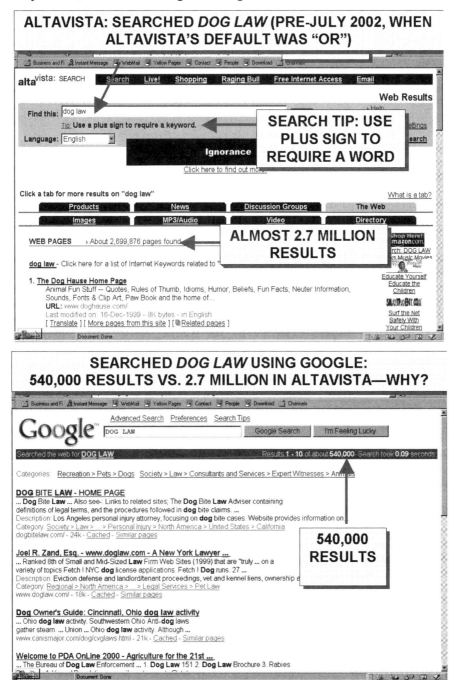

Most search engines allow you to search two or more keywords as phrases by surrounding them with quotation marks (e.g., *"dog law"* or *"negligence per se"*). This is a more limiting search than a search employing the *AND* Boolean connector. The phrase search locates your terms in the exact order in which you have entered them and with no intervening words in between the keywords you have enclosed in quotation marks.

Will a search for the phrase *"dog law"* find documents with either of the following phrases?

- The law of a dog
- The dog in Western law

The answer is *no*, because the search engine is instructed to search for documents with both of the words *dog* **and** *law* next to one another and in that exact order.

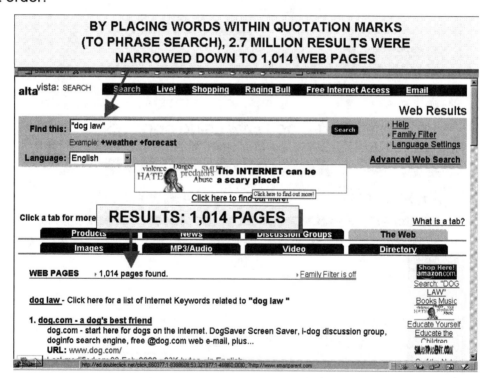

Proximity Connectors

Some search engines allow you to indicate that you want a keyword or phrase to appear in a returned resulting document in close proximity to another keyword or phrase. To do this, these search engines utilize "Proximity Connectors." Unfortunately, not many free search engines offer this flexibility. When it is available however, using it can result in much more precise results.

Unlike an *AND* Boolean search that instructs the search engine only to find documents where both search terms appear anywhere in the document, a search utilizing a Proximity Connector instructs the search engine to find both those search terms but in close proximity to one another. Thus, with an *AND* search, one search term could appear in the first paragraph of a document and the second search term could appear many paragraphs later. Even though the first term could be completely unconnected to the second search term, such a page could still turn up in results.

On the other hand, with a search utilizing proximity connectors, the two terms on the resulting page would be closer together and probably related to one another — more in line with how a searcher intended them to be. The most commonly recognized Proximity Connector used by free search engines and Web sites is *NEAR*.

There is no standard however, for how near *NEAR* means. For example, placing the *NEAR* connector between words (or phrases) when using **FindLaw's California Case Law Search** means that the site will return results where the search terms can be separated by as many as fifty words, while a different search engine might deem *NEAR* to mean within three words of each other.

Google uses an asterisk to indicate a *NEAR* proximity search. Typing "*" between your keywords or phrases takes the place of one, or more than one, word. For example, searching for *George * Bush* could return the following results: *George W. Bush*, *George Bush*, *George H.W. and Jeb Bush*, *George A. Bush*, *George Walker Bush* or a page with a sentence that reads, "*George trimmed the large bush.*" **Google** does not tell us how near *NEAR* is, so using the asterisk in a **Google** search may be of limited value, as there is no way to define how many words the asterisk represents. On the other hand, it can be an excellent way to search for individuals if they are referred to with an unknown middle name (or names).

Adding additional asterisks <u>does</u> change the search results; it pushes our keywords further apart. So, adding two asterisks together in between two keywords does not bring back search results that only include the first keyword separated from the second keyword by two words.

If we add quotation marks to our proximity search (e.g. for *"Carole * Levitt"*) this does not turn our search into an exact phrase search where the asterisk takes the place of only one word. It does, however, limit our results to just the exact spelling of our keywords. For example, our search for *"Carole * Levitt"* brings back only the exact name *Carole* and the exact name *Levitt* (but they could be separated by multiple other words) while a search for *Carole * Levitt* (without the quotation marks) also brings back results that include the name *Carol* and the name *Leavitt.*

Yahoo! also utilizes the "***" as a Proximity Connector but quite differently from **Google** and most other search engines — it is limited only to phrase searching. To conduct a proximity search at **Yahoo!**, the search terms must be contained within quotation marks and must be separated by the asterisk (e.g., *"Mark * Rosch"*). Using the asterisk in this way (at **Yahoo!**) indicates that you want the first keyword to be separated from the second keyword by one other word and that the words must appear in that order. The asterisk essentially takes the place of one word in such a search. Note that you cannot search **Yahoo!** with multiple asterisks to take the place of multiple words.

Searching with Wildcards

"Wildcards" can have many different functions. Generally speaking, the wildcard is a single symbol or character that can be entered to take the place of one or more characters in a search term.

For example, wildcards can be used:

- at the end of a word
  - to stem or extend the root of a word (a search for *child** would find *child, child's, children*, etc.).
- in the middle of a word
  - to take the place of any letter — this is useful when the same word is spelled different ways (e.g., a search for *mari*uana* would find *marijuana* or *marihuana*).

WARNING: The asterisk (*) is often used as the wildcard, but some search engines or Web sites might use the exclamation point (!). Most free search engines do not employ any wildcards at all. Some employ selected ones. As noted earlier, **Google** and **Yahoo!** utilize the asterisk like a "Proximity Connector" to take the place of one or more entire words instead of one or more characters within only one word.

Google automatically stems keywords in a search, so a search for *child* would find *child, child's, children*, etc. **Yahoo**, on the other hand, does not stem as extensively. Test searches at **Yahoo** for the keyword *child* yielded results that included *child* and *child's* but not *children*.

Organizing Your Search with Parentheses

Parentheses are used to clarify a complex Boolean search or to change the "logic" of the Boolean logic. Unfortunately, not many major search engines (currently only Microsoft's **Bing**) recognize parentheses as a search parameter. Here is an example of a Parentheses search (using **Bing**) *("Barack Obama" "Joe Biden") NOT (Iran OR Iraq)*. The parentheses instruct the search engine which search terms to group together. Your search results would include both the names *Barack Obama* and *Joe Biden* but they would not include the *words Iran* or *Iraq*. The same search conducted without parentheses — *"Barack Obama" "Joe Biden" NOT Iran OR Iraq* — would yield very different results. The results would not include the *word Iran*, but they could include:

- *Iraq* on its own
- *Barack Obama* and *Joe Biden* (both names together)
- *Iraq* and *Barack Obama* and *Joe Biden*

Search Engine Help Pages and Features Comparison Chart

As we've discussed, every search engine is different. They offer different features and different ways of implementing similar features. Every search engine offers help pages to help you learn about each search engine's limitations or unique features. This is a screenshot of **Google's** main help page. (http://www.google.com/support).

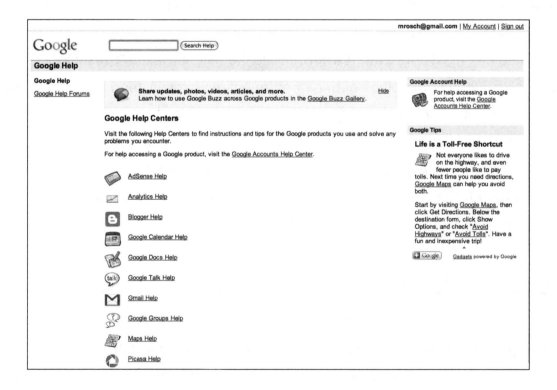

We have created a handy chart (http://linkon.in/8XULKZ) to illustrate a comparison between some of the most popular search engines. The chart includes information on the search engines' *Default Boolean Connector*, *Other Boolean Connectors Recognized*, *Proximity Search*, availability of *Cached Pages*, and more. It also includes direct links to each search engine's help pages. (See the back of this book for an enlarged, tear-out version of this chart.)

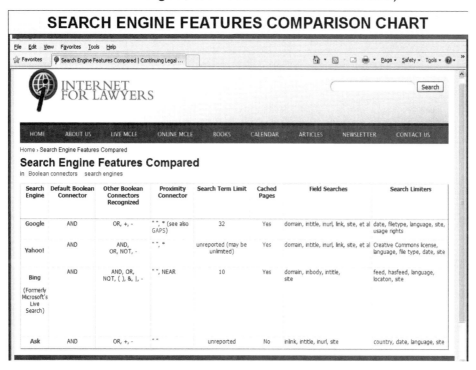

Chapter Four

SEARCH ENGINES: GOOGLE

There are literally thousands of search engines on the Internet — each of which claims to deliver the most relevant results. While we have not reviewed all of them, we have compiled this list of our favorite search engines and directories (in order of our preference). **Google** is our top pick for general research with **Yahoo!** coming in a close second, and Microsoft's **Bing** rounding out the top three. **Justia's Legal Web Search** and **USA.gov** are the top picks for law-related and government document research, respectively. (You can also limit your **Google** search to government sources using **Google's** *U.S. Government Search* page. (http://www.google.com/unclesam).

In this chapter though, we will focus on **Google** because:

- Many believe that **Google** delivers the most relevant results of any major search engine.
- Nearly three-quarters of all English language searches are run through **Google** in one way or another.
- A majority of the advanced search features found at many of the major search engines were first introduced by **Google** and later adopted by those other search engines.

This discussion of **Google** will focus on the most useful features, but we will not be able to delve as deeply into **Google** as we would like to because this book is not just about searching — it also covers investigative research, legal research Web sites, and tips. For those who want to delve deeper into **Google**, look for our *Google For Lawyers* book (published by the American Bar Association Law Practice Management Section; http://linkon.in/acf4MI).

In the next chapter, we will discuss our other favorite search engines.

Why Google? (http://www.google.com)

As we will discuss in the next chapter, while **Yahoo!** and **Bing** have made major advances in the past few years, we still feel that **Google** consistently returns the most useful results. That said, no one search engine holds the best answer for every search. There are some occasions when we have found the precise answer we've needed using a search engine other than **Google**.

Google delivers relevant results through the proprietary "PageRank" technology it employs to determine a Web page's relevance and importance based on each page's content, the number and types of other Web pages that link to it (in-bound links), and other criteria. The **Google** spider updates the entirety of its index every 28 days (on average), although some Web sites are spidered more often — with some spidered every day (or multiple times per day).

Google also offers many advanced features and search functions that help it return relevant results. **Google** pioneered many of these advanced features and when we wrote the first edition of this book in 1999, **Google** was the only search engine that offered most of them. For instance, **Google** was the first major search engine to search and index many types of files (i.e., Microsoft Word documents and PDFs) that until then had been relegated to the "Invisible Web" (In other words, although the documents were on the Web, search engines could not locate them so they were invisible to researchers.)

In the intervening years, **Google's** basic and advanced search features have become the *de facto* search industry standards, as the other major search engines have developed and implemented similar features. As we discuss the use of these basic and advanced search features, we will use **Google** to illustrate those features and to "stand in" for those other search engines as well. Where there are significant differences between search engines, we will point those out.

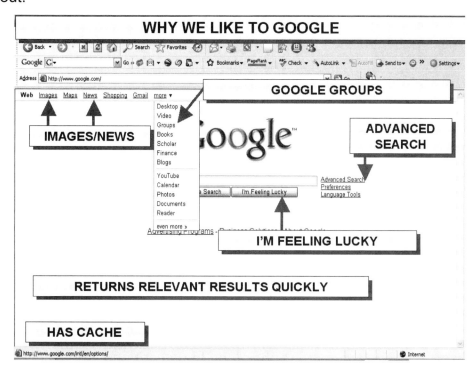

"Basic" Google Search Strategies

Google's Boolean default connector is *AND*. Therefore, there is no need to type the word *AND* between keywords to connect them. **Google** will do this automatically, behind the scenes for you.

Google is not case sensitive, so there is no need to capitalize proper names.

GOOGLE SEARCHING USING THE "AND" DEFAULT, A PHRASE, AND A COMMON (AKA "NOISE") WORD OR NUMBER

Google™

NUMBER +1 LAW FIRM "UNITED STATES"

[Google Search] [I'm Feeling Lucky]

Advanced Search
Preferences
Language Tools

Advertising Programs · Business Solutions · About Google

©2009 · Privacy

Google automatically excludes common words and also numbers (e.g., *the*, or *1*). These are referred to as "noise" words. This exclusion rule can be overridden by adding a *plus sign* (**+**) in front of the word or words, without any spaces (e.g., *of mice +and men*). **Yahoo!**, on the other hand, seemingly excludes no words from its search results. If you were to search for *the wings of eagles* (without quotation marks), **Yahoo!** would return results not only with that phrase, but also Web pages that included all of those words — but not necessarily in that order.

"Instant" Search Results with "Google Instant"

On the morning of September 8, 2010, **Google** announced a major innovation to the way it processes queries and delivers results - **Google Instant**.

Google Instant takes the auto-complete, predictive suggestions that have been automatically displayed under the **Google** search box as you type your keywords one step further. **Google Instant** not only displays those predictive suggestions for your search, it also displays a full list of results for those suggestions.

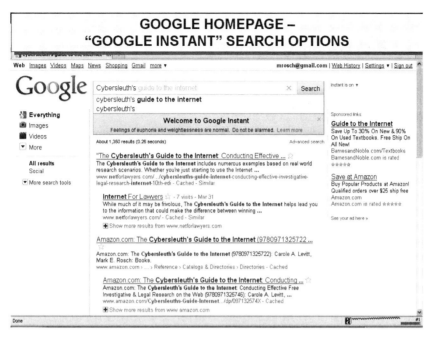

In the above example, the results begin appearing as we type each character of our keyword. The list changes with each additional character.

You can use your keyboard shortcuts to access the selections on the list of suggested keywords/phrases. Use the down arrow to highlight a particular entry. Use the right arrow to perform an *I'm Feeling Lucky Search* (as described in the next section), or you can use the *Return* key to select the highlighted entry and perform a "regular" **Google** Web search (as described in the next section).

Google's official blog post announcing **Google Instant**, describes a few of the core features in **Google Instant** as:

- Dynamic Results - **Google** dynamically displays relevant search results as you type so you can quickly interact and click through to the web content you need.

- Predictions - One of the key technologies in **Google Instant** is that we predict the rest of your query (in light gray text) before you finish typing. See what you need? Stop typing, look down and find what you're looking for.

- Scroll to search - Scroll through predictions and see results instantly for each as you arrow down.

Based on test searches, it appears that the predictive search suggestions displayed under the search box are determined by some mix of preset **Google** "guesses" of popular searches, an individual user's prior Web search history and the searchers physical location (based on **Google's** automatic detection of the Internet connection). As this book is going to press, we have been unable to determine how these criteria are weighted in determining results.

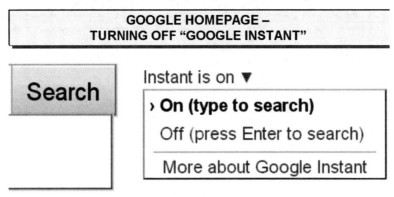

GOOGLE HOMEPAGE –
TURNING OFF "GOOGLE INSTANT"

Search

Instant is on ▼
› **On (type to search)**
Off (press Enter to search)
More about Google Instant

If the predictive keyword suggestions and accompanying results are distracting or unsettling to you, you can turn off **Google Instant** using the *Instant is on* drop-down menu to the right of the search box.

Google Instant works with newer versions of the Chrome, Explorer, Firefox, and Safari browsers. The service began to roll out to users in the United States on the day of the announcement. The United Kingdom, France, Italy, and Germany are expected to follow soon thereafter.

There are three primary methods of searching **Google**, one of which is found on its *Advanced Search* page and two of which are displayed on its home page. The two home page search methods are indicated by the two search buttons located beneath **Google's** query box:

- *Google Search*
- *I'm Feeling Lucky* (See page 59.)

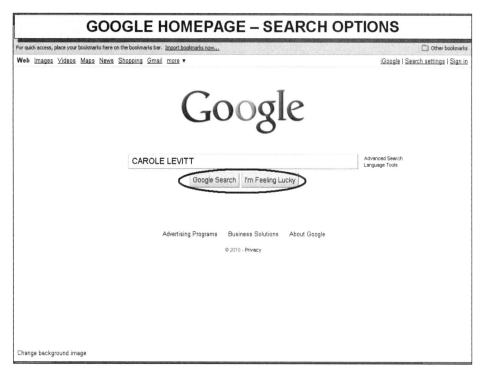

Google Search: After typing keywords into the query box on the home page, most people typically click on the *Google Search* button (or just tap the *Enter* key on their computer). This instructs **Google** to search its entire index. The searcher is then presented with a list of results (that could reach into the thousands or millions).

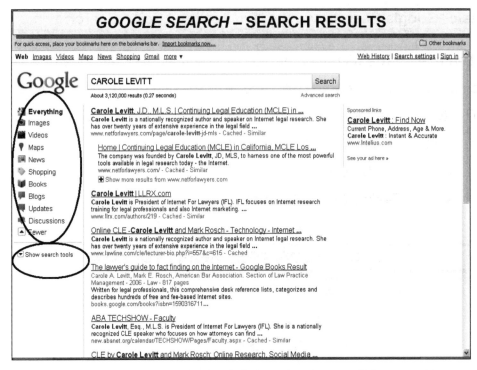

After you enter your search, the left-hand column of the results page offers you ways to narrow down your search by selecting the *More* link or the *Show search tools* link. The default display of results is *Everything*.

If you click the *More* link, a drop-down menu is displayed, from which you can narrow your search results to:

- *Images*
- *Videos*
- *Maps*
- *News*
- *Shopping*
- *Books*
- *Blogs*
- *Updates*
- *Discussions*

We will discuss most of the features noted above later in this chapter but want to draw your attention to *Updates* at this juncture because it's a very different type of result than other **Google** results. The first difference is the type of sources from which *Updates* are drawn, such as **Twitter**, **Facebook**, **MySpace**, and **FriendFeed** — with the majority of them coming from **Twitter**.

Another major difference about *Updates* results is that **Google** continues to run your search and if it detects new *Updates* while you're browsing the results list, those new *Updates* are added to the top of the results list. This is the closest thing to "real-time" Web search results currently available on the Web.

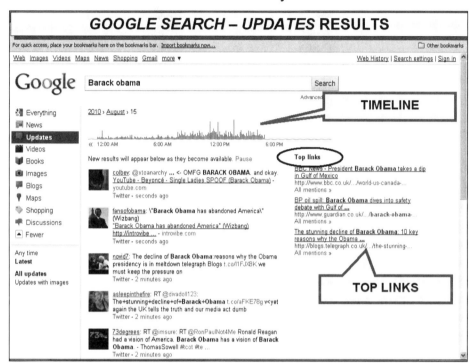

The *Updates* (mostly tweets from **Twitter**) are displayed in reverse chronological order. Displayed above the tweets results list you will also see a *Timeline*. (*Timelines* are discussed just after the next bulleted list.) The *Top Links* column to the right lists the most popular (e.g., recurrent) resources cited (e.g., linked to) from within the *Updates*. (As of our summer 2010 publication deadline, *Updates* results were only displayed as far back as February 2010.)

If you click the *Show search tools* link, (on the **Google** *Search* results page) a drop-down menu is displayed, from which you can narrow (or expand) your search results to:

- ***Any time***
    - *Latest*
    - *Past 24 hours*
    - *Past week*
    - *Past month*
    - *Past year*
    - *Custom range...*
- ***All results***
    - *Nearby*
- ***Standard view***
    - *Related searches*
    - *Wonder wheel*
    - *Timeline*
- ***Standard results***
    - *Sites with images*
    - *Fewer shopping sites*
    - *More shopping sites*
    - *Page previews*
    - *Translated search*

While most of these search tools are self-explanatory, we will discuss the ones that are not, such as the *Wonder wheel, Timeline,* and *Page previews* tools.

The *Timeline* link generates a graphical representation of the date distribution of the results and reorders the results into "chronological" order. You can click anywhere along the timeline to display results only from the point in time you've selected. Clicking the month or the year (similar to those seen in the *Updates Results* illustration on page 55) adjusts the timeline to access *Updates* for that time period.

One drawback to the *Timeline* view is that the dates **Google** uses to create the chronological order are not necessarily the dates on which the documents in the results list were published/created — sometimes it's the date when **Google** found the page or it might be a date that's included in the text of the document/page.

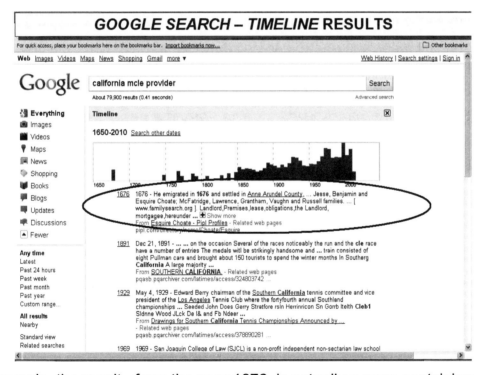

For example, the result , from the year 1676, is actually a page containing information randomly aggregated from multiple sources that includes our keywords (*California mcle provider* and the date *1676* — and although the two terms are not related, that's apparently how **Google** decided the date origin of this particular document).

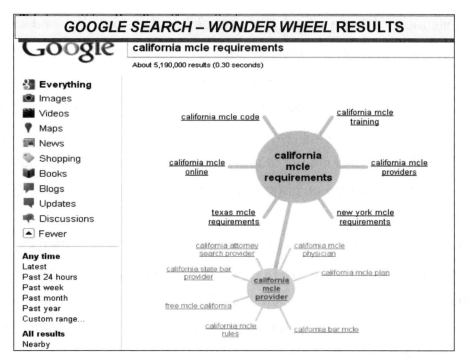

Clicking the *Wonder wheel* tool gives you a visual representation of various key terms that recur in the search results list. By clicking any of the terms on the *Wonder wheel*, you are able to drill down to retrieve more specific information from various Web sites.

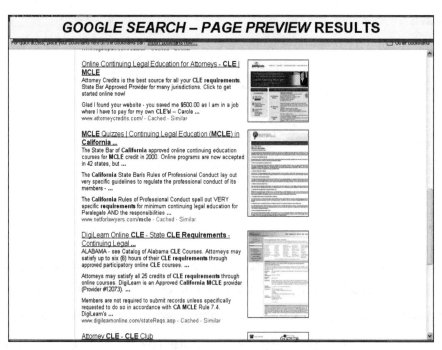

Clicking the *Page previews* link allows you to view a small preview image of each Web site in your results list.

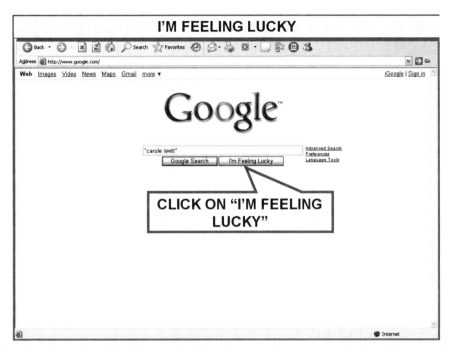

I'm Feeling Lucky Search: For those who run out of patience when they see too many results — feeling compelled to review as many as possible — try using the *I'm Feeling Lucky* button. It rewards searchers with just one site — often just the one they need. No other major search engine offers a similar function.

Once you have completed a search and the results are presented, you can narrow your search further by using **Google's** *Search within results* feature instead of running a new search.

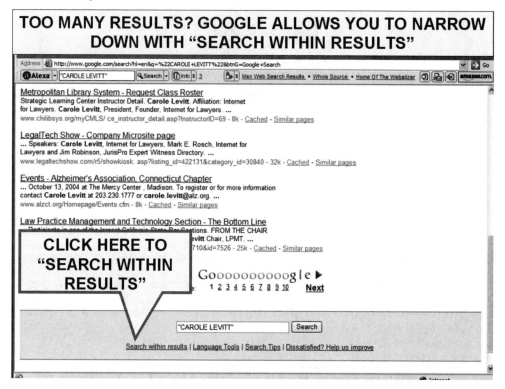

This feature can be invoked by scrolling down to the bottom of any of the results pages and clicking on the *Search within results* link. A new search page will be presented where you can type in additional words or phrases to narrow down your search.

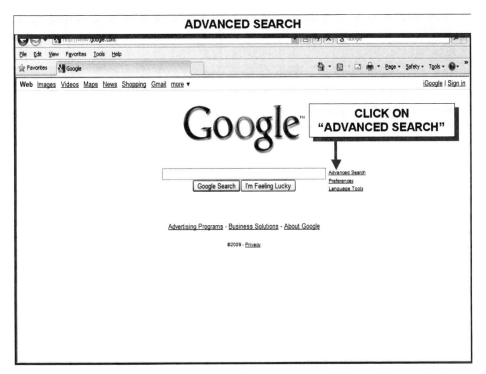

All of the major search engines offer *Advanced Search* templates, where users can create very sophisticated Boolean searches or search for information from very specific sources by entering information into the *Advanced Search* template or choosing options from various drop-down menus. The link to access the *Advanced Search* page at **Google** (and **AltaVista**) is located to the right of the main search box on each search engine's home page. Most other search engines, such as **Bing** and **Yahoo!** hide their *Advanced Search* option (we will reveal their hiding place later when we discuss these two seach engines at more length in *Chapter Five*).

We'll use the **Google** *Advanced Search* page to illustrate how these *Advanced Search* tools can be used to create more effective searches. It offers a query template that makes Boolean and phrase searching easier (as illustrated in the image below), by entering your search terms into one or more of the following search boxes: *all these words, this exact wording or phrase, one or more of these words, But don't show pages that have...any of these unwanted words.*

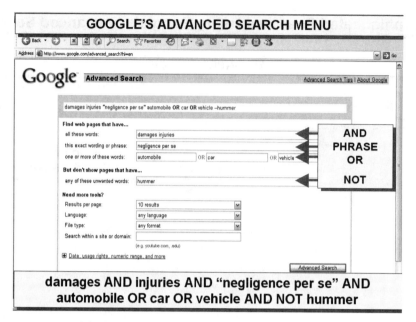

GOOGLE'S ADVANCED SEARCH MENU

damages AND injuries AND "negligence per se" AND
automobile OR car OR vehicle AND NOT hummer

It also offers more sophisticated search options, such as the ability to search by:

- *Language* (returns pages written in any language or a specific language);
- *File type* (returns results in any file format or only a specific format);
- *Domain* (returns results from a specific site or domain—discussed in detail later in this chapter);
- *Date, usage rights, numeric range, and more* (click on this link to reveal the following options):
    - *Date* (returns Web pages updated any time or within the past year, six months, or three months);
    - *Usage Rights* (returns results that are *free to use or share*; *free to use or share, even commercially*; *free to use, share, or modify*; or *free to use, share, or modify, even commercially*);
    - *Where your keywords show up* (returns results where search terms occur: anywhere on the page or in the text, URL, links, or title);
    - *Region* (choose *any region* to indicate all countries or select a specific country from the drop-down list);
    - *Numeric Range* (e.g. a dollar range or an address range).
    - *Page- Specific Searches;*
        - *Similar* (finds Web pages similar to a specific page);
        - *Links* (finds Web pages that link to a specific URL— discussed later in this chapter after the *Domain* discussion).

You can also use the *Results per page* drop-down menu to determine the number of results displayed per page (e.g., 10, 20, 30, 50, or 100).

The following is an example of a sophisticated *Advanced Search* where we entered one search term into the *all these words* search box and selected options from four different drop-down menus to narrow down our search results. We created a search for the word *negligence* in the *title* of a document where the document must be in the *Word file format*, is written in *English,* and has been indexed by **Google** in the *past year*.

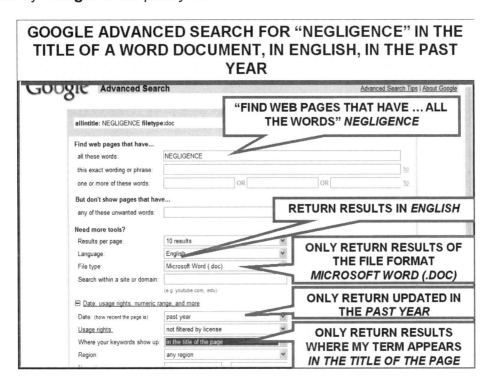

If you have ever had trouble locating information on a specific Web site but you are certain the information is on that site, you might have better luck using **Google's** *Search within a site or domain* search feature (located on the *Advanced Search* page) rather than a site's own internal search engine. Utilizing the *Search within a site or domain* feature, you can essentially superimpose the **Google** search engine onto another Web site (assuming it's a site that **Google** has previously indexed).

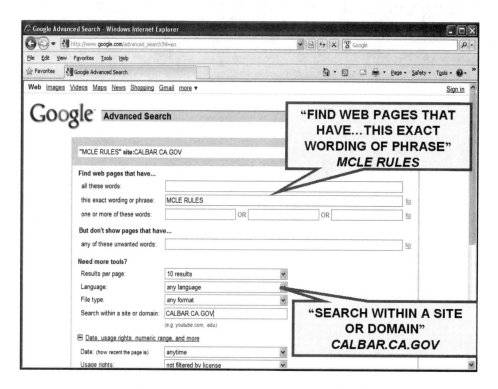

You can combine **Google's** *Search within a site or domain* feature with keywords and phrases entered into the *Advanced Search* page's query boxes to restrict **Google** to searching only a specific domain that you've specified. This is achieved by entering the URL of the site you want to search into the *Search within a site or domain* query box.

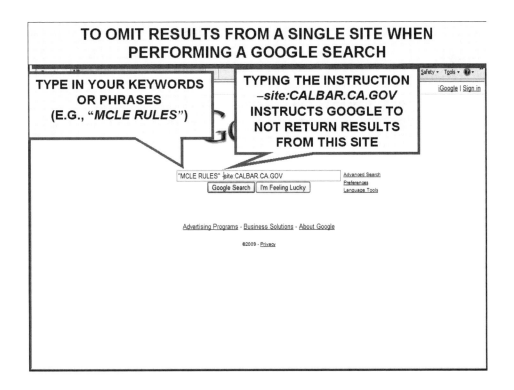

TO OMIT RESULTS FROM A SINGLE SITE WHEN PERFORMING A GOOGLE SEARCH

TYPE IN YOUR KEYWORDS OR PHRASES (E.G., "*MCLE RULES*")

TYPING THE INSTRUCTION *–site:CALBAR.CA.GOV* INSTRUCTS GOOGLE TO NOT RETURN RESULTS FROM THIS SITE

Google used to offer the option to exclude an entire site or domain with the *Domain…Don't return results from the site or domain instruction* from a drop-down menu that accompanied this feature. Now, to exclude a certain domain from your search, you must type the instruction directly into **Google's** search box yourself as illustrated in the screenshot above

The domain-specific searches at **Yahoo!**, **AltaVista**, and **Bing** are all presented in a very similar manner, however, only **Bing** and **Dogpile** still offer the ability to exclude a specific URL or domain directly from their respective *Advanced Search* templates

Using Google's Advanced Search to Discover Who is Linking to Whom

You can also use the *Advanced Search* page to determine potential relationships between individuals or companies by learning who is linking to whom on the Web. In the *Page-specific tools* section of **Google's** *Advanced Search* page (which is hidden behind the *Date, usage rights, numeric range, and more* link noted on page 62), you can type your target URL into the *Find pages* *that link to the page* search box to retrieve a list of sites that link to the site you have entered.

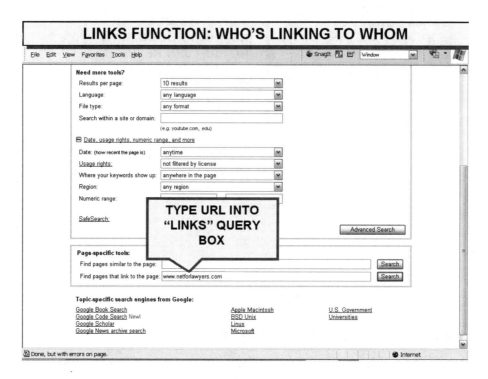

This can help to identify some "unofficial" relationships between companies, between companies and distributors, or between people.

None of the other search engines we've been discussing offer this search in the same way. The majority of the major search engines used to let you conduct a similar search by typing *links:sitename* into the main search box (where *sitename* is the URL of the site you're investigating; note that there is no space after the colon) and then click on the *Web search* button. Using that same search strategy at **AltaVista** returns many pages that link to the target *sitename* URL you've entered, but also returns pages that include the keyword *links* and *sitename*. However, **Bing** does not offer the ability to perform this kind of search (and returns far inferior results when you do).

Using Google's Advanced Search *File Type* Drop-Down Menu to Locate Specific File Types

In 2001 **Google** began indexing file types created in Adobe's popular Portable Document Format (PDF). This marked one of the first significant steps to index anything other than HTML documents on the Web. This was a boon to all Web searchers, who could now find the PDF documents that numerous government agencies, researchers, and universities posted to the Web. Up until 2001, these file formats could not be easily found by researchers because search engines did not index them, so they were considered "invisible." This moved many documents from the "Invisible Web" to the "Visible Web." (See page 35 in *Chapter Three* for more information about the "Invisible Web.")

Later in 2001, **Google** announced that it was also able to index files stored in file formats generated by the Microsoft Office suite (e.g., Word, Excel, and PowerPoint), all of which had been invisible up until then. Eventually, other major search engines like **Yahoo!**, **AltaVista**, **Bing**, and **USA.gov** added the ability to index these file formats as **Google** and return them in relevant searches. Use the *File Type* drop-down menu found on each search engine's respective *Advanced Search* page to limit a search to returning only files in a specific format.

Using Google's Advanced Search *File Type* Drop-Down Menu to Locate PowerPoint Presentations

PowerPoint presentations (once invisible as noted above) can be extremely useful when looking for material on a "hot" topic that has been the subject of conference presentations. The individuals making these presentations could also make good expert witnesses. Similarly, you may be able to find presentations from a particular expert using this strategy.

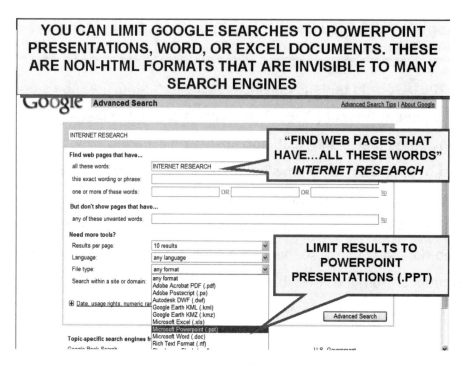

To do this, enter your search terms in the appropriate search boxes (e.g., *Find web pages that have all these words*, *Find web pages that have exact wording or phrase*) and then select *Microsoft PowerPoint (.ppt)* from the *File type* drop-down menu. The screen shot above illustrates how to limit a search to return only PowerPoint presentations on the subject of *Internet research*.

The results list displays only PowerPoint presentations that include your keywords.

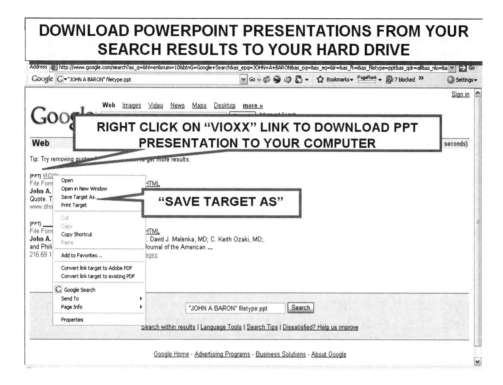

Once you've found a PowerPoint presentation that looks useful, you have the choice of viewing it in your Web browser or downloading it to your hard drive where you can then open it using PowerPoint. Downloading the presentation is a good choice because you can view it in the "editing" mode and read the presenter's notes (if there are any).

Using Google's Advanced Search *File Type* Drop-Down Menu to Locate PDFs

As mentioned on page 6, documents on the Web may be in the PDF file format. While they were once invisible, advances in search engine technology mean that they now reside on the visible Web. Web site owners might post documents as PDFs in order to maintain the integrity, layout, or design of a document so that it looks the same regardless of the type of computer on which it is displayed. Some common examples of this include court forms, tax forms and client intake sheets.

When returning PDFs in search results, **Google** (and some other search engines, such as **Yahoo!**) also give you the option of viewing the PDF document as an HTML document. Viewing a file in HTML, rather than PDF, can help the file open faster and make it easier to copy text from the document to quote in your own document by pasting it into the body of your document. (Note that even though **Bing** searches can be limited to only return PDF documents by entering *keyword filetype:PDF* into the search box, it does not offer an obvious option of viewing those files as HTML. Clicking the *Cached page* link that accompanies a PDF result will display a text-only HTML version of the document. See page 99 for more information on conducting *filetype* searches at Bing.)

The screenshot below presents a side-by-side comparison of a document returned in a **Google** search in the HTML (left) and PDF (right) formats.

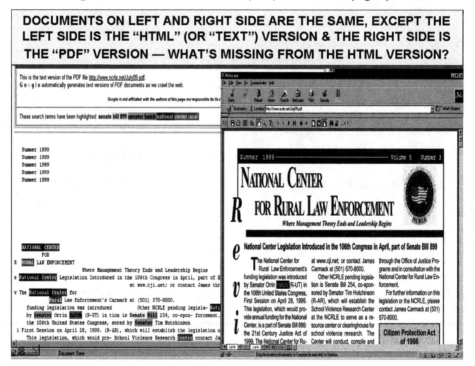

Using the Tools on the Specialty PDF Toolbar

You can be sure that you're viewing a PDF document in your Web browser if you see the specialty Adobe Reader toolbar underneath the browser's Address Bar. This toolbar is different from the standard browser tool bar that is visible when viewing HTML documents. The PDF tool bar provides a number of features to help you get the most out of the PDF documents you find on the Web. The PDF toolbar will look different, depending on which version of the free Adobe Reader you have installed on your computer. The illustration below points out some of the most useful of those features.

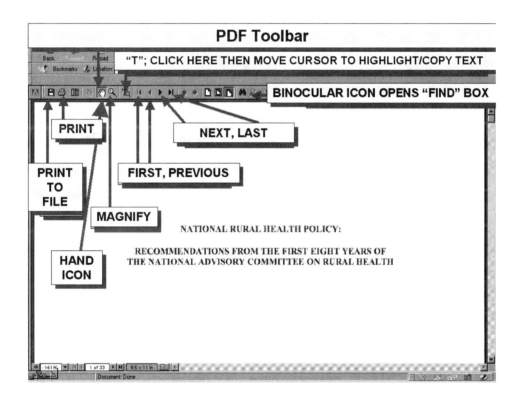

Finding Your Keywords in Web Documents

To scan Web pages to locate your keywords quickly, you need to know about the power of the *Find* function. It lets you jump directly to any search word or phrase in a Web document that you choose. To initiate the *Find* function:

- Visit a Web page

- If you are looking at a PDF document, click on the *Binocular* icon. Depending on which version of the Adobe Reader you are using, the *Binocular* icon will be located in a different place on the PDF document and the look of the *Find* dialog box will differ (see the screen shots of version 5 and 9 below for an example of the differences).

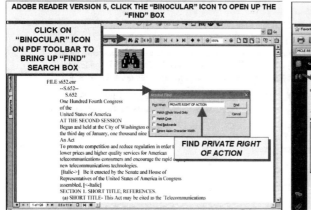 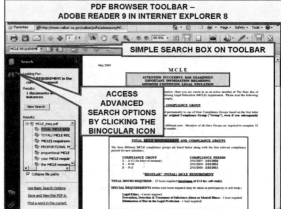

- If you are looking at a non-PDF document (e.g., HTML, Word, WordPerfect, PowerPoint, etc.), go to the browser's *Edit* pull-down menu and select *Find* (or hold down the *Control* key and the *F* key together). See page 9 for a detailed discussion of this feature.

- The *Find* dialog box will pop up

- Type any word or phrase into the dialog box

- Click on *Find next*

- You will be brought directly to your search word or phrase

- It will be highlighted

- To scan through the document to find the next occurrence of a word or phrase:

  - In a PDF; click on the other *Binocular* icon (the one with the arrow), a *page* icon (with a right- facing arrow next to it), or select an occurrence from the results list if you are looking at a PDF document

  - In a non-PDF document; click on *Find next* (located on the *Find* dialog box)

Over the years, **Google** has created a set of "tabs" or links, displayed on its home pages, to give searchers direct access to other file types, databases, and services (other than traditional Web sites). (**Yahoo!** and many other search engines including meta-search sites such as **Dogpile** and **Yippy** also include tabs.) The tabs on **Google's** home page include the following file types, databases, and services:

- *Images*
- *Videos*
- *Maps*
- *News*
- *Shopping*
- *Gmail*
- *More*

Google has added so many file types, databases, and services that they ran out of room to display all of the tabs on their home page, thus, many are hidden behind **Google's** *More* drop-down menu. (**Yahoo!** also includes a *More* tab on its home page.)

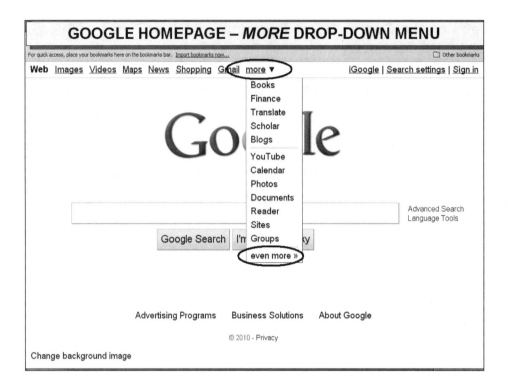

Some of the file types, databases, and services lurking behind **Google's** *More* drop-down menu include:

- *Books*
- *Finance*
- *Translate*
- *Scholar* (See pages 295-299.)
- *Blogs* (See pages 80-82.)
- *Groups* (Seepages 133-134.)

We will discuss many of these file types, databases, and services in detail in this chapter.

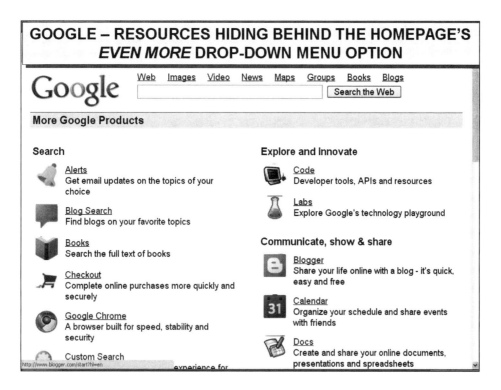

GOOGLE – RESOURCES HIDING BEHIND THE HOMEPAGE'S *EVEN MORE* DROP-DOWN MENU OPTION

Only **Google** has an *even more* link (found on the drop-down menu once you click *More* from the home page; see the previous illustration). Some of the file types, databases, and services lurking behind the *even more* tab include:

- *Alerts*
- *Google Chrome*
- *Earth*
- *iGoogle*
- *Patent Search*

Google Web searches also include a few news items as part of the results page — placing them at the top of the first page of results.

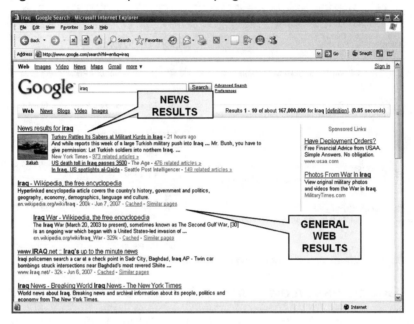

However, to search <u>only</u> current news, **Google** offers a *News* tab on its home page (see illustration on page 73). The *News* database contains only the past thirty days of news. In the summer of 2009, **Google News** results made the name(s) of the articles' reporter(s) into clickable links. Clicking on them retrieves a list of other articles also written by that same reporter.

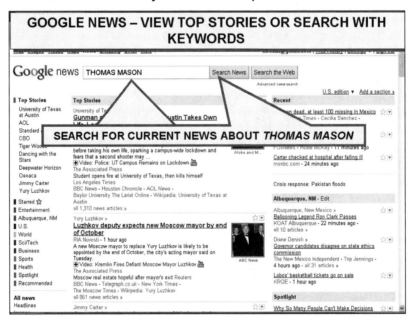

(Other search engines and meta-search sites also find current news, such as **AltaVista.com**, **AllTheWeb.com**, **Bing.com**, **Yahoo!**, **Dogpile**, and **Yippy**.)

Google News Advanced Search

Many of the basic and advanced search functions of the **Google News** database are similar to its general Web search.

However, the *News Advanced Search* also includes some unique features such as the ability to limit a search to:

- *News source: Return only articles from the news source named (e.g. CNN, New York Times)*
- *Source Location: Return only articles from news sources located in (A country or a U.S. state)*
- *Location: Return only articles about a local area (City, State, or Zip Code)*
- *Author: Return only articles written by*

In addition, the *News Advanced Search* includes a link to *Try archive search for articles added more than 30 days ago*, which we will discuss later in this chapter.

As you review your **Google News** results, notice the following features displayed at the bottom of the page

- *Stay up to date on these results:*
  - *Create an email alert for* [your search term] (*Alerts* are discussed in the next section of this chapter)
  - *Add a custom section for* [your search term] *to Google News*
  - *Search Google Fast Flip for* [your search term] (*Fast Flip* is a "web application that lets users … 'flip' through pages online as quickly as flipping through a magazine."*

Using Google Alerts to Keep Up to Date with Information Automatically

Google Alerts (http://www.google.com/alerts), allows you to set up an alert service based on your chosen keywords (or phrases). You are then notified (via e-mail) when your chosen keywords (or phrases) appear online in one (or all) of the following: *Blogs, Discussions, Video,* or *News.* To set your **Google Alert** to include all of the sources, choose **Google Alerts'** *Everything* option from the drop-down menu. You can request notification on a *once a week, once a day,* or *as it happens* basis.

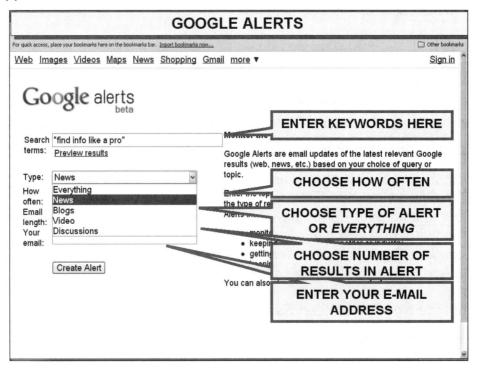

Both **Yahoo!** and **Bing** have introduced *News alerts.* (See pages 96 and 100 for details about **Yahoo!** and **Bing's** *News alerts.*)

In 2006, **Google** extended the date range of its news search and the sources from which it draws results with its launch of the **Google News Archive** search (http://news.google.com/archivesearch).

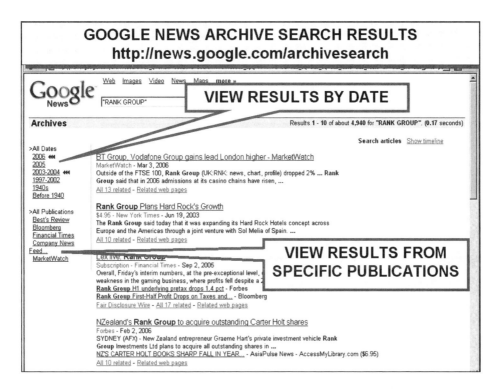

The date coverage of the **Google News Archive** is not documented, but in one of our test searches we found an August 16, 1879 article from *The Sydney Morning Herald*. While access to many of the **Archive's** articles is free, access to some articles (mostly from newspapers such as the Washington Post Archives and the New York Times Archives), requires a fee. The **Google News Archive** search allows you to display results in a variety of ways, including by relevancy (which is the default display), by source, by date range, or in a timeline.

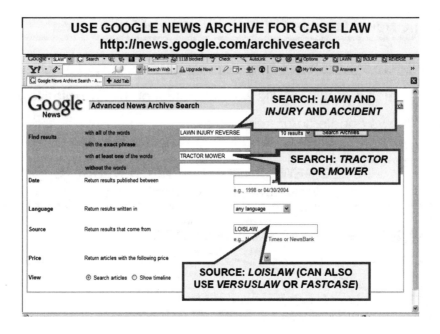

For lawyers, the addition of court opinions to the *Archive* is important to note. The opinions come from several case law databases (Fastcase, Loislaw, and Versuslaw), all of which charge an access fee. To limit results to one of the case law databases, you would use the *Source…Return results that come from* box on the *News Archive* search's *Advanced Archive Search* page.

Before you pay for court opinions returned as search results via the **Archive**, read about free access to court opinions at **Google Scholar** and other databases, discussed in *Chapter Twelve*. And, before you pay for news articles found by the **Archive**, read the section about remote access to public library databases on pages 145-146.

Using Google to Locate Blogs

Since 2001, "personal Web logs" (or "blogs") have become a popular and powerful means of expression and communication on the Internet. Many blogs are like a personal journal or diary. Others are used as an individual professional publishing platform for marketing purposes. Made up of short, frequently updated posts, blogs are arranged in reverse chronological order — with the newest posts at the top of the page. Many blogs present more of an attitude (or at least a personality) than a regular Web site.

The contents and purposes of blogs vary with the personalities of the "bloggers" who create them. Blogs can contain everything from links and commentary on current events, to news about a specific topic or company. A personal blog might resemble an online diary and include photos, poetry, essays, project updates, or fiction. Often these blogs are no more than a chronicle of what's on the mind of the blogger at any given time. Professional blogs might include current awareness or commentary on a particular industry or area of law. Regardless of their content, blogs are Web sites, but not every search engine has added them to their respective indices or treats results from blogs equally. Blogs' ease of development and updating make it extremely easy for anyone, even those with limited technical ability, to create, host, and update their own Web site. Blogs can be an excellent source of news or commentary on "hot" topics and public opinion regarding companies or their products.

Google has created a separate search engine for information posted to blogs (http://blogsearch.google.com). On the home page, there is the standard search box and a link to the *Advanced Blog Search* (http://linkon.in/a5Kbqd) — pictured below.

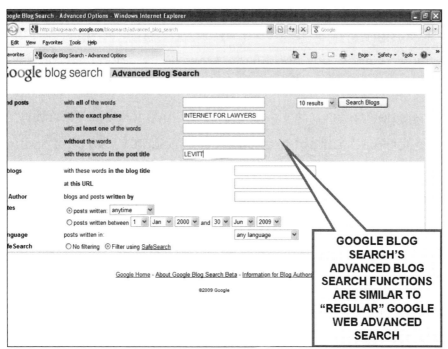

GOOGLE BLOG SEARCH'S ADVANCED BLOG SEARCH FUNCTIONS ARE SIMILAR TO "REGULAR" GOOGLE WEB ADVANCED SEARCH

Using the *Advanced Blog Search,* you can narrow your results by searching for words *in the post title, in the blog title, at this URL, blogs and posts written by*, *Dates*, and *Language*.

You can be alerted to new blog postings on your subject by creating a **Google Alert** (discussed earlier in this chapter) or subscribing to the Atom or RSS feeds. The link to these services is found to the left of the search results page. For more information on Atom or RSS feeds, see pages 447-448.

For information on using blogs for investigative research, see pages 134–135.

Using Google to Locate Non-Text Files Such as Sound/Audio/Podcasts and Video

Audio and video can be found online if you know where to look. **YouTube.com** (owned by **Google**), is obviously one of the largest repositories but you can limit results to video-only results right from the **Google** search engine's home page by choosing the *Videos* tab. **Google Video** search (http://video.google.com) was developed as "an open video marketplace." Searches return a variety of results ranging from amateur video that can be submitted to **Google's** video database by any Web user to episodes of popular TV shows, music videos, and short films. Most of the videos can be viewed for free, while some videos are offered for sale. (The video's owners, not **Google**, determine the sales prices of a video. However, even videos that carry a fee can be previewed for free.) **Yahoo!** and **Bing** both include *Video* tabs on their home pages.

Podcasts are a more recent phenomenon in delivering audio content via the Internet. You can think of podcasts as "radio delivered via the Internet." Instead of listening to a live broadcast, however, listeners download audio files to their computers or portable media players (e.g., an iPod) to play them back when it is convenient. Like other kinds of content available on the Internet, podcasts are relatively easy to create and cover a wide array of topics. Most podcasts are saved in the MP3 format, allowing maximum portability and flexibility in playing back the audio content. A recent **Google** search for *podcasts* returned over 583 million results (compared to 79 million a year earlier).

In the legal arena, some lawyers are creating podcasts for marketing purposes and to educate clients and potential clients on a variety of topics. (Legal podcasts are occasionally referred to as "plawdcasts," but the term has not gained the popularity of the term "blawg.") As listeners, legal professionals can use podcasts to get up-to-speed or keep up-to-date on numerous legal and non-legal topics.

To find podcasts on all topics, you can use an online directory of podcasts, such as **PodcastAlley.com**. For legal blogs, see **Blawgs.fm** (thttp://blawgsfm.justia.com), **The Blogs of Law** (http://www.theblogsoflaw.com), or simply use a search engine. For example, to find a podcast about *copyright infringement*, we searched **Google** for *podcast*, *copyright,* and *infringement*. Nearly half a million results were returned. One of the results was the "This Week in Law" podcast (http://www.twit.tv/twil) hosted by IP attorney Denise Howell, along with a revolving panel of experts. She posts a new podcast each month on various intellectual property and technology issues.

Once you have located podcasts that you find useful (or entertaining), you can either check back with the host site frequently to download new installments, or subscribe to the podcast via RSS. Similar to RSS feeds of text content (discussed in the *RSS Feeds Bring Information to You* on pages 447-448), podcast RSS feeds alert you automatically when new content is available and even send the files to you automatically. These specialty RSS aggregators are sometimes called "podcatchers." Some of the more popular podcatchers include **iTunes** (http://www.apple.com/itunes/) for Mac and Windows; **Juice** (http://juicereceiver.sourceforge.net) for Mac, Windows, and Linux; and **Google Reader** (http://www.google.com/reader/), which is web-based.

FindSounds (http://www.findsounds.com) is a specialty search engine where you can locate specific sounds to add sound to a presentation.

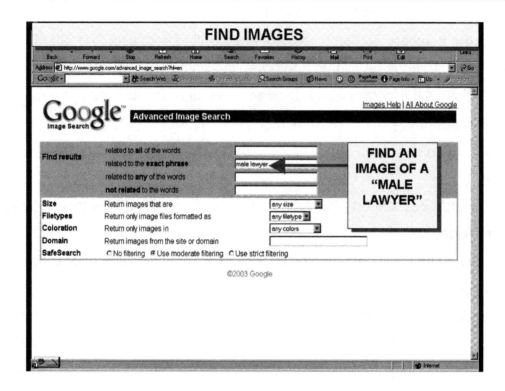

It's often useful to find out, in advance, what a person looks like, whether you are investigating that person or simply need to identify someone you are meeting for the first time (such as a new client) at a public place. Entering the person's name into an image search engine can sometimes help you find his or her picture. You can also conduct an image search for places, concepts, or products by using the appropriate keywords to describe them.

Click the *Images* tab on **Google's** home page (or **AltaVista**, **Yahoo!**, or **Bing**) to search for images on the Internet. Be sure to use **Google's** *Advanced Image Search* for a more precise search (**Google's** *Advanced Image Search* is shown above). As of July 2010, **Google** claims to have over ten billion images in this database.

(**Yahoo!** and **Bing** also have *Advanced Image Searches* but they are not offered until after you run an *Image* search.)

For those who are curious about upcoming Google features, visit **Google Labs** (http://labs.google.com/). According to **Google**, it "showcases a few of our favorite ideas that aren't quite ready for prime time." Despite that designation, many of the features and services that start out in **Labs** are very useful.

"Hidden" Search Engine Features Not Even Found Behind Google's *Even More* Menu

Google *Glossary*: One "graduate" of the **Google Labs** is **Google Glossary**. To use the **Google Glossary**, type the word *define* followed by a colon and the word you want defined (with no spaces) into the query box on the **Google** home page (e.g., *define:clew*). Several definitions of the word are displayed, from various dictionaries (general and topical) and Web sites. Using our example of *clew*, definitions came from **Wordnetweb** (http://wordnet.princeton.edu/) which is a "lexical database of English" created by a professor at Princeton and **GJW Direct** (http://gjwdirect.co.uk/boatterms), which is the UK's largest direct boat insurer. **Wordnetweb** gave a general definition of the word ("a ball of yarn or cord or thread") while the **GJW** site gave a more specific definition relating to boats ("An aft corner of a triangular sail").

Synonyms: Another of **Google's** lesser-known features is its ability to return synonyms of a search term you enter. To invoke the synonym search, add a *tilde* ("~") next to the term (or terms) for which you want to retrieve synonyms. For example, entering *~broken ~femur* will return results that not only include those keywords, but also synonyms for either word, such as *fractured* or *bone*.

Google Patent Search (http://www.google.com/patents) offers a searchable database of more than seven million patent records. It includes images of patents back to 1790. Granted patents from 1920 to the present are full-text searchable in varying degrees. Patent applications are searchable from 2001 to the present and include multi-page images for all included applications.

Despite its name, this database also includes trademark data, including applications searchable from 1884 to the present. Registered trademark images are available from 1870 to the present.

Using Google as a Phone Directory or Address Directory

From **Google's** home page query box, one can actually use the search engine as a telephone or address directory and even a reverse directory. If you enter a person's name and their city (or state abbreviation, ZIP, or area code) into the query box, **Google** will display the phone number and address of that person (above the list of Web page results). These results include only publicly listed U.S. street address and phone numbers.

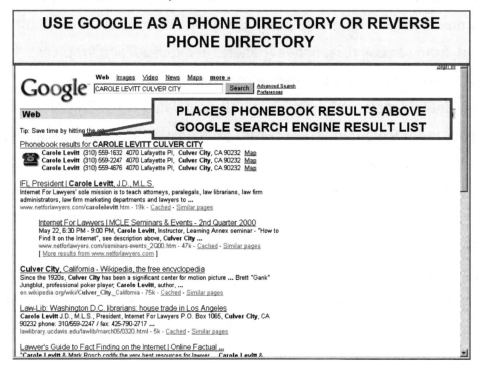

To find listings for a U.S. business, type the business name, city, and state, or type the business name and ZIP Code into **Google's** search box. This also works with reverse searching (e.g., type in a phone number or address, and the name[s] tied to the number or address will be displayed above the results list).

Anyone can fill out **Google's** online form (http://www.google.com/help/pbremoval.html) to request removal of their own personal listing information from the **Google** phone book. That page also contains an address where one can send a hard-copy request (signed and on company letterhead) to remove one's own business information from the **Google** phone book.

Yahoo! will return similar results for a phone number or address search. **Yahoo!** does not maintain its own phone book database as **Google** does. **Yahoo!** pulls its phone number results from **Intelius.com** and its address results from its own **Yahoo!** *Maps* service (http://maps.yahoo.com).

Search Tips and Tricks: How to Locate "Invisible" Data in Databases

As we dicussed on page 34, most search engines do not readily index data found in databases, but they can locate databases for you to search so you can locate the "invisible" data they contain. Use **Google.com** (or any other search engine) to locate databases on specific topics by typing the word *database* into the *With All The Words* query box on the *Advanced Search* page and then add other words and phrases to describe the data you are seeking. For example, to find a database of all California State Bar members, type in the phrase *California state bar* and the keywords *member* and *database*.

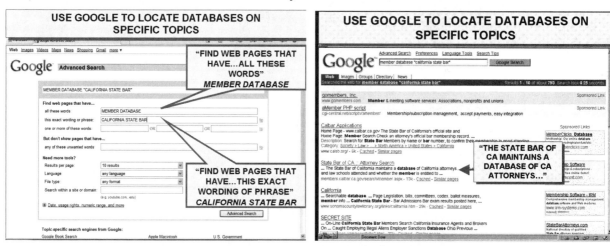

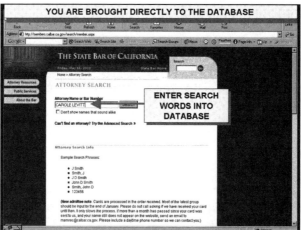

That said, some databases are built in such a way that some search engines **can** retrieve information from them — the trick, though, is knowing what specific search terms to use to help the search engine locate the database with the information.

GOOGLE CAN RETRIEVE INFORMATION FROM CERTAIN DATABASES – DEPENDING ON HOW THE DATABASE IS BUILT

Google Advanced Search   Advanced Search Tips | About Google

CAROLE LEVITT CALIFORNIA "ATTORNEY SEARCH"

Find web pages that have...

all these words: CAROLE LEVITT CALIFORNIA

this exact wording or phrase: ATTORNEY SEARCH

GOOGLE – RESULTS OF THIS SEARCH INCLUDE RECORDS FROM THE CALIFORNIA STATE BAR'S MEMBERSHIP DATABASE

Show search tools

4 California attorneys that match levitt - State Bar of CA ...
Attorney Search Attorney Name or Bar Number Advanced Search » . Levitt, Carole Ann, Inactive, 143511, Rio Rancho, December 1989 ... members.calbar.ca.gov/search/member_search.aspx? ms=levitt - Cached

in Local Directory!
www.USdirectory.com

California Attorney List
Providing Detailed Profiles Of Attorneys In CA. Search Now!
Lawyers.FindLaw.com

See your ad here »

Taking the previous California State Bar example one step further, we can use very specific keywords and phrases, to get information on Carole Levitt's license to practice law in California. If we type *Carole Levitt California* into the *all these words* query box on **Google's** *Advanced Search* page and *attorney search* into the *this exact wording or phrase* box, the first search result returned is Carole's attorney registration record from the California State Bar's Web site (see above). This search works for two reasons: 1) The California State Bar's membership database stores and displays information in such a way that **Google** can access it and 2) the phrase *attorney search* appears on the California State Bar's results page when conducting a search for licensed attorneys at its Web site. Realistically, though, you wouldn't know in advance whether a database that would answer your question was built in such a way as to allow **Google** access.

HUMAN SEARCH ENGINES

The **Library of Congress** (http://www.loc.gov/rr/askalib/) allows you to submit text questions online to the librarians at the **Library of Congress**, and also offers designated times when you can "chat" with them live. Also, see page

288 for information about the **Internet Public Library's** *Ask an ipl2 Librarian* service.

Yahoo! *Answers* (http://answers.yahoo.com/) allows its users to submit text questions online to be answered by other **Yahoo!** *Answers* users. **Yahoo!** *Answers* users earn points through participation. For example, answering a question earns a user two points and asking a question "costs" five points (but you can "earn" 100 points just for creating a free account). Similarly, **Mahalo** *Answers* (http://www.mahalo.com/answers) awards points and "Mahalo Dollars" (M$) for answers voted as the best. Mahalo Dollars are convertible to U.S. Dollars at a rate of $0.75 to M$1. (**Google** had previously offered a similar service but discontinued it at the end of 2006).

FINDING "SPECIAL TOPIC" SEARCH ENGINES AND DIRECTORIES

For links to a variety of topical search engines and directories, use **CompletePlanet** (http://www.completeplanet.com).

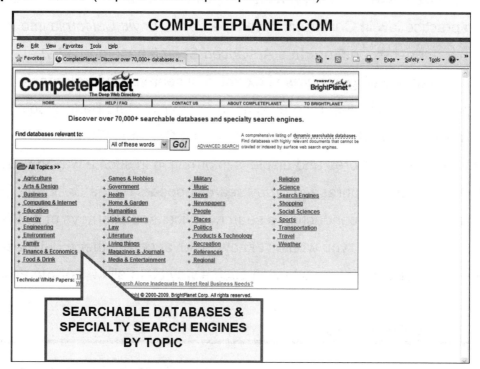

When we cover legal research later in this book, we'll discuss **Justia** (see pages 104 and 247), a search engine that searches Web sites focused on only one topic — law.

At the end of an Internet research seminar, we often hear the following comment: "That was a great seminar. I really understand the Web better now and everything I can find on it. But, where do I go now to find someone to do it for me?" The goal of our seminars is twofold: (1) to teach lawyers how they can use the Web for research on their own, and (2) for those lawyers who don't have the time (or inclination) to use the Web on their own, to inform them of what's available on the Web so they know what to ask for when handing a research assignment over to an associate, librarian, or paralegal. However, for many of you in a small or solo practice, there is no one else to take over the research task! Or maybe you have an assistant, but the subject matter or depth of research is out of their area of expertise. In either case, this is the time to seek expert research support.

For those determined lawyers who insisted that you "needed" us to locate the information you were missing, we formed our **Information For Lawyers** investigative division (http://www.infoforlawyers.com) in late 2005.

The research focus is on the six information categories with which attendees and readers have repeatedly asked us to help them:

- People Finding (e.g., missing witnesses, missing heirs)
- Competitive Intelligence (e.g., profiling an opposing counsel, expert, prospective client)
- Asset Searching
- Company Background
- Criminal Records (note: availability of information varies widely from jurisdiction to jurisdiction)
- Legal Research

We have assembled a seasoned staff of research professionals to handle your requests. These degreed law librarians and lawyers have over fifty combined years of experience conducting research for attorneys at some of the country's most respected law firms and for large corporate clients. While no electronic search is absolutely complete, we have access to some of the most comprehensive pay databases available for locating information about people. Our experienced team reviews and cross-matches their results, combining them with other information they have located from sources available on the Internet, to deliver a dossier of information that can help make or break your case.

Pricing varies by project, but most are billed at $100/hour ($25 minimum). Per search fees incurred when using pay databases are billed to clients (at cost, with no mark-up) in addition to the hourly fee.

Chapter Five

OTHER FAVORITE SEARCH ENGINES AND META-SEARCH SITES

Until recently, **Google** had very little competition in the relevance of its results, or the types and numbers of documents in its index, but **Yahoo! Search** and **Bing** have made impressive progress. Beginning in mid-2004, **Google** claimed to index nearly 8.2 billion pages of the Internet (although it is important to note that there is no way to independently confirm this self-reported number). In late 2005, after attempting to refute **Yahoo!'s** claim of indexing more than 20 billion items (see below), **Google** removed the reference to the size of its index from their home page. (**Google** had not updated the number posted on its home page since first claiming 8.2 billion pages in 2004.) Currently, the major search engines no longer display the number of pages in their respective indices.

Yahoo! (http://www.yahoo.com)

In February 2004, **Yahoo!** implemented a new search index of its own (reportedly based on an index and spidering technology created by Inktomi, which Yahoo! acquired in 2002). Previously, **Yahoo!** had been receiving its Web search results from **Google**. It quickly became clear that this new index was returning relevant, high quality results — many of which are very similar to

Google results, for the same search (in terms of number and order of the search results). In an August 2005 posting to the **Yahoo**! *Search Blog*, **Yahoo!** claimed that its search index had grown "to over 20 billion items…this update includes just over 19.2 billion Web documents, 1.6 billion images, and over 50 million audio and video files" (http://www.ysearchblog.com/archives/000172.html). Because the seach engines are no longer touting the size of their indices and there is no independent auditing, we have to take their word for it. Some veteran search engine watchers didn't embrace Yahoo's claim (http://linkon.in/cIjDrr; http://linkon.in/cA2kYs).

When you visit **Yahoo!** you can conduct a search using the search box at the top of the page or you can click on one of the many "tabs" or links to limit your search to specific file types, databases, and services (other than traditional Web sites). The tabs on **Yahoo!'s** home page are located above the search box and also on the left-hand side of the page. The tabs located above the search box include the following file types, databases, and services.

- *Images*
- *Videos*
- *Local*
- *Shopping*
- *More*

Some of the tabs located on the left-hand side of the home page include

- *Mail*
- *Finance*
- *Groups*
- *Maps*
- *Weather*

Although **Yahoo!** (http://www.yahoo.com/) and **Yahoo! Search** (http://search.yahoo.com), both offer the *Advanced Search* feature, it is hidden on the home page behind the *More* link where you can select it from the drop-down menu. It is also displayed as an option after you run a search, and even then it is still hidden (behind the *Options* link to the right of the query box).

Yahoo! offers many of the same search features and functions as **Google**. The following are some of the different features found at **Yahoo!** (or some of the same features, but implemented differently from **Google**):

- **Yahoo!** uses the asterisk (*) as a Proximity Connector but only for phrase searching. (See *Chapter Three*, page 41 for a full discussion of Proximity Connectors) To conduct a proximity search at **Yahoo**, the search terms must be contained within quotation marks and must be separated by the asterisk (e.g., *"Mark * Rosch"*). Using the asterisk in this way (at **Yahoo!**) indicates that you want the first keyword to be separated from the second keyword by one other word and that the words must appear in that order. The asterisk essentially takes the place of one word in such a search. Note that you cannot use multiple asterisks to take the place of multiple words.

- The *links* search (discussed in *Chapter Four* on page 65) is not offered on the **Yahoo!** *Advanced Search* page as it is at **Google**. To conduct a *links* search at **Yahoo!**, you must enter the *links* instruction, then a colon, and then the URL of the site you're investigating; without any spaces (into the search box). Your search would look like this if you were running a *links* search for netforlawyers.com:

  link:www.netforlawyers.com

- While **Yahoo!** does not maintain its own phone book database as **Google** does, **Yahoo!** allows you to conduct a phone number or address search and pulls its phone number results from **Intelius.com** and its address results from its own **Yahoo! Maps** service (http://maps.yahoo.com).

- **Yahoo!** offers a *News alerts* service (not as extensive as **Google Alerts**). **Yahoo!** requires you to create a **Yahoo!** account to set up *News alerts* (http://alerts.yahoo.com/home.php).

- **Yahoo! Answers** (http://answers.yahoo.com/) allows users to submit text questions online to be answered by other **Yahoo! Answers** users. **Yahoo! Answers** users earn points through participation. For example, answering a question earns a user two points and asking a question "costs" five points (but you can "earn" 100 points just for creating a free account). **Google** had previously offered a similar service but discontinued it at the end of 2006).

While it doesn't maintain a public area where users can access tools that are still in development, **Yahoo!** maintains a separate blog (http://www.ysearchblog.com/) that offers "a look inside the world of search from the people of Yahoo!" where many of the search engine's newest functions have been announced first. (For example, that's how we learned that **Yahoo!** has a *Glossary* (*define*) feature that functions similarly to **Google's**.) For various **Yahoo!** shortcut search tips, such as how to use **Yahoo!** as a Glossary using its *define* shortcut or how to find a synonym using its *synonym* shortcut, see http://tools.search.yahoo.com/newsearch/resources. To find a synonym for the word lawyer enter this shortcut into the search box: *synonym lawyer.*

    Yahoo! has even created a sparse (more **Google**-like) search interface that features just its search box and a few content tabs (e.g., *Images, Videos, Local*) at http://search.yahoo.com.

    See the **Bing** entry (in the next section) for more recent news about **Yahoo!**.

In May 2009, **Microsoft** relaunched its search initiative with a new "decision engine" named **Bing**. At launch, **Microsoft** described **Bing** as being "designed to empower people to gain insight and knowledge from the Web, moving more quickly to important decisions." The idea is to present information to help users make decisions in four major categories: *Travel*, *Shopping*, *Health*, and *Local* — rather than just displaying a list of links. If your searches don't fall into those categories, then your results may not look all that different than what you're used to. On the surface, the results for test investigative and background research searches we've run have been very similar to those from the company's previous search engine **Live Search**. That's not a bad thing, though, because those results tend to be very relevant to the keywords for which we searched.

On July 2009, "**Microsoft**…acquire[d] an exclusive 10 year license to **Yahoo!'s** core search technologies, and **Microsoft** will have the ability to integrate **Yahoo!** search technologies into its existing web search platforms. **Microsoft's Bing** will be the exclusive algorithmic search and paid search platform for **Yahoo!** sites. **Yahoo!** will continue to use its technology and data in other areas of its business such as enhancing display advertising technology," (http://www.microsoft.com/Presspass/press/2009/jul09/07-29release.mspx). On February 18, 2010 — **Microsoft** and **Yahoo!** announced that they "received clearance for their search agreement, without restrictions, from both the U.S. Department of Justice and the European Commission, and will now turn their attention to beginning the process of implementing the deal." As of September 2010, researchers can still search at either **Bing** or **Yahoo!**. In our identical test searches of both search engines, we found similar results for those identical searches, although some of the results were in a different order. **Bing** displays the number of search results at the top of the list of links to those results. **Yahoo!** displays (not always the same number) in the left-hand column.

Bing has the following tabs on its home page for you to limit your search to various databases (or to use various services):

- *Images*
- *Videos*
- *Shopping*
- *News*
- *Maps*
- *Travel*
- *Entertainment*

Bing only makes its *Advanced Search* functions available after your search results are returned (via a link labeled *Advanced* that appears near the top of the search results list; just below the search box). Clicking on the *Advanced* link opens up the *Advanced Search* box at the top of the search results list. Here you can add additional search keywords or phrases. Clicking the *Add to Search* button returns new, narrower results. You can also use other *Advanced Search* functions to narrow your search to:

- *Site/Domain*
- *Country/Region*
- *Language*

One option not offered on the *Advanced Search* page is the ability to restrict a search to specific types of files. However, you can instruct Bing to do just that by typing a special instruction into the search box, for specific document types, including:

- Microsoft Word – *[keyword] filetype:doc* or *[keyword] filetype:docx*
- Microsoft Powerpoint – *[keyword] filetype:ppt* or *[keyword] filetype:pptx*
- Microsoft Excel – *[keyword] filetype:xls* or *[keyword] filetype:xlsx*
- PDF – *[keyword] filetype:pdf*

While **Bing** offers many of the same types of searches as **Google** and **Yahoo!**, of the three search engines, only **Bing** recognizes parentheses as a search parameter (see page 43 for details) and the ability to exclude a specific URL or domain directly from the *Advanced Search* template. Be careful when using the *NOT* and *OR* Boolean connectors at **Bing**. Like **Google** and **Yahoo!**, you must capitalize your Boolean connectors; otherwise, **Bing** will ignore them as stop (or "noise") words. (See page 50 for an explanation of stop (or "noise") words.) At **Bing**, you can also use the minus sign in the place of the NOT Boolean connector, as you would at **Google** and **Yahoo!**.

Bing offers *News alerts*. To use the *News alerts*, **Bing** requires you to have, and sign in to Windows Live account (click on *News* from the **Bing** home page and then click on *News alerts*). **Bing's** *News alerts* only runs your search through its *News* database. (**Google Alerts**, on the other hand, allows you to opt to run your search through several other databases in addition to its *News* database, as discussed in *Chapter Four*). After you enter your search into **Bing's** *Create a news alert about* search box, select how often you want to be alerted: *Once a day*, *Twice a day*, or *Weekly*.

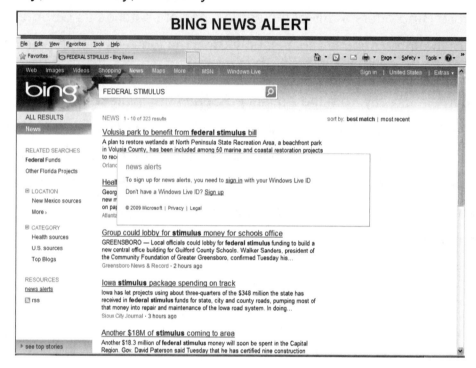

META-SEARCH SITES: SEARCHING A "SEARCH ENGINE OF SEARCH ENGINES"

Meta-search sites function like a "search engine of search engines" — submitting your search to multiple search engines at once. They do not maintain their own index, but rely on the indices of other search engines from which they draw results. Currently, one of the more popular is **Yippy** (http://www.yippy.com). One feature that makes **Yippy** stand out from other meta-search sites like **Dogpile** (http://www.dogpile.com) is the grouping of results into topical folders (Yippy refers to these as *Clouds*) displayed on the left side of the page, in conjunction with the "regular" list of results down the center of the page.

While meta-search sites can help return large amounts of information on a subject, they are limited in that (1) they search only a limited number of sources and (2) some of those sources may be too busy (e.g., experiencing high searching volume) to reply back to the meta-search site's query. There would be no way of knowing if one of the search resources did not return any results to a search without (in the case of **Yippy**) clicking the *details* link (see illustration in the next section) to view their individual results. None of the other meta-search sites offer a similar feature.

Another of our favorite, if more specialized, meta-search site is **Twingine**.

Meta-Search Sites: Twingine.com (http://www.twingine.com — formerly Yagoohoogle.com)

Twingine is also a meta-search site but only submits searches to two search engines — **Yahoo!** and **Google**.

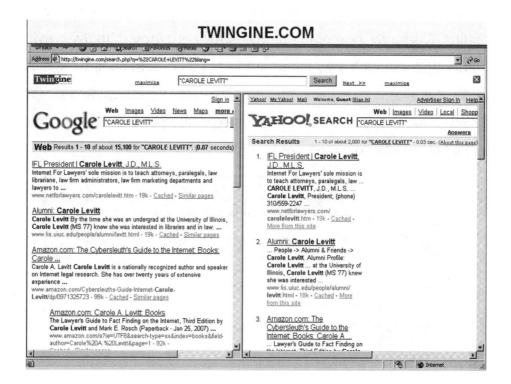

The site was originally conceived as an April Fools' Day prank that made it appear that **Yahoo!** and **Google** had joined together to form one giant search engine called "**Yagoohoogle.**" Traffic to the fictitious site was so heavy that the prankster created an actual meta-search site to run searches simultaneously on **Yahoo!** and **Google** and display the results side by side. Reportedly after receiving cease and desist letters from both **Yahoo!** and **Google**, the developer chose the less-infringing **Twingine** name for his creation.

Meta-Search Sites: Yippy.com (http://yippy.com/ — formerly Clusty.com; formerly Vivisimo.com)

Yippy is a meta-search site that submits your query to multiple search engines simultaneously. **Yippy** aggregates the results from those various search engines into one familiar-looking list of results down the center of the page.

Unlike other meta-search sites, **Yippy** creates a set of topical folders (they call *Clouds*; displayed on the left side of the page). A small number (in parentheses to the right of each folder's name) indicates the number of results in that folder. Folders can be expanded to show their contents by clicking on the "plus sign" or the triangle to the right of the folder. Folders may contain links to resources or sub-topical folders related to the topic of the main folder.

Additionally, **Yippy** offers specific details about how many results each search engines (to which it submitted your query) returned for your search. This level of information can be useful in case one of the search engines is too busy processing other search requests or otherwise does not respond to **Yippy's** query. This information is accessible by clicking the details link above the search results (circled in the illustration above).

Justia's Legal Web Search (http://www.justia.com)

Justia (http://www.justia.com) is a free legal portal and does not require registration. Aside from offering a comprehensive directory to help researchers find legal research Web sites, **Justia** also offers a sophisticated search engine, *Legal Web*, which locates legal-specific information on the Web. It is powered by **Google's** search engine technology.

To actually run a *Legal Web* search at **Justia**, do not enter any keywords into the search box at **Justia.com**. Instead, click the *Search Justia* button to the right of the search box on the home page (see next illustration).

Then you are offered a *Legal Web* (see next illustration) search.

JUSTIA LEGAL WEB SEARCH (STEP 2)

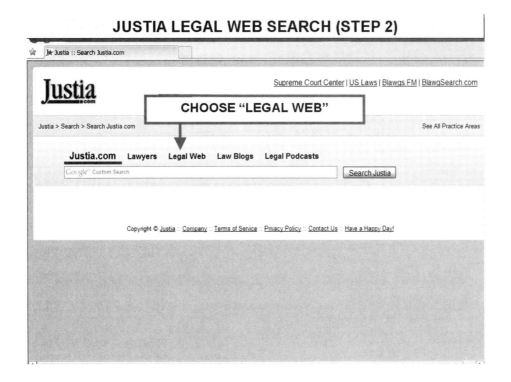

After selecting *Legal Web*, enter your search into the search box and click the *Search Legal Web button*.

JUSTIA LEGAL WEB SEARCH (STEP 3)

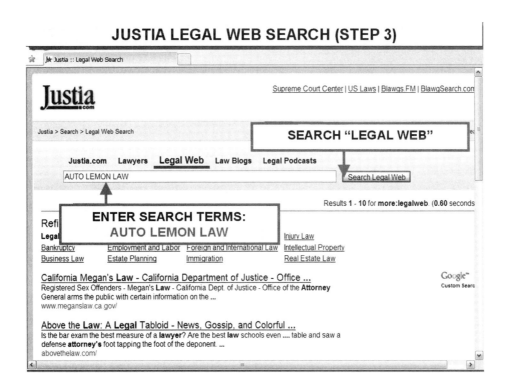

The search results page (see next illustration) will first display paid **Google Ads**. Above your search results, a group of suggestions are displayed to help you refine the initial results list. Finally, the organic list of your search results is displayed. For more details about **Justia** and its free case law and docket databases see pages 247-253.

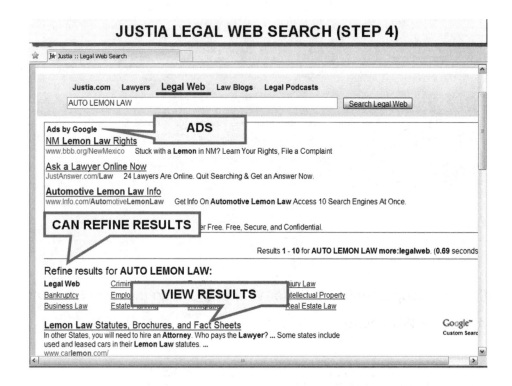

USA.gov, at http://www.usa.gov, is the federal government's portal that includes a custom search engine powered by **Bing**. It searches millions of pages of federal, state, local, territorial, and tribal government documents, many of which would not be found through searches anywhere else (or at least not as easily). Like **Bing**, a link to **USA.gov's** *Advanced Search* page is only visible after you've run a search. To access **USA.gov's** *Advanced Search* page directly, visit http://search.usa.gov/search/advanced. There you can limit your search to specific jurisdictions, file formats, domains (e.g., www.doe.gov), and more. (See pages 276–279 for more information)

USASEARCH.GOV ADVANCED SEARCH FOR "ENEMY COMBATANT" IN A PDF DOCUMENT FROM THE FEDERAL GOVERNMENT

For more information about locating other special topic search engines, see page 90.

Chapter Six

FINDING OLDER VERSIONS OF WEB PAGES THAT HAVE BEEN DELETED OR REVISED

To find older versions of Web pages that have been deleted or revised, use **Google Cache**, **Yahoo! Cache**, **Bing Cache**, and **The Way Back Machine** (also known as **Internet Archive** or by its URL **Archive.org**).

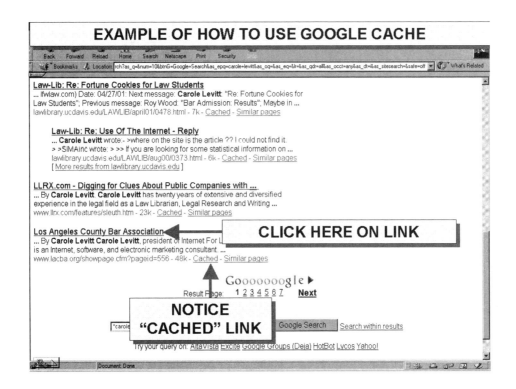

If a page listed in **Bing**, **Google**, or **Yahoo!** search results is no longer available (e.g., you receive the dreaded "404 error" message when you click on it), look for the *Cached* link (see the illustration on page 109) to access an archived version of the page stored by the search engine. The "cached" version is a copy of that particular page as it appeared at the time of the search engine robot's last visit to that page. The search engine stores a copy of the information from that page on the search engine's own server for future reference and/or retrieval.

Bing, **Google**, and **Yahoo!** only offer access to the most recent version of a page that has been captured in its cache. **Bing** and **Google** both include the date on which the cached copy was made (**Google** also includes the time). **Yahoo!** does not include date or time information for the pages it has cached. (Note that none of these search engines offers cached versions of all pages in its search index.)

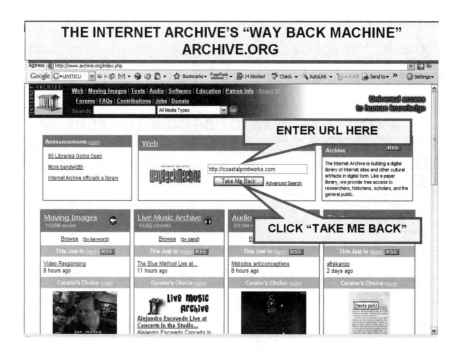

To find old versions of revised or deleted Web pages, you can also try the **Way Back Machine** (http://www.archive.org), which is an archive of more than 150 billion old Web pages from 1996 to date (as of August 2010). Unlike the traditional search engines that offer access only to the most recent cached versions of the old Web pages they've captured, the **Way Back Machine** offers access to all of the versions of any Web page it has captured. It is important to note, however, that you cannot do a keyword search through this collection of pages. To locate any of these old pages, you must enter the URL of the specific site (or page) you're interested in locating into the search box on **Archive.org's** home page and click the *Take Me Back* button.

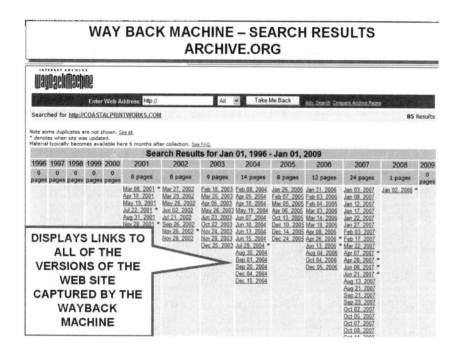

The search results will display a chronological list of all of the versions of the URL searched for that are available in the **Archive's** collection. Clicking on any of the links will display that old Web page as it appeared on the date selected.

While **Archive.org** is continuously collecting these pages, it takes a minimum of six months (and in some cases up to 24 months) before particular Web pages are available in search results.

Admissibility of Information from the Internet Archive

Getting information from the Internet admitted into evidence should be no different than getting other traditional evidence admitted. Like traditional evidence, it too must be: (1) relevant and (2) authentic in order to be deemed admissable. While a judge makes the determination whether evidence is relevant and can be heard by the jury, it becomes the jury's responsibility to ascertain authenticity after an attorney makes a prima facie showing of genuineness. Relevancy is generally the easier of the two hurdles to overcome.

Proving the authenticity of Web page evidence might be straight-forward when information is still posted on the opposition's Web site, but can prove to be problematic if the information you wish to get entered into evidence is no longer available at the original Web site, but is only available via **Archive.org**.

A Federal Magistrate Judge's Memorandum Opinion and Order in a *Motion in limine* hearing in the unreported *Telewizja Polska USA, Inc.* v. *Echostar Satellite*, Case No. 02C3293 (N.D. Ill. Oct. 15, 2004), *available at* http://cyberlaw.stanford.edu/packets/echostar.pdf, is widely cited as an example of the court allowing copies of Web pages from **Archive.org** into evidence. In that Memorandum Opinion, the magistrate rejected the plaintiff's claim that Web pages from the Internet Archive Web site were not properly authenticated and further rejected plaintiff's attack on the Internet Archive Web site as an unreliable source. The magistrate stated that Federal Rules of Evidence Rule 901 requires only a prima facie showing of genuineness and leaves it to the jury to determine the true authenticity.

Finally, as to admissibility, many prior courts have indicated that hearsay objections to Internet evidence could be overcome. In the *Telewizja* Memorandum Opinion, the magistrate rejected plaintiff's contention that the archived Web pages stored at the Internet Archive constituted hearsay, holding that they were not "statements" but merely images and text showing what a Web site once looked like. (The plaintiff had alleged they were "double hearsay," no less.) The magistrate also found that the Web site pages were an admission by a party-opponent and were admissible under the "best evidence" rule.

This would seem to be a worthwhile precedent to cite when trying to get Web pages retrieved from **Archive.org's** collection admitted into evidence — if the U.S. District Court judge hadn't over-ruled the magistrate in an unwritten opinion. It is surprising (and a bit disturbing) that the only source we have found that correctly cites the judge's ruling in this case has been **Wikipedia**, *available at http://en.wikipedia.org/wiki/Internet_Archive#Telewizja_Polska* (the online encyclopedia to which anyone can make a contribution discussed in *Chapter Two*).

Attempting to verify this **Wikipedia** entry, we sifted through the extensive docket for this case on **PACER** (Public Access to Court Electronic Records; discussed in *Chapter Fourteen*) and were not able to locate the judge's order over-ruling the magistrate. Finally, we resorted to one of the oldest (and un-cyber) research methods — we picked up the phone and called the prevailing attorney who represented Telewizja Polska. He confirmed that the judge had indeed over-ruled the magistrate during the course of the trial but that there was no written opinion.

We do not recommend taking information found at **Wikipedia** as absolute fact. Cross-checking and verifying information found on the Internet is important. (Some courts have allowed information found at **Wikipedia** into evidence (e.g. *Allegheny Defense Project* v. United States Forest Service, 423 F.3d 215, (W.D. PA 2005) while others have not (e.g. *Palisades Collection* v. *Graubard,* Docket No. A-1338-07T3 (NJ Superior Court April 17, 2009). See page 29 for more information about these cases.

Novak v. *Tucows*, No. 06-CV-1909, 2007 U.S. Dist. Lexis 21269 (E.D.N.Y. March 26, 2007), is another unreported federal case in which the court would not admit Web pages obtained from **Archive.org** into evidence. As part of his reasoning for this denial, the judge cited the *St. Clair* opinion (which we discussed earlier in *Chapter Two*) and its characterization of information located on the Internet as "voodoo information."

On the other hand, in another unreported case, *SP Technologies* v. *Garmin International,* No. 08 C 3248. (N.D. Illinois, September 30, 2009), the court admitted into evidence a printout of a Web site's content from the **Archive.org's** collection, explaining:

> According to Plaintiff, the Web site has not been authenticated pursuant to Federal Rule of Evidence 901. That rule, however, requires only "evidence sufficient to support a finding that the matter in question is what its proponent claims." FED. R. EVID. 901(a). Here, Defendant has attached an affidavit from a manager at the Internet Archive, who explained how that Web site saves old web pages and that Defendant's Exhibit D was created in 1999. (Butler Aff. [182].) Plaintiff's argument amounts to a suggestion that the printout of this Web site would be admissible only if a person with direct knowledge of the Web site's existence in 1999 testified that the printout was a true and accurate copy of the contents of the Web site on that date. Such a high standard is not required for other types of evidence, and is beyond what Rule 901 requires. See *United States* v. *Harvey*, 117 F.3d 1044, 1049 (7th Cir. 1997) (Rule 901 "requires only a prima facie showing of genuineness and leaves it to the jury to decide the true authenticity and probative value of the evidence"). The court therefore notes Plaintiff's concerns about the reliability of the printout, but nevertheless concludes that the printout is admissible as evidence and denies the motion to strike. Accord *Telewizja Polska USA, Inc.* v. *Echostar Satellite Corp.*,No. 02 C 3293, 2004 WL 2367740, at *6 (N.D. Ill. Oct. 15, 2004) (admitting evidence from the Internet Archive when accompanied by an affidavit from an Internet Archive official).

Note that the court in *SP Technologies* relied upon the unreported Magistrate's decision in *Telewizja* (discussed on page 112).

Chapter Seven

FREE INVESTIGATIVE RESEARCH RESOURCES TO LOCATE AND BACKGROUND PEOPLE

Public Records vs. "Publicly Available" Information

Public records refer to records filed with a governmental agency. They often offer the best way to find and investigate people and companies. "Publicly available" information refers to information that is not filed with a government agency but is public nevertheless. For example, your phone number is publicly available if you allowed the telephone company to list it. An association that you belong to may list your contact information on its Web site, making the information publicly available.

The definition of what constitutes a public record varies from jurisdiction to jurisdiction. What is considered public in one state may not be considered public in another.

The availability of public records also varies from jurisdiction to jurisdiction. Just because a record is considered public, does not mean that it must be available on the Web – or even available for free. In some instances, records that are available online from one county office might not be available online from the equivalent office in another county in the same state.

In jurisdictions that do not provide free Web access to the information, you may be forced to resort either to using a pay database, "snail mail," or actually visiting the offices of the repository agency in person. Some states, such as

Florida, not only have a plethora of free public record information on the Web (such as liens, judgments, trademark owner names, corporate records, and annual reports), they also provide the actual images of the full public record (http://www.sunbiz.org).

Public Records and "Personal" Information

In the realm of public records, personal information refers to information that identifies you personally, such as your name, Social Security Number, date of birth, address, or phone number. (See pages 206-208 for sources of "personally identifying" information.)

Public Records and "Sensitive" Information

Some public records contain sensitive information. Sensitive information is any information in a public record that, if released, could cause embarrassment, bias, or harm (such as a divorce decree that includes children's names or a bankruptcy record that includes bank names and account numbers). This information is often redacted, thus portions of public records can become private. (See below.)

Private Records

Some entire records filed with government agencies are considered private, such as tax returns and driver's license information. In other cases, as noted above, only portions of some records are considered private. Private records can be accessed if the subject of the record consents or if there are laws providing for exceptions.

In 2000, the U.S. Supreme Court (*Reno v. Condon*, 528 U.S. 141, available at http://caselaw.lp.findlaw.com/scripts/getcase.pl?court=us&vol=000&invol=98-1464) deemed driver's license records to be private under the Driver's Privacy Protection Act, 18 U.S.C. 2721 (DPPA), but the DPPA does allow access to driver's license information, in specified instances, without the licensee's consent under 18 U.S.C. 2721(b):

(4) For use in connection with any civil, criminal, administrative, or arbitral proceeding in any Federal, State, or local court or agency or before any self-regulatory body, including the service of process, investigation in anticipation of litigation, and the execution or enforcement of judgments and orders, or pursuant to an order of a Federal, State, or local court.

(6) For use by any insurer or insurance support organization, or by a self-insured entity, or its agents, employees, or contractors, in connection with claims investigation activities, antifraud activities, rating or underwriting.

(8) For use by any licensed private investigative agency or licensed security service for any purpose permitted under this subsection.

Methods of accessing these records vary from state to state. **BRB Publications** has compiled a comprehensive book (*The MVR Book*, available at http://www.brbpub.com/books/) detailing how to access driver's license information; driving histories; VIN (Vehicle Identification Numbers); and registration information for vehicles and vessels in the United States (on a state-by-state basis), Guam, Puerto Rico, the Virgin Islands, and Canada.

Merlin, a commercial investigative database (http://www.merlindata.com/), contains driver's license information from fifty states. However, only ten states offer current data "government sources:" Connecticut, Florida, Maine, Michigan, Minnesota, Ohio, Tennessee, Texas, Wisconsin, and Wyoming. Merlin's database provides, "historical government data and data from non-government sources" for the remaining states. In order to search this database, you must select a DPPA-compliant use (see page 117) for accessing the data from the *Disclosure Reason* drop-down menu and a GLBA-compliant use (see pages 208-212) from the *Authorized Purpose* drop-down menu. **LexisNexis's Accurint** also offers a *Driver's License* database that contains information from twenty-four states but only ten are current.

FINDING PORTALS, DIRECTORIES, AND ARTICLES POINTING TO PUBLIC RECORDS AND PUBLICLY AVAILABLE INFORMATION

To help you find the ever-changing landscape of public records and publicly available information available on the Internet, we have prepared an online article (with links to many public record sites discussed in this section) at the **Internet For Lawyers** Web site (http://www.netforlawyers.com/article_public_records.htm). Attorneys and paralegals in many jurisdictions can also earn CLE credit by reading the article and answering questions about Web sites visited.

The following are some of the most useful portals, directories, and a meta-search site for accessing free public records and publicly available information online, with the most useful listed first:

- **Search Systems** (http://www.searchsystems.net/)
- **Rootsweb** (http://www.rootsweb.com)
- **USGenWeb** (http://www.usgenweb.com/)
- **Portico** (http://indorgs.virginia.edu/portico/)
- **BRB Publications** (http://www.brbpub.com/freeresources/pubrecsites.aspx)
- **Zabasearch.com** (http://www.zabasearch.com)
- **Black Book Online** (http://www.blackbookonline.info)
- **ZoomInfo.com** (http://www.zoominfo.com/Search/)
- **123People.com** (http://www.123People.com)
- **Pipl.com** (http://www.Pipl.com; pronounced "people")

Search Systems (http://www.searchsystems.net) provides nearly 50,000 links to free (and some pay) searchable public record resources. Recent site redesigns have made **Search Systems's** free database a little less obvious on the home page though.

For example, users might be drawn to the prominent headings in the left-hand column (*Search Intelius*, *Search Unlimited*, and *SearchSystems.net Services*) that all lead to pay sites. (**Intelius** and **Search Systems's** pay databases will be discussed in *Chapter Ten*). Similarly, the *Public Records Search* box placed directly above the links to the free public records database might lead some to believe that results of searches entered there would yield links to free sites – they do not.

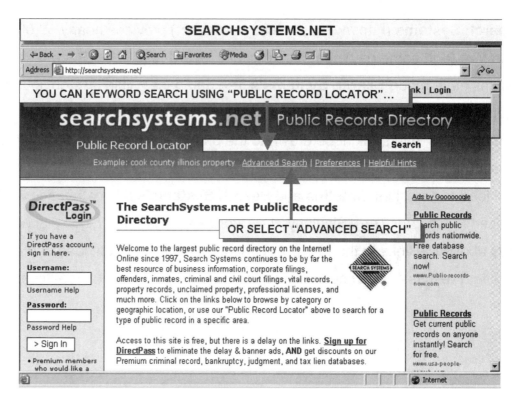

There are three ways to locate public records in the **Search Systems** database:

- Browsing by jurisdiction (Select *United States Free Public Records by State*, *United States Free Public Records Nationwide*, *Free Public Records in Other Nations* [includes Canada, Australia, and Mexico, among other countries], or an individual state. If browsing by state, choose by type [e.g., *Professional & Business Licenses*], *Regional*, *Counties* or *City & Town,* and then read through the alphabetical list of public records available for that jurisdiction.

- Searching by keywords, using the *Public Records Locator* database at the top of the home page (or clicking on *Advanced Search* for more precise keyword searching).

- Browsing by category, such as *Birth Records*, *Court Records*, *Criminal Records*, *Deaths*, *Licenses*, *Marriage Records*, *Property Records*, *Sex Offenders*, *Unclaimed Property*, or *Uniform Commercial Code*.

To their credit, **Search Systems's** *Public Records Locator*, which does return results from the site's free database of sources, is located in a fairly prominent spot near the top of the home page.

You can use the *Public Records Locator* to search through the site's database of sources by the type of public record (e.g., *license*) using the *By Type of Record* drop-down menu, by jurisdiction (e.g., *California*) using the *By State* drop-down menu, or relevant keywords (e.g., *accountant*) using the *By Keyword(s)* box. Unfortunately, one drawback is that you can only search by one of these criteria at a time.

Another drawback of *Public Records Locator* results is that for some searches the first set of links displayed under the heading, *Featured Links*, all lead to pay databases. You have to scroll down to the results under the heading *Links* to find the links to (mostly) free sites.

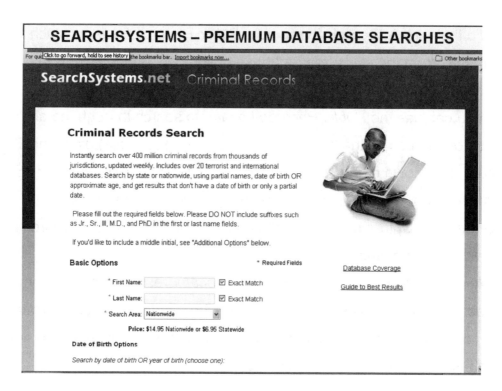

SEARCHSYSTEMS – PREMIUM DATABASE SEARCHES

SearchSystems.net Criminal Records

Criminal Records Search

Instantly search over 400 million criminal records from thousands of jurisdictions, updated weekly. Includes over 20 terrorist and international databases. Search by state or nationwide, using partial names, date of birth OR approximate age, and get results that don't have a date of birth or only a partial date.

Please fill out the required fields below. Please DO NOT include suffixes such as Jr., Sr., III, M.D., and PhD in the first or last name fields.

If you'd like to include a middle initial, see "Additional Options" below.

Basic Options   * Required Fields

* First Name: ☑ Exact Match
* Last Name: ☑ Exact Match
* Search Area: Nationwide

Price: $14.95 Nationwide or $6.95 Statewide

Date of Birth Options

Search by date of birth OR year of birth (choose one):

Database Coverage

Guide to Best Results

In addition to its database of free links to public records resources, **Search Systems** provides paid access to select premium databases on a per-search basis (e.g., their *Criminal Records Search*; https://www.searchsystems.net/springapp/funnel/newSearch.do). As pictured above, **Search Systems** offers a *Nationwide* criminal record search for $14.95 and a *Statewide* search for $6.95. (To their credit, **Search Systems** does a good job of explaining the limitations of these kinds of criminal record searches, albeit on a separate page – http://premium.searchsystems.net/cr-guide-funnel.php.)

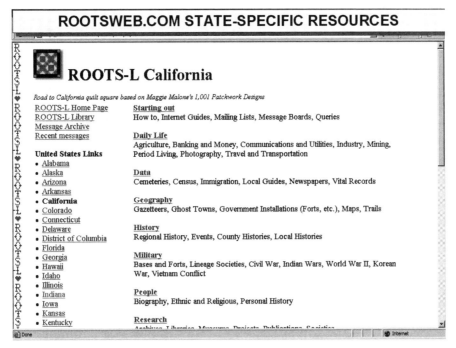

ROOTSWEB.COM STATE-SPECIFIC RESOURCES

ROOTS-L California

Road to California quilt square based on Maggie Malone's 1,001 Patchwork Designs

ROOTS-L Home Page
ROOTS-L Library
Message Archive
Recent messages

United States Links
- Alabama
- Alaska
- Arizona
- Arkansas
- **California**
- Colorado
- Connecticut
- Delaware
- District of Columbia
- Florida
- Georgia
- Hawaii
- Idaho
- Illinois
- Indiana
- Iowa
- Kansas
- Kentucky

Starting out
How to, Internet Guides, Mailing Lists, Message Boards, Queries

Daily Life
Agriculture, Banking and Money, Communications and Utilities, Industry, Mining, Period Living, Photography, Travel and Transportation

Data
Cemeteries, Census, Immigration, Local Guides, Newspapers, Vital Records

Geography
Gazetteers, Ghost Towns, Government Installations (Forts, etc.), Maps, Trails

History
Regional History, Events, County Histories, Local Histories

Military
Bases and Forts, Lineage Societies, Civil War, Indian Wars, World War II, Korean War, Vietnam Conflict

People
Biography, Ethnic and Religious, Personal History

Research
Archives, Libraries, Museums, Projects, Publications, Societies

Done   Internet

Rootsweb.com, though primarily a genealogy site, has links to public records (such as the *Social Security Death Index*; see pages 128-129) and other publicly available information resources (such as cemetery records and historical societies). The *U.S. Town/County Database* provides access to geographical collections based on the parameters you enter. Some of the resources returned are free and some require fees/subscription to access their data.

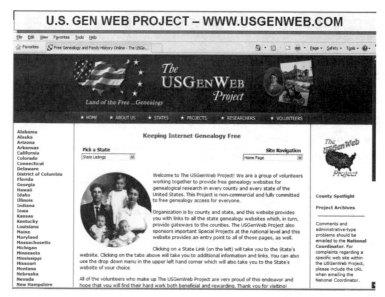

USGen Web (http://www.usgenweb.com/) is a genealogical site that links to other Web sites that contain information at the state and county levels. Because volunteers maintain this site, the volume of resources available varies from state to state. For example, the California page includes *Table of Contents - Counties*, *State Counties - Clickable Map*, *CAGenWeb Archives*, *CAGen Web Mailing List*, *California Research Help*, *CAGenWeb Supporters*, *About CAGenWeb Project*, *History of California*, and *Search CAGenWeb*.

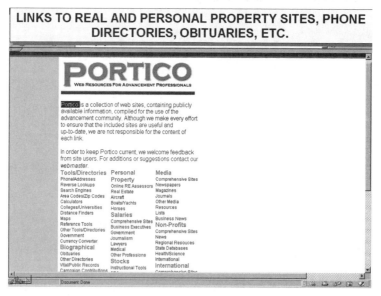

Portico (http://www.indorgs.virginia.edu/portico/home.html) links to publicly available information and public records. Links are arranged topically, then jurisdictionally.

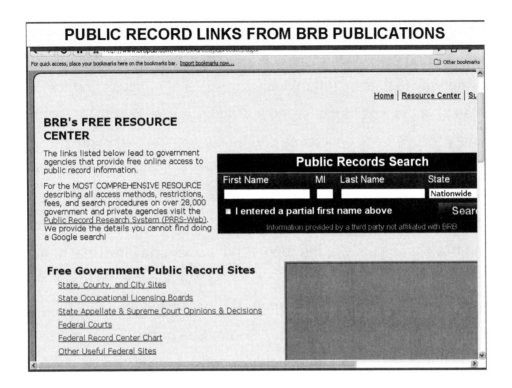

PUBLIC RECORD LINKS FROM BRB PUBLICATIONS

BRB's FREE RESOURCE CENTER

The links listed below lead to government agencies that provide free online access to public record information.

For the MOST COMPREHENSIVE RESOURCE describing all access methods, restrictions, fees, and search procedures on over 28,000 government and private agencies visit the Public Record Research System (PRRS-Web). We provide the details you cannot find doing a Google search!

Free Government Public Record Sites
- State, County, and City Sites
- State Occupational Licensing Boards
- State Appellate & Supreme Court Opinions & Decisions
- Federal Courts
- Federal Record Center Chart
- Other Useful Federal Sites

Home | Resource Center | Su

Public Records Search

First Name   MI   Last Name   State
                                 Nationwide

■ I entered a partial first name above   Sear

Information provided by a third party not affiliated with BRB.

BRB Publications
(http://www.brbpub.com/freeresources/pubrecsites.aspx) presents an extensive collection of free links to numerous sources for locating public records including civil records, criminal records, driving records, real estate records, legislation, and state occupational licensing boards, as well as public record vendors and record retrievers, among other categories. **BRB** also offers its *Public Record Research System (PRRS)-Web*, a subscription database product ($124 annually or $10.95 monthly) that details how to access records from more than 26,000 government agencies, and provides information on verifying attendance at more than 4,000 accredited colleges and universities, among other types of information. The data are updated weekly.

Zabasearch.com (http://www.zabasearch.com/) offers a free search of public records and publicly available information by *Name* and *State* or by *Phone Number*. You can also narrow down your search results further by clicking the *Advanced Search* link (displayed only after your results are displayed) to add additional search criteria, including *City/Town* and *Birth Year*. Only basic information is displayed in search results for free (e.g., birth year, telephone number, and address). The *Get the Dirt* and *Run a Background Check* links that accompany search results take you to a fee-based service — **Intelius**. The **Intelius** summary results do (often) include names of *relatives* and the cities/states of addresses found for the individual you've searched. Beyond that, the summary results page only teases at the information that might be available in their complete report, like in its *Statewide Criminal Check*, *Bankrupcties & Liens*, *Neighbors* (all with the disclaimer *when available*). A background search at Intelius costs $49.95. (Note that there may also be a $39.95 discount offer. Seleceting this option gets you the report and a seven-day free trial of **Intelius's** Identity Protect service. If you do not cancel this membership before the trial period ends, your credit card will automatically be charged the $19.95 monthly membership fee for this service – every month. See page 228 for more information on **Intelius**.) More reasonably priced searches can be conducted using **Merlin** (see pages 214–220 for more information on this service).

The **Godfrey Memorial Library** (http://www.godfrey.org) is located in Connecticut and specializes in genealogical materials. Its holdings include the *American Genealogical-Biographical Index* (*AGBI*), the largest genealogical reference set ever published. At over 225 volumes, the *AGBI* contains, "approximately 4 million names from over 800 genealogically related research books." Members have access to a wide range of genealogical and reference databases via their Internet connections. (Information from the AGBI is available via e-mail request.) Memberships range from $45 to $125 per year. Note, many of these databases may also be available for free through your own public library's Web site. See pages 145–146 for a more detailed discussion of databases that might be available through your library.

Black Book Online (http://www.blackbookonline.info) is sponsored by Crime Time Publishing, a publisher of books geared toward private investigators and owned by a Los Angeles-area private investigator. **Black Book Online** provides links to a variety of databases with useful annotations telling you what each database contains. Resources include telephone directories, reverse look-ups, business information, news, skip tracing resources, and death records.

Social Security Numbers can be validated online, in real time, and for free (to determine if a Social Security Number is valid and if the holder has been reported as deceased). Not all database searches at **Black Book Online** are free, but those that are not clearly include a green *Pay Site* designation.

ZoomInfo.com (http://www.zoominfo.com/Search/) calls itself a "summarization search engine" because it extracts information from millions of online sources (such as Web sites, press releases, electronic news services, and SEC filings) and summarizes the information into a standard, comprehensive format. The site claims to contain information about 45 million businesspeople and 5 million businesses. You can search for a person just by name. You can also add a *Company Name*, *Job Title*, *Industry Keywords,* or geographic limiters to narrow down your search. With a free registration, you can claim and edit your **ZoomInfo** profile to "manage your Web presence." The site offers premium *ZoomInfo PowerSell* access that includes additional search criteria.

123People.com (http://www.123People.com) is a meta-search site that retrieves information from a variety of publicly available sources simultaneously. Searching is as simple as entering a first and last name into the search box and clicking *Search*. You can also add a *City/ZIP*, or futher narrow your search to one of twelve countries (the United States is the default) or opt to search anywhere in the *World*. Results are arranged in categories that include *Picture*, *Phone Numbers*, *E-mail Addresses*, *Weblinks*, *Amazon*, *News*, *Social Networking Profiles*, *Blogs*, and *IM/Microblogs*, among others. A sample search for *Mark Rosch* did find an impressive amount of information, including numerous images of this book's co-author posted at different Web sites, his current home address and phone number, links to different Web sites and blog posts where he is mentioned, links to news articles in which he is interviewed, and links to his **LinkedIn** and **Facebook** profiles. Not all of the results related to this book's co-author however. The results included images not of him that appeared on Web pages where his name did appear, addresses and phone numbers for five other *Mark Rosch*s, and links to Web pages mentioning some of those other *Mark Rosch*s. While **123People.com** does cast a wide net, the results should not be considered comprehensive. Results for this sample search did not include a full e-mail address, a link to the co-author's **Twitter** profile, or links to books he has authored, despite this information being posted widely on the Internet.

FINDING OR INVESTIGATING PEOPLE

Begin by Ascertaining Whether They're Alive: The Social Security Death Index

Before spending the time and money to find or investigate someone, first make sure they are still alive. A good place to check is the free *Social Security Death Index (SSDI)* located at **Rootsweb.com** (http://ssdi.rootsweb.ancestry.com/cgi-bin/ssdi.cgi). If a death (since 1962 only) has been reported to the Social Security Administration, the death record will be found in the *SSDI*.

Do not enter your information into the first search screen shown.

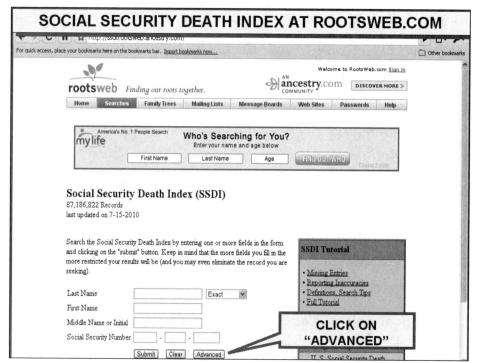

Instead, click on *Advanced Search* to reach the advanced search page shown in the next illustration.

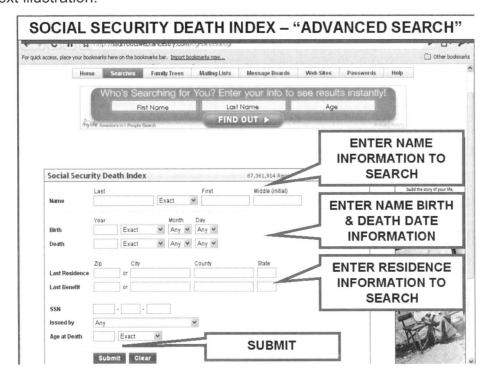

On the **Social Security Death Index's** *Advanced Search* page, you can enter significantly more search criteria (e.g., *ZIP Code, state, county* and/or *city of last residence*) to help narrow your search down to the particular individual for whom you are looking. Unfortunately, not all of the records in the **Death Index** contain all of this data. So, if you have a last known address where your subject may have died, including it in your search might not return information about your subject, even if they are dead and their name is contained in the database. If you don't find your subject, delete some information and conduct a broad first and last name only search and then match other information you have about your subject with information in the returned records.

Ancestry.com also offers access to the SSDI, as well as other vital record databases, but access to many of these resources is only available via a paid subscription.

See pages 178–182 for information on state and local death records.

PUBLICLY AVAILABLE INFORMATION

Publicly available information is that information that you voluntarily provide to a private entity or publish in a public place (such as the Internet). As discussed on page 115, if you provide your phone number and address to a private entity — such as the telephone company — it becomes publicly available. If you publish information on the Internet (e.g., postings to an online community or social networking site; information on your or someone else's Web site; or information you provide to commercial sites such as **Classmates.com**), this information also becomes publicly available and may be found by anyone surfing the Internet. It may also be sold to marketing companies or investigative research database companies.

Gravesites

Looking for a relative's will but can't find a death record through the Social Security Death Index? You're also unsure of where they died or were buried, but you are sure they are dead. You may be able to glean this information by finding their gravesite. **Findagrave** (http://www.findagrave.com) can be searched to locate the gravesite locations of more than 50 million people. Obituaries are another good tool to verify deaths.

Similarly, **Interment.net** contains "published transcriptions from 5,000+ cemeteries across the world." You can search for grave information about an individual you think might be dead by name or you can browse for information from specific cemeteries by location. You can search by as little as a last name, but that will probably return too many results. The site's search is powered by **Google**, so you can conduct a full name (phrase) search by enclosing the name in quotation marks. Note however, that names in this collection are listed *Last Name, First Name* so that is how you should construct your full name search (e.g., *"Rosch, Cornelius"*). You might also try separating the first and last names with an asterisk (e.g., *Cornelius * Rosch*; as described on page 43). The asterisk search will yield different results from the quotation mark search.

Tributes.com (http://www.tributes.com) contains a searchable database of "over 86 million current and historical death records dating back to the 1930s." Clicking the *Search Obituaries* button allows you to search by as little as a last name. You can add additional criteria, including a *First Name*, *City*, or *State*. You can also narrow down your search further by adding *Keywords* that might appear in the obituary, or by using the *Date Range* drop-down menu.

Obituary Daily Times (http://www.rootsweb.ancestry.com/~obituary/) provides a searchable index of millions of obituaries published in newspapers around the United States and Canada. The search results do not link to the actual obituary online, but rather they return a citation to the newspaper in which the obituary was published. (See page 145 to learn how to access full-text newspaper archives for free.) According to the site, the database's daily updates contain approximately 2,500 entries each. A list of newspapers included in the database is also available at http://www.rootsweb.ancestry.com/~obituary/publications.html.

The **National Obituary Archive** (http://www.arrangeonline.com/), with nearly 60 million obituaries online, is another site to search for an obituary.

Using a Search Engine to Find or Investigate People

Searching for information about people using a search engine is very hit or miss, but can be worth the time. If the subject always uses their full name, search it as a phrase. But if they sometimes use one (or more) middle names or middle initials, connect the names with the *and* Boolean connector. To search **Google** using a proximity connector, use the asterisk (*) which acts as a NEAR connector, keeping the first and last name in close proximity to one another on the resulting pages. **Yahoo!** also offers the ability to conduct a "within one word" proximity search. See pages 37–41 for details on Boolean and proximity search connectors.

See page 127 for a description of **123People.com**, a meta-search site that is designed to retrieve information about people through a name search.

Searching Usenet (Discussion) Groups, Forums, Message Boards, Blogs, and Social Networking Sites to Find and Investigate People

Another "sometimes useful" way to find or investigate people is by searching Usenet (discussion) group postings (e.g., **Google Groups**), forums, message boards, blogs (personal Web logs), and social networking sites (e.g., **MySpace**, **Facebook**, or **Twitter**). In these online forums, one might encounter information ranging from factual and personal information to rumors and public opinion.

The place to start this kind of search is **Google Groups** (http://groups.google.com), an archive of over one billion Usenet postings (also referred to as *messages*) sent to public Usenet groups since 1981. Search with the advanced search page template by clicking on *Advanced Group Search*.

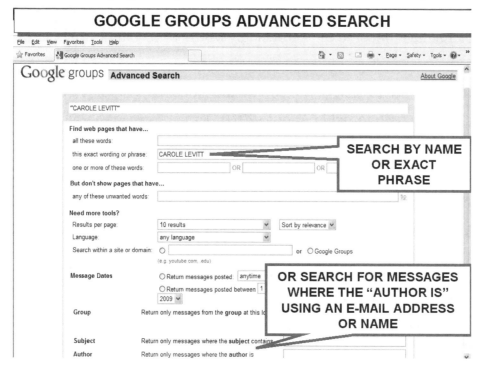

Google Groups can be searched by:

- keywords describing a topic or issue
- the name of a person or company
- a product name
- a product model number
- an author of a message by the *author's name* or *e-mail address*

E-mail addresses are being masked in the returned **Google Groups** messages, but there is a way to uncover them. First, click on the *More options* link and a partial address will be displayed with ellipses inserted between the first part of the address and the domain (e.g., *m...@aol.com*). Click on the ellipses. Instead of displaying the full e-mail address, an *Unlock e-mail addresses* screen appears. A randomly generated string of characters will be displayed, which you will be instructed to enter into the query box as a security/verification process. Once you have done that and clicked *Enter,* the message will be displayed. While the e-mail address will still be masked, clicking *Show options* now will reveal it.

Searching Blogs

Blogs have become an increasingly useful and voluminous source of information about individuals and various topics. According to data compiled by **BlogPulse.com**, a division of Nielsen Media Research, there were over over 144 million blogs on the Internet in August 2010. Those blogs generated 1 million posts per day according to **BlogPulse**. That comes to over 11 posts per second.

The following sites offer the ability to search additional discussion forums and Web logs (blogs):

- **BoardReader** (http://www.boardreader.com): Searches thousands of forums, message boards, and microblogging sites.

- **Technorati** (http://www.technorati.com): Searches over 133 million blogs in "real time," every day.

- **BlogPulse** (http://www.blogpulse.com): Searches millions of blogs every day.

- **Google Blog Search** (http//www.blogsearch.google.com/): Provides a separate search engine to locate information posted to blogs. Its goal is to search "every blog that publishes a site feed (either RSS or Atom)." You can take advantage of the *Advanced Blog Search* to refine your search by exact phrase, blog author, date, etc. The site also offers a *Safe Search* filter to screen out adult sites from your results. If you want to be automatically alerted to new blog postings on your search terms, there are links to Atom or RSS feeds on the left-hand side of each results page where you can subscribe. See pages 80-81 for a more detailed, illustrated description.

THEBLOGSOFLAW.COM

For an annotated index of legal blogs, arranged by topic, see **TheBlogsofLaw** (http://www.theblogsoflaw.com).

JUSTIA – BLOG SEARCH

To keyword search law-related blogs, see **Justia.com** (http://www.justia.com) and click on the *Law Blogs* link above the search box.

For those interested in creating their own blogs, see **Blogger.com** (http://www.blogger.com), **Journal Space** (http://www.journalspace.com), **Moveable Type** (http://www.moveabletype.org), **WordPress.org** (http://www.wordpress.org), or one of the numerous other blogging tools available.

Searching Social Networking Sites

One of the most-talked-about areas of content growth on the Internet are the social networking sites. The term "social network" was coined in the mid-1950s by sociologist J. A. Barnes to describe interactions between people in the real world. When applied to the Web, it refers to Web sites where individuals with similar personal and/or professional interests can create an online "profile" and share information about those interests so others can read about them.

Friendster (http://www.friendster.com) was one of the first sites referred to by the social network label, however, later arrivals such as **MySpace** (http://www.myspace.com) and **Facebook** (http://www.facebook.com) have become better known. Most of these sites give users the ability to post text, images, sound, and other information to their profiles. They often also include the ability to create a blog and/or chat with other users.

Social networking sites were originally the domains of the 20-and-under crowd, but a February 2010 survey by the Pew Internet & American Life Project found that 47 percent of adults already online also use social networking sites, with more than half of those (52 percent) reporting that they have two or more profiles. The survey also found that those online adults preferred **Facebook** by a wide margin. Seventy three percent reported having a profile on **Facebook**, 48 percent have a profile on **MySpace** and 14 percent have a **LinkedIn** profile. (Social Media & Mobile Internet Use Among Teens and Young Adults, *available at* http://www.pewinternet.org/Reports/2010/Social-Media-and_Young-Adults.aspx.)

Recently, attorneys have been able to find information in social networking profiles that has made a difference in the outcomes of their cases. For example, Santa Barbara, California, prosecutors said information a woman posted about her partying lifestyle on **MySpace.com** was the difference between a judge ordering a prison sentence rather than probation in a drunken driving crash that had killed her passenger. One attorney recently told us that his wife (also an attorney) was able to locate an elusive individual and serve her based on information the individual had posted in her **Facebook** profile. Another attorney was able to locate a missing witness using **MySpace.com**, even though the witness did not have a profile — her young daughter did. Judges and law firm recruiters have also been known to use social networking sites to sift through profiles of potential hires.

MySpace

MySpace claims 113 million active monthly users around the world. (The actual number of profiles is likely higher.) The basic profile includes pre-defined categories of information into which members can add their own information. It is not necessary to create a **MySpace** account to be able to browse or search through the "public" profiles on the site. Any information a member adds to their public profile would be visible to anyone else who visits that profile — including the list of their *Friends* and *Comments* those *Friends* have sent to the member. Because the majority of profiles are not "private," you can access a large number of profiles to see if a particular person you're interested in has created a **MySpace** profile for themselves, and what information they have posted about themselves there.

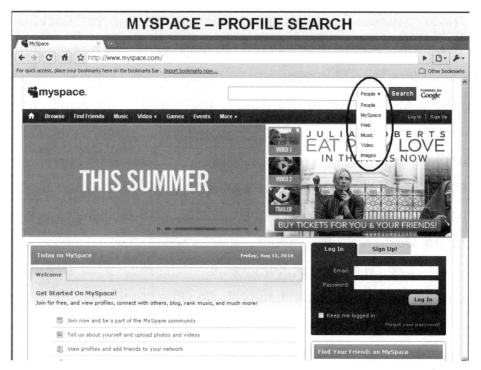

MySpace provides a *Search* box, located at the top of each **MySpace** page, which includes a number of limiters (in a drop-down menu) to help you narrow in on the types of information you are looking for in the profiles. The two most useful limiters to online researchers are *MySpace* (which allows you to search using names and/or keywords and presumably searches through all visible content contained in **MySpace** profiles) and *People* (which allows you to search using names and appears to search through the registration database of **MySpace**). The beauty of searching the *People* limiter is that it allows you to search by a person's real name or e-mail address (if they registered with their real name or e-mail address) even if they don't display it on the visible portion of their profile. Many people register with their real name, but when they create their profile, they realize that they should not display it on their profile — but it's too late if they've already registered with their real name, since we can search it by using the *People* limiter. **MySpace** requires a valid e-mail address in order to create an account. The *People* limiter is not explained anywhere on the **MySpace** search page. You just have to know about it, and now you do! (Note, however, that after **MySpace** users create their account they can change the names they used to register their account, even deleting the last name entirely.)

Facebook

Facebook contains self-created profiles of more than 500 million people around the world. Members are broken down into "networks" based on their attendance at specific schools, employment at specific workplaces, etc. Looking at the **Facebook** home page it is not apparent that it is possible to search through the profiles without having your own account. There is however, a separate search page at http://www.facebook.com/srch.php that allows you to search by name to determine whether someone has a profile.

Even if a search returns a result indicating that the subject of your search has a profile, you cannot access that profile unless you (at least) register and create a profile of your own. This requires you to give **Facebook** at least a name and an e-mail address. The e-mail address that you register with determines which network you are a member of and allows you to view many other profiles in that particular network. For example, if you have a University of Illinois student or alumni e-mail address and you register with it, you automatically become part of that network. If you lack a network e-mail, you can still register, but you are restricted to a regional network — such as *Los Angeles*.

Individual users have the option of leaving their profile open to everyone on the Web, or everyone in their network. They can also choose to make their profiles more private and restrict access only to their online friends, or to make their profile available to their online friends and the friends' friends.

Classmates

Classmates.com (http://www.classmates.com), which offers many of the same functions as **Facebook** and **MySpace**, pre-dates those other sites, but was launched long before the social network label was applied to Web sites. **Classmates.com's** database contains over 40 million people from 130,000 schools located in the United States and Canada.

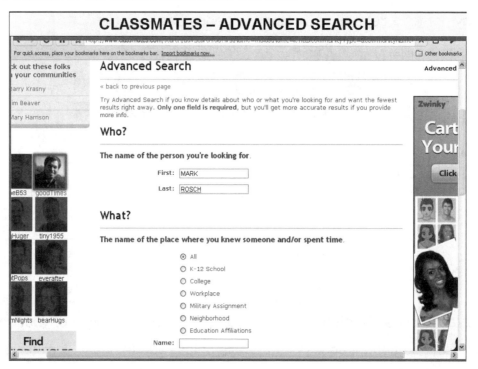

Use the *Advanced Search* functions to refine your query and search using a person's *Name* and *City*, *State/Province*, *K-12 School*, *College*, *Workplace*, *Military Assignment*, *Neighborhood*, or *Education Affiliations*. A link to the *Advanced Search* menu is only visible after you've conducted a "simple" search using the boxes in the upper right hand corner of the welcome page. Because people using **Classmates.com** <u>want</u> to be found (by their fellow classmates), they tend to use their real names. Both married and maiden names are often listed for women members. This makes the site popular with private investigators. Some information can be obtained free with registration. Taking full advantage of this site requires a $39 annual fee (often discounted to a fraction of that amount).

LinkedIn (http://www.linkedin.com/), a <u>professional</u> networking site, can be used by attorneys in much the same way that they use social networking sites (to find missing people and obtain background information about people). Like **Classmates.com**, those using **LinkedIn** <u>want</u> to be found — thus, they tend to use their real names. This makes the **LinkedIn** site an ideal tool for finding people.

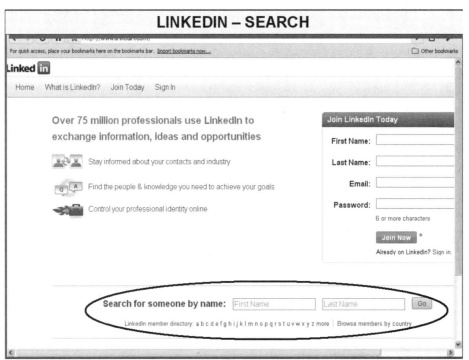

You can search the site's more than 70 million profiles of professionals worldwide, in hundreds of industries, using the *Name* search boxes at the bottom of the home page. (**LinkedIn** claims that executives at all of the Fortune 500 have profiles on the site.) Searching does not require having a **LinkedIn** account of your own. If you are logged into your own **LinkedIn** account, however, you can search with additional criteria like a *Company* name in addition to, or instead of, an individual's name.

Microblogging Sites (e.g., Twitter)

"Microblogging" sites are an even more recent development in the online social networking scene. As the name implies, micoblogging sites consist of short posts — very short. **Twitter** (http://www.twitter.com), the most popular microblogging site, limits posts (known as "tweets") to just 140 characters. Microblogging sites are even easier to update than the "traditional" social networking sites already discussed. These posts often address the answer to the question, "What's happening?" and can include detailed information about the individual poster's daily activities. Increasingly, users are posting links to, and commentary about, news stories and current events. Reviewing this information for indicators of an individual's, interests, points of view, or even political leanings can be very useful to attorneys conducting juror research.

Twitter's simple search box is right on the home page. There, you can keyword search through the millions of individual tweets – from (roughly) the last two weeks. You can also use **Twitter's** *Advanced Search* page (http://search.twitter.com/advanced) to create more sophisticated, specific searches.

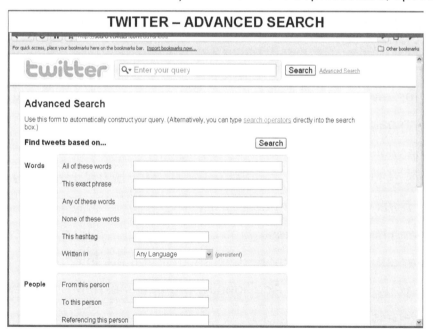

The *Advanced Search* page includes numerous Boolean search options, similar to **Google's** *Advanced Search* page, to locate tweets with *All of these words*, *Any of these words*, *None of these words*, and *This exact phrase*.

Further down the page are search options to locate tweets: *From this person, To this person*, or *Referencing this person*. These are a bit misleading because you have to know the "user name" that an individual tweets under. You cannot search by their real name from this page (although a number of people tweet under some form of their real names; e.g., one of the authors of this book tweets as MarkRosch; so you may still be able to locate someone this way). You must have a **Twitter** account of your own and be logged into it, to search for another (potential) **Twitter** user by their real name. Once logged in, click the *Find People* link in the upper right-hand corner of the screen and enter the name of the person for whom you are searching into the search box and click the *Search* button. If your subject used their real name to create their account (even if their user name is a pseudonym) a link to their profile will be returned in the results. Remember, however, that many people may share the same name.

Other popular microblogging sites like **Jaiku** (http://www.jaiku.com) and **Plurk** (http://www.plurk.com) do not have the search capabilities of **Twitter**, making them less useful for investigative research.

Professional Networking Sites for Lawyers

Recently, a number of professional networking sites have been launched specifically for lawyers. Their profiles can contain useful information about the attorneys who participate. Some of the most popular sites are **LawLink** (http://www.lawlink.com), the **A.B.A.'s LegallyMinded** (http://www.legallyminded.com), and **Martindale-Hubbell Connected** (http://www.martindale.com/connected).

Knowing how to mine these sites can be useful if you need background information about another lawyer (e.g., someone you are interviewing for the firm or someone you are opposing. Additionally, professional networking sites can be useful for referrals.

Many public libraries provide free remote access to useful, current databases (that would be very costly if you had to pay to use them). Most databases are full-text and updated regularly (some as often as daily). The database topics range from business, news, financial, and science, to medical. These databases can be used for finding background information about clients, the opposition, a company, a product, or a topic you need to get up to speed about. Every library offers a different group of databases, ranging from the **Wall Street Journal** (full-text) to **Gale's Business Directory** (which includes background information, broker reports, and more) to **RefUSA** (which provides addresses and phone numbers for millions of people and businesses).

The only trick to accessing these databases is that you must have a library card. To locate your library's Web site and learn what valuable databases you have been missing out on, see **Libdex** (http://www.libdex.com). Enter the name of your city or town to locate a link to your local public library.

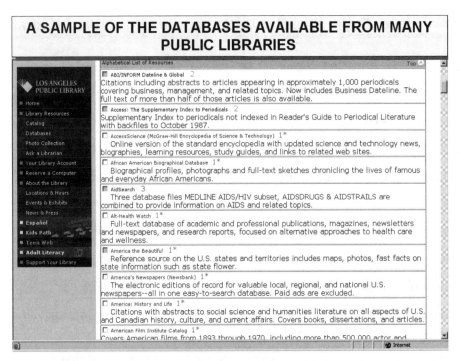

A SAMPLE OF THE DATABASES AVAILABLE FROM MANY PUBLIC LIBRARIES

Above is an example of the remote access offerings from **Los Angeles Public Library** (http://www.lapl.org).

Locating Pictures and Photographs of People, Products, or Places

Whether you are investigating a person or just want to be able to identify someone you are meeting at a public place (such as a new client), it's often useful to know what someone looks like. Entering the person's name into an image search engine can sometimes enable you to find his or her picture. You can go directly to **Google Images** (http://images.google.com/), which has billions of images in its index, **Yahoo! Images** (http://images.search.yahoo.com), **Bing Images** (http://www.bing.com/images), or **AltaVista Images** (http://www.altavista.com/image/default) to search for images, or you can visit **Alltheweb.com** (http://www.alltheweb.com) and click on the *Images* or *Pictures* tab above the search box. In addition to finding images of people, you can also conduct an image search for places, concepts, or products by using the appropriate keywords to describe them.

Additionally, there are search engines that specialize in returning image results, such as **PicSearch** (http://www.picsearch.com) and **ImageToss** (http://www.imagetoss.com).

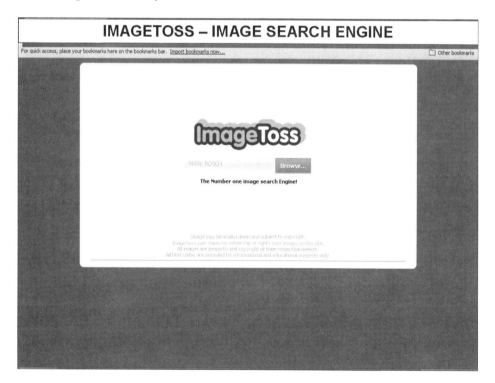

There are many free and pay telephone directory Web sites that list businesses and people in the United States and abroad. The pay sites are usually more up-to-date (often updated daily). These directories can help you find one or more of the following pieces of information:

- home address
- company address
- e-mail address
- phone number (land-line or cellular)
- neighbors

Many of the directories have both regular look-ups (by name) and reverse look-ups (e.g., by phone number, area code, or address).

The Ultimates (http://www.theultimates.com/) provides links to various white and yellow page, and e-mail directories. While numerous search sites are listed per page, each one must be searched separately, so you must enter the name of the person or company you're searching for, and city (and/or state), individually into each site's search form.

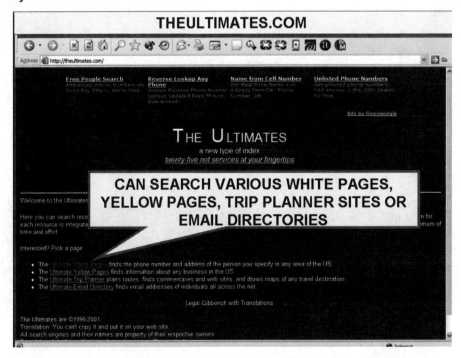

WhitePages.com (http://www.whitepages.com) offers the ability to search U.S. and Canadian people or companies by name and to perform a *Reverse Phone* or *Reverse Address* lookup . The *Basic People Search* requires only a last name (including a first name or initial is optional). The site also allows you to broaden a search by selecting the *Begins With* box when you're uncertain of the full spelling of a particular name (accessed by clicking on the *People* tab and then the *Advanced Search* link). Once a full result is displayed, clicking the *Map & Directions* link will display a map to the address to which the phone number is registered.

Clicking the *Neighbors* link generates a list of phone listings in close geographic proximity to the search result you are viewing. This can be useful for contacting the neighbors of missing witnesses or heirs – or anyone avoiding service of process – because now you can contact those neighbors by phone to see if they have information about your subject and address the neighbors by name.

Oddly, instead of displaying results for some searches, **WhitePages.com** first asks for name and telephone information from the searcher. There seems to be no rhyme or reason as to when this occurs. The first of two consecutive searches (on the same computer) might request information from the searcher, while the second yields the phone listing results without supplying any additional information. We have been able to ignore the request for information form and just click the *Submit* button to continue onto the phone listing results of our search.

While the site indicates that they are "continually updating" their data, it goes on to say, "generally speaking, listing information…is 60-90 days old."

You can also use **WhitePages.com** to determine domestic area codes and ZIP Codes by clicking the *Area & ZIP Code* link on the home page or the *Area Code Maps* link at the bottom of the home page. You can also use the site to locate international calling codes and phone directories by clicking the *International* link at the bottom of the home page. Hidden at the bottom of the home page, behind a link labeled *More*, is the *Neighbor* search that allows you to search just with an address to retrieve a list of names, addreses, and phone numbers in close proximity to that address.

Anywho.com (http://www.anywho.com/), with its compilation of millions of consumer and businesses phone listings, is another favorite phone listing search site. It can be searched by a person's or a company's name (or business category). Its *Find a Person* search requires as little as a last name. The site also allows searching for partial first names with as little as a first initial. **Anywho.com** also offers the ability to perform a *Reverse Lookup* by phone number and area code. While the site is owned by AT&T, it goes out of its way to inform users that, "the personal identifying information available on **AnyWho** is provided solely by Intelius, Inc. … none of the listings contained in the White Pages are obtained from AT&T billing records." **Anywho.com** no longer provides information on the currency of the information found on the site. Previously it said listings were updated "weekly" (and prior to that it listed the update timetable as "regularly" and "monthly").

At **Yahoo!** *People Search* (http://people.yahoo.com/), you can perform a *U.S. Phone & Address* search with just a last name — here, too, a first name is optional (and you can also add as little as a first initial), *City/Town*, and *State*.

The site also offers a reverse phone number search and an *E-mail Search*. Note that while an *E-mail Search* for *Carole Levitt* did turn up her correct e-mail address, a search for *Mark Rosch* did not, despite his e-mail address being posted on numerous pages already indexed by **Yahoo!'s** robot.

It is a good idea to use a few "people and business finder" sites to compare the information provided at each. It's also important to remember to always try several of these sites before giving up after striking out at one of them. **Google** and other search engines can also be searched (and reverse searched) to find contact information; all you have to do is enter a phone number, name, or address into the search engine's query box. If **Google** finds the contact information, it sometimes places it at the top of the results list (with a telephone icon to the left; see page 86 for more information about **Google's Phonebook** search); other times, the phone number or address will be returned in **Google** Web search results, just like any other information listed on a Web site. Finally, you might try a pay database, such as **Merlin** (http://www.merlindata.com), where listings are updated daily. (See pages 214–220 for details about **Merlin.**)

Infobel.com (http://www.infobel.com/en/world) provides links to the Web-based telephone directories of over 200 countries. Choose a country and language and **Infobel** will link you to the local online phone directories available in the chosen country. These directories are maintained by the local phone companies, so search functions and parameters (including available search language) vary widely from site to site.

The telephone listing sites and other databases we have discussed so far obtain their information about telephone numbers from publicly available sources. Usually, the information comes from the yellow or white page phone books that we are all familiar with; public records; or is divulged by individuals on warranty cards, rebate forms, sweepstakes entries, and the like, and then resold for marketing purposes.

There was a time when information providers would obtain information from an individual's telephone account (e.g., address, numbers called) by contacting the phone company and pretending to be that individual — an activity known as "pretexting." Other information providers may also have been able to obtain this kind of information with the help of an employee of the phone company who would be paid to retrieve the information about specific individuals. You should be wary how providers are obtaining information from phone records, because these methods are no longer legal. The Telephone Records and Privacy Act of 2006 (Public Law No. 109-476, *available at* http://www.gpo.gov:80/fdsys/pkg/PLAW-109publ476/pdf/PLAW-109publ476.pdf) criminalizes the obtaining of telephone records by these means. However, the law does not apply to "any lawfully authorized investigative, protective, or intelligence activity of a law enforcement agency of the United States, a State, or political subdivision of a State, or of an intelligence agency of the United States."

The following sites are not phone directories, but you can sometimes find people's phone numbers or other contact information using them.

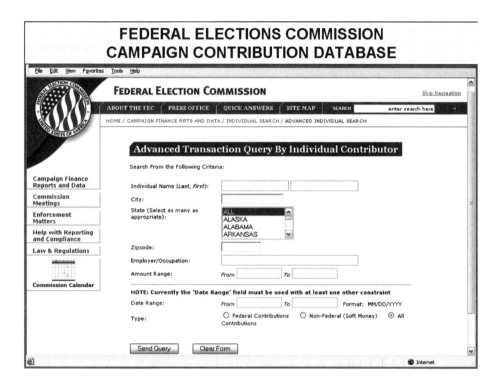

The **Federal Elections Commission** (http://www.fec.gov/finance/disclosure/norindsea.shtml) tracks federal political campaign contributions of over $200. It can be useful in locating the name and address of a person's employer, not to mention their political persuasion, if your subject has made such a political contribution. The basic search allows only for *First* and *Last* name searches. Clicking the *Advanced Search* link gives you the ability to narrow your results with additional search criteria, including *City*, *State*, *Zip Code*, and *Employer/Occupation*, among others.

Individual states typically have a similar database or list for state political campaign contributions. To find a specific state's political contribution database, visit **Search Systems** (http://www.searchsystems.net) and choose a state. Look for an entry under *Campaign Finance* or *Campaign Contributions*.

To learn who's behind a Web site (or at least who the contact person is and their address and telephone number), visit **Betterwhois.com** (http://www.betterwhois.com). It searches multiple domain name registries. After typing in a domain name, click the *Search* button, and then scroll down to see the results.

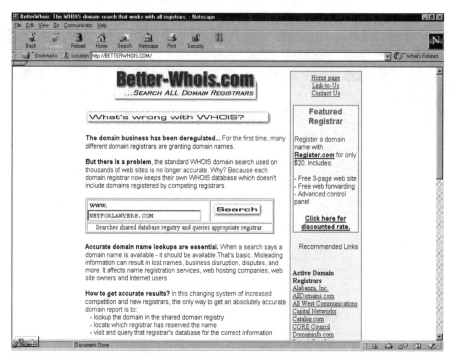

Domain Tools (http://www.domaintools.com/), like **Betterwhois**, searches through multiple registries. Advanced search functions, such as locating domain names that start or end with a specific word or phrase, can be accessed on the *Domain Search* page (http://domain-search.domaintools.com/).

While there is, unfortunately, no single registry Web site that contains data on all domains, **Betterwhois.com** and **Domain Tools** search a large number of the individual registries. For a full list of accredited domain name registries (that can be searched individually), visit **ICANN's** site (http://www.icann.org/registrars/accredited-list.html). Reverse searching by a person's name to see what domains an individual owns is no longer offered anywhere free. **DomainTools** does offer the ability to search for domains owned by a particular person or company (http://www.domaintools.com/reverse-whois). Pricing is based on the number of results returned by the search — from $79.98 for 1–9 domains to $999.98 for 500–999 domains.

If you have tried unsuccessfully to sue or subpoena someone, it is possible they may be in the military and thus, legitimately unavailable. To verify if someone is currently in the military, you may access the **DMDC (Defense Manpower Data Center) Military Verification** database (https://www.dmdc.osd.mil/appj/scra/scraHome.do). You must search with a minimum of a *Last Name* and a *Social Security Number* or *Birth Year*, *Month*, and *Day*. (See page 181 for information on locating dates of birth.) Results indicate only whether the individual is or is not on active duty. Presumably, out of privacy and military tactical concerns, it does not give any specific information regarding duty station. There is no charge to search the database. Previously, it was necessary to write or call to establish an account before searching this database. This is no longer necessary in order to search.

The pay service **Military Search** (http://www.militarysearch.org/) provides verification of the current military status of any person (directly from the "Department of Defense Data Center"). If you have the *Name* and *Social Security Number* of the individual you are searching for, the search costs $10. However, with this information, you could run the same search yourself for free (as noted above). Without the *Social Security Number*, **Military Search** will track it down for you and run the search for $35. Results of either search will be sent to you by fax, postal mail, or express delivery.

GI Search (http://www.gisearch.com) is a social networking site for people who wish to get in touch with others with whom they served in the armed forces. You can search using a *Last Name* and *First Name*, *Nickname/AKA*, or *Installation*. Registration is free but not required to search. A military background is not needed to become a member.

Using Asset Searches to Find People and Investigate Backgrounds

There are two main reasons to search for assets. The first reason is to locate a person. Locating a person's assets is often the most direct route to locating the person's address or telephone number. The second reason to locate a person's assets is to gather investigative information about a person. For example, in a divorce action, we need to locate assets for proper division of property. In another case, we might need to locate assets to ascertain whether a defendant has assets or is judgment-proof. This could help us decide whether to file a lawsuit in the first place.

Locating Assets — Real Property

Trying to trace real property assets for a divorce client? Trying to find a person's whereabouts by finding their home address — assuming they own a home? If you don't know where the person lives or if you want to conduct a nationwide search to trace assets held anywhere, a pay database search is required. But, if you only need to target one county or city, you might be able to do a free search if that county or city's assessor, recorder, or treasurer records are available for free online and are searchable by owner name. However, many jurisdictions only offer free address searching, which brings you back to pay databases if you need to search by owner name. (See *Chapter Ten* for information regarding pay databases.)

BRB Publications (http://www.brbpub.com/prs/searchfirms.aspx) offers a searchable database of more than 600 vendors offering paid access to numerous types of public records around the country. The database is searchable by state, type of record, or company name. (Also, see *Chapter Ten* for more information on pay investigative databases.)

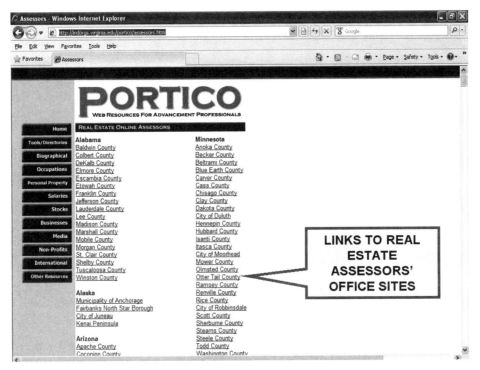

Search Systems (http://www.searchsystems.net), **Portico** (http://indorgs.virginia.edu/portico/assessors.html), and **BRB Publications** (http://www.brbpub.com/freeresources/pubrecsitesStates.aspx) each link to hundreds of free state and local assessor's, recorder's and/or treasurer's offices that are on the Web.

To find the sales price of a home, register free at **Domania.com** (http://www.domania.com). Type an *Address* and *ZIP Code* (or *City and State*) into the query boxes and you might find the date of sale and the sales price for the home if it has sold recently. You can also display a list of properties within a certain radius (from a half mile to two miles) and a minimum sales price. Not every state or every county is included in **Domania's** database. Displayed results will include up to the fifty most recent sales in the vicinity of the address searched. Thus, the exact address you entered might not be displayed at all if it was not sold recently.

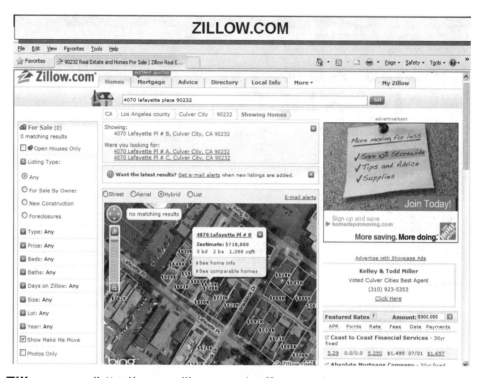

Zillow.com (http://www.zillow.com) offers real estate sales prices, current "for sale" listings, and estimated sales values ("Zestimates"). The site gathers information from a variety of public record and publicly available sources to display recent sales prices, current asking prices (for homes listed for sale), and "Zestimated" values for almost any house, based partially on the latter two other criteria. Zestimates are generated automatically, based on the available information, without property-specific information like current condition, renovations, etc. Because of this, further research and cross-checking as to the actual market value of a property may be necessary.

In addition to locating property valuation information for a specific address, you can also retrieve broader data by searching with as little as a *Street* or *Neighborhood* name or a *ZIP Code*.

Searching for a specific address returns an aerial map pinpointing the address and displaying the Zestimate for that property and the properties surrounding it. Square footage and the number of bedrooms and bathrooms are also displayed. Clicking on the orange house that serves as a pinpoint for the address you've searched opens a pop-up that contains a "bird's eye" aerial view of the home, as well as property tax information, "Zestimated" sales price trends for the property and the neighborhood, and a list of recent, nearby home sales in the area.

Registration (which is free) gives you access to additional features, including keeping track of value information on specific homes. Registered users can also post a *Make Me Move*™ price for other site visitors who might be interested in purchasing their home. (Zillow maintains "registration" and "claiming" processes to help confirm the legal owner of the home before users can input data about a specific address.)

Neither **Zillow** nor **Domania** return the property owner's name.

Money

The National Association of Unclaimed Property Administrators (NAUPA) sponsors the **Unclaimed.org** Web site (http://www.unclaimed.org). It links to the unclaimed property databases in all fifty states, the District of Columbia, Puerto Rico, and the Canadian provinces of Alberta, British Columbia, and Quebec. The search results from many states provide addresses of those who have unclaimed property. Occasionally, these addresses are current, making these databases useful for locating a specific person (besides finding their money).

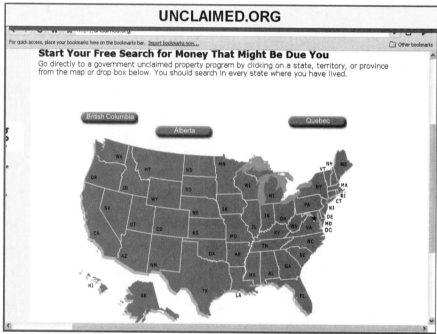

NAUPA also sponsors a free multistate searching database, **MissingMoney.com** (http://www.missingmoney.com/), which covers thirty-eight states, the District of Columbia, Puerto Rico, and the Canadian province of Alberta. Select *Search all states and provinces* from the *State/Province* drop-down menu to search all available jurtisdicitons simultaneously. An *Advanced Search* option is offered once your basic search results are displayed. There, you can specify up to two additional previous last names to search. In the case of common names, you can limit your search to up to four states, or choose to search all available state databases.

Landings.com (http://www.landings.com) and the **F.A.A. Registry Aircraft Registration Inquiry** site can both be used to verify pilot certifications, to discover aircraft ownership, and locate addresses for those individuals.

To discover aircraft ownerships at the **Landings.com** site, click on *Databases* (located toward the bottom of the page, under the *Search/Ref* column), and then click on *U.S.* or *World* under the *A/C Registrations* heading. Click *Owner Search* in either database to access the search screens. *U.S.* registration information is updated monthly. The update cycle varies from country to country when conducting *World* searches.

The **F.A.A. Registry Aircraft Registration Inquiry** site is updated daily. For aircraft ownership (http://registry.faa.gov/aircraftinquiry/defimg.asp), search the database by *Name*, *N–Number* (F.A.A.-issued registration number), *Serial number*, *Make/model*, etc. One advantage to the **F.A.A. Registry** is that even if a plane has been deregistered and/or exported out of the United States, searching by its N–Number will return information on the last U.S.–registered owner and the country to which it was exported.

Pilot Certification

To verify pilot certifications at **Landings.com** (http://www.landings.com), click on *Databases,* then on *Pilots* under the *Certifications* heading, and then enter your query. Typically, you will be searching by *Name*, but you can also search by other criteria, such as by *City* or *ZIP Code* (if you need to know, for example, the names of certified pilots in a specific city or ZIP Code) or to narrow down your search for a common name.

To verify pilot certifications at the **F.A.A.** site (http://www.faa.gov/about/office_org/headquarters_offices/avs/offices/afs/afs700/), click on *Airmen Certification* and then click on *Search Airmen Certification Information* under the *Online Services* heading. You must supply the following information about yourself before you can conduct a pilot certification search: your *Last Name*, *Employer*, *Street*, *City*, and *Country*. Because the searcher's personal information is not required at the **Landings.com** site, we would prefer using that site to the **F.A.A.** site. However, when we searched the same name at both sites, we obtained differing results, indicating that a search at both sites might be necessary.

Boat Registration

Ownership information regarding domestic commercial vessels is not available online, but at the **U.S. Coast Guard Vessel Documentation Center** site (http://www.uscg.mil/hq/cg5/nvdc/), *Abstracts of Title* can be ordered online for $25, by clicking *Order Products On-Line* in the left-hand column; other documents are also available. It's not that easy to find information about recreational and smaller commercial boats because their registration is handled at the state level (usually by the Department of Motor Vehicles or by the Department of Fish and Wildlife). It varies from state to state as to whether this information is available for free on the Internet.

Intellectual Property (Patents, Trademarks, and Copyrights)

In a hunt for a person's assets, do not overlook intellectual property – patents, trademarks, and copyrights.

Patents

The **U.S. Patent and Trademark Office (U.S.P.T.O.)** offers a full-text searchable database of patents back to 1976 at http://patft.uspto.gov. The database also includes full-page images of patents from 1790-1975 searchable only by *Issue Date*, *Patent Number,* and *Current U.S. Classification*. Patents from 1976-present can also be field searched (e.g., *Inventor's name*). Patent applications are also searchable back to March 2001. Also, see page 85 for information on **Google's Patent Search**.

Trademarks

Use **TESS** (**Trademark Electronic Search System**) to search over 4 million pending, registered, and dead federal trademarks at the **U.S.P.T.O.** site (http://www.uspto.gov/trademarks/index.jsp). Click the *Search Marks* link near the center of the page to begin searching. *Basic*, *Boolean*, and *Advanced* searches are available. Also, see page 86 for information on **Google's Trademark Search**, which is included in its **Patent Search**.

Copyrights

The **U.S. Copyright Office** consists of one integrated catalog (instead of what had been three separate databases) of over 20 million records for registered works and recorded documents since January 1, 1978 (http://www.copyright.gov/records/). The catalog includes registrations and preregistrations for books, music, films, sound recordings, maps, software, photographs, art, multimedia, periodicals, magazines, journals, newspapers, etc. Also included are records for assignments, transfers, and miscellaneous documents relating to copyright ownership. To search the database, click the *Search the Catalog* link. This link leads to the *Basic Search* page where you can search by *Title, Name, Keyword, Registration Number, Document Number*, or *Command Keyword* (Boolean, phrase, and wildcard searching). Sample searches are located on the search page and should be referred to before beginning a search. For more detailed searching, click the *Other Search Options* link. (Also see pages 409-410.)

Locating Assets — Businesses

Company Ownership, Registered Agents, and Fictitious Business Names (FBNs)

Secretary of State sites and County or City Recorder sites are useful for the following three tasks:

    (1) Identifying company ownership when conducting an asset search

    (2) Finding the registered agent's name and address if trying to serve a corporation

    (3) Finding a company's address

Residentagentinfo.com

(http://www.residentagentinfo.com) has compiled a helpful list of links to the Secretary of State sites in all fifty states, the District of Columbia, Guam, and Puerto Rico. Forty-eight states, the District of Columbia, and Puerto Rico offer corporation records free online, searchable by company name (and some offer registered agent name or officer name searching). The amount of information displayed varies from state to state. For instance, some states do not display officer names or the registered agent's name. Usually, the missing information can be ordered online for a fee. Two states (Indiana and New Jersey) charge for accessing corporate information online, but Indiana will provide the information free over the telephone. Guam does not offer a free online search. The site lists no information for the U.S. Virgin Islands, but this territory also does not offer a free online search of corporate records. For multistate searching or to search by criteria not available for free (such as a registered agent name), a pay database search will be necessary. See *Chapter Ten* for pay database information.

ResidentAgentInfo also links to similar resources in Australia, Canada, and the United Kingdom.

Many companies are incorporated in Delaware. **Delaware's Division of Corporations** site (http://www.corp.delaware.gov/onlinestatus.shtml) offers free searching. You can search by *Entity Name* or *File Number*. You can also search with a partial *Entity Name,* but the results list will be incomplete. For example, a search for *Universal* returns a list of only 50 entities of the "999 matches found" that begin with *Universal*. The site's search results include *Entity Name, File Number, Incorporation/Formation Date, Entity Kind, Registered Agent Name, Address, Phone Number*, and *Residency*. Note that even though you are conducting these searches online yourself, the service is only available "during normal business hours from 7:00 a.m. to 11:59 p.m. EST, Monday through Friday."

To link to County or City Recorder Offices (or similar county or city agencies that handle fictitious business name [FBN] filings), search for a specific county's or city's Web site at the **State and Local Government on the Net** Web site (http://www.statelocalgov.net). (Note that Fictitious Business Names are also referred to as "Doing Business As" names [DBAs].) Click on the state in which the county or city is located and then scroll down to *County* or *City* and select whichever one you need from the list. Then browse to find the county's or the city's Web site for the Recorder's (or Clerk's) office. When it comes to FBN filngs, every county and city offers different information and different methods for accessing and searching the information. Some may not offer FBN searches at all. When the FBN databases can be searched for free, it varies as to whether one can search by the FBN only or also by the owner's name.

SEC Info (http://www.secinfo.com) offers free, full-text searching of U.S. Securities and Exchange Commission (S.E.C.) filings and also Canada's SEDAR filings (Canadian Securities Administrators System for Electronic Document Analysis and Retrieval) back to 1994 for some companies. The following search options are available: *Name*, *Industry*, *Business*, *SIC Code* (Standard Industrial Classification Code — the government's numerical classification system that describes a company's business), *Area Code*, *Topic*, *CIK* (Central Index Key — the unique identifying number the S.E.C. assigns each company, *Accession Number*, *File Number*, *Date*, and *ZIP Code*. Additionally, although not listed as one of the available criteria next to the *Search* box, you can also search by NAICS (North American Industrial Classification System numbers — the government's newer numerical classification system that describes a company's business; adopted to replace the SIC Codes). While you can search the site (and receive a list of results) without registering, registation is required to view full-text filings.

The Federal Government's official **S.E.C.** site, **EDGAR** (http://www.sec.gov), is free and provides access to data in "real time." Since 2006, **EDGAR** has provided full-text searching http://searchwww.sec.gov/EDGARFSClient/jsp/EDGAR_MainAccess.jsp (currently covering the most recent four years of filings). This has made **EDGAR** significantly more useful.

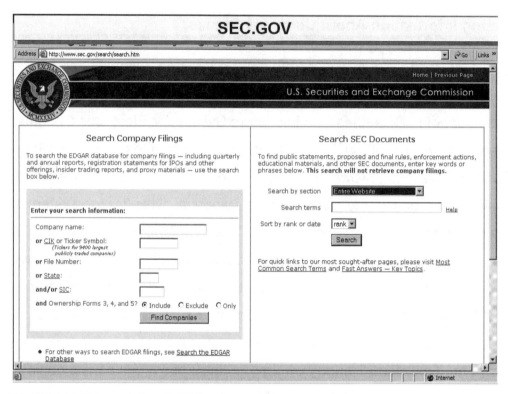

Field searching at the S.E.C. site can be done at
http://sec.gov/search/search.htm by *Company name*, *Ticker Symbol*, *CIK*, or *SIC*,
and can be further limited by state. You cannot search the S.E.C. site using NAICS
numbers.

Morningstar Document Research (formerly **10kWizard**;
http://www.10kwizard.com) is a fee-based service offering realtime, full-text
searching of current U.S. Securities and Exchange Commission (S.E.C.) EDGAR
filings, Pre-EDGAR filings back to 1966, and archival EDGAR filings back to
1994. The following search options are provided: *Company Name*, *Industry*,
Keywords, *Phrases*, *CIK*, *SIC*, *Type of Form*, and *Date Restrictors*. Automated
company alerts are also available. When launched, the site offered free access
to these searches and was one of the first sites to do so. Access is now available
through a number of different subscription packages ranging in price from $249
to $2,275 per year.

PACER (Public Access To Court Electronic Records) (http://pacer.psc.uscourts.gov/), is the government's low cost federal docket database. It is particularly useful for searching federal bankruptcy court dockets (and the underlying documents for many cases) because all of the bankruptcy courts participate in **PACER**. Search the *Case Locator* portion of **PACER** (foremerly known as the *U.S. Party/Case Index*) when you are unsure where the subject might have filed bankruptcy. Searching is permitted by *Name* (personal or company), *Docket Number*, *SSN* (Social Security Number), a combined *Four Digit SSN* and *Party Name* search, or a *TIN (Taxpayer Identification Number)*. See pages 383–387 for complete details about **PACER**.

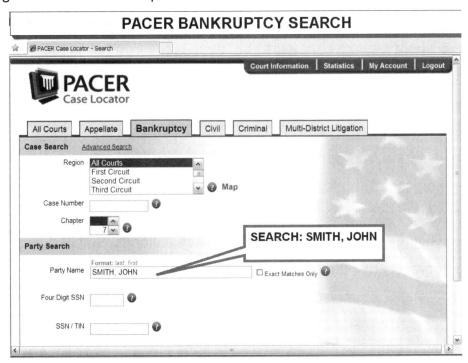

Freecourtdockets.com offers free bankruptcy court docket searching, but the underlying documents are not available. See page 390 for more details.

Bankruptcy dockets and the underlying documents can also be searched (for a fee) at **West CourtExpress** (http://www.courtexpress.westlaw.com) and **LexisNexis CourtLink** (http://www.lexisnexis.com/courtlink). See page 391 for more details.

Some pay investigative databases, such as **Merlin** (http://www.merlindata.com/), **Accurint** (http://www.accurint.com), and **West's PeopleMap** (http://west.thomson.com/westlaw/public-records/libraries/peoplemap/default.aspx), indicate if someone has declared bankruptcy. See pages 214–224 for details about these databases.

UCCs, Judgments, and Liens Databases

Search Systems's free *Public Records Locator* search engine is a good resource to locate UCC, judgment, and liens databases (http://www.searchsystems.net/) available on the Internet. Simply type in the appropriate keyword (e.g., to search for UCCs, type in *ucc*) or select a jurisdiction from the *By state* drop-down menu to locate a relevant database. Links to those databases, where available, may also be found in the free public record directories hosted by **BRB Publications** (http://www.brbpub.com/freeresources/pubrecsites.aspx) and **Portico** (http://indorgs.virginia.edu/portico/).

The **National Association of Secretaries of State** Web site (http://nass.org/index.php?option=contact_display) offers direct links to the Secretaries of State's Web sites in all fifty states, American Samoa, the District of Columbia, Guam, Puerto Rico, and the U.S. Virgin Islands. Select a jurisdiction from the drop-down menu for information about its Secretrary of State and a link to their Web site. Some jurisdictions offer free searchable UCC databases while others do not. If a free search is not available, a pay database (discussed later in *Chapter Ten* of this book) may offer UCC or judgment and liens databases for that jurisdiction.

At the pay databases, you can often conduct multistate searching (e.g., an "all state" UCC search) or multi-type record searching (e.g., search UCC, judgment and liens records simultaneously in one or more states or counties). These types of multijurisdictional and multi-type searches are not available through the free search resources on the Internet.

Locating criminal record information online, whether for free or a fee, is hit or miss because there is no national criminal records database available to the general public or legal professionals. We've been told by some law enforcement officers that even the FBI's **National Crime Information Center (NCIC)** database (available to federal and local criminal justice agencies; as well as some select, authorized, non-criminal justice agencies) is not a complete collection of criminal record information. The **NCIC** relies on local law enforcement agencies and courts to report information for inclusion in the **NCIC** database. Our law enforcement sources have told us that agencies in smaller jurisdictions often do not enter warrants for criminals if the jurisdiction is unwilling/unable to pay for the criminals' extradition back to their jurisdiction for trial.

Individual resources covering different jurisdictions can provide some information about arrests, criminal convictions, or incarcerations.

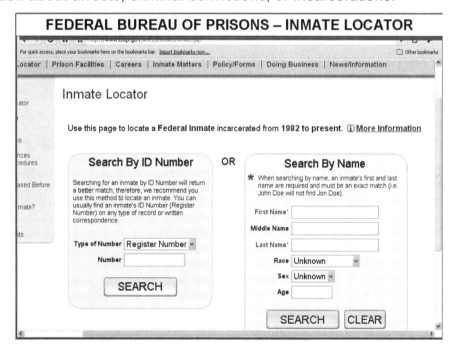

The **Federal Bureau of Prisons' Inmate Locator** (http://www.bop.gov/iloc2/LocateInmate.jsp) can be used to search for federal inmates using their *Register Number*, DCDC *Number*, *FBI Number*, *INS Number*, or *Name* (a full first and last name are both required). The site includes information on all federal inmates from 1982 to present. Information regarding federal inmates released prior to 1982 can be obtained by sending a request to the Bureau via postal mail. See http://www.bop.gov/inmate_locator/inmates_b4_1982.jsp for details.

Corrections.com

(http://www.corrections.com/links/viewlinks.asp?Cat=30) provides links to the Departments of Correction in all fifty states. That does not mean that every state provides a searchable database of inmates. Even in those states that do offer such searchable databases, the criteria by which you can search and the amount of information displayed will vary from state to state. For example, Illinois makes inmate information available online, with searches available by *Name*, *Birthdate*, or *IDOC* number, while California offers no online search option.

VineLink.com (http://www.vinelink.com) allows you to find out when an offender has been arrested, released, or is scheduled to appear in court in forty-seven states and the District of Columbia. The system was originally created to protect crime victims by providing them with the release date of offenders. The opening screen prompts you to select a state in which to search. Depending on coverage for the state you choose, you will be able to search city, county and/or statewide records. Searching is uniform in all jurisdictions covered. You can search with a *First name* and *Last Name* or *Offender ID*. You can also add a *Date of Birth* or *Age Range* if you have this information. After finding the individual in the database, the victim (or anyone) may register to receive a phone call or e-mail before an offender's release date.

Free Inmate Locator (http://www.inmatesplus.com/) has compiled links to the forty-one states that offer free information and photographs of incarcerated inmates. For those states that do not have an online inmate locator, a link is provided to the Department of Corrections of that state. The site also includes a link to the **Federal Bureau of Prisons' Federal Inmate Locator** database. A *County Jails* link leads to a state-by-state list of counties with links to their individual searchable inmate databases.

CriminalSearches.com searches multiple sites simultaneously to retrieve information about individuals. You can search for information from all fifty states and the District of Columbia with as little as a last name. You can search all jurisdictions simultaneously, or select just one from the *State* drop-down menu. The *Advanced Search* page allows you to narrow your search down further with the addition of a *Middle Name*, *Age Range*, or *DOB* (Date of Birth). Sample searches returned results from official state and county court sites and state departments of corrections. Despite the wide net cast by the site, it is far from comprehensive. In fact, because many of the records come from court dockets, some results may only indicate charges that were filed and tried but not convictions. While a number of the results of our test searches did reveal charges that had been dismissed, this site can be useful when used in conjunction with other information sources.

BRB Publications's (http://www.brbpub.com/prrn/search.aspx) **Public Record Retriever Network** database of public records vendors includes numerous companies that provide *ad hoc* access to criminal records in multiple jurisdictions.

LLRX.com's court rules database (http://www.llrx.com/courtrules) links to numerous courts that place criminal (and civil) docket sheets or case summaries online (mostly for free). Some courts provide docket number searching only, while others offer more search functions (such as party or attorney name). Not all courts post criminal dockets.

Some law enforcement agencies place their booking logs on the Web, while others provide lists of delinquent parents or jail escapees. For an example of a booking log, view the **Los Angeles Sheriff's Inmate Information Center** (http://app4.lasd.org/iic/ajis_search.cfm). For an example of a list of delinquent parents, see **Los Angeles County's Most Delinquent Parents** site (http://childsupport.co.la.ca.us/dlparents.htm). For a database of escapees, see the **Florida State Department of Corrections' Inmate Escape Information Search** (http://www.dc.state.fl.us/EscapedInmates/). If similar information is available in other jurisdictions, try a search engine search with appropriate keywords (e.g., *"San Diego" county california warrants search*).

Search Systems offers access to criminal information on a "pay as you go" basis. Criminal records searches by state are $6.95, and a "nationwide" search is $14.95. See pages 119–122 for more information on the coverage of these records.

DEPARTMENT OF JUSTICE NATIONAL SEX OFFENDER DATABASE ADVANCED SEARCH

Wonder if your new neighbor is a sex offender? The U.S. Department of Justice (DOJ) **National Sex Offender Public Registry** (http://www.nsopr.gov/) offers one-stop access to registries from fifty states, Guam, the District of Columbia, Puerto Rico, and Indian Country.

The site's *Standard Search* requires a *Last Name* and (at least) a first initial to conduct a search through all the participating jurisdictions. The *Advanced Search* page gives you the ability to conduct a more focused search. On the *Advanced Search* page you can choose to *Search all States, Territories, and Indian Country*, select a single jurisdiction to search from the *State/Territory* drop-down menu, or select a single jurisdiction to search using the *Indian Country* drop-down menu. You can also search by *County*, *City*, or *ZIP Code*. It's important to note that the DOJ has only created an overlay of the existing sex offender database maintained by each jurisdiction. The DOJ has not created a master national database of sex offenders that it maintains separately.

You can also link directly to each state's full sex offender registries online by visiting the **FBI State Sex Offender Registry** Web site (http://www.fbi.gov/hq/cid/cac/registry.htm).

Verifying Occupational Licenses of Professionals, Experts, and Others

Portico has a free *Occupations* page (http://indorgs.virginia.edu/portico/occupations.html) that links to various licensing boards throughout the country. Occupations range from *Artist* and *Architect* to *Medical Professions* and *Lawyers/Judges*. It also includes links to thirty-four state bar associations' and the District of Columbia's searchable databases of members.

IsHeReallyaLawyer.com provides links to forty-seven state bar associations', and the District of Columbia's searchable member databases. The site also includes a link to the U.S. Patent Bar's searchable database of patent attorneys.

BRB Publications (http://www.brbpub.com/freeresources/pubrecsitesOccStates.aspx) has an extensive collection of free links to state *Occupational Licensing* agencies, browseable by state.

Search Systems (http://www.searchsystems.nct) also links to occupational licensing boards. Choose a state and scroll through the alphabetical list of agencies and information sources.

To verify medical licenses (and in some states, doctors' discipline records), use the links found at the **Federation of State Medical Boards of the United States'** Web site (http://www.fsmb.org/directory_smb.html), an organization of seventy-one medical licensing authorities in fifty states, the District of Columbia, Guam, Puerto Rico, the Northern Mariana Islands, and the U.S. Virgin Islands. The Federation also operates **DocInfo.org** which provides disciplinary sanction information about, "medical doctors, osteopathic physicians and the majority of physician assistants licensed in the United States." Searches must include the individual's *First Name, Last Name, City* and *State.* To narrow your results even further, you have the option of adding a *Middle Name/Initial, ZIP Code, Degree Code* (e.g., MD, DO, PA), or *Specialty.* An individual report costs $9.95.

Another good source of information about medical professionals can be their associations' Web sites, from the general **American Medical Association** (**A.M.A.**) site to specialty medical association sites. Some include disciplinary, contact, or biographical information in addition to licensing information.

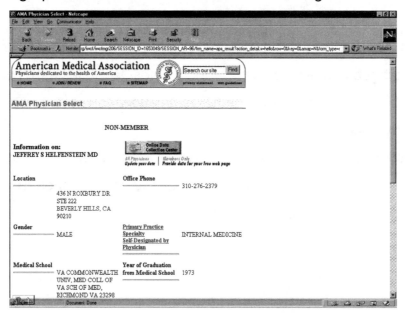

For example, to locate information beyond licensing about doctors, such as office addresses and where they graduated from medical school, visit the **A.M.A.'s** site (https://extapps.ama-assn.org/doctorfinder/html/patient.jsp) and choose the *for Patients* link on the right-hand side. The **A.M.A.** site searches "virtually" every licensed physician (814,000) or doctor of osteopathy in the U.S. and its possessions, by either *Name* or *Specialty* (whether or not they are a member of the **A.M.A.**).

Finding Background Information About Attorneys and Judges

See page 175 and *Chapter Nine* (pages 195–201) of this book.

Vital Statistics: Births, Deaths, Marriages, Divorces, and Social Security Numbers

Whether vital statistic public records are available free on the Internet varies widely from jurisdiction to jurisdiction. Many states have confidentiality laws that prohibit you from requesting a copy of a vital statistic record (especially birth certificates) unless you are requesting your own (or your parent's, your spouse's, or your child's). Also, whether these various vital statistics are kept at the state level or county level varies widely. If vital statistics are available online for a particular state, dates of coverage and geographic coverage within the state vary widely, as does the type of vital statistics available.

VitalChek (http://www.vitalchek.com) is a "one-stop-shop" of sorts to which 400 U.S. agencies have outsourced the function of providing online access to vital statistic public records (for a fee). A limited number of U.S. territorial agencies and agencies in Canada, Mexico, and the United Kingdom are also affiliated with **VitalChek**.

There are several online directories that are helpful to discover if these vital statistics are available online directly from your county or state. We have found different resources at each, so check them all before deciding a vital record is not online.

Search Systems (http://www.searchsystems.net) offers both its *Public Records Locator* search engine and its browseable topical directory (choose a relevant topic, from *Births* and *Deaths* to *Marriages* and *Divorces*, etc.), or browse its jurisdictional directory.

BRB Publications's (http://www.brbpub.com/pubrecsites.asp) free collection of links to *State, County and City* public records sites (browseable by state) includes numerous vital statistics databases.

Various genealogy-related sites also provide links to other sites that are useful for locating vital statistics. For example, **Rootsweb** links to state, regional, and local historical societies and libraries where birth and death records might be posted. Some of these sources are free and some require payment. **Rootsweb** offers a state resources page (http://www.rootsweb.ancestry.com/roots-l/usa.html), where you can review what's available state by state.

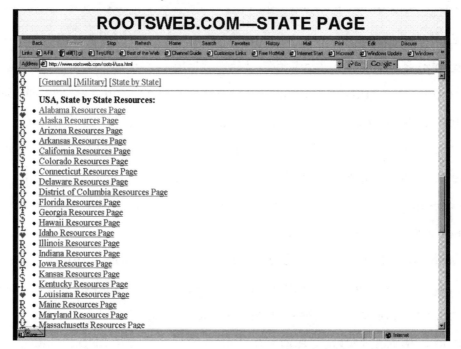

There are also "volunteer project" databases hosted at **Rootsweb** such as obituary and cemetery records and family trees that might be useful for finding someone's vital records. The state resources pages found at **Rootsweb** also provide links describing how to obtain vital records from particular government agencies. After choosing a state from the list of *State by State Resources* page (http://www.rootsweb.ancestry.com/roots-l/usa.html), scroll all the way down to *Vital Records* and select the type of record that you need (except for California – where you'll choose *Data* and then *Vital Records*).

The **VitalSearch Company Worldwide, Inc.** (http://www.vitalsearch-worldwide.com) site provides vital records databases for nineteen states including Alabama, California, Florida, Georgia, Kentucky, Oregon, Texas, Washington, and Wisconsin. (No records are available for the additional states listed as *Shell only*.) Until the Summer of 2010, the site provided free (if somewhat limited) access to many of its databases. That is no longer the case. The majority of it resources are now only available to paid subscribers. Using the site's remaining free databases takes nerves of steel because there are many annoying advertisements. To use the free databases, first choose a state (for the following description, we have chosen *California*). Focus on the *Database* list (near the top of the page): *Births: 1905-2000*, *Deaths: 1905-2000*, *Marriages: 1949-1986*, *Divorces -*, and *Additional Vital Records: 1880-1920*. However, as soon as we selected *Deaths: 1905-2000*, we learned that free access is now limited to the years 1905-1929 only and requires registration as a *Guest Searcher* if you are not already a *Premium* (paid) subscriber. Click *You Will Need A Free Guest Pass* and after filling in and submitting a brief form, a user name and password will be e-mailed back to you within seconds. At this point you will be able to click on *All Other Searchers Enter Here* and enter your new user name and password. A huge advertisement appears for *Net Detective* on the subsequent page. Ignore this and scroll down the page to the *Surname* search box and enter the last name of the individual whose records you are searching for and click on *Begin Search* located on the bottom right-hand corner. (Searches are limited to the first six characters of the last name.) The only other of the site's California databases available to *Guest Searchers* is *1986 Marriages-Bride Indexed*. The **VitalSearch** site also provides access to information in specific counties by selecting from the drop-down menu near the center of the state resource page. Single user subscriptions are available for $57.95 per year or $24.95 for 90 days of access.

Marriage and Divorce Records

California marriage and divorce records are a prime example of how geographic coverage varies widely when searching for vital statistics. On the *Marriage Records* page found at **Search Systems,** there are links to marriage data for just twelve out of California's sixty-eight counties and some of those records are only historical. In addition, there is a link to a statewide site that pulls data from **Brigham Young University's Western States Historical Marriage Records Index**. (For nearly three decades, BYU-Idaho has been extracting early marriage records from counties in the western part of the United States.)

Texas marriage and divorce records are a prime example of records once kept at the county level now being kept at the state level. There are two places to obtain the Texas state records free online. The first place is the official state Web site, but the records are not in a user-friendly searchable database. Instead, the records must be downloaded and then opened in Excel. Texas marriage records (1966-2008) can be found at http://www.dshs.state.tx.us/vs/marriagedivorce/mindex.shtm and divorce records (1968-2008) can be found at http://www.dshs.state.tx.us/vs/marriagedivorce/dindex.shtm (each year's records are held in a separate file). Earlier records are found at individual county Web sites. The second place to obtain Texas marriage and divorce records is at **Courthouse Direct**. For searchability, **Courthouse Direct** is better than the state's site because it provides user-friendly searchable databases. On the other hand, the state's site is more up-to-date (by five years) and **Courthouse Direct** charges a $3.25 per document surcharge and $1.00 per page (e.g., a one page document would cost $4.25 and a two page document would cost $5.25, etc.). **Courthouse Direct's** database of Texas marriage records (1966-2003) can be found at http://linkon.in/aKFh1R and its database of divorce records (1966-2003) can be found at http://linkon.in/cQe9Fx. Both the marriage and divorce databases allow you to include a date range to narrow down your results. Oddly, when searching the divorce database, the date range also applies to the marriage date included in the record. So if a couple was divorced between 1966 and 2003, but were married before 1968, searching the divorce database for the bride or groom's last name and dates at least as early as 1925 can return these wedding dates as well.

To find whether other states post marriage and divorce records on the Web, visit the directories noted earlier in this section.

After September 11, 2001, it became harder to find free databases with birth records. Before September 11, 2001, databases containing California and Texas birth records, for example, were hosted free at **Rootsweb** but have now been removed. Early in 2003, **VitalSearch Worldwide** added their searchable databases of California births from 1905-2001 back onto the site (http://www.vitalsearch-ca.com/gen/ca/_vitals/cabirthm.htm) although it is no longer free to access. You'll notice though that new data have not been made available by the state of California since 2001. (See the discussion on page 178-179 for details on how to search **VitalSearch's** collections of California, Kentucky, and Texas birth records; and death, marriage, and divorce records in various other states).

If you don't find links to a state's birth records at **VitalSearch**, **Rootsweb's** state pages, **Search Systems**, or **BRB Publications**, you might try **Birthdatabase.com** (http://www.birthdatabase.com). While it's not an official birth record by any means, for those who only need to obtain or verify a date of birth, it allows you to search for birthdays for free. Since so many people have the same name, it's not always easy to determine if your search has turned up the correct person. **Birthdatabase.com** allows you to narrow the search by entering an estimated age (within two years). Another birthday site, **Stevemorse.org** (http://stevemorse.org/birthday/birthday2.html), gives users more search options to what seems to be the same 120 million birthdate records. Neither of these birthday sites provides any documentation as to where the data come from, but we have had success locating birthdays for a variety of individuals who live in various parts of the country.

While the **Social Security Death Index (SSDI)** (noted on pages 128-129) is a national death index, many state and local governments also maintain death indices. However, not every state will provide access to its death records for free online.

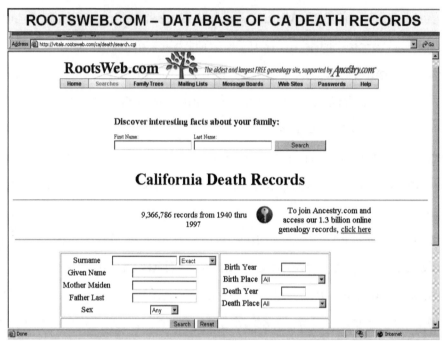

Use **Rootsweb's** state resources page (http://www.Rootsweb.com/roots-l/usa.html) to find state and local death records. Select a state and scroll down to *Vital Records* (but for California, click on *Data* and then scroll down to *Vital Records*). **Rootsweb** offers a searchable database of 9,366,786 California deaths from 1940 through 1997 (http://vitals.rootsweb.ancestry.com/ca/death/search.cgi).

VitalSearch Worldwide offers a searchable database of over 12 million California deaths from 1905-2000 (http://www.vitalsearch-ca.com/gen/ca/_vitals/cadeathm.htm). Paid subscribers can obtain detailed death information from **VitalSearch Worldwide** over the entire range of the databases while non-subscribers can obtain summary information only through 1929. See the discussion of **VitalSearch Company Worldwide, Inc.** on pages 178-179 for tips on searching this site and to learn which states **VitalSearch's** death records databases cover.

Social Security Numbers (SSNs) of dead people are available to the public and are posted on the **SSDI** at **Rootsweb** (see pages 128-129). Social Security Numbers of people still alive are not public records.

However, if you only need to verify a Social Security Number, you can search for free at Crimetime Publishing. The company provides instant validation of the Social Security Number that you enter on its **SSN Validator** site (http://www.ssnvalidator.com). Information included in the validation results include *State of Issuance*, *Approx. Date of Issuance*, and *SSA Death Masterfile* which indicates whether the Social Security Number for which you searched was issued to an individual listed in the **SSDI**.

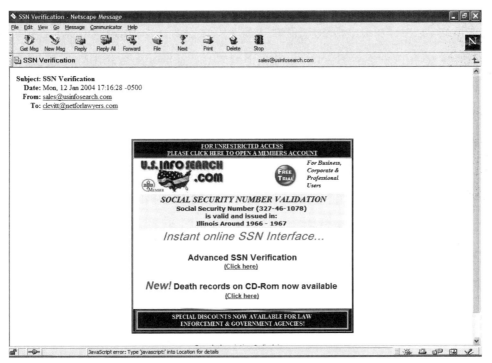

U.S. InfoSearch (http://www.free-ssn-id-verification.usinfosearch.com/) identifies whether the Social Secutiy Number you provide is valid (and not fabricated) or if it belongs to a dead person. It requires you to provide your e-mail address in order to receive the validation information via e-mail (see screen shot above).

Neither site's results show to whom the number belongs.

To find out to whom a Social Security Number belongs, you'll usually need a pay investigative research database (detailed in *Chapter Ten,* beginning on page 203). On occasion, Social Security Numbers will appear as part of a filing recovered from a free public record database, such as a lien database. However many states, such as California and New York, are retroactively redacting identifying information like Social Security Numbers from historical filings.

Recent security breaches in public record databases have resulted in pay databases restricting access to full Social Security Numbers although there is no law mandating the restriction (yet). While one can still search by a full Social Security Number, the pay databases' search results will display only a truncated Social Security Number, unless the searcher is an authorized user, in which case the searcher can have access to full Social Security Numbers. Different database vendors interpret "authorized" in different manners, so vendors may differ as to who qualifies as an "authorized" user. For example, a number of pay databases grant access to full Social Security Number data to lawyers if they agree to a site visit to verify their identities, security of the location, etc., while some others do not require such a visit. Additionally, some vendors only give full Social Security Number access to lawyers whose primary practice is collections work, while other vendors do not make this distinction. Most of these pay databases require users to attest that they have a permissible use to access this information as per the Gramm-Leach-Bliley Act (GLBA), 15 U.S.C. 6802, each time a search is performed. (See pages 207-212 to learn about the GLBA's exceptions). Other databases are cutting lawyers off completely from access to full Social Security Numbers.

In the commercial pay databases, a truncated Social Security Number displays only the first five digits, while the government's **PACER** bankruptcy docket database displays the last four digits. Therefore, even if you do not have access to full Social Security Numbers from a commercial database, if the individual you're researching has filed for bankruptcy, you can combine the truncated Social Security Number from the commercial database and the **PACER** database to identify the full Social Security Number.

Locating Information Via a Freedom of Information Act Request

When it's not available anywhere, try a Freedom of Information Act (FOIA) request.

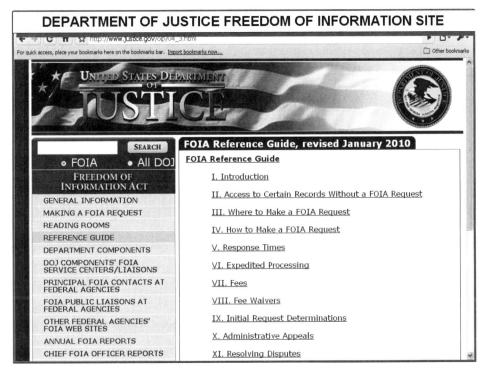

The **U.S. Department of Justice** provides a primer on how to file a federal FOIA request at http://www.justice.gov/oip/04_3.html.

The National Freedom of Information site provides links to individual state FOIA information (http://www.nfoic.org/states/).

Chapter Eight

FINDING EXPERTS
AND VERIFYING THEIR CREDENTIALS

Before you begin your search for an expert, it's often a good idea to do some background reading about the subject for which you need an expert witness. This can also help you identify experts by finding the names of the leading authors in the field. Instead of traveling to the library to perform a literature search, you can view a library's catalog (by title, subject, and author) over the Internet and you can also tap into their valuable databases remotely (as noted on pages 145-146) to perform a literature search and download the articles for free.

Finding Experts by Searching Free National Expert Witness Directory Databases

There are many types of free sites where you can find experts. A logical place to begin a search is at a national expert witness directory database. These sites may include the expert's profile, *Curriculum Vitae* (CV), deposition transcripts, references, trial transcripts, and articles.

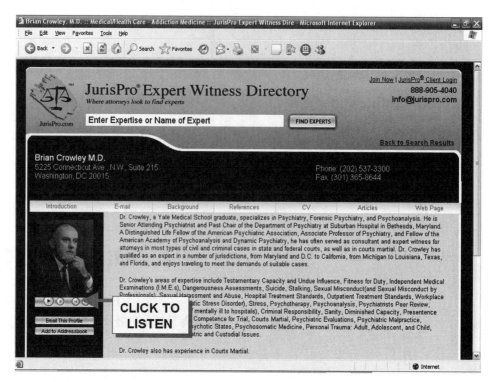

Jurispro.com (http://www.jurispro.com) is a free expert witness database with a unique feature. The site gives you the ability to view an expert's photograph and listen to their voice. The expert's *CV, Background, Publications*, and *References* are also included, in addition to a link to their Web site (where applicable) and an e-mail contact form.

ALMexperts.com (http://www.almexperts.com/ExpertWitness/) has a database of expert witnesses searchable by *Name of Expert or Company, Area of Expertise*, or *Keyword*. Search results can include the expert's *Profile, Resume*, picture, link to their Web site, and an e-mail contact form.

IDEX (https://www.idex.lexisnexis.com/) allows searching by an expert's name to retrieve trial transcripts, deposition transcripts, articles, challenges to the expert, and *Curriculum Vitae*. You can also perform a *Similar Case Search* to find cases with similar fact patterns to a case you are handling and information on the experts who testified in those previous cases. The site's *Testimonial History Search* is priced at $140. A *State License Discipline Search* is available for $30. See page 175-177 to learn about the possible availability of free searches for disciplinary information by jurisdiction.

Experts.com's (http://www.experts.com/) directory lists experts in over 1,200 categories of expertise. Search criteria are similar to **Jurispro** and **ALMExperts**, but the search results offer less detail than those other sites. Results include a profile of the expert, contact information, links to the expert's Web site, and e-mail. Some results also include links to books or articles the expert has written. While the site has reportedly added audio, in test searches we have not found any experts taking advantage of this option. Additionally, their *Name* search seems less precise than some of the other sites discussed in this section. For example, we were able to locate a particular expert by conducting a *Keywords* search for *Psychiatry*, but not by conducting a *Name* search for his last name.

MoreLaw (http://www.morelaw.com/experts) also has a free directory of experts that is browseable by state and area of expertise or searchable by *Name*, *Company Name*, *Phone Number*, etc. Results include the least information of the directories discussed here. Profiles include contact information, Web site and e-mail links, and a description of the expert's areas of expertise. See page 194 for other ways to locate experts using **MoreLaw**.

Finding Experts by Searching a Search Engine, Discussion Group, or Social Network

To locate an expert in a specific field, use a search engine and enter the phrase *"expert witness"* (in quotation marks) or the word *expert*, along with any other keyword or phrase that describes the expertise, such as *"child custody"* into the query box. This will often turn up the Web sites of expert witnesses in that particular area, or sites where experts you may be interested in have been mentioned.

Discussion group postings, as discussed on page 133 in *Chapter Seven*, are another place to search for experts (or to search for their opinions) assuming they participate in any of the numerous discussion groups available online. Archives of discussion group postings, such as **Google Groups** (http://groups.google.com), can be searched by keywords and phrases, by a person's name (if included in the body of message), or even by the author of the message (using the person's name or e-mail address). See page 123 for details about searching **Google Groups**.

Experts may also be participating in social and professional networking sites such as **LinkedIn**, **Facebook**, or **Twitter**. See pages 136–144 for more information on conducting searches at these sites.

Finding Experts by Searching Law Association Web Sites

Many specialty law association Web sites sponsor expert witness directories. Usually, these require a paid membership to the association in order to access them.

The **Defense Research Institute** (**DRI**; http://www.dri.org) offers an expert witnesses database free to its members (who are all defense attorneys) searchable by expert *Name*, *Expertise*, and *Locale*.

TrialSmith (formerly known as **DepoConnect**; http://www.trialsmith.com/ts/) is a subsidiary corporation of the Texas Trial Lawyers Association. **TrialSmith** offers a database where plaintiff's attorneys can access an online litigation bank with more than 270,000 deposition transcripts and more than 2.2 million other database items that reference experts and case topics. Access to **TrialSmith's** collection is available only to the plaintiff's bar. Annual subscription fees vary depending on membership in one of the site's nearly 90 partner associations. Non-members of any of **TrialSmith's** partner associations pay from $179 to $999 annually depending on the level of membership. Per-search charges also vary depending on the level of membership. Click *Services* on the site's home page and then *Subscription Plans* from the subsequent drop-down menu for more details.

Many state and county bar associations offer expert witness directories on their Web sites, often for free. For example, the **Illinois State Bar Association** offers a browseable list of experts organized by category (http://www.illinoisbar.org/experts/), while the **Los Angeles County Bar Association's** database, **Expert4law** (http://www.expert4law.org), offers a keyword searchable directory of experts, private judges, consultants, researchers, and more.

Another useful way to locate an expert, especially when it's an unusual expertise, is to get a referral from an association based on the particular expertise you are dealing with. There's an expert in every field and there's an association for every field, or so it seems. If you know the association's exact name, use a search engine to find its Web site. If you don't know the exact name of the association (or if you are unsure if one even exists), you can still use a search engine and enter the topic of the association (e.g., *banana*) and the word *association*. (By the way, there are at least five associations related to the banana.)

There are also two useful databases where you can keyword search for an association:

- **Associations Unlimited** (formerly titled **Encyclopedia of Associations**): Some libraries provide their library cardholders free remote access to this database. Use **Libdex** (http://www.libdex.com) to find your library's URL and discover if they offer this database.

- **Guidestar** (http://www2.guidestar.org/AdvancedSearch.aspx) has information on more than 1.8 million non-profit associations searchable by *Organization Name/Location*, or *Keywords*. Access to basic information from the results (e.g., *Organizational Statistics*, *Form 990s*, *Revenue and Expenses*) is available with a free registration. Additional information (e.g., *Financial Statement*, *Balance Sheet*, Highest Paid Employees & Their Compensation) is available to subscribers paying $350 per month for "Premium" access.

Finding Experts by Searching a Product Directory

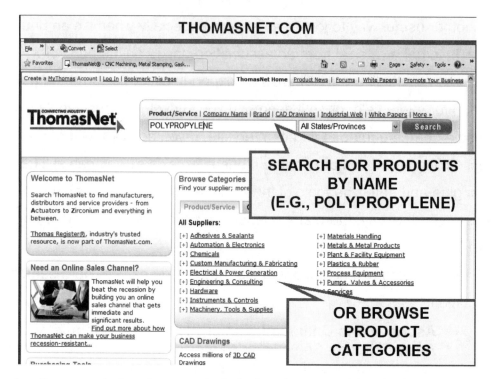

Another way to locate experts is to locate companies in the industry in which you need an expert. This is useful when you need to find an expert knowledgeable about a specific product but you don't know who manufactures it or you are looking to locate an expert from a particular company's rival. **ThomasNet.com** (http://www.thomasnet.com), allows you to search for companies by *Company Name*, *Product/Service*, or *Brand*.

Finding Experts by Searching a College or University Web Site

College professors often make good experts. If you plan to hire or depose experts who are professors, go to the university's Web site for a look at their *Curricula Vitae* (CV), courses they've taught, and articles or books they've published. Links to college and university home pages can be found at **American Universities'** Web site (http://www.clas.ufl.edu/au/). Often the institution will have a search page to locate experts among its faculty that is searchable by subject or name. For example, **Florida State University's College of Medicine** (http://www.med.fsu.edu/Directory/browsedir.aspx) lists its faculty's specialties and links to those professors who have Web pages that include their CV, list of research projects, and publications, etc.

Finding Experts Via a Literature Search Through Topical Article Databases

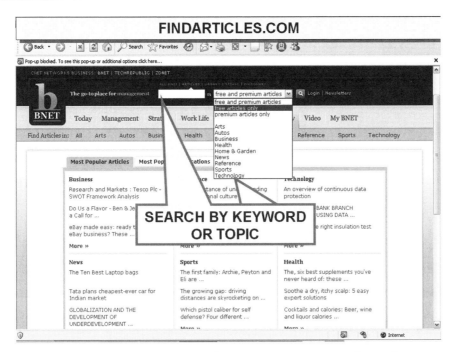

If you need an expert in a specific area, you can perform literature searches by topic (or by a given expert's name to verify their expertise) to locate their writings:

- using your library's remote databases of full-text, free newspaper and magazine articles (see pages 145-146)

- directly at **BNET FindArticles.com** (http://www.findarticles.com; see page 418)

- by visiting **IngentaConnect** (http://www.ingentaconnect.com; see page 418)

- searching journals and other scholarly publications at **Google Scholar** (http://scholar.google.com; see pages 295-299)

- searching for publications on medical topics at **The U.S. National Library of Medicine Gateway** (http://www.nlm.nih.gov; see page 422)

Finding Experts Through Jury Verdict, Settlement, Case Law, and Brief Bank Web Sites

Sometimes the best way to find experts is by searching through documents (such as such as jury verdicts, settlements, case law, and brief banks) where they have been mentioned as the expert of record.

MoreLaw.com (http://www.morelaw.com/) provides a free jury verdicts and settlements database. To locate experts who have previously testified in cases similar to one that you are handling, search by keywords describing your case.

Law.com has a pay database, **VerdictSearch.com**, of over 150,000 jury verdicts (http://www.verdictsearch.com/). Annual subscription prices are based on law firm. Day passes are available to any practitioner for $349.

JuryVerdicts.com (http://www.juryverdicts.com) is maintained by **The National Association of State Jury Verdict Publishers** (NASJVP). It links to its members that publish jury verdict summaries throughout the United States. You cannot search for verdicts from this site. You must follow the links to the publisher(s) that cover the jurisdiction(s) in which you're searching. Fees to access summaries of the cases, jury verdicts, or awards in which the experts testified, varies from publisher to publisher. Access to the site's expert witness directory is free. However, it only lists names of experts (culled from jury verdicts) and an area of expertise, without contact information.

Expert witnesses might be mentioned by name in court briefs or case law. See pages 291–299 (free case law databases), page 378 (free U.S. Supreme Court briefs), and pages 383–387 (paid sources for lower federal court briefs) for tips on locating information on expert witnesses from those sources.

Verifying Experts' Professional or Trade Licenses

For more information on verifying an expert's professional or trade license, see pages 175–177.

Chapter Nine

LOCATING AND BACKGROUNDING ATTORNEYS, JUDGES, AND OTHER LEGAL PROFESSIONALS

Contact Information, Biographies, and Directories

It's always a good idea to check into the status of an attorney with whom you are associating, opposing, or hiring. For information about an attorney's license status, disciplinary action taken against them, and their contact data, check the appropriate state bar site if the state bar is unified in that jurisdiction. But if the state bar is voluntary, check the state's attorney licensing site (often the state supreme court). To learn if a state bar is unified or voluntary, use the **A.B.A. Division for Bar Services** color-coded map of the United States (voluntary bar associations are indicated in green). From here, you can also link to the association (http://www.abanet.org/barserv/stlobar.html).

If the association is voluntary, do not assume an attorney is unlicensed if their name is missing from the association's directory. You can search their name at the licensing board for that state by visiting **Ishereallyalawyer.com** (http://www.ishereallyalawyer.com), which links directly to the searchable databases of attorney licensing boards (or to the unified state bar association) in forty-six states, as well as the District of Columbia, and the U.S. Patent Bar.

LexisNexis's Martindale-Hubbell Directory (Martindale) (http://www.martindale.com),

FindLaw's Lawyer Directory (http://lawyers.findlaw.com/), and **Justia's Lawyer Directory** (http://lawyers.justia.com/) are three of the major free lawyer directories (discussed below), but there are several newer directories, some of which attempt to rate lawyers (see page 198 for details).

Martindale (http://www.martindale.com) allows you to find a lawyer anywhere in the world (some judges are also included). At the **Martindale** site, click on the *Advanced Search* link and select either the *People*, *Law Firms*, or *Company* tab to begin narrowing down your search. Depending upon which category is chosen, the search criteria will vary. For example, on the *Law Firms* tab, one of the criterion is to search by size of firm, but this criterion is not shown after selecting *People*. The following search criteria are offered when selecting *People* (which is the default search option): *Keywords, First Name, Last Name, Current Organization, Job Title, City, U.S. State/Canadian Province, Country, Practice Area (10 Maximum), Law School Attended, Bar Admissions, Years In Practice, Languages Spoken, Area of Focus,* and *Major Memberships*. Results of *People* searches can also be limited to *Search for lawyers only* and/or to only display individuals who have been *Peer Review Rated*. Searches can include a mix of criteria. For example, you can search for all attorneys who practice in Los Angeles, California, attended Pepperdine Law School, and speak French; or you can search by an attorney's first name only (if you don't know the last name), but be sure to add in other identifying information such as city and state. Not selecting the *Search for lawyers only* might include other legal professionals, such as administrators, paralegals, or librarians, in your search results, however, **Martindale** no longer provides separate search options to locate these professionals. There is an *Advanced Search* menu for a database of *Experts and Services* (http://experts.martindale.com/Advanced-Expert-Search.html) that includes some *Practice Management & Service* and *Attorney & Litigation Support* vendors (among other categories).

FindLaw's Lawyer Directory** provides a basic search at http://lawyers.findlaw.com. There are two search boxes where you can search by *Legal Issue* (enter a practice area) and/or *Location* (enter a city, ZIP Code, or state). The consumer focus of this database is made clear by the *I want a lawyer to contact me* checkbox that accompanies these search options. To search by a lawyer's name, click on the *Name Search* link on the home page, to the right of the basic search box. Using the *Advanced Options* link located below the basic search box, you can select *Lawyers Only* or *Lawfirms Only* and additionally limit the search by *Languages*, *Credit Card Accepted*, or *Free Consultation Offered.* Further down the **Directory's** home page, there is also a *Browse For a Lawyer* option, that can be limited by *Top Cities*, *By State*, or *By Legal Issue.*

Justia's Lawyer Directory** provides a basic search at http://lawyers.justia.com. There are two search boxes where you can search by *Legal Issue or Lawyer/Firm Name* and/or location (a city and state are automatically detected and filled in based on your Internet connection, but can be easily changed). Using the tabs beneath the search boxes, you can *Browse By Practice Areas* or *States*. Users can also browse an alphabetical listing of names using the *Lawyer Name Directory* links near the bottom of the page. No *Advanced Search* options are offered.

The following are some newer directories, some of which attempt to rate lawyers:

- **Nolo** (http://lawyers.nolo.com) can be searched by *State*, *County*, *ZIP Code*, and *Legal Issue.* The directoy can also be browsed by *Legal Issue*, *City*, or *State*.

- **Superlawyers.com** (http://www.superlawyers.com) includes "outstanding lawyers from more than 70 practice areas who have attained a high degree of peer recognition and professional achievement." After selecting a state, you can search the directory by *Keyword* (e.g., attorney name, law firm name, or city) and *Practice Area*.

- **Avvo.com** (http://www.avvo.com) is a directory that also includes a rating system for lawyers that employs, "[a] mathematical model that considers the information shown in a lawyer's profile, including a lawyer's years in practice, disciplinary history, professional achievements and industry recognition." You can search the directory by keyword (e.g., attorney name, law firm name, or city) and/or location (a city and state are automatically detected and filled in based on your Internet connection, but can be easily changed). Users can also *Browse lawyers by practice area*.

Contact Information and Biographies: Judicial Directories

All current and former federal judges since 1789, except bankruptcy judges, can be searched by name at the **Federal Judicial Center's Biographical Directory of Federal Judges** site or by clicking on a letter of the alphabet to browse through a list of names that begin with that letter (http://www.fjc.gov/public/home.nsf/hisj).

FEDERAL JUDICIAL CENTER: BIOGRAPHICAL DIRECTORY OF FEDERAL JUDGES (AND DATABASE)

Research questions regarding groups of judges (e.g., How many women judges are there in the federal district courts?) can be conducted by clicking on the *Select research categories* link.

There is no directory of all state judges online for free, but some states provide profiles of their state and local judges (or at least contact information) at the court's official site. For example, profiles of the California Supreme Court's seven sitting justices appear online (http://www.courtinfo.ca.gov/courts/supreme/justices.htm) and now includes a video of the justices.

Also, check your state or local bar association for judicial profiles. The **Los Angeles County Bar** (http://www.lacba.org/), for example, offers judicial profiles at its site (click on *Know Your Judges*). They are free only to its members, however. While the **Dallas, Texas Bar Association** provides its collection of judicial profiles to all Web site visitors (http://www.dallasbar.com/judiciary/profilelinks.asp). (To locate links to state or local bar associations, see **FindLaw** (http://www.findlaw.com/06associations/state.html) or the **A.B.A.'s Division for Bar Services** site (http://www.abanet.org/barserv/stlobar.html).

Articles by and About Judges or Attorneys

Some libraries allow free remote access to the **LegalTrac** database, which indexes articles from legal periodicals and legal newspapers. Many of the articles are about lawyers and judges, or are written by them. **LegalTrac** primarily offers abstracts of the articles although some articles are available full-text. See **Libdex** (http://www.libdex.com) to find your library's URL and learn if it offers remote access to **LegalTrac** or other legal and general newspaper and magazine sources that may contain articles by or about judges and attorneys. See pages 145–146 for details about free remote access to other databases.

Legal newspapers often profile lawyers and judges or feature articles by them. **Law.com** (http://www.law.com) provides access to articles by and about attorneys and judges that have been published in various ALM (formerly American Lawyer Media) legal newspapers. **Law.com** features a *Quest* search where you can search either the *Law.com Network* or the *Legal Web*. While the search and the brief annotation results from *Law.com Network* and the *Legal Web* are free, a paid subscription is often necessary to read the full story if it derives from any of the ALM publications. *Legal Web* results will also include information from legal bloggers/blawgers. (See the next section for information about blawgs.) Those who have paid subscriptions to individual ALM legal newspapers can search the archives for free at **Law.com**.

Blogs, Blawgs, and Tweets by and About Judges or Attorneys

More and more lawyers and judges are creating blawgs (a play on the word "blogs" used if the blog is law-related). Blawgs may help you learn about a lawyer's practice area or about the lawyer's or judge's personality. To find a blawg (or blog) on a particular topic, visit **TheBlogsoflaw** (http://www.theblogsoflaw.com), which can be browsed by topic, or **Justia's Blawgsearch** (http://blawgsearch.justia.com/), which can be keyword searched in addition to browsing.

More recently, attorneys and judges have begun microblogging (posting information to sites that allow only short updates such as **Twitter**). **Justia** created **LegalBirds** (http://legalbirds.justia.com/) to capture these law-related tweets. The tweets can be keyword or name searched or browsed by topic (use the *Categories and Practice Area* directory). One can also view *Top Legal Birds'* tweets. For more information about blogs see pages 80–81. For more information about microblogging (Twitter) see pages 143–144.

Chapter Ten

PAY INVESTIGATIVE RESEARCH DATABASES

What are Pay Investigative Research Databases?

Unlike most free investigative resources on the Web, pay investigative research databases allow you to create much more sophisticated searches. The pay investigative databases also integrate many different types of data into their databases to create their search results. Some of the most well-known pay investigative research databases are: **Merlin Information Services** (http://www.merlindata.com), **LexisNexis Accurint** (http://www.accurint.com), and **Westlaw's PeopleMap** (http://linkon.in/aDhjwl). We'll discuss these, and a few others, in more detail later in this chapter.

When Should You Use a Pay Investigative Research Database?

Use a pay investigative research database when you need to:

- Access public records that are not free on the Web

- Conduct a combined search of publicly available information, public records, and non-public information (e.g., information from credit headers)

- Search simultaneously through multiple states for one record type

- Search simultaneously through multiple record types in one (or more than one) state

- Find relationships between people

- Find relationships between a person and various public records associated with that person

- Find a full Social Security Number (See pages 208-213 and 225-227 to learn about limitations of finding a full Social Security Number.)

- Find a full date of birth (See pages 181 and 208 to learn about limitations of finding a full date of birth.)

- Conduct a sophisticated search, using one or more clues you have about a person, such as: their name (sometimes even just a first name if you can add other identifying information); Social Security Number (full); date of birth; estimate of the person's age; or a previous or current phone number, city, state, or ZIP Code

What Type of Records are Found In Pay Investigative Research Databases?

The following records and information might be found in pay investigative research databases:

- Names (maiden and married) and aliases
- Associates (e.g., individuals who may have worked with your subject), neighbors, and relatives of your subject
- Current and past addresses
- Current and past telephone numbers (land-lines)
- Cellular phone numbers
- E-mail addresses
- Various cross (reverse) directories to search by number (e.g., phone or Social Security Number) or address (e.g., physical or e-mail) instead of just by name
- Partial Social Security Numbers,unless you have been approved to view full Social Security Numbers (see pages 208-213)
- Real property records (could include assessor or tax data and mortgages)
- Personal property (could include watercraft, motor vehicles, aircraft registrations, and FAA certifications)
- Bankruptcy records
- Criminal records, including sex offenders, arrests, and wants and warrants
- Full or truncated dates of birth (often truncated to only the month and year), unless you have been approved to view the full date (see page 181)
- Date of death
- Marriages and divorces
- Business profiles
- Company ownerships (usually corporate, but could include other forms of ownership)
- Subject's place of employment
- Liens, judgments, and UCCs
- Driver's License information
- Various professional licenses (e.g., contractors) and permits/licenses for controlled substances, drivers license, hunting/fishing, and concealed weapons
- Credit headers
- Voter's Registration

Some pay databases provide other enhancements, such as a graphical presentation of the results to help visualize connections or an e-alert feature to notify the researcher when someone's information has changed. Note that the amount of information (and whether it is available at all) will vary from state to state and from database company to database company.

Where Do Pay Investigative Research Databases Obtain Their Data?

Depending on which pay investigative research database you are using, the data listed above might come from one or more of the following sources:

- Public records (e.g., bankruptcies and real estate assessor records)
- Publicly available information (e.g., telephone and address listings from telephone companies or even from utility companies; and more recently, information scraped from Web sites, blogs, and even social networking sites such as **MySpace**, **Facebook**, and **LinkedIn**)
- Non-public information derived from credit headers such as addresses, phone numbers, full Social Security Numbers, and full dates of birth (See the next page for an explanation of credit headers and see pages 208-213 for an explanation about who qualifies to receive full Social Security Numbers in search results.)

Pay Investigative Research Databases Restrict Access to Social Security Numbers

Although searching with a full Social Security Number usually will return more targeted results than a name search, all pay investigative research databases restrict access to full Social Security Numbers, unless you go through an approval process, which includes submitting to a site visit (except for **LocatePlus**, discussed later in this chapter).

It is important to understand that pay investigative research databases allow you to <u>search</u> by a full Social Security Number, but the full Social Security Number will still not be displayed in your results (unless you are approved to access them). Of course, if you are already searching with the full Social Security Number then you already know the full Social Security Number so not seeing it displayed wouldn't matter.

Pay Investigative Research Databases are Relational Databases

In addition to returning results about the particular individual you are searching for, most investigative research databases have created a "relational" component. The relational component is two-fold: The first feature of the relational component consists of finding connections between a person and various types of records associated with that person, thereby creating a virtual dossier about the person. The second feature of the relational component consists of finding connections between a person and their neighbors, associates, and relatives. This can be a useful tool for finding someone who might know the whereabouts of the person you are searching for if they have gone missing. With that said, these relational databases have limitations of their own. Typically, they only link people who share the same name and address (or different names but same address) and the date coverage is (generally) only back to the mid-1980s. Thus, these databases might miss some crucial relationships. For example, a "complete" report on a subject might not include information on their parents or siblings if they haven't shared an address or owned property with them anytime since the mid-1980s. However, former in-laws might be included if they shared or owned real property with the subject of the report anytime after the mid-1980s.

Some Pay Investigative Research Databases Include "Credit Headers" from Credit Reports

Some of the information found in investigative research databases comes from credit bureaus that compile credit reports. Although credit reports include financial information, the financial information is not what credit bureaus sell to the investigative research database companies. Instead, they sell the "personally identifying" information, such as one's name, address, telephone number, full Social Security Number, and full date of birth, found at the top (at the "head") of the credit report (hence the name "credit headers").

Credit header information is considered "non-public." In other words, it is not "public" in the sense that it is neither "publicly available" (because the information isn't freely available as one's published telephone number for instance) nor is it a "public record" (because it is not held by a government agency).

Information from credit headers is considered by many researchers to be the most up-to-date. However, not all pay investigative research databases include credit header information. For example, **KnowX**, **Intelius**, and **US Search** do not include credit header information. Therefore, these database vendors would not be able to provide full Social Security Numbers to their subscribers. It is possible; however, that they might be able to retrieve full dates of birth from sources other than credit headers. While **West's PeopleMap** does integrate credit header information into its database, it does not provide full Social Security Numbers to anyone.

Access to non-public credit header information is only allowed to those who fall within one of the exceptions of the Gramm-Leach-Bliley Act (GLBA), 15 U.S.C. 6802(e). To read the original Act, see http://linkon.in/bpnCDt. Our focus is on Section 6802 of the Act, *available at* http://linkon.in/cofH3Z, which prevents financial institutions (including credit bureaus) from disclosing (and selling) nonfinancial/non-public, personal information to third parties, such as investigative research databases unless they come within one of the "General Exceptions" of Section 6802(e)(1)–(e)(8). (See pages 210-212 to read this section.) Thus, financial institutions can extract the nonfinancial/nonpublic, personal information from credit reports to sell the remaining information to the investigative pay database vendors. The vendors in turn can sell the information to subscribers (such as lawyers) who come within the GLBA General Exceptions, but the subscribers must attest that they fall within one of the GLBA exceptions each time they conduct a search.

Typically there is a pull-down menu listing the GLBA exceptions and subscribers must select one.

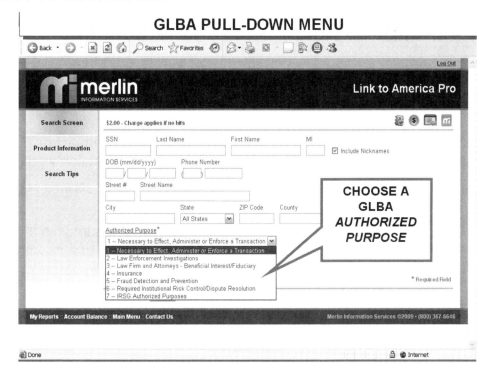

If you have no GLBA authorized purpose, you can select the *ISRG Authorized Purposes* option. This will allow you to access information from the investigative research databases that include credit headers, but the current credit header data will be excluded from your search results (however, data that pre-dates GLBA might appear in your search results, but remember, it will be old information and not necessarily that helpful). See the next section for details about GLBA.

If you are in the legal profession, read the Gramm-Leach-Bliley Act and focus on Section 6802(e)(3). It states:

(e) General Exceptions

Subsections (a) and (b) of this section shall not prohibit the disclosure of nonpublic personal information —

(1) as necessary to effect, administer, or enforce a transaction requested or authorized by the consumer, or in connection with —

(A) servicing or processing a financial product or service requested or authorized by the consumer;

(B) maintaining or servicing the consumer's account with the financial institution, or with another entity as part of a private label credit card program or other extension of credit on behalf of such entity; or

(C) a proposed or actual securitization, secondary market sale (including sales of servicing rights), or similar transaction related to a transaction of the consumer;

(2) with the consent or at the direction of the consumer;

(3)

(A) to protect the confidentiality or security of the financial institution's records pertaining to the consumer, the service or product, or the transaction therein;

(B) to protect against or prevent actual or potential fraud, unauthorized transactions, claims, or other liability;

(C) for required institutional risk control, or for resolving customer disputes or inquiries;

(D) to persons holding a legal or beneficial interest relating to the consumer; or

(E) to persons acting in a fiduciary or representative capacity on behalf of the consumer;

Now that you've read this portion of the act, you will probably agree that GLBA is a prime example of "legalese." Most database vendors will not offer a legal opinion about what it means and who is and who isn't entitled to view GLBA credit header information. However, on Merlin's site, they offer some interpretation of GLBA's General Exceptions. Legal professionals, such as attorneys, paralegals, and law librarians, will probably fall under exceptions 4, 6, and 8 (see below). The following information is found at Merlin's site (https://www.merlindata.com/SearchASPs/authorizedpurpose_exp.ASP):

> The information that this service provides contains information governed by the Gramm-Leach-Bliley (GLB) Act and the Individual Reference Services Group (IRSG). A violation of the privacy laws of the GLB may subject a company, individual or management to civil and/or criminal penalties pursuant to 15 U.S.C. 6821 and 15 U.S.C. 6823. The following are the only Authorized Purposes for which this information may be accessed.
>
> GLB Authorized Purposes
> 1. Transactions Authorized by Consumer
>
> As necessary to effect, administer or enforce a transaction that was requested or authorized by the consumer.
>
> This Authorized Purpose is restricted to specific uses. Based on your company's industry classification, options may include some of the following
>
> 1(a) Asset Verification
> 1(b) Credit & Collections Activity
> 1(c) Credit & Collections or Skiptracing (Locating Debtors)
> 1(d) Credit & Collections or Skiptracing (Locating References)
> 1(e) Locating Existing Customers for Legal Purposes
>
> 2. Transactions Authorized by Consumer (Application Verification Only)
>
> As necessary to effect, administer, or enforce a transaction requested or authorized by the consumer by verifying the identification information contained in applications for employment, housing, or insurance.
>
> This Authorized Purpose is restricted to specific uses. Based on your company's industry classification, options may include some of the following:
>
> 2(f) Employment Verification
> 2(g) Pre-Employment Screening
>
> 3. Law Enforcement Purposes
>
> To the extent specifically permitted or required under other provisions of law and in accordance with the Right to Financial Privacy Act of 1978, to law enforcement agencies, self-regulatory organizations, or for an investigation on a matter related to public safety.
>
> This Authorized Purpose is restricted to specific uses. Based on your company's industry classification, options may include some of the following:
>
> 3(h) Apprehending Criminals

4. Use by Persons Holding a Legal or Beneficial Interest Relating to the Consumer

For use by persons holding a legal or beneficial interest relating to the consumer.

This Authorized Purpose is restricted to specific uses. Based on your company's industry classification, options may include some of the following:

4(i) Locating Beneficiaries & Heirs
4(j) Locating Owners of Unclaimed Goods

6. Fraud Prevention or Detection

For use to protect against or prevent actual or potential fraud, unauthorized transactions, claims, or other liability.

This Authorized Purpose is restricted to specific uses. Based on your company's industry classification, options may include some of the following:

6(k) Fraud Prevention
6(l) Insurance Claims Investigations/Subrogation
6(m) Locating Fraud Victims

8. Legal Compliance

For use to comply with Federal, State, or local laws, rules, and other applicable legal requirements.

This Authorized Purpose is restricted to specific uses. Based on your company's industry classification, options may include some of the following:

8(n) Child Support Enforcement
8(o) Legal Process Service
8(p) Locating Witnesses & Victims
8(q) Locating Former Patients

A violation of the privacy laws of the GLB may subject a company, individual, or management to civil and/or criminal penalties pursuant to 15 U.S.C. 6821 and 15 U.S.C. 6823.

Pricing varies from one investigative database to the next. Some offer flat-rate pricing while others offer a "per search" fee. Some require a monthly subscription while others do not.

The investigative research databases that include credit header information in their search results have a fairly extensive application and approval process to insure that the vendor is not selling information to identity thieves or others who should not have access to the information. Several years ago, **LexisNexis** tightened access to its **Accurint** database (as did other vendors, such as **ChoicePoint**). According to some attorneys to whom we have spoken, **Accurint** would only approve full Social Security Number access for those attorneys whose primary function was collections work. This was later confirmed by **Accurint**. During this same period, attorneys who were not collections attorneys, but who wanted access to full Social Security Numbers could access them through **Merlin** if they submitted to a site visit of their office from a **Merlin** representative and met certain security standards. At some point, **Accurint** changed its policy and said it would decide whether subscribers were entitled to full Social Security Number access after they performed a site visit of the applicant's office. More recently, we have heard reports from law firms that **Accurint** has returned to its "collections work" policy and has denied access to full Social Security Numbers to many attorneys. **Merlin** charges $100 for the site visit. **LocatePLUS** does not require a site visit for access to full Social Security Numbers, but does require that applicants complete an application prior to approval. (See page 226 for more information on **LocatePLUS**.)

MAJOR PAY INVESTIGATIVE RESEARCH DATABASES

While there are many pay investigative research databases available on the Web, we will highlight the three major ones geared to legal professionals. They each contain information from credit headers, have the broadest range of data, and tend to be more up-to-date. We will focus on the following:

- **Merlin Information Services** (http://www.merlindata.com)
- **LexisNexis Accurint** (http://www.accurint.com)
- **Westlaw's PeopleMap** (http://west.thomson.com/westlaw/public-records/libraries/peoplemap/default.aspx)

At the end of this chapter we will list other investigative research databases. Some require pre-approval because, like the major databases, they contain information from credit headers. Some are geared more toward business people or the general public and do not require pre-approval because they do not contain information from credit headers.

Merlin Information Services Investigative Research Databases

Merlin Information Services (http://www.merlindata.com) is one of the pay investigative research databases favored by private investigators (and should be considered by other searchers too). Its database is comprised of public records and publicly available information, in addition to credit headers. As noted earlier, only those who meet GLBA exceptions can access the live credit header information. An important distinction between **Merlin's** credit headers and other vendors is that **Merlin's** are "live," which means they are updated daily. (Although we have heard that **Accurint's** are updated weekly, **Accurint** refused to confirm or deny this.) While **Merlin** is a national database, it is especially strong in its California resources. Many of the national record types listed on page 205 are available at **Merlin**. We will highlight some of **Merlin's** most useful databases and also ones that are unique.

MERLIN INFORMATION SERVICES

On July 13, 2009, **Merlin** redesigned its Web site and added advanced search capabilities with its *MerLink* database that searches national credit headers, national white pages data, national assets, and various current and historical California databases simultaneously.

MERLIN INFORMATION SERVICES: LINK TO AMERICA PRO SEARCH

When we are searching **Merlin**, we usually begin either with **Merlin's** *Link to America Pro* search ($2.00) or its *Link to America* search ($1.00). Each is updated monthly. The search fee applies whether or not results are found at *Link to America Pro* and *Link to America.*

Both databases search through the same 5 billion records but *Link to America Pro* also searches through <u>credit headers</u>. They both allow you to search by one or more of the following: *SSN, Phone Number, Date of Birth, Address, County, and Name* (*Last name, First name, middle initial* and you can also instruct **Merlin** to include nicknames). You can search *All States*, but you might be informed there are too many results and be asked to narrow your search. You can narrow down by state or with any of the other criteria (e.g., middle initial or date of birth).

Link to America Pro and *Link to America* results will be similar. They will display: *Name, Month/Year of Birth, Age, Address, SSN* (truncated if you don't have full Social Security Number access approval), *Date First Reported, Date Last Reported*, and *Multiple Phone Numbers*. In addition, *Link to America Pro* includes a *Death Reported Date*, a *Map*, and a free *Current & Historical Phones at the Address,* plus a *Neighbors* report. According to Merlin, "This report includes current and historical phone listings for each address, geographical relatives (people with the same last name as the subject in the same geographical area as the subject), and up to twenty business and residential neighbors' phone numbers." In contrast, each *Link to America* search result includes a free report of current and archived phone listings for residents that have been at the address since 1999 and stretching back two years for businesses. Merlin claims that it is "common to find addresses, Social Security Numbers, maiden names and AKAs dating back thirty years in your results." In some of our test searches, no Social Security Numbers (not even partial numbers) were displayed.

To obtain more data than *Link to America Pro* or *Link to America* search results provide, look for records that also include Social Security Numbers (not all records include a Social Security Number). Depending on your subscription, the Social Security Numbers might be full or partial. In either case, (whether the record has a full or partial Social Security Number), it will offer a *Report Menu* icon.

If you click on the icon, you can run an *Investigator Background Report* for a $4.00 fee. (Note: you can also search the *Investigator Background Report* database directly.) The *Investigator Background Report* includes the following information:

- Current & historical (back to 1999) residential names and phone listings with name and address information for households with unlisted phones (sometimes only a partial phone number is included); California addresses also include California civil court records, California business filings and some older California birth and California marriage records

- Current & historical business names and phone listings

- Contact name, business name, address, and phone number including two years of historical business listings, with an "archived" date when the listing was no longer current

- Neighbors

- Property ownership

- Social Security Number verifier

- Possible family members (which includes names and most addresses of people with the same last name as the subject who have shared an address with the subject, current and historical phone listings, and neighbors, for each possible family member's address)

- Bankruptcies

- Watercraft registrations

- Federal Aviation Administration certificates

- Federal Aviation Administration aircraft registration, pilot licenses, airmen certificates, and other certifications

- Criminal record(s) are optional because there is an extra fee. To add a single state criminal search to the report will increase the fee to $7.00 and to add a "national" criminal search will increase the fee to $11.50. (Note, however, that a "national" criminal search is not a comprehensive national criminal search. This "national" criminal search will only search those jurisdictions that have accessible digital criminal records.)

The following data aren't included in the *Investigator's Background Report* but are included in the *Complete Report* — which is a report, that since February 2010, attorneys have not been allowed to access: *Drivers License* information, *Judgments*, and a more in-depth *Relatives* summary.

The following industries can access the *Complete Report:*

- Collections Agencies (if an attorney is a collections attorney, they can probably gain access to the *Complete Report)*
- Financial Institutions (e.g., banks and credit card companies)
- Healthcare
- Private Investigators
- Process Servers and Attorney Service Companies
- Universities
- Utilities

The fee for the *Complete Report* is $15

Merlin offers five phone databases:

- *Cell Phones* contains millions of records, searchable by name or address. If you perform a name search, you must also include a city and state or a state and ZIP code. **Merlin** warns us that "all information is consumer reported, which sometimes leads to incorrectly reported information." Results will display: name, address, phone number, and source ("source" does not mean the name of the source, just a code, such as *s2* or *s3*, which simply lets the researcher know that multiple sources found the same information). Results may also include the carrier name. The data is updated in "real time." The cost to search this database is $2.50 and there is no charge if no results are returned.

- *Cross-Directory* contains what Merlin describes as, "the most complete listing of current and archived names, addresses, phone numbers and dates of birth available anywhere. Both residential and business information can be returned in one search. Sources include white pages, directory assistance, marketing lists, postal change of addresses, and numerous public record filings." You can search by any combination of name, address, county, city, state, ZIP code, phone, fax, business name, or SIC code. This is probably the only **Merlin** database where you can even search only by first name, but you must also have your subject's date of birth. The data are updated monthly. The cost to search this database is $1.00 and there is no charge if no results are returned.

- *Reverse Phone Number Lookup* is a reverse search by phone number of 65 million listed and unlisted residential and business land-line phone numbers and over 60 percent of all cellular phone numbers in the U.S. **Merlin** states that, "This unique database is continuously maintained with nearly a half-million, real time daily updates…provided by over 20 million daily transactions by consumers who purchase products either online or over the telephone." Most important, both phone companies are listed if the phone number has been ported from one company to another. Frequently, people port their land-lines over to a cell phone, so this can be useful information to help you know which phone company to serve with a subpoena. The cost to search this database is $5.00 and there is no charge if no results are returned.

- *PhoneSour¢e - Electronic, Directory Assistance* is a residential and business phone database, updated continually throughout the day. The database can be searched by name, phone number, or address. Results can be limited to residential listings only or business/governmental listings. You can retrieve all listings on a specific street by entering the street name, city, and state or search a more generalized area by entering a city and a radius (in miles) up to 100 miles. A national name search is also possible and will return a state-by-state results list. The cost to search this database is $0.25 and, unlike the four other phone databases discussed above, there is a charge if no results are returned. The results list displays only the first 30 hits. To retrieve any additional results will cost another $0.25 for every 30 listings.

- *Phones Plus* (not accessible to attorneys) is searchable by name or address, and is described by **Merlin** as, "the industry's most comprehensive source of phone numbers." This 75 million record database returns name, address, and non-electronic directory assistance phone numbers as well as telephone numbers not found in a traditional directory assistance search such as cell phone numbers and unlisted phone numbers. The data are updated monthly. The cost to search this database is $2.00 and there is no charge if no results are returned.

Other databases offered by **Merlin**:

- The *Drivers License* database, contains driver's license information from fifty states. However, only ten states offer current data "government sources:" Connecticut, Florida, Maine, Michigan, Minnesota, Ohio, Tennessee, Texas, Wisconsin, and Wyoming. The information for the remaining states is archived, with different coverage dates for each jurisdiction. (See pages 117-118 for more information on accessing this database.)

- *CarFacts* offers over 105 million records from public and private sources (including DMV information from some state agencies) searchable by owner, address, or VIN. Most results will display the owner name, address, vehicle make, and vehicle year, while some results could include license plate number, phone number, VIN, and vehicle model. Thus, this may be a valuable database for finding addresses and phone numbers and not just information about someone's car. The data are updated monthly. The cost to search this database is $3.00 and there is no charge if no results are returned.

- *Western Evictions Database* includes information about individuals who have been evicted from their homes in four Western states: California, Nevada, Oregon, and Washington.

- *California Ultimate Weapon* is a simultaneous search of various California databases that allows you to preview results before deciding which ones to buy.

- *Credit Headers* is a database that only contains credit header information.

Merlin offers some useful features such as the *First Date Reported* and *Last Date Reported* for each record. Another function we find quite useful (once unique to **Merlin** but now adopted by others, such as **West's PeopleMap** discussed on page 224), is the ability to sort the columns of your results list to create a customized report (e.g., sort by last name, or by city, or by state).

While **Merlin** doesn't require a monthly subscription fee *per se*, it does require an initial deposit of $100 to open a debit account. **Merlin** then deducts a minimum usage fee of $20 monthly whether or not you use their database but this fee is waived if users spend over $35 in searches each month. There are also flat rate subscription options.

Lawyers can qualify for a free trial by using the ***Merlin Free Trial Certificate*** in the back of this book, but you will have to fill out an application and go through the usual approval process.

Merlin also offers skiptracing and research services which can be accessed by clicking the *Locate Services* link located just beneath the *Professional Services* heading on the far right side of the menu of options (https://www.merlindata.com/SearchASPs/MainMenu.ASP). These services include: skiptracing services, public record asset reports, place of employment searches, EIN (Employer Identification Number) searches, reverse phone/wireless searches, cell phone searches, welfare searches, Supplemental Security Income (SSI) searches, and utilities searches.

LexisNexis Investigative Research Databases: Accurint (and Other Databases Owned by LexisNexis)

In addition to its legal research databases, **LexisNexis** (whose parent company is **Reed Elsevier**) has offered public records at **Lexis.com** (http://www.lexis.com/) for over 25 years. While **LexisNexis** requires an annual subscription, the occasional user can use the **LexisONE Community** Web site (http://linkon.in/a3PMvd) for public record research on a "pay as you go" basis for one day, one week, or one or more months. A credit card is required for payment. An example of one of the **LexisONE Community** databases is its

Finder & Assets Records database, which includes the following public records: corporate filings, death & criminal records, F.A.A. pilots, marriage and divorces, real property, and a military locator. Prices range from $34/day to $55/week to $112/month. It's important to note that these searches do not include credit header information or any of the other proprietary information available in an investigative research database. (For more information on free case law databases found at **LexisONE Community**, see page 254.)

To access more than just public records, you will need to use one of **Lexis's** investigative research databases discussed in the upcoming pages.

Over time, **LexisNexis** has acquired many once-independent investigative research database companies, many of which included publicly available and credit header information. Two of those acquisitions were **Accurint** at http://www.accurint.com (and its parent company **Seisent**) and **ChoicePoint**. With the **ChoicePoint** acquisition, **LexisNexis** became the owner of other databases that **ChoicePoint** had previously acquired, including **KnowX** (http://knowx.com/), **Rapsheets** (now rolled into **KnowX**), and **AutoTrackXP** (http://www.autotrack.com). (Sometime between 2009 and 2010 we noticed that despite the **ChoicePoint** name appearing on various **LexisNexis** Web pages, you are redirected from http://www.choicepoint.com to http://www.lexisnexis.com/risk where the **ChoicePoint** name does not appear. However, at **AutoTrackXP** the **ChoicePoint** name does appear.) While some of the **Lexis** acquisitions are still accessible as separate databases (with the same familiar search interfaces that each of their subscriber bases are used to using), it is possible that they will all be integrated into one database at some point.

Accurint and **AutoTrackXP** users must be approved before becoming subscribers because these databases include information from credit headers. In addition, a site visit of their office is required if a user wants access to full Social Security Numbers (see page 213). **KnowX** does not require a subscription or pre-approval (because it does not access information from credit headers).

The remainder of this discussion will focus on **Accurint** (http://www.accurint.com), which is the **LexisNexis** database most used by legal professionals who perform investigative research. When **Accurint** was an independent database, its "per search" price for a basic report (address, telephone number, and a full Social Security Number) was $0.25 and did not require a monthly subscription. By 2005, a year after the **LexisNexis** acquisition, **LexisNexis** increased the pricing and created various pricing plans. Eventually, full Social Security Numbers became unavailable to any attorneys using **Accurint**. We can't provide up-to-date prices because **LexisNexis** customizes many of its contracts, usually dependent on your volume of use.

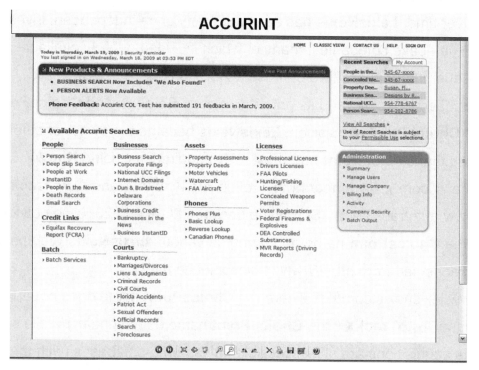

The above illustration shows the great number and types of individual databases available through **Accurint**.

We'll highlight some of the databases and some of their niftier features.

- The *Phones Plus* database contains 80 million phone numbers (30-40 million of them are cellular). *Phones Plus* receives a weekly update when land-line phone numbers are ported over to a cellular phone and this information is displayed in your results. (Not all databases provide this information. For instance, in a test search of **Westlaw's** *Reverse Phone* database, a phone number search failed to indicate that the number, originally a land line, had been ported over to a cellular phone, despite several years elapsing since the porting over.)

- The *E-mail* database includes 600 million U.S. e-mail addresses. While **Accurint** tells us this database is quite popular, it did not include the e-mail address for a name we tested even though that person's e-mail address is listed on her Web site and other places on the Internet.

- The *People at Work* database has added 50 million new records so you can now search over 100 million individuals to learn where they work.

- The *Voter's Registration* database covers twenty-two states, but only eighteen are current.

- The *Canadian Phones* database contains 12 million residential and 1.8 million business phone numbers.

- The *Driver's License* database contains data from twenty-four state governments but only ten are current. In addition, **Accurint** has Driver's License information from non-governmental sources from all fifty states.

- The *Vehicle Identification Number* database (VIN) covers forty-three states, but only twenty-four are current.

- The *Contact Card Report* lists names and contact information of your subject and others who may help you contact your subject. The named people also include a "relative designation," such as "wife." Disconnected phone numbers will be indicated and a relocation search can be performed.

- The *People Alert* service alerts you by e-mail if there are any changes to the report of a person for whom you've searched.

- The *Deep Skip* search displays contact information for the search subject and names of household members (and their contact information).

- The *Feedback* feature gives a researcher the opportunity to indicate whether a phone number provided by **Accurint** was correct. The feedback is integrated into the *Deep Skip* search results and used internally at **Accurint** for quality control.

- *Relavint* is a relational feature that helps you to visualize relationships between people and their possible relatives and associates (and vehicles, property, and even businesses) by allowing you to create diagrams. *Relavint* costs $2.00 per diagram.

In addition to its well-known legal research database, **Westlaw** (http://web2.westlaw.com), which is part of the **Thomson/Reuters** Corporation, offers one public record database (**Public Records**) and one investigative research "tool" (**PeopleMap**). (Because **PeopleMap** searches through so many individual databases, they have asked us to refer to **PeopleMap** as an investigative research "tool" instead of a database.)

Westlaw informs us that **Public Records** and **PeopleMap** can be subscribed to on a stand-alone basis, but, like **Accurint**, were unwilling to give us exact pricing. Pre-approval is required before one can become a subscriber.

The **Public Records** database (http://west.thomson.com/westlaw/public-records/libraries/default.aspx) is used primarily when a researcher wants to search a name through a specific type of public record or through all available public records, in one or all jurisdictions.

PeopleMap (http://linkon.in/aDhjwl) is used to uncover information about a person by searching their name through public records, publicly available information, and credit header information. In addition, **PeopleMap** attempts to uncover relationships between people.

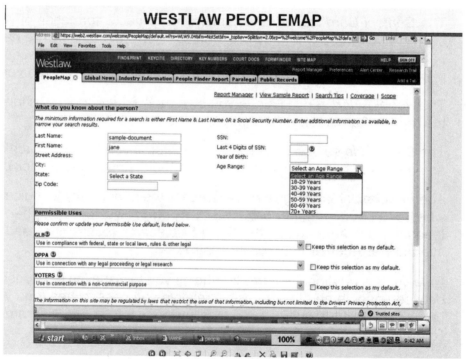

Aside from providing the text of the information contained in a record (and sometimes an image of the actual record), **PeopleMap** also provides a graphical representation to display relationships. It also geographically pinpoints your subject's possible location using Microsoft Virtual Earth's mapping feature. The first step of a **PeopleMap** search runs the subject's name through the **Experian** credit header database to make a match with individuals in that database. (**Experian** is a national credit reporting company whose database is updated daily. It is also used by **Merlin**.) **PeopleMap** then searches through thirty-five "content sets" which include civil lawsuit abstracts, dockets, arrest records, World Watch List Profiles, and marriage and divorce records. Once you have identified your subject from the results list, you can create customized reports. Like **Merlin**, the results can be sorted by name, city, state, and year of birth, or, unlike **Merlin**, viewed by type of document. The reports can be retrieved for fourteen days, without an additional charge, by clicking on the *Report Manager* tab.

While **Accurint** has a *Foreclosure* database, **Westlaw** has a *Pre-Foreclosure* database, which includes *lis pendens* or notices of defaults.

Despite **PeopleMap's** power, it would not be the right choice for those who need to discover full Social Security Numbers because **PeopleMap** (and other **Westlaw** public record databases) do not provide full Social Security Numbers to anyone but a "qualified" government employee (and even they must qualify annually).

OTHER PAY INVESTIGATIVE RESEARCH DATABASES

In addition to the major pay investigative databases already discussed, there are others that warrant mention, as they also include useful (and sometimes free) information, including: **LocatePLUS** (https://www.locateplus.com/welcome.asp), **Intelius** http://www.intelius.com), and **US Search** (http://www.ussearch.com/consumer/index.jsp). Of these three databases, only **LocatePLUS** requires pre-approval because it's the only one of the three that contains information from credit headers. Even though **Intelius** and **US Search** appear to be geared more to the business person and the general public rather than the legal professional, we mention them in this book because many of our seminar attendees, in their visits to free telephone directory sites, have encountered links to **US Search** and **Intelius**. When they click on the links, they are offered background checks and other research services. As an enticement, some free summary information is displayed. Sometimes we find this free information useful and you might too. The three major pay investigative databases discussed earlier (**Merlin**, **Accurint**, and **PeopleMap**) do not offer any information for free, although **KnowX**, noted briefly in the **LexisNexis** section, does.)

LocatePLUS

The following types of searches are available at **LocatePLUS** (https://www.locateplus.com/welcome.asp):

- *Person* (by Full or Partial Name or Social Security Number)
- *Current and Historical Address*
- *Common Residence*
- *Criminal Background* (coverage varies from jurisdiction to jurisdiction)
- *Name-to-Wireless Phone Number* (Fifty percent of all U.S. cell numbers are available.)
- *Name-to-Non-published Number*
- *Reverse Cell Phone and Non-published Number* (The search defaults to a $5 enhanced search, but one can override the default and select a $1 basic search. If there are no results, there is no fee.)
- *E-mail Address By E-mail address or By Name*
- *MVR* (Motor Vehicle Records; searches 31 states)
- *Corporate Record Search*

LocatePLUS's pricing ranges from a pay-per-click plan (which requires a $15 minimum monthly subscription) to plans that do not require any minimum, to the site's *Choice Savings Plan* (which is more like an annual flat-rate plan). **LocatePLUS** is quite user friendly and it is one of the only databases we know of to provide full Social Security Numbers without requiring a site visit. You must, however, go through **LocatePLUS's** approval process before your account is created and you have access to their data.

LocatePLUS is one of the few databases with records dating back far enough to find Carole Levitt's childhood home address. However, in some of our test searches, **LocatePLUS's** data was not as fresh as other investigative pay databases' data, which seems strange because **LocatePLUS** does contain information from credit headers. For instance, **LocatePLUS** did not find Carole Levitt's current phone number, her e-mail address, nor the corporate record for her company (Internet For Lawyers), although some of the other investigative databases did find this information.

US Search

If you performed a search at the free **Whitepages.com** site, you used to see a link in your search results for *Background Information*. Clicking this link would take you to **US Search** (http://www.ussearch.com/consumer/index.jsp). (More recently, **Whitepages.com** seems to have shifted its allegiance from **US Search** to another company, **PeopleFinders**.)

US Search's prices range from $9.95 to $99.95, which seems high to us, but their $9.95 twenty-four hour pass may be worthwhile for those who can batch their searches and only need current addresses, phone numbers, or property ownership information. To obtain more information about your subject beyond current addresses, phone numbers, or property ownerships, you will need to use other **US Search** databases (and pay more).

US Search allows you to view some information for free. For instance, in our search for *Carole Levitt* at the **US Search** site, the following information was provided for free as part of the results: the current city and state of her home and business, eight "aliases" (common mis-spellings of her name, her maiden name, and her former married name), her correct age, past cities where she once lived (back to the 1980s), and one relative (Mark E. Levitt). Only the last bit of information was incorrect.

Intelius

If you performed a search at the free **Infospace.com** phone directory site, you used to see a sponsored link to **Intelius** offering additional information about the person for whom you searched (for a fee). You will now need to visit the **Intelius** site directly at http://www.intelius.com because **Infospace.com** no longer serves as a phone directory site (and no longer links to **Intelius**) or you can access **Intelius** from **Search Systems's** home page (http://publicrecords.searchsystems.net/index.php). (See pages 119-122 for information about **Search Systems**.)

After running an **Intelius** *People Search* for *Carole Levitt*, the free summary results displayed her age, her middle initial, and the names of four cities and states where she had lived. Although an incorrect middle initial was displayed among correct ones, the cities and states matched up with our subject. One of the displayed cities was the city of her current residence. In contrast, **KnowX's** free results did not find a current city for *Carole Levitt*.

To obtain more information from **Intelius** will cost between $1.95 and $44.95 depending on the amount of information included in the report. Prices are discounted if you agree to an *Identity Protect* membership. In our opinion, this seems like a ploy to wring more money out of searchers who don't read the fine print informing them that the *Identity Protect's* $19.95 monthly membership fee is automatically billed to your credit card if you fail to cancel after the seven day free trial.

Your search results could include all or some of the following information about people: address; phone number; real property ownership; selected lawsuit information (bankruptcies, marriage and divorce records, criminal records, tax liens, and judgments); licenses; birth and death records, names, addresses, and phone numbers of neighbors and of associates; relatives; and others linked to the same addresses as the subject. There are no business name searches available in this database.

Should Legal Professionals Use Databases Like Intelius or US Search?

You will need to consider what types of information you need, how often you'll need it, and then test out each database to evaluate the results to determine which database is best for your particular search needs. We recommend using your own name for the test. For those who frequently need to access investigative databases, a subscription to one of the major databases may turn out to be less expensive and include more up-to-date results (since they include credit headers), but we have had varying luck retrieving correct information from all of the databases we've discussed.

Court dockets can be useful investigative tools to discover the following information: (1) how litigious someone is, (2) if someone has a criminal background, or (3) if there is a bankruptcy in someone's past. These sites offer access to federal dockets:

- **PACER** (https://pacer.login.uscourts.gov/cgi-bin/login.pl?court_id=00idx) is the government's pay federal docket database. See the full discussion on pages 383-388.

- **Justia** (http://dockets.justia.com/) provides free access to the last four years of U.S. District Court dockets (civil only) and some U.S. Courts of Appeal dockets. See the full discussion on pages 251-252.

- **Freecourtdockets.com** (http://www.freecourtdockets.com) provides free access to twenty years worth of dockets from the following courts: U.S. District (Civil and Criminal); U.S. Bankruptcy, U.S. Federal Claims, and U.S. International Trade (the U.S. Courts of Appeal are not yet available). See the full discussion on pages 391.

- The **U.S. Supreme Court** offers free dockets at its site (http://www.supremecourt.gov/docket/docket.aspx). See pages 372–373 for details.

- **FindLaw** also offers a free U.S. Supreme Court docket database at its **Supreme Court Center** site (http://supreme.lp.findlaw.com/supreme_court/docket/termindex.html). See page 269 for details.

- **RECAP** offers free access to millions of U.S. District (Civil and Criminal) and Bankruptcy Court documents. See page 388 for details.

For federal and selected state and local dockets, see the following pay sites:

- **Westlaw's CourtExpress** (http://courtexpress.westlaw.com/).
- **LexisNexis CourtLink** (http://www.lexisnexis.com/courtlink).

Some state and local courts place their docket sheets or a summary of the docket sheet online at the court's official site, while other courts place nothing online. In addition to the docket sheet, some courts even place images of the court documents online. Sometimes they are available for free and other times you will need to pay for them. It varies widely from jurisdiction to jurisdiction. For more information about state and local court dockets, see the information about **LLRX**'s database of links to court dockets on page 273.

Chapter Eleven

USING THE INTERNET FOR SUBSTANTIVE LEGAL RESEARCH

Putting Internet Search Tools to Work for Legal Research

For those who are conducting investigative and business research and want reams of information from various sites (or for those who are researching in unknown territory and want to get an overview of what's available), general search engines are useful. But, for those doing <u>legal</u> research (case law, statutory, and regulatory), it would practically be malpractice to rely on a free, general search engine to locate the most current statutory law or regulatory law or use it as the only source to conduct a case law search. (Although the **Google News Archive** could be used to conduct case law research, the resources it points to are not free; and while **Google Scholar's** new offering of case law research is free (http://scholar.google.com/advanced_scholar_search), you need to visit that specific portion of **Google** and not simply conduct a general **Google** Web search at **Google.com**. See pages 79–80 for details about **Google News Archive** and see pages 295-299 for details about **Google Scholar's** free case law research.)

For legal research, other search tools, such as Internet legal research books and also legal-specific portals and directories, come into play. They narrow the Internet down to relevant and reliable law-related Web sites that have already been evaluated for you. They also home in on sites and databases that a search engine can miss altogether. Estimates suggest that only a small percentage of the billions of pages on the Web are even indexed by search engines and that it can take up to one month for a Web page to be indexed by a search engine.

Finding a Subject Specialist or an Internet Research Book Arranged by Subject

Since people can be thought of as "search tools," ask someone who is knowledgeable in the field in which you are conducting research to recommend reliable sites. If you don't know a subject specialist, buy an Internet reference book that is geared to legal professionals (like this one). The best ones list Web sites by subject and offer recommendations. Be sure to buy the most recent edition available. This book, for instance, is updated annually.

LEGAL PORTALS AND LEGAL DIRECTORIES

Legal directories attempt to categorize Web sites by areas of law and/or jurisdiction, and then provide links to those legal content Web sites. Legal portals, in addition to providing directories, also provide "added value," such as a full-text keyword searchable database of court cases or subject-specific articles about an area of law. Thus, portals are more than a directory of links to other legal content sites because they include substantive legal content right on their site. Even with this "added value," most portals are still free (or partially free) because advertisers (and other alliances) support the cost of running the site.

Portals and directories are quite different from a search engine. Search engines return their results via automated programs that do not rely on human intervention. In contrast, legal portals and directories employ humans to create their product. These humans (usually law librarians or lawyers) have the subject expertise to be able to categorize the sites (just as a librarian would catalog a book by subject) and judge whether a site is reliable, before adding it to the portal or directory. This insures that you will be able to easily pinpoint relevant and reliable sites.

Free legal portals and directories are usually sponsored by one of five different groups, all of which have their own reasons for sponsorship: (1) commercial entities, using the free portion of their site to generate revenue either through advertising or marketing related pay products, such as **FindLaw** or **Justia**, who both create Web sites for lawyers, for a fee; (2) law firms, using their sites to attract clients; (3) governmental entities, using their sites to make government documents and services more accessible to the public; (4) academic institutions, using their sites for scholarly reasons; and (5) associations, using their sites to offer value to their members (and sometimes to educate the general public).

Assessing Legal Portals and Legal Directories

If you want to use a portal or directory that we have not mentioned in this book, you will need to assess its quality before relying upon it. A high-quality, useful legal portal or directory should do the following: (1) include a subject (or practice area) directory and preferably also include a jurisdictional directory, (2) include an internal search engine so you can search the site with keywords, (3) be user-friendly (intuitive); (4) link directly to many relevant sites, (5) include "added value" (and make it easy to access this "added value"), and (6) be reliable (by being credible, up-to-date, and objective). An example of a legal portal that meets these qualifications is **Justia** (http://www.justia.com).

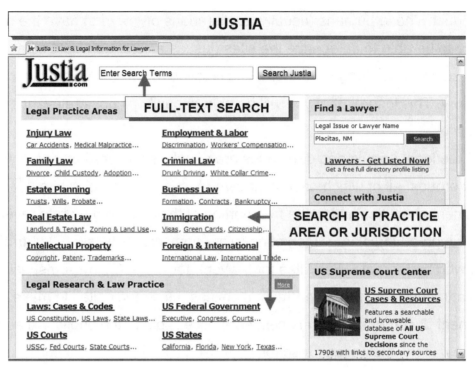

As you review the home page, it's easy to see that it meets the first five "quality" tests (noted on page 235) by (1) having a practice area directory and a jurisdictional directory, (2) offering a keyword search box, (3) being user-friendly (intuitive) by providing an easy-to-read and easy-to-navigate home page, (4) linking directly to many relevant sites that appear once you start clicking on the practice areas or jurisdiction link, and (5) displaying its added value (in the right-hand column there are links to searchable databases). Scroll down the home page to locate the *Company* link. Clicking this link and then selecting the *About Us* link helps you decide that **Justia** meets the final criteria of the quality test – reliability. As to credibility, Tim Stanley, former **FindLaw** CEO and co-founder, is listed as the leader of the **Justia** team. Tim is well-known in the Internet legal research field. He also notes that his team is "comprised of computer scientists, lawyers, librarians and marketing professionals with over 100 years of legal online and engineering development experience." The **Justia** toll-free number is also prominently displayed. As to objectivity, **Justia** clearly states its purpose for offering free information: "Justia is focused on making legal information, resources and services easy to find on the Internet. The company provides Internet users with free case law, codes, regulations, legal articles and legal blog databases, as well as community resources. Justia works with educational, public interest and other socially focused organizations to bring legal and consumer information to the online community." As to being up-to-date, **Justia's** case law and docket databases show today's date when we began reviewing the dates when cases and dockets were last added to its database.

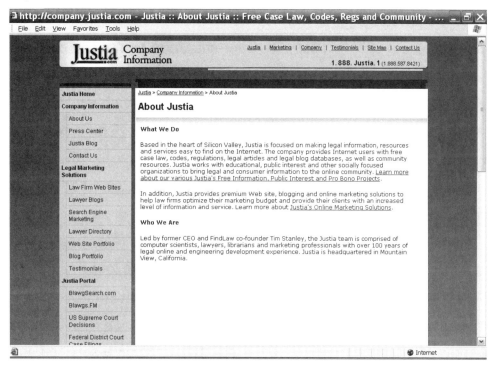

The Top Legal Directories and Portals

Some of the top legal directories and portals are **FindLaw, Justia.com, LexisONE Community, LexisNexis, Nolo.com, Law.com, HG.org, LLRX, USA.gov, Cornell Law School's Legal Information Institute (LII)**, and the **American Bar Association**. Each of which will be discussed in this section.

Free Commercial Legal Portals and Directories

FindLaw

FindLaw (http://www.findlaw.com) is one of the easiest to use and most comprehensive of the free legal portals. **FindLaw's** portal includes directories and "added value," ranging from full-text searchable case law databases (see pages 241–246) to a brief bank of U.S. Supreme Court briefs (see page 244) to e-newsletters and more.

FindLaw has undergone many changes since its inception in 1995. (**FindLaw** began as a list of Internet resources compiled by computer engineer/ attorney Tim Stanley and attorney Stacy Stern for a workshop of the Northern California Law Librarians Association). One of the most noteworthy changes was its purchase in 2001 by Thomson/West (now Thomson Reuters). Though it is still a free portal, there are now links to **Westlaw** pay services (e.g., case law and **KeyCite**). Also, certain services that were once free are no longer available or have been changed to such an extent that they are not as useful (e.g., the *Lawcrawler* search engine which originally retrieved law-related results from the Web but now only retrieves results from **FindLaw**), and some services, though available, are not as easy to find (such as free full-text case law databases for selected courts, which we'll point out later in *Chapter Twelve*). In late 2005, **FindLaw** underwent a design change, and its links (many of which had become outdated) were updated. In 2009, another design change took place to reflect the fact that **FindLaw** (http://findlaw.com/) focuses on two audiences: the legal professional and the public. Thus, the site is now divided into those two categories. If you use the direct URL http://www.findlaw.com/, you will find yourself on the consumer side of the site.

Probably the most useful data on that side (for both consumers and legal professionals) is **FindLaw's Lawyer Directory**. See page 197 for details.

To reach the site created for legal professionals, click on the link at the top of the home page (see above) labeled *Visit our professional site* or you can, in the alternative, use this URL to go directly to the professional site: http://lp.findlaw.com/.

The **FindLaw** *Legal Professional* site's home page has a lot going on. Much of its information can be accessed by clicking the tabs located in one of the two rows of tabs running horizontally beneath the **FindLaw** logo, such as *Cases & Codes* on the top row (left side) or *Newsletters* from the second row (right side). The *Cases & Codes* section contains links to state, local, and federal resources (constitutions, statutes, cases, ordinances, and more) and various **FindLaw**-created case law databases, discussed in next section (below). The *Forms* tab on the second row of tabs brings you to free sample business contracts and free forms (and also pay forms).

FindLaw's Free Case Law Databases

Free case law databases at **FindLaw's** portal are an example of the "added value" discussed earlier when we explained one of the distinctions between a directory and a portal. Cases are uploaded to the database as soon as they are released. Case law can be accessed from two places: from the *Cases & Codes* tab at the top of the home page or from the *Research the Law* search box in the middle of the home page (which also offers a keyword searchable database of articles). The *Research the Law* option and the *Cases & Codes* option are different from each other and will be explained below.

All of **FindLaw's** full-text databases discussed in the upcoming pages can be searched using the same protocol. See pages 243–246 for details.

Research the Law: FindLaw's Free Archive of Summaries of Published Opinions

Using the *Research the Law* search box, one can search (by party name) **Findlaw's** *Opinion Summaries Archive* back to September 2000, covering the U.S. Supreme Court, all thirteen U.S. Circuit Courts of Appeals, and select state supreme and/or appellate courts (California, Florida, Texas, Illinois, Delaware, and New York).

There is also an *Advanced Search* link to search by *Court, Legal topic, Industry, Docket Number, Party Name, Date,* and *Date Range.* To search with keywords, click the *Full Text* tab.

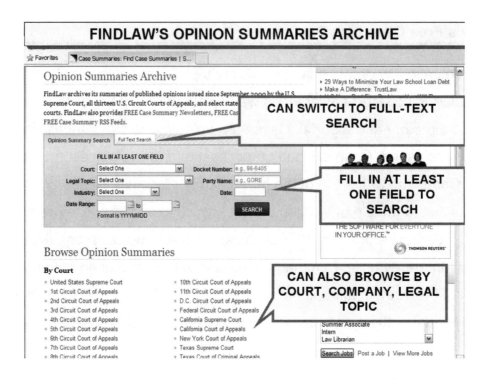

After you run your search, there will be a results list displaying the summary of the case. Click the case name and then click the *Read* link to view the full text of the case (you must be logged into your free **FindLaw** account to view the full text). To register for a free account, see http://linkon.in/csv4n0.

After selecting the *Cases & Codes* tab (see page 240 for an illustration), you will find case law databases for the U.S. Supreme Court, all thirteen U.S. Circuit Courts of Appeal, and all fifty states (in contrast to only the five states found at the *Opinion Summaries Archive*, explained on page 241). Most of the databases found by selecting the *Cases & Codes* tab go back further in time than the *Opinion Summaries Archive.* To access these databases, you will need to scroll down to *Browse Cases and Codes* and select the U.S. Supreme Court, one of the available U.S. Courts of Appeal, or a state.

For all the states (with the exception of California, which will be described on page 245), **FindLaw** has created databases that are browsable by *Date* or *Court* and searchable by *Docket Number* or *Party Name* (a *Date Range* can also be added to the *Docket Number* or *Party Name* search). To keyword search, click the *Full Text* tab. (For Florida, Texas, Illinois, Delaware, and New York, researchers may prefer to use the *Opinion Summaries Archive* because there are additional search options, such as *Legal Topic* or *Industry*.)

To locate a state case law database, visit the **FindLaw** *Cases & Codes* page (http://findlaw.com/casecode/) and follow these steps:

- Scroll down to *State Resources*
- Select a state
- Scroll down to *State Court Opinions*
- Click on the link that has the notation *From FindLaw.* It will look like this: *Supreme Court of Arkansas and Appellate Court Opinion—From FindLaw.*

FindLaw will also link to the official state court site (which might include a searchable state case law database) and any other site that has created a searchable case law database for the state.

FindLaw has created full-text searchable databases for the U.S. Supreme Court and the U.S. Courts of Appeal cases. **FindLaw's** *U.S. Supreme Court Opinions* database goes back to 1893 (http://www.findlaw.com/casecode/supreme.html). (See page 377 for information about **FindLaw's Supreme Court Center**, which offers briefs and more.) To search **FindLaw's** *U.S. Appellate Court Opinions* database, visit http://www.findlaw.com/casecode and select a specific circuit. Dates of coverage vary by circuit, with most going back to 1994.

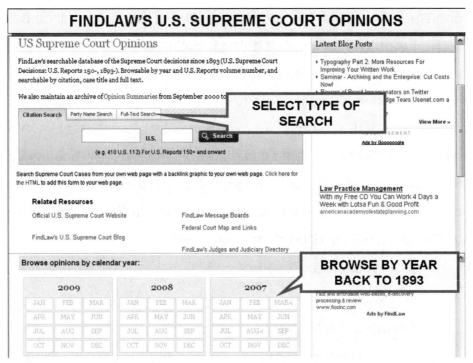

For both the Supreme and Appellate courts, cases can also be searched by *Full text* (keywords and phrases) and *Party name*. While the Supreme Court cases can be searched by their official U.S. Reports citation (by entering it into the *Citation* search box), the Appellate courts' search menu does not offer a *Citation* search box. Instead, it offers a docket number search box. Both the Supreme and Appellate court cases can be browsed by year. Select a year, and cases will be listed alphabetically by plaintiff. You can choose to reverse the list to appear alphabetically by defendant. At the *Cases and Codes* page (http://www.findlaw.com/casecode/), it appears that you can only search one circuit at a time. However, there is an *All Circuit Courts* search at http://linkon.in/9pdMMD (but we find that it doesn't always seem to work correctly).

Free California Supreme and Appellate Court Case Law Databases

To use the *California Supreme and Appellate Court Cases* database (http://www.findlaw.com/cacases/index.html), which extends back to 1934, you must be logged into your free **FindLaw** account (to register for the free account, see http://linkon.in/csv4n0). To begin using the database, do not get misled by the *Opinion Summaries* link or any of the *Related Resources* links. Instead, you must scroll down the main page to the *Powered By AccessLaw* database. Although it defaults to a *Citation* search, an *Advanced Search* is also offered where cases can be browsed by date or volume, or searched by the following criteria:

- *Keywords* and *Phrases (full text)*
- *Docket Number*
- *Party Name*
- *Judge Name*
- *Attorney Name*
- *Cite Check* (see pages 263-269 for details on the *Cite Check* feature)

FindLaw has posted a warning about relying on this database (and the same goes for most free databases):

> Please note that "slip opinions" are the "as filed" opinions of the court that have not yet been enhanced and edited for publication in the California Official Reports and may not yet be final as to the issuing court. In addition to clerical corrections, opinions on this page are subject to modification and rehearing until final, and Court of Appeal opinions are subject to a grant of review or depublication order by the Supreme Court. Opinions certified or ordered partially published are set forth in their entirety on this page. (See rules 976, 976.1, and 977, Cal. Rules of Court.) Modifications to previously posted opinions will appear as separate documents on the day modifications are filed.

As with any case law research, be sure to cite check your cases before filing a brief. (See pages 263-269 for information on how to cite check for free and see page 255 to learn about "renting" **Lexis's Shepard's** database for the day, week, or month.

Full-Text Search Tips

All of **FindLaw's** full-text databases, discussed in the previous sections, can be searched using the same protocol. The Boolean operators *AND*, *OR*, and *NOT*; and the proximity operator *NEAR* (which places words within 50 words of each other) can be used to connect keywords and phrases. To search for an exact phrase, enclose it in quotation marks. The asterisk (*) wildcard is used to expand the root of a word. For more details about full-text searches, visit http://www.findlaw.com/info/helpers/searchhelp.html or look for the *options* link to the right of the *Search* box, if available (the link is not available at every database).

As noted at the beginning of this chapter, **Justia** (http://www.justia.com) is a free legal portal and does not require registration. It offers a comprehensive directory to help researchers find legal research Web sites.

There are two directories below the search box for those who prefer to browse rather than keyword search. The first directory, *Legal Practice Areas,* can be browsed by legal topic (e.g., *Family Law*) and the second directory, *Legal Research & Law Practice*, can be browsed primarily by jurisdiction (e.g., *U.S. Federal Government*). **Justia's** *Legal Research & Law Practice* directory is broken down by jurisdiction (e.g., *US Federal Government*, *US States*), primary materials (*Laws: Cases & Codes*), *Legal Forms*, and more. (For general information about **Justia.com**, see pages 104 and for information on how to search its *Legal Web*, see pages 105-106.)

On **Justia's** home page, you can also select the *Lawyer Directory*, *Law Blogs*, or *More* tabs to search other areas of **Justia**. While *Lawyer Directory* and *Law Blogs* are self-explanatory, the *More* tab deserves some explanation. From this tab, you can select to search some of the same material you find listed on the home page, but there are also some materials not listed on the home page such as *Mexico Law*, *Argentina Law*, *Justia Blog*, and *Legal Forms*.

JUSTIA CASE LAW DATABASES AND REGULATION TRACKER

U.S. SUPREME COURT CASES AND RESOURCES

US Constitution, US Laws, State Laws... | Executive, Congress, Courts...

US Courts
USSC, Fed Courts, State Courts...

US States
California, Florida, New York, Texas...

Law Schools
Law Reviews, Outlines, Law Prof Blogs...

Legal Forms
US Federal, US States, Biz Contracts...

Lawyers, Legal Aid & Services
Injury Lawyers, Criminal Lawyers...

Experts & Expert Witnesses
Accident Experts, Medical Experts...

Law Blogs
Business Law, Family Law, IP Law ...

Legal PodCasts
Constitutional Law, Technology...

US Supreme Court Cases & Resources

Features a searchable and browsable database of **All US Supreme Court Decisions** since the 1790s with links to secondary sources including legal blogs and online databases like Google Book Search. There is also access to mp3 audio of Supreme Court oral arguments of case summaries from Oyez.org.

Visit the US Supreme Court Center

BlawgSearch

U.S. DISTRICT COURT'S CIVIL CASE FILINGS

Cases in the News - Documents

Facebook Lawsuits - Copyright, patent, contract and other lawsuits involving Facebook, including Ceglia v. Zuckerberg & Facebook.

U.S. REGULATION TRACKER

Yahoo! Lawsuits - Copyright, patent, contract and other lawsuits involving Yahoo!, including Xiaoning et al v. Yahoo! Inc. et al.

US Federal Resources

US District Courts' Civil Case Filings. Search new cases by state, court, lawsuit type (eg patent law) or party name. Subscribe to RSS feeds of search results to receive updates of new cases.

US Regulation Tracker. Track new regulations of specific federal agencies and subscribe to RSS feeds for daily updates.

Justia, like **FindLaw**, also offers several free case law databases. Unlike **FindLaw**, you will also find a free regulation tracking database and a free docket database at **Justia**. However, **Justia's** free case law and docket databases are undergoing extensive upgrading and updating as this book goes to press, so we will discuss what is currently available.

Justia's *U.S. Supreme Court Center* database can be reached by either clicking on the *US Supreme Court Cases & Resources* link found on the left-hand column of the home page or by using this URL: http://supreme.justia.com. The database coverage reaches back to Volume 1 of the U.S. Reports (1791). You can browse by *Volume*, *Year*, or *Recent Opinions*.

Although there is a **Google** search box at the top of the page where you can enter keywords or phrases and connect them with Boolean connectors, this full-text search option of **Justia's** *Supreme Court Cases and Resources* does not work properly at this time. This database is being upgraded. Until the upgrade is complete, we do not recommend using the full-text search option for keyword or phrase searching. You will probably have luck using the **Google** search box for citation searches (e.g., "1 U.S. 1") and party name searches. If you want to *Share* you search results or a specific case, click on the *Share* button (see prior illustration) to email the case or post it to one of your social networking sites, for example.

The *U.S. Court of Appeals Opinions* database is not highlighted on the home page of **Justia** but can be found at http://cases.justia.com/us-court-of-appeals. It goes back to 1950 and allows you to search one circuit individually or all federal circuits together. Note: As of September 2010, the database only goes up to 2007 (we were informed that more current cases would be added).

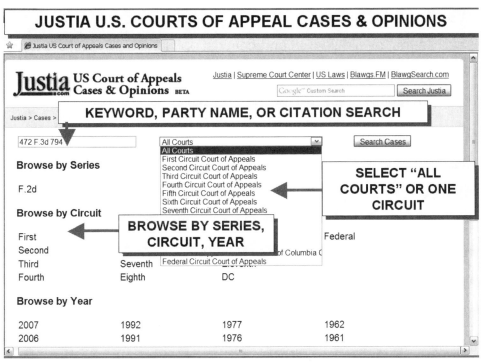

There is very little documentation explaining how to search this database (possibly because the database is in "Beta" mode), but from our testing, it does not seem to be powered by **Google** (as the Supreme Court database discussed in the previous section is). This means that only simple keyword searching is available (keywords are automatically linked with the *AND* Boolean connector) and that the other Boolean connectors and also phrase searching are unavailable. The inability to search by phrases (such as citations, party name[s], or attorney name[s]), may give you false hits. For example, a search for the citation *472 F.3d 794* will bring back results for that exact case but also cases that include the *472* as a numbered footnote and the abbreviation *F.3d as part of the citation 252 F.3d 1124*. In addition to keyword searching, one can also *Browse by Series* (Federal Reporter 2nd or 3rd series), *Browse by Circuit,* or *Browse by Year.* If you see a blank screen after selecting a case from the results list, scroll down and the case will appear below. Hopefully, by the time you read this book, the database search experience will have improved.

Justia's Free U.S. District Courts Case Law Database

Justia's *Federal District Court Opinions and Orders* database is currently offline. **Justia** was the first free site to offer full-text keyword searching of all the U.S. District Courts' available civil and criminal opinions and orders (but only back to 2004). (See pages 293-299 to learn about other sites that now offer free searchable databases of U.S. District Courts' opinions.)

Justia's Free U.S. Regulation Tracker

Justia's *U.S. Regulation Tracker* (http://regulations.justia.com) allows researchers to track new regulations of specific federal agencies back to 2005 by *Department or Agency, Regulations Filed* (date), *Full Text*, or by a combination of these search options. Search results can also be restricted to *Rules* (final), *Proposed Rules*, etc.

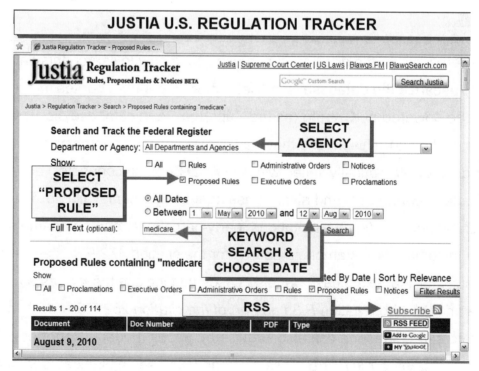

Researchers can subscribe to RSS feeds for daily regulation updates. The *U.S. Regulation Tracker* database, like the *U.S. Court of Appeals Opinions* database discussed in the previous section, also does not seem to be powered by **Google**; therefore, use the U.S. Court of Appeals search tips explained on page 251. Results can be sorted by *Date* or by *Relevance.* You can also select (from the home page) to *Browse by Government Agency* or *Browse by Date.*

Justia's Free Federal Court Docket Database

Another database first offered for free by **Justia** is the *Federal District Court Filings and Dockets* (civil only) database (http://dockets.justia.com). It now also includes dockets from the U.S. Courts of Appeals. See page 391-394 for complete details.

LexisONE Community (http://law.lexisnexis.com/webcenters/lexisone) is a legal portal (partially free and partially pay) offered by the commercial legal vendor **LexisNexis**. It was originally launched in July 2000 as **LexisONE** and re-launched as **LexisONE Community** in December 2008. (For brevity's sake, we'll refer to it as **LexisONE.**) To use even the free portion of the portal requires registration.

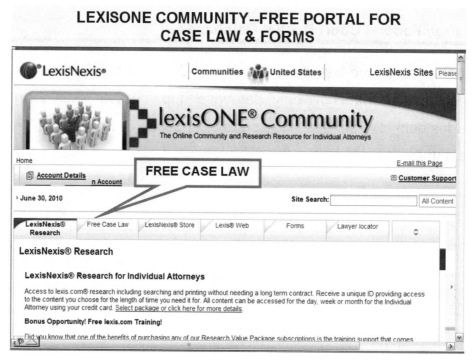

LEXISONE COMMUNITY--FREE PORTAL FOR CASE LAW & FORMS

The highlights of the portal's <u>free</u> "added value" resources are accessible from the tabs on the home page, beginning with (1) *Free Case Law* (full-text searchable), (2) *Lexis Web* ("search engine that delivers free web content specifically from legal sites validated by LexisNexis® attorney editors"), (3) *Forms* (ranging from free forms to interactive pay forms), and (4) *Lawyer locator* (see page 196 where we discuss the **LexisNexis Martindale Directory**).

In addition to the free content above, there are several "pay as you go" options (using a credit card) for individual attorneys who wish to search selected **LexisNexis** databases, such as case law, annotated codes, news, **Shepard's**, and public records (for more information about accessing the public record database, which **Lexis** refers to as its *Finder & Assets* research package, see pages 220-221). To access these options, click the *LexisNexis® Research* tab on the home page (or visit http://linkon.in/a3PMvd). Pricing varies depending on which database is selected and whether one selects a daily, weekly, or monthly payment package (e.g., the daily package for unlimited access to **Shepard's** is $43, the weekly package is $69, and the monthly package is $146).

LexisONE's Free Case Law Databases

LexisONE posts cases to its free case law database as soon as they are released. The following courts' cases are included in the **LexisONE** case law database:

- U.S. Supreme Court (back to 1781)
- Federal Courts of Appeal (covers only the most current 10 years). You can search one circuit or you can search all circuits with the U.S. Supreme Court together (by choosing *Combined Federal Cases*). There is no way to perform an all-circuits search without including the Supreme Court (**Justia**, as noted on page 251, allows an all-circuits search).
- All fifty states' Supreme and Appellate courts (covers only the most current 10 years). One can search all states together or one state (but not multiple states).

LexisONE's case law databases can be searched by the following criteria:

- *Keywords or Phrases* (Do not use quotation marks.)
- *Citation*
- *Parties*
- *Judges*
- *Counsel*
- *Date*

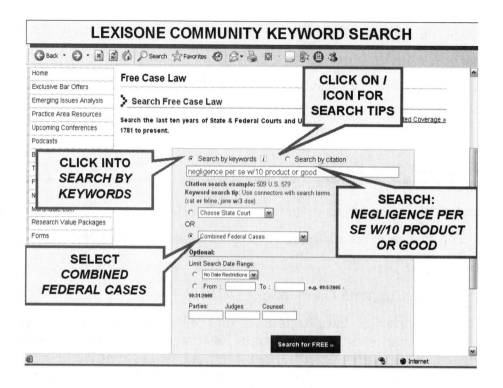

To keyword search **LexisONE** (see the illustration above), you need to click into the *Search by Keywords* radio button and then enter your keywords or phrases into the search box. The **LexisONE** (http://linkon.in/9JXU58) free case law database can be keyword/phrase searched using the same Boolean and proximity connectors used with **LexisNexis's** pay database. If you are not a pay **LexisNexis** user, see detailed instructions on how to search by clicking into the information icon (which is indicated by the letter *i*) to the right of *Search by Keywords* or visit http://linkon.in/amxM10.

The above search *negligence per se w/10 product or good* is a request for cases that include the phrase *negligence per se* (unlike **Google**, phrases are <u>not</u> placed within quotation marks) within ten words of the words *product* or *good* (*w/* is a proximity connector that stands for "within" and any number up to 255 can be added to it). Note that a search for a singular word will also bring back the plural and the possessive, so it's usually best to search for the singular form if you also want to include the plural in your results. We have chosen to search the *Combined Federal Cases* database. **LexisONE** recognizes the use of parentheses to organize keywords (see page 43 for a full explanation of using parentheses).

The various search boxes can be mixed and matched to create a more targeted search. For instance, you can enter a name into the "segment" search boxes (*Judge*, *Counsel*, or *Party*) and ALSO add a keyword into the *Search by Keywords* search box. To view every reported case where Lloyd Levitt was the counsel of record in cases involving class actions, for example, you would (1) select the appropriate court; (2) enter the phrase *class action* into the *Search by Keyword* box; and (3) enter the counsel's last name and first name into the *Counsel* segment search box (use proximity connectors to indicate that the first name is within three words of the last name in case a middle name or middle initial is used). Your search would look like the illustration below:

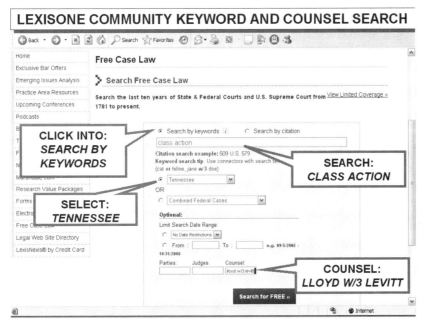

You can also conduct a segment-only search (without entering keywords into the *Search by keywords* box) if you want to bring up every case with a specific party, counsel, or judge name.

LexisONE does not offer free access to its **Shepard's** database, but by clicking on the *Shepardize this citation for $6.00* link (to the right of any case returned in search results) you will have the option to Shepardize for a fee. You will first need to register a credit card with your **LexisONE** account. If you need to Shepardize more than seven cases, it makes sense to explore the day rate of $43 noted earlier. (See pages 263–269 for information on a free, but more laborious, alternative to **Shepard's** and **KeyCite**.)

While you can search for all state cases (for free) back ten years at **LexisONE** (http://law.lexisnexis.com/webcenters/lexisone), coverage is much further back if you use another free **Lexis** database, but only for California cases, which can be searched back to 1850 at the free database **LexisNexis** provides at the California state court's official site (http://www.lexisnexis.com/clients/CACourts/). (Check your state court's official site to find out if **LexisNexis** (or another company) has provided a similar database for your state with deeper date coverage. Also, see *Chapter Thirteen* for information about free member benefit legal research databases (with deeper date and jurisdiction coverage) that may be found at many state bar association Web sites.

From the home page (see next illustration), California Appellate and Supreme Courts can be searched together or separately. The basic search page offers a *Get Opinion by Cite* search and a *Natural Language* search. *Natural Language* searches are very basic and allow you to type your research issue into the search box using terms, phrases, lists, or even a sentence (e.g., *Where can I find cases about "negligence per se" and also products or goods?*). Note: Only in the *Natural Language* search are you instructed to enclose phrases in quotation marks. In all other **Lexis** searches, you do NOT enclose phrases in quotation marks. Also, wildcard characters (such as ! or *) are not available in a *Natural Language* search, but they are available in all other **LexisNexis** databases we discuss in this chapter.

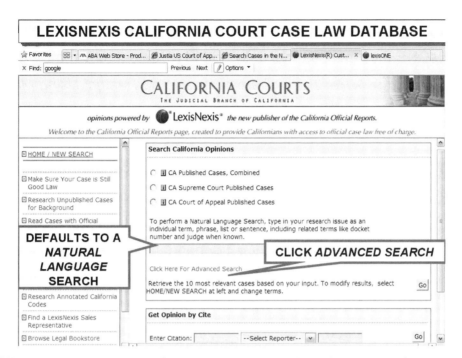

Click on the *Advanced Search* link to search with more options.

The *Advanced Search* page defaults to the *Natural Language* search, but you can select a *Terms & Connector* search or an *Easy Search* instead.

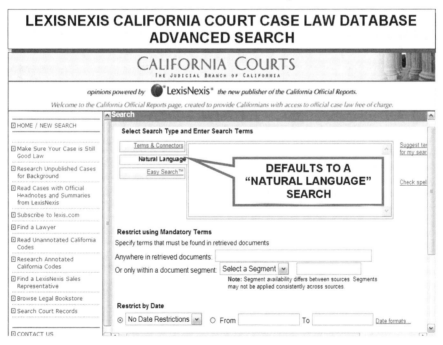

The *Natural Language* option of the *Advanced Search* page, offers a *Document Segment* search option, but unlike **LexisONE's** *Parties*, *Judges*, and *Counsel Segments* discussed on page 257, you are offered many more segments here (see the first illustration on page 257). Note: the same additional segments, such as *opinionby,* can also be used on the *Terms & Connectors* and at **LexisONE**. But at **LexisONE** they must be manually added to the searches this way: *opinionby (ginsburg).* A *Restrict by Date* segment and *Restrict Using Mandatory Terms* segment are also included.

To change to the *Terms & Connector* search, simply click on the tab above the *Natural Language* tab (see the illustration below). While the same *Restrict by Date* segment and *Document Segment* search (see the first illustration on the next page) discussed above in the *Natural Language* search are also included on the *Terms & Connector* page, there are some major differences between the two searches. For instance, in a *Terms & Connector* search: (1) you can link your terms with Boolean connectors, (2) when using the *Document Segment* search, be sure to click the *Add* tab to the right of where you enter your keywords as illustrated in the next screen shot on the next page, (3) you can add multiple *Document Segments* to create a very sophisticated search, and (4) there is no *Restrict Using Mandatory Terms* segment.

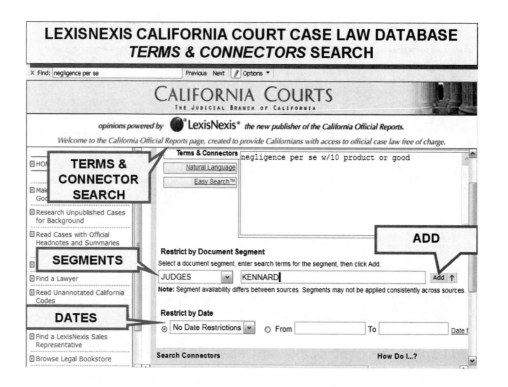

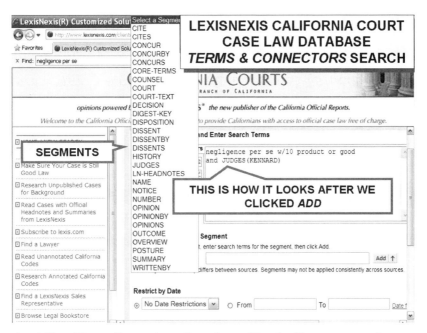

LEXISNEXIS CALIFORNIA COURT CASE LAW DATABASE
TERMS & CONNECTORS **SEARCH**

To select the *Easy Search* option (see illustration on previous page) on the *Advanced Search* page, click on the tab below the *Natural Language* tab. As the name implies, "*Easy Search* is optimized for short search queries (two or three terms), and does not require specific search syntax."

Once a case is being viewed, notice that there are colored "treatment" flags to indicate how other cases have treated your case (e.g., positive, negative, or possible negative treatment).

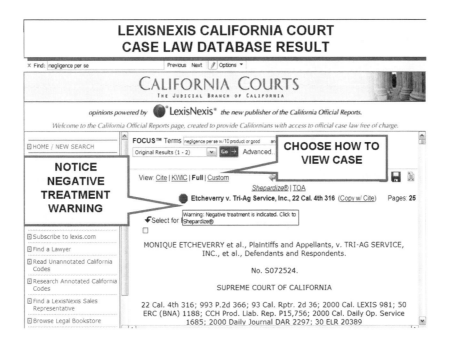

LEXISNEXIS CALIFORNIA COURT CASE LAW DATABASE RESULT

Important Note: This **LexisNexis** California database is only updated monthly. For more current California cases, use **LexisONE** (http://law.lexisnexis.com/webcenters/lexisone) and restrict your search to *California* (by selecting *California* from the *Choose State Court* drop-down menu) and also restrict your search to the last month of opinions (by entering a date range into the *Limit Search Date Range* search boxes). See the illustration on page 264.

For a comparison of the free **LexisONE** to the pay **LexisNexis**, see http://www.netforlawyers.com/article_lexis_one.htm.

Cite-Checking Cases:
A Free Alternative to Shepard's (LexisNexis) and KeyCite (Westlaw)

Cite-checking cases to verify that they are still "good law" is the final step in a research project. Sometimes it's also the first step if you want to find more and/or later cases that cite to your cases. Most researchers are familiar with paying for the print or online cite-checking services provided by **Shepard's** and **KeyCite**. One of the questions that people conducting legal research on the Internet most often ask us is, "Can I **Shepardize** (or **KeyCite**) cases anywhere for free on the Internet?" The answer in the strictest sense is "no." However, there is a free, alternative process to **Shepard's** and **KeyCite**, which we call the "party name as keyword plus" citation search but it is quite rudimentary and the results do <u>not</u> include the editorial treatment that the pay services **Shepard's** or **KeyCite** do include. It's up to you to determine how these new cases treated your case (you will need to decide if a court overruled your case, or if it reversed, affirmed, harmonized it, etc.). We only recommend using the "party name as keyword plus" citation search for fairly recent cases because cite-checking older cases with this method might bring back a large number of citing cases, all of which you would have to read to determine if they were at all relevant. At that point, it might be a better idea to use the "pay as you go" **Shepard's** service at http://linkon.in/a3PMvd, discussed on page 255.

The "party name as keyword plus" citation search process can be accomplished by first searching the party names from the case that you hope to rely on as keywords through a free, full-text searchable case law database that contains cases published <u>after</u> the date of your case. We'll use **LexisONE** for our example of how to cite check this way. (In addition, **FindLaw** has an alternative to **Shepard's** and **KeyCite** that does not involve the "party name as keyword plus" search method, but only for California cases [see page 266] and U.S. Supreme Court cases [see page 269]. There is still no editorial treatment to explain how the resulting cases have affected your case, however.)

LEXISONE COMMUNITY--FREE ALTERNATIVE TO SHEPARD'S

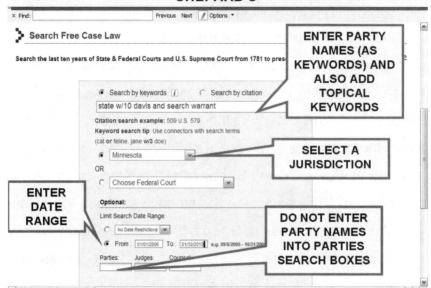

Follow these steps to cite-check a case for free using our "party name as keyword plus" search method:

- Enter the plaintiff's and defendant's names (from the case you want to cite-check—*State and Davis*, a 2006 Minnesota Appellate Court case) into the *Search by Keywords* box.

- Place a Boolean connector between the names. For example, in the case of *State vs. Davis*, 711 N.W.2d 841, 2006 Minn. App. LEXIS 48 (2006). your search would look like this:

    - *state w/10 davis* (if using **LexisONE**)

    - *state davis* (if using **FindLaw**)

    - and then, if you have too many irrelevant cases, add the "plus," such as:

        - a keyword or phrase from the case being cite-checked. For instance, if the issue in *State vs. Davis* was about search warrants, you could add the phrase *search warrants* to the keywords *state* and *davis* to find all cases citing *State vs. Davis* that concerned search warrants.

        - a date restrictor (e.g., our case was decided in 2006, so we will restrict the search to cases between January 1, 2006 and today's date). Your search would look like this:

            - *state w/10 davis and search warrants* (if using **LexisONE**)

            - *state davis "search warrants"* (if using **FindLaw**)

LEXISONE COMMUNITY--FREE ALTERNATIVE TO SHEPARD'S

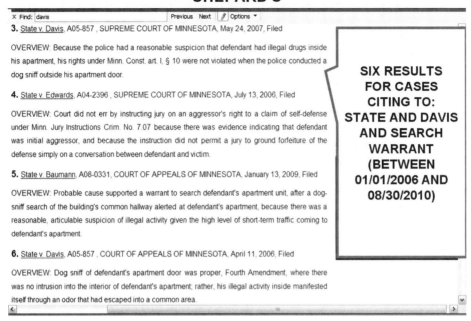

This will return a list of cases that cite to your case, including your case (six in the example illustrated above).

Rather than reading through each case on the results list in its entirety to find the place where the new case cites to your original case, scan the case by using the Web browser's *Find* function. If the document is a PDF, use the *Binocular* icon to bring up the *Find* search box. If the document is not a PDF, select *Edit* and then select *Find* from the browser's Menu Bar at the top of the screen (or simply enter the shortcut *Control f*). Enter one of the party names (e.g., *Davis*) from your original case to instantly be taken to the place in the new case where your original case is cited. You'll still have to read that part of the case to see how (or if) the new case affects your case, but what do you expect when it's free?

FindLaw's *California Case Law* and *U.S. Supreme Court Opinions* databases are the only case law databases on **FindLaw** (http://www.findlaw.com/cacases/) that allow you to run a free alternative to **Shepard's** or **KeyCite** without searching the party names as keywords in the manner explained on page 264. However, as noted earlier, there is no editorial treatment to explain how the resulting cases have affected your case.

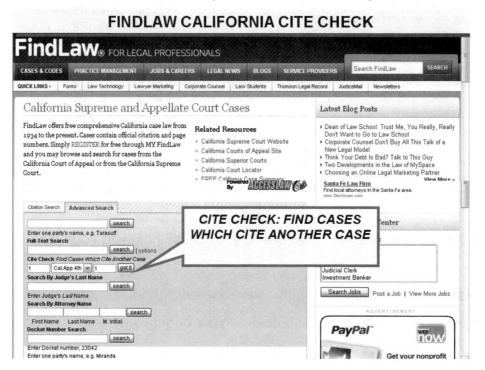

There are two ways to cite-check a California case at **FindLaw**:

- Type a citation into the *Cite Check:Find Cases Which Cite Another Case* search box found on the California case law database's *Advanced Search* menu at http://www.findlaw.com/cacases/#dirsearch2 (see preceeding illustration; remember, you will need to be logged in to your free account). A list of reported cases citing your original case will be displayed (see next illustration).

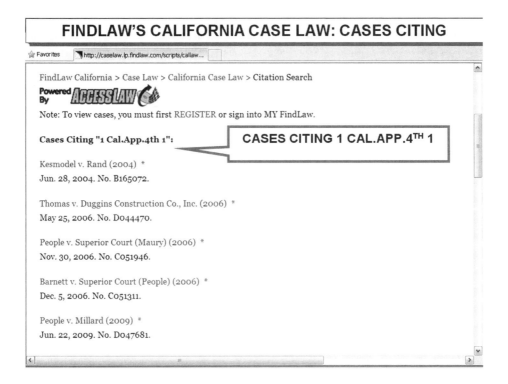

FINDLAW'S CALIFORNIA CASE LAW: CASES CITING

Favorites http://caselaw.lp.findlaw.com/scripts/callaw...

FindLaw California > Case Law > California Case Law > Citation Search

Powered By ACCESSLAW

Note: To view cases, you must first REGISTER or sign into MY FindLaw.

Cases Citing "1 Cal.App.4th 1":

CASES CITING 1 CAL.APP.4TH 1

Kesmodel v. Rand (2004) *
Jun. 28, 2004. No. B165072.

Thomas v. Duggins Construction Co., Inc. (2006) *
May 25, 2006. No. D044470.

People v. Superior Court (Maury) (2006) *
Nov. 30, 2006. No. C051946.

Barnett v. Superior Court (People) (2006) *
Dec. 5, 2006. No. C051311.

People v. Millard (2009) *
Jun. 22, 2009. No. D047681.

- If you are already viewing a case, click the *Cases Citing this Case* link in the upper left-hand corner of the case that you are viewing. A list of reported cases citing your original case will be displayed.

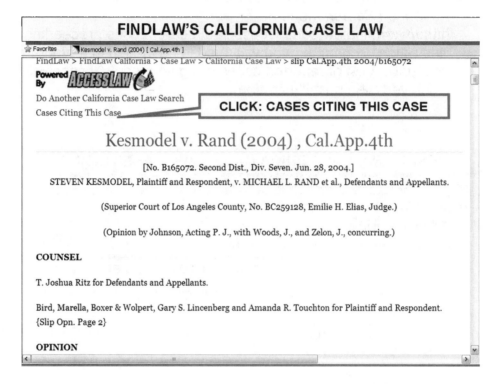

After searching the *U.S. Supreme Court Opinions* database at **FindLaw** (http://www.findlaw.com/casecode/supreme.html#dirsearch2) and viewing a case result, note the four links on the top left (see next illustration):

- *View enhanced case on Westlaw*
- *KeyCite this case on Westlaw*
- *Cases citing this case: Supreme Court*
- *Cases citing this case: Circuit Courts*

FINDLAW U.S. SUPREME COURT SEARCH RESULTS WITH CASES CITING THIS CASE

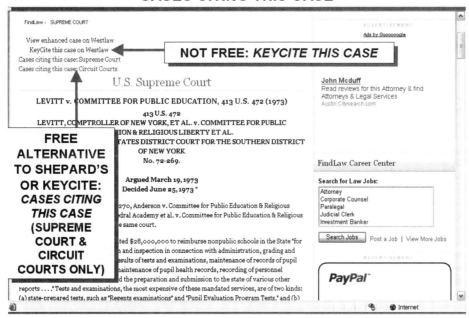

The last two links will bring you to a free list of cases that cite your case, without any editorial treatment you would have found at a pay citation service. Meanwhile, the first two links will bring you to **Westlaw's** *Westlaw By CreditCard* service where you can pay to retrieve documents and check citations in **KeyCite**. You do not have to be a **Westlaw** subscriber to use this service; anyone with a credit card can use it on an *ad hoc* basis. If you have more than a few citations to check, it might be worth your time to use this or **Shepard's** pay service discussed in the **LexisONE** section on page 255. Although pay databases other than **Lexis** and **Westlaw** offer cite checking, they are generally not much better than the free rudimentary methods we've just discussed.

Law.com (http://www.law.com) is a legal portal owned by **ALM** (**American Lawyer Media**); **ALM** was originally known for its print legal publications (such as *The American Lawyer, National Law Journal, New York Law Journal,* and *Legal Times),* all of which are also available online via **Law.com**. **Law.com** slices and dices its legal news to meet the needs of all types of lawyers as suggested by its links labeled *Legal Technology, Corporate Counsel, Small Law Firms, Large Law Firms,* or *International News.* Under the **ALM** *Publications Site* heading (located in the left-hand column), there are links with drop-down menus to *National Legal News* and *Regional Legal News* and also to *Law Journal Newsletters.* Some of these are free and some require pay subscriptions (some of the paid newsletters offer a thirty-day free trial).

In addition to its legal publications, **Law.com** is divided into several other sections (some free, some free but requiring registration, some partially free, and some fee-based).

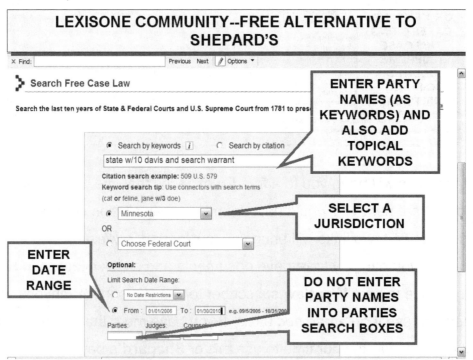

An example of a section that is partially free is **Law.com's** keyword search engine *Quest* (its search box is on the top right-hand side of the home page), used to search the internal *Law.com Network* or the external *Legal Web.*

While the *Quest* search and the results (brief annotations) are free, a paid subscription is often necessary to read the full story if it originated in certain **ALM** publications. *Legal Web* results will also include information from legal bloggers (accessible for free). You can register to receive an e-newsletter (**Law.com** *Newswire*; at https://store.law.com/Registration/Default.aspx?promoCode=nw) of the day's top legal news and feature stories, culled from **ALM's** publications, with clickable links to the full stories. We are never sure when we click on a link to the full story in **Law.com** whether we will receive the full story, a message informing us that "*The page you have requested is available only to premium subscribers,*" or a request to log in. This is one of our main beefs with **Law.com**, along with more pop-up ads than ever, many of which block the text of the story and are often hard to close. On the other hand, **Law.com** is incredibly useful to us for keeping us up-to-date with the legal field, especially its *Newswire* (noted above) that comes into our e-mail box daily (and sometimes more often than daily if there is a breaking story).

The *Jobs, Verdicts,* and *CLE Center* links (listed in the lower left-hand column of the home page under the *Law.com Network* heading) provide access to non-news services. Some of the services are free and some are fee-based. For example, the *Jobs* link offers free job searching at **LawJobs.com** while the *Verdicts* link brings you to a fee-based verdict and settlement database, **VerdictSearch.com** (see page 194 for details) and the *CLE Center* link brings you to the fee based online **Law.com CLE Center**, where you will find courses accredited in more than thirty states.

HG.org (http://www.hg.org/index.html) was one of the very first online law and government sites, founded in January of 1995 by Lex Mundi, a network of independent law firms. **HG.org** is a bit of a mix between **Law.com** and **FindLaw** or **Justia**. Like **Law.com**, **HG.org** provides an expert witness directory (free) and an employment search.

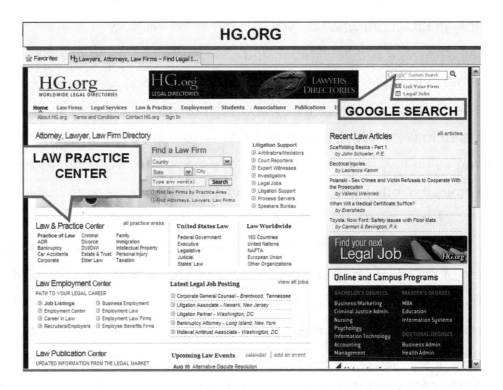

Like **FindLaw** and **Justia**, **HG** provides a lawyer directory and a directory of law-related Web sites arranged by subject and jurisdictional categories. Scrolling down to the *Law & Practice Center* and then clicking on *all practice areas* takes you to a page with seventy "core areas of law" and one hundred thirty "sub areas of practice." **HG** explains that, "Pages are presented in a consistent format and provide information on US (Federal and State), European and International Laws. An abundance of information dealing with the specific area of law is also integrated into each page, including: Publications, Articles, Organizations, Resources, Attorneys and Law Firms." When we chose *Bankruptcy Law,* **HG** displayed links to: Web sites (primarily U.S.) explaining bankruptcy, the U.S. Bankruptcy Code, the U.S. Bankruptcy courts' organizations related to Bankruptcy, Bankruptcy lawyers, and articles about Bankruptcy.

There is a **Google**-powered search box on the top right-hand side of the home page to keyword search the site (see preceeding illustration). Searching the two words *Dubai escrow* brought up an article titled "Property Development and Escrow Law in Dubai." We especially like **HG** for its foreign and international links.

LLRX.com

LLRX (http://www.llrx.com) is a cross between an e-magazine and a portal. The e-magazine portion provides Internet research articles that discuss Web sites and then links directly to them. There are also articles and news items about emerging Internet issues and lawyer-related technology. Meanwhile, the portal portion of the site is illustrated by **LLRX's** database of 1,400 links to state, federal, and local court rules; forms; and dockets. This database can be browsed by type of court (e.g., Bankruptcy), by jurisdiction (e.g., federal or state), or searched with keywords. There is a **Google**-powered search box on the top of the home page to keyword search *LLRX.com,* or *LLRX.com* together with *beSpacific* (blog), or the *Legal Web*. To learn when new articles are added to **LLRX**, subscribe to its monthly e-mail alert.

Besides offering access to online ordering of legal books, software, and forms, **Nolo's** portal offers free information useful to both legal professionals and the general public (http://www.nolo.com). To read free legal articles, select a topic (ranging in from *Accidents* to *Wills*) listed under the *Free Legal Information* column located on the left-hand side of the home page. Notice the other *Free Legal Information* links, found below the *Find a Lawyer* portion of the site. Here you will find links to: a *Law Dictionary*, *State Laws & Resources*, *Law Blogs*, *Law Podcasts,* the *Supreme Court Center* (a searchable database of U.S. Supreme Court cases), and *Selected Books for Free.* The book titles range from *Everybody's Guide to Small Claims Court* to *The Foreclosure Survival Guide.*

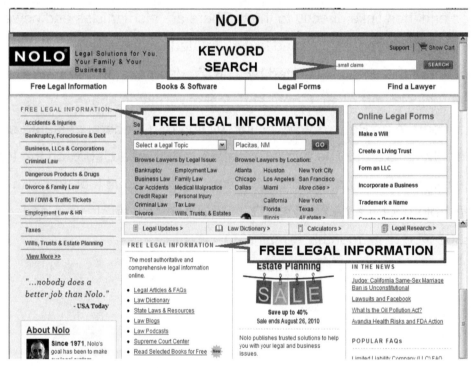

Zimmerman's Research Guide, hosted at the **LexisNexis InfoPro** site (http://law.lexisnexis.com/infopro/zimmermans/), is a free, handy, annotated subject guide that links to various Web sites (both free and pay), print resources, and even specific libraries that have collections on the subject you are researching. It is keyword searchable and can also be browsed by subject (legal and non-legal).

Law Firm Portals

Siskind Susser's **Visalaw.com** (http://www.visalaw.com/index.html) was probably the first law firm-sponsored Web site. In addition to promoting its firm, the site offers enormous amounts of free information about immigration law, from articles and forms, to links to government sites and several free e-newsletters, such as *Siskind's Immigration Bulletin.*

There are many other law firms offering free information. For another example, see page 412 where we discuss **Illinoisdivorce.com** (http://illinoisdivorce.com/) in the "Family Law" section.

Government Portals and Directories

USA.gov (formerly FirstGov.gov)

USA.gov (http://www.usa.gov/) is the Federal Government's document search portal and is powered by **Bing**. **USA.gov** searches millions of Web pages from all levels of the United States government: federal, state, local, tribal, the District of Columbia, and the U.S. territories.

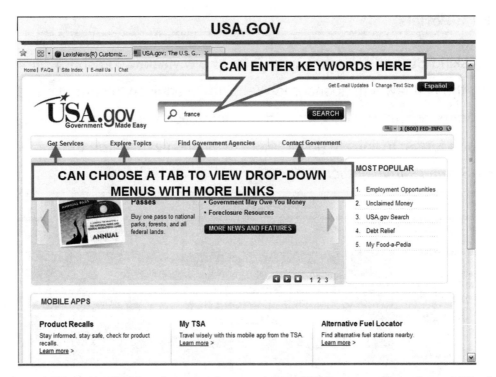

In addition to offering keyword searching, **USA.gov** offers the ability to browse by a government service, topic, agency, or government contact. To browse instead of keyword search, select one of the four tabs listed below the search box on **USA.gov's** home page (*Get Services, Explore Topics, Find Government Agencies,* and *Contact Government).* Once you select one of these tabs, such as the *Find Government Agencies* tab, for example, a drop-down menu appears, where more links are revealed (as displayed in the next illustration). Clicking any of these general links will then display more sub-topical links from which to choose.

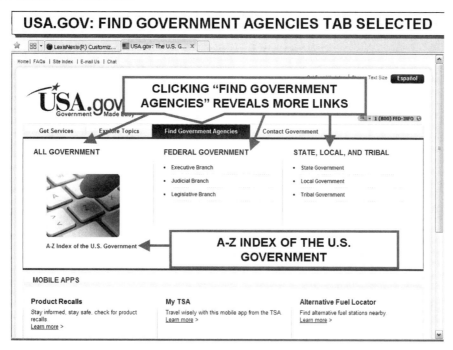

If you select the *Get Services* tab, you will see that **USA.gov** also serves as a forum in which to conduct business online with government agencies. For instance, you can buy stamps or coins, print forms online, e-file your taxes, and more.

Use the search box on **USA.gov's** home page to keyword or phrase search government documents (state, federal, local, tribal, and territorial). (Although results occasionally bring back court opinions, this is not the right site to search for them. Instead, see the sites on pages 241-253, 291-300 , and 367-382 where free case law research is discussed.)

USA.gov was recently redesigned and its search is now powered by **Bing**. Unfortnately, there are no search tips with this redesign, so you will need to review the section in this book that covers searching with **Bing** (see pages 97-99). (Briefly, Boolean connectors can be used to link keywords and phrases and the default is *AND*, so leaving a space between words automatically connects your keywords/phrases with the *AND* Boolean connector.)

Our search of the phrase *"homeland security"* and the keywords (and Boolean connector) *washington OR nevada,* brought back results containing all of those keywords. Related search results are displayed on the left-hand side of the page while the organic results are displayed down the center of the page. However, the *Related Searches* result list inexplicably showed no related *washington* results.

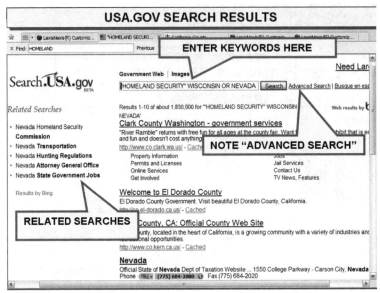

Unfortunately, the link to the *Advanced Search* was taken off the home page a number of years ago, and it is only visible after you run your search and receive results (as noted in the above illustration). In the alternative, it can be reached by visiting **Search.USA.gov** (http://www.search.usa.gov/) and clicking on its *Advanced Search* (see illustration below).

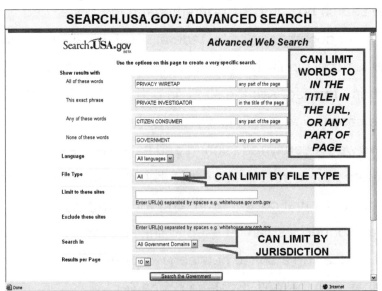

At **Search.USA.Gov**, you will then be able to construct your search in the following ways:

- Enter keywords into the following search boxes:
    - *All of these words, This exact phrase, Any of these words, None of these words*
- Limit the keywords to these places:
    - *Any Part of the Page, In the Title of the Page,* or *In the URL of the Page*
- Select the *File Format* drop-down menu to limit search results to the following formats:
    - *PDF, Excel, Word,* or *PowerPoint*
- The *Search In* drop-down menu (see illustration below) defaults to *All Government Domains*, but to limit search results to specific jurisdictions, select one of these:
    - *Federally Focused, Non-Federal* (searches all resources except federal level), *Tribal Sites, U.S. territories*, or select one specific state or territory.

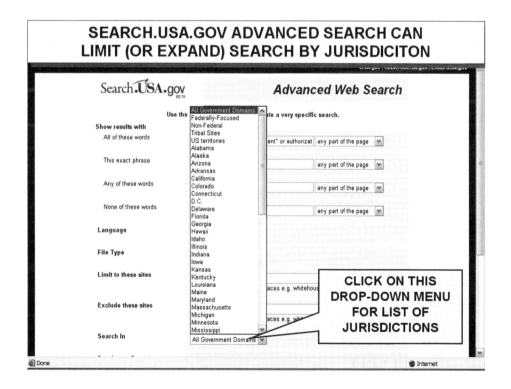

SEARCH.USA.GOV ADVANCED SEARCH CAN LIMIT (OR EXPAND) SEARCH BY JURISDICITON

While still in its infancy, keep an eye out for **Law.Gov** (http://resource.org/law.gov/index.html). Three groups, AALL, the Law Library of Congress, and Public.Resource.Org (founded by Carl Malamud), have joined forces to create **Law.Gov**, a government-wide collection of all primary legal materials of the United States <u>and</u> international governmental bodies. **Law.Gov** is intended to be a one-stop site for this information. As of the publication deadline for this book, by the admissions of its founders, **Law.Gov** is still in the "idea" phase. Shortly thereafter, in September 2010, **Law.Gov** received a $2 million grant from **Google**. We recommend you stay tuned.

There are many excellent academic portals and directories for Internet legal and government research, with most created by law schools. Academic portals are particularly useful for linking to their own state and local legal research and government Web sites; you will probably want to visit your state's law school sites first for local links. For a list of all law school Web sites, see **FindLaw** (http://stu.findlaw.com/schools/fulllist.html). Once you link to the relevant law school, you will most likely need to locate the library's page to find their list of legal research and government links.

One of the better law school Web sites for legal professionals is the **Legal Information Institute (LII)** portal created by **Cornell Law School** at http://www.law.cornell.edu. Like **FindLaw** and **Justia**, **Cornell's LII** provides links to material available from other Internet Web sites, but has also created a good deal of "added value" with its collections of searchable legal databases held on **LII's** own servers. Many of these databases and outside Web sites can be accessed by conducting a keyword search from the home page's search box or by clicking on the links found (on the home page) beneath sections labeled: *Read the law, Learn more, Popular topics, Get help, Keep up,* and *Help out*.

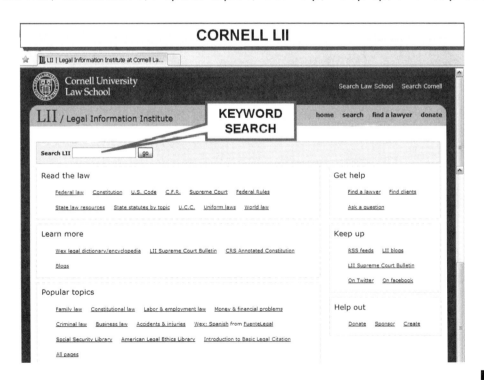

CORNELL LII

Beneath the section labled *Read the law,* there are links to the following resources, many of which are searchable databases, such as:

- *Federal law* (Among other resources, this is where you will find the searchable database of *U.S. Court of Appeals decisions* where you can search all circuit court opinions or select just one circuit to search.)

- *Constitution*

- *U.S. Code* (discussed in more detail on pages 331-332)

- *C.F.R.* (discussed in more detail on pages 333-334)

- *Supreme Court*

- *Federal Rules*

- *State law resources*

- *State statutes by topic* (see page 285)

- *U.C.C.*

- *Uniform laws*

- *World law*

Beneath the section labled *Learn more*, there are links to the following resources, some of which are searchable databases, such as:

- *Wex legal dictionary/ LII Supreme Court Bulletin*
- *CRS Annotated Constitution*
- *Blogs*

Beneath the section labled *Popular topics,* there are links to popular *Wex* articles (such as *Family Law*) and other resources, some of which are searchable databases such as:

- *American Legal Ethics Library* (see page 419)
- *Introduction to Basic Legal Citation* (see page 428)
- *Social Security Library*
- *Uniform Commercial Code*

Beneath the section labled *Get help,* there are links to various resources, including a lawyer directory (*Find a lawyer*).

To search *Wex,* link to it from the *Learn More* section of the **Cornell LII** home page. At the *Wex* home page, you can either choose to browse topics or keyword search (see next illustration).

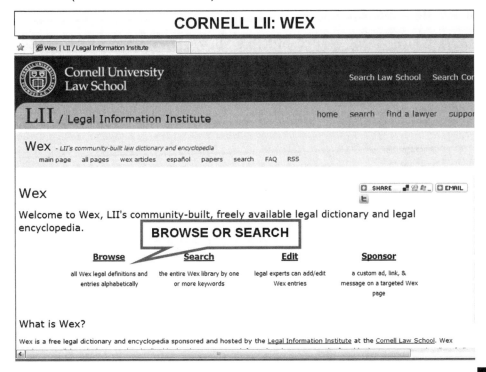

After selecting *Search* (see prior illustration), the subsequent screen displays the search box and various search options, such as searching *with all the words, with the exact phrase,* etc. In the next illustration, we are searching for the keyword *mortgage.*

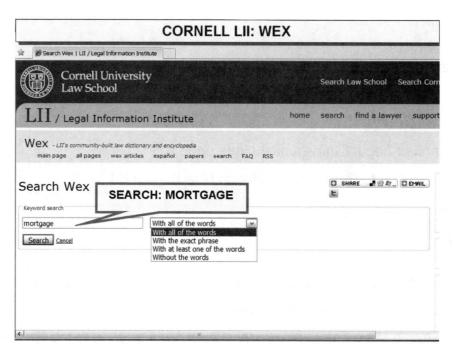

The next image illustrates **Wex's** *Overview* of the topic and a tab labeled *Resources.* (*Resources* include links to leading federal and state cases and relevant statutes and regulations.)

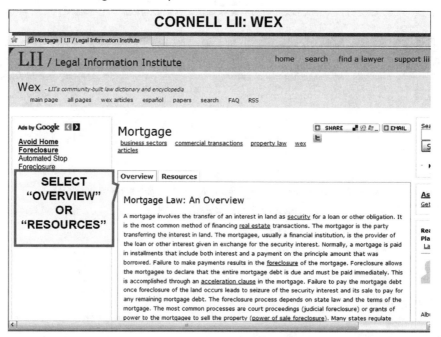

Another highlight of **LII** is its *State Statutes by Topic* database (http://topics.law.cornell.edu/wex/state_statutes), which links to all fifty states' statutes on topics ranging from *Agriculture* to *Water Code*. Not every state's statutory scheme is organized in a topical breakdown similar to this database. Thus, some topics will display a state's name with a link to the home page of that state's statutory database.

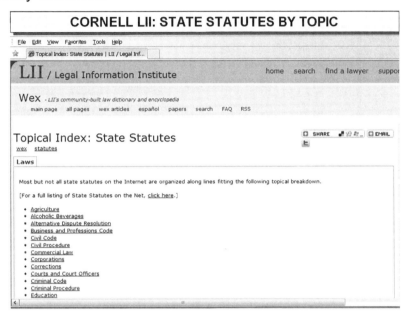

Legal Associations' Portals

Many legal associations have created Web sites that not only provide information about the association, but also provide links to law-related Web sites that relate to the association's area of focus and may be of interest to their members. Many have also added original content such as online seminars and discussion groups. While some association sites are restricted to members only, they often make some information available to the public. For example, anyone can access the list of legal research links at the **American Association for Justice** (**AAJ**) site (formerly **The Association of Trial Lawyers of America**; http://www.justice.org/cps/rde/xchg/justice/hs.xsl/485.htm). But, only **AAJ** members have access to the full archive of *Trial* magazine online (and other publications), and *AAJ Exchange* (http://www.justice.org/cps/rde/xchg/justice/hs.xsl/678.htm), an online, full-text searchable database for members to share over 155,000 documents (pleadings, verdicts and settlements, court strategies, and information about experts).

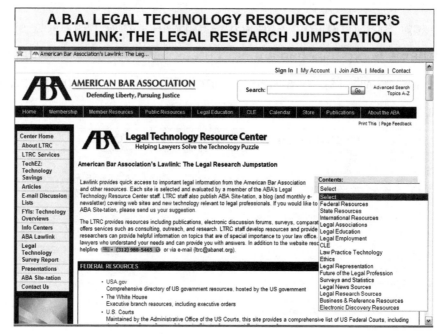

The American Bar Association (http://www.abanet.org), like AAJ, has information on its Web site available to members and non-members. Legal research links from the A.B.A. Legal Technology Resource Center's LawLink: Legal Research Jumpstation are found (free) at http://linkon.in/aMfOyT.

Check your state or local bar associations for their list of links. To find links to legal related associations and bar associations, see FindLaw's *Legal Associations & Organizations* list (http://linkon.in/ckXXLy) or the A.B.A.'s *State and Local Bar Associations* list (http://linkon.in/adcRDE).

Attorneys often need access to subject areas outside the law. For instance, an attorney may need access to scientific information for an environmental case or economic information for a damages issue.

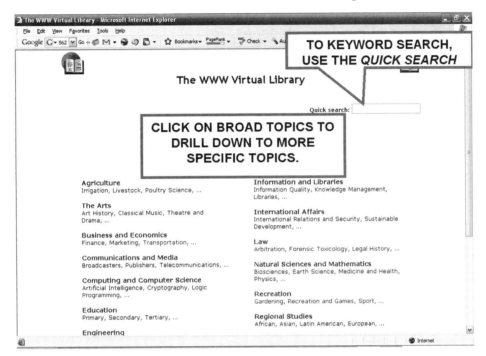

The **WWW Virtual Library** (http://vlib.org/) is the oldest directory on the Web, created by Tim Berners-Lee, who is credited with creating HTML and "inventing" the Web. It is considered one of the highest-quality directories to Web sites and is run by a group of volunteers who are experts in various fields, ranging from *Aboriginal Language* to *Zoos*. They have provided links to sites they consider to be the most useful in their respective field of expertise. Besides using the traditional "drilling down" method of a directory (clicking from broad topics to more narrow topics until you find the most relevant topic), there is also a keyword search feature (*Quick Search*) located on the top right-hand side of the home page. The keyword search feature is also referred to as *VL Search* (http://vlsearch.org/VLsearch?). In addition, an *Advanced* search feature is available from the *VL Search* page. Although the **WWW Virtual Library** is more useful for non-law links, it does have a good collection of international and comparative law links. However, it is not strong in American law, so use the legal directories and portals noted earlier in this chapter.

The **ipl2** at http://www.ipl.org (a January 2010 merger of the **Librarians' Internet Index** and the **Internet Public Library**) offers both a keyword searchable database and an annotated directory of Internet resources. Resources are divided into five categories (*Resources by Subject; Newspapers and Magazines; Special Collections Created by ipl2; For Kids;* and *For Teens*). *Resources by Subject* is organized into twelve main topics and numerous sub-topics that range from art and science to sports. *Special Collections Created by ipl2* consists of links (annotated) to various Internet resources based on topics ranging from *Deaf and Hard of Hearing* and *Associations on the Net* to *German Ready Reference.* The sites are hand-selected by librarians after they have tested and evaluated the sites for reliability. A free newsletter, highlighting new sites, can be read at http://theipl.wordpress.com/ or you can subscribe to the RSS feed at http://theipl.wordpress.com/feed/. The **ipl2** site also provides the *Ask an ipl2 Librarian* service (http://www.ipl.org/div/askus/index.html) to answer reference questions twenty-four hours a day, seven days a week (during most of the year). For other "librarian question/answer" services, see the *Human Search Engines* section on page 89.

REFDESK

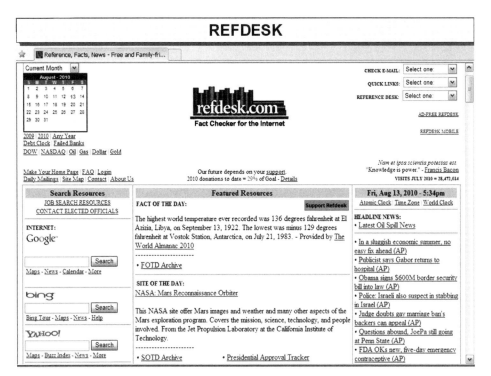

Refdesk.com (http://www.refdesk.com) is a directory created in 1995 by Bob Drudge (he is the father of Matthew Drudge, editor of the **Drudge Report**). **Refdesk.com** offers links to myriad reference sites, including general and topic-specific encyclopedias (e.g., legal, medical), dictionaries, newspapers, and calendars, calculators, and even **The Old Farmer's Almanac** site.

Chapter Twelve

FREE ONLINE CASE LAW DATABASES

This chapter will focus on some of the non-governmental Web sites that provide free online case law databases (**The Public Library of Law** (**PLoL**), **FindACase Network**, and **Google Scholar**). Other free online case law databases, which are included in various legal portals, were discussed in *Chapter Eleven* (e.g., **FindLaw**, **Justia**, **Cornell Legal Information Institute**, **LexisONE Community**, and **LexisNexis**). Free governmental online case law databases are discussed in *Chapter Fourteen*.

The Public Library of Law (PLoL): Free Case Law Database

According to the **PLoL** Web site (http://www.plol.org), **Fastcase** launched the **PLoL** "to make it easy to find the law online." Anyone can search **PLoL** for free, although registration is required to view the full text of cases. **PLoL** provides a free, full-text keyword-searchable database of case law from the following sources:

- All fifty states' Appellate and Supreme Court cases from 1997 to present
- All U.S. Supreme Court cases from 1754 to present
- All Federal Circuit Courts of Appeals cases from 1950 to present

The **PLoL** case law database does <u>not</u> include federal district cases, federal bankruptcy cases, or any other non-case law legal materials. The tabs to the right of the *Case Law* tab (*Statutes, Regulations, Court Rules, Constitutions,* and *Legal Forms*) only link to the official government Web sites where you can search those materials.

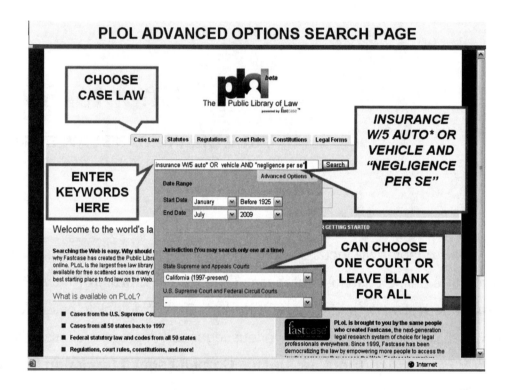

To search case law, select the *Case Law* tab and enter a citation, docket number, party name, or keywords and phrases into the search box. This will search all jurisdictions for which **PLoL** has cases. Choose the *Advanced Options* link to limit your search by a date range, a specific state's case law, a specific Federal Circuit, or the U.S. Supreme Court. (You can leave the court search boxes blank to search all courts included in the **PLoL** database.) **PLoL** only allows researchers to select one jurisdiction or all jurisdictions. **PLoL** searches can include Boolean connectors (*AND, OR, NOT*), phrase searching, wildcard characters (the asterisk), and proximity connectors (*W/N*).

PLoL also includes a link to the paid content found at **Fastcase**. (See the **Fastcase** entry beginning on page 308.)

The pay case law database, **VersusLaw**, also offers the free **FindACase Network** case law database (http://www.findacase.com). **FindACase** distinguishes itself from **PLoL** by offering free access to federal district court cases and by offering broader date coverage for most of the courts included in its database.

The following courts are included in the **FindACase** database:

- U.S. Supreme Court: 1886–present
- Federal Circuit Courts of Appeal: Date coverage varies, but some circuits go as far back as 1930.
- Federal District Courts: Date coverage varies, but some districts go as far back as 1930.
- State and D.C. Appellate Courts: Date coverage varies, but some states go as far back as 1910.

FindACase only allows you to search state and federal case law grouped by state. Grouping by states means that you can't search all state court cases together or all federal court cases together. Instead, you must select one state at a time. However, within a particular state, you can search one or multiple courts within that state.

For example, as illustrated below, after we selected *New York*, we could search one or more of the following: *New York Appellate Courts, U.S. District Courts of New York, 2nd Federal Circuit Court*, or *U.S. Supreme Court*. To search an additional state, we would have to start this process over again by picking another state from the list, then selecting the available courts in that state, etc.

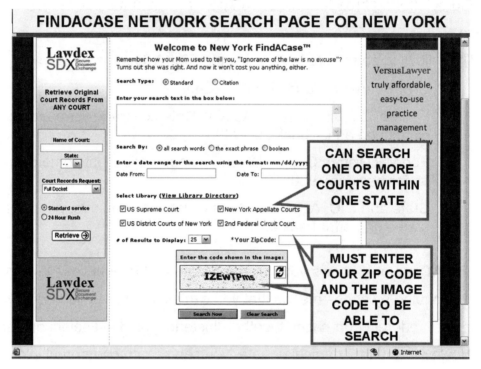

After selecting a state in which to search, **FindACase** provides two search options: *Standard* (keywords/phrases) or *Citation*. After choosing the *Standard* search, enter your keywords/phrases into the search box and then select whether to search by: *all search words*, *the exact phrase,* or *Boolean*. (There is little documentation on this site. For example, there is no indication as to whether you should use the *AND* Boolean connector or the plus sign [+] to connect words. Our test searches indicate that the plus sign does not work.) A date range can also be entered. Finally, one chooses which courts to search.

Although **FindACase** is free to search, you must enter a ZIP Code and an image code (Captcha) before conducting a search. The request for an image and ZIP Code is quite annoying for two reasons: (1) for every search you must re-enter them and (2) the image code is case sensitive (so pay attention to your upper and lower cases when typing in the text string in the image).

Late in the evening of November 17, 2009 a **Google** employee tweeted that something was new at **Google Scholar** and challenged readers to figure out what it was... One of the authors of this book, a well-known late-night type, visited **Google** *Scholar* that evening and learned that **Google** had launched a free case law database (*Legal Opinions and Journals*). It contained opinions from: all U.S. state appellate and state supreme courts back to 1950, the U.S. federal district, appellate, tax, and bankruptcy courts back to 1923, and the U.S. Supreme Court back to 1791. Also included in this database are legal journal articles. You can reach **Google Scholar** from the **Google.com** home page by selecting the *More* tab, and then selecting **Scholar** or you can use this direct URL: http://scholar.google.com/.

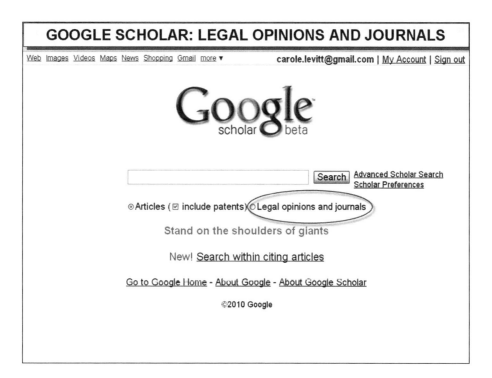

To reach the site's *Advanced Search*, click the *Advanced Search* link (to the right of the search box as displayed in the prior illustration) or directly via http://linkon.in/dxq6WC. The cases come from a variety of sources, such as **Cornell LII**, **Justia**, **Public.Resource.org**, and official court sites.

Google provides this disclaimer about using its case law database: "Legal opinions in Google Scholar are provided for informational purposes only and should not be relied on as a substitute for legal advice from a licensed lawyer. Google does not warrant that the information is complete or accurate" (http://scholar.google.com/intl/en/scholar/help.html). Disclaimers like this can even be found at official courts' Web sites where they are providing a database of their legal opinions. As with any case law research, it's imperative that you determine that you are using cases that have not been overruled or reversed (by using the citation features at **Google Scholar** (see page 299), or conducting a citation check at **KeyCite**, **Shepard's**, or other free alternatives discussed on pages 263-269.

Searching **Google** *Scholar* is similar to searching **Google.com** (as far as Boolean and proximity searching are concerned), but for **Google Scholar**-specific search tips, visit the *Advanced Scholar Search Tips* page at http://scholar.google.com/intl/en/scholar/refinesearch.html#legalrestrict.

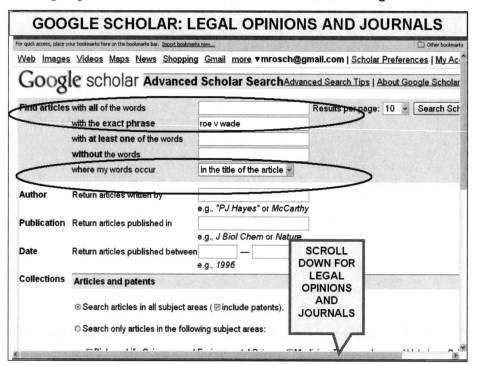

Unfortunately, the *Advanced Scholar Search Tips* page provides very little documentation about how to use the case law portion of **Google Scholar**, so we have run a number of test searches to offer searchers some guidance.

From those test searches, we learned, first of all, that you will be able to create better and more targeted searches at the **Google** *Advanced Scholar Search* page at http://scholar.google.com/advanced_scholar_search (see next illustration), where you can limit results to:

- all legal opinions and journals, but you cannot limit your search to just journals or just legal opinions

- only U.S. federal court opinions, but you cannot limit your search to just one type of federal court (such as the U.S. Supreme Court)

- any combination (one, multiple, or all) of the fifty states' court opinions (plus the database includes the District of Columbia)

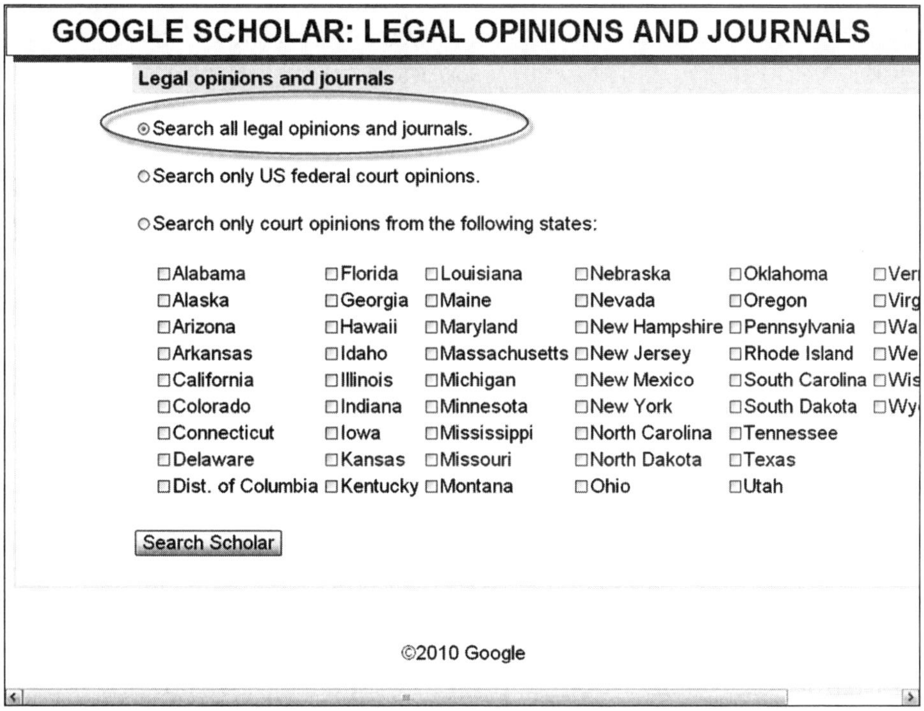

GOOGLE SCHOLAR: LEGAL OPINIONS AND JOURNALS

Another thing we learned from our test searches was how to force a citation, a party name, and a judge name search, despite the lack of dedicated "field" search boxes to conduct these types of searches:

- To force a search by citation, enter it (in Bluebook style) into the *Find articles with the exact phrase* search box on the *Advanced Scholar Search* page. (Even though a case citation is not an "article," the results will include cases.)

- To force a search by party name (see the *Roe v Wade* illustration on page 296), enter the party names (e.g., *Roe v Wade*) into the *Find articles with the exact phrase* search box, limit your results to *Search only US federal court opinions*, and from the *Find articles where my words occur* drop-down menu, select *in the title of the article* (this search will bring back cases, not articles, because you selected *Search only US federal court opinions*). This search brought back two results (the U.S. Supreme Court decision and the Federal District Court decision). Be sure to use "v" and not "versus" or "vs." If you wanted to research the case *Roe* v. *Wade* and all cases relating to that case, you would enter the two party names, *Roe* and *Wade*, into the *Find articles with all of the words* search box, click into the *Search all legal opinions and journals* radio button, and from the *Find articles where my words occur* drop-down menu, select anywhere in the article (this search will bring back both cases and articles that include the keywords *Roe* and *Wade*).

- To force a search by judge's name, first enter the judge's last name into the search box labeled *Return articles written by* and then either click into the radio button labeled *Search only US federal court opinions* or *Search only court opinions from the following states* (and then choose a state). At the U.S. Supreme Court level, this search will bring back any case in which the specified judge delivered the opinion, concurred with it, or dissented from it. If you want only cases in which a specified U.S. Supreme Court judge delivered the opinion, for example, you could try adding the word *delivered* into the *Find articles with all of the words* search box. This is very hit-or-miss. It's possible that a result (or results) could include cases in which someone else delivered the opinion but the specified judge was mentioned regarding his or her delivery of another opinion cited to in the case you are viewing.

After you have conducted a case law search, clicking any of the results on the list will display the full-text of the case (*View this case* mode).

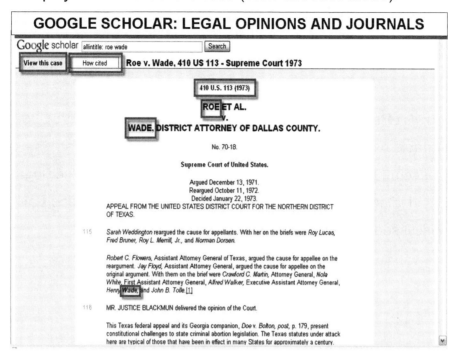

Each of your keywords will be highlighted in different colors. The *How cited* tab (to the right of the *View this case* tab), will help you conduct a rudimentary citation check of your case to ascertain whether it is still good law. The next illustration shows the *How cited* page.

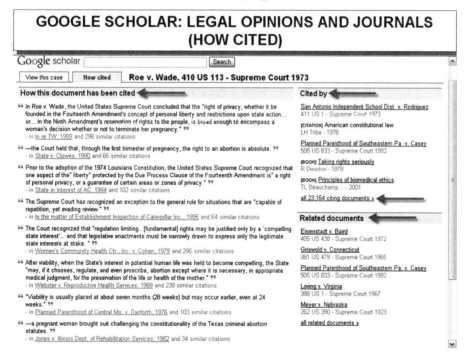

Two other free case law databases, **PreCYdent** and **AltLaw,** which we tagged as "works in progress" in the last edition of this book, are no longer in existence. **AltLaw** attributes its demise to the new **Google Scholar** case law database.

If you visit **Public.Resource.Org** (http://public.resource.org), you will not find a searchable case law database, but will instead find raw data that may eventually become the basis for a database of case law (and other legal material) for all U.S. and international law. For more information on this, see **Law.Gov**, which we discussed on page 280.

Chapter Thirteen

FREE "MEMBER BENEFIT TO LAWYERS" ONLINE LEGAL RESEARCH DATABASES: CASE LAW AND MORE

Free legal research databases, which include case law and other legal materials, are provided as a "member benefit" to lawyers whose state or local bars (or other legal professional associations) subscribe on behalf of all members. Typically you will need to enter your bar association membership number and a password to access these member benefit databases.

Forty-seven state bar associations currently provide access to this type of database. (The bar associations of California, Delaware, and Montana are the states that do not yet offer this member benefit.) The majority of states are subscribing either to **Casemaker** or **Fastcase** as a member benefit. Arkansas offers **VersusLaw**, Pennsylvania offers **InCite**, and New York offers **Loislaw** (but **Loislaw's** New York subscription only offers the most current three years for free). Visit your state or local bar association's Web site (or the Web sites of other legal associations to which you belong) to learn if they offer this member benefit.

These "member benefit to lawyers" legal research databases typically offer more material than just case law, more sophisticated search options, and broader date coverage than the free case law databases found at (1) official court Web sites (discussed in *Chapter Twelve*), (2) Web sites discussed in the next chapter, and (3) legal portals such as **FindLaw**, **Justia**, **Cornell Legal Information Institute**, **LexisONE Community**, and **LexisNexis** discussed in *Chapter Eleven*.

Casemaker: Free Member Benefit Database of Online Case Law (Plus Other Legal Materials)

Casemaker is an online legal research database subscribed to by a consortium of twenty-eight state bar associations: Alabama, Alaska, Colorado, Connecticut, Georgia, Hawaii, Idaho, Indiana, Kansas, Kentucky, Maine, Massachusetts, Michigan, Mississippi, Nebraska, New Hampshire, New Mexico, North Carolina, North Dakota, Ohio, Rhode Island, South Carolina, Texas, Utah, Vermont, Washington, and Wyoming. If your bar association is part of the consortium, visit your bar's Web site and click on the link to **Casemaker** to access its materials. In the near future, **Casemaker** plans to offer individual subscriptions (at $29.95 per month) in non-consortium states. Members of the consortium have access to all fifty states' basic *Books* as well as the entire federal library. All law students have free access to **Casemaker** (**CasemakerX**). The **Casemaker** Consortium was originally launched by the Ohio State Bar Association in 1998. In February 2008, Collexis Holdings, Inc. (a developer of search and knowledge discovery software) acquired Lawriter LLC (**Casemaker's** parent) and began upgrading the database. In 2009, Collexis sold Lawriter to SSN Holdings, Inc.

Casemaker is divided into two section: a *Federal Libraries* and *State Libraries* with each *Library* divided into *Books* (types of legal materials, such as cases, statutes, etc.).

Most **Casemaker** *State Libraries* contain the following *Books*:

- *Case Law*
- *Statutes* (or *Codes*)
- *Constitution*
- *State Court Rules*
- *Session Laws*

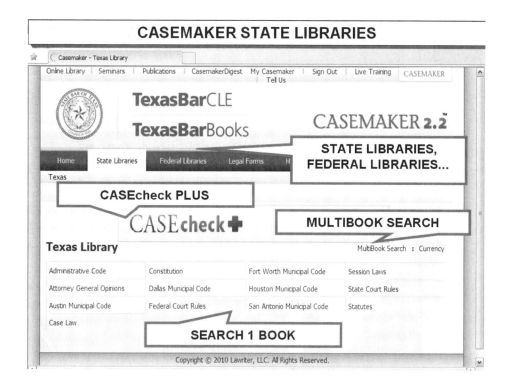

CASEMAKER STATE LIBRARIES

Some states offer additional materials, such as *Attorney General Opinions* and *Municipal Codes* (see the Texas Bar's **Casemaker** menu in the preceding illustration), or *Ethics Opinions*.

The *Federal Library* contains the following *Books*, among others:

- *Court Opinions*: *Supreme Court* (1754 to current), *Circuit Court* (1930 to current), *District Court* (1930 to current), *Bankruptcy Court* (1979 to current), and various specialty courts, such as the *Tax Court*

- *Federal Court Rules*

- *United States Code* (Users can also search the last 3 years of session laws in addition to the code.)

- *Code of Regulations* (*CFR*)

- *Public Laws*

- *Constitution*

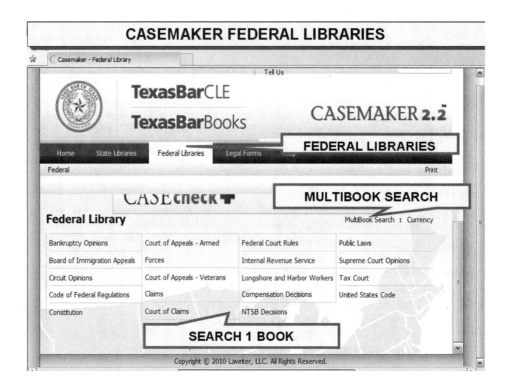

Multiple *Book*s (or all of the *Book*s) of one state can be searched together (by selecting *Multi-book Search*) or an individual *Book* can be searched separately. If you choose *State Libraries* and then *Multi-State Case Law*, you can search the case law of multiple states or all states, and new with version 2.2, you can also search Federal Courts of Appeal cases together with state cases. The only *Book* that you can multi-state search is the *Case Law Book*, so you cannot search the statutes of all states together, for example.

Multiple *Book*s or all of the *Book*s of the *Federal Libraries* can be searched together (by selecting *Federal Libraries* and then *Multi-book Search*) or an individual *Book* can be searched separately.

CASEMAKER CASE LAW SEARCH MENU

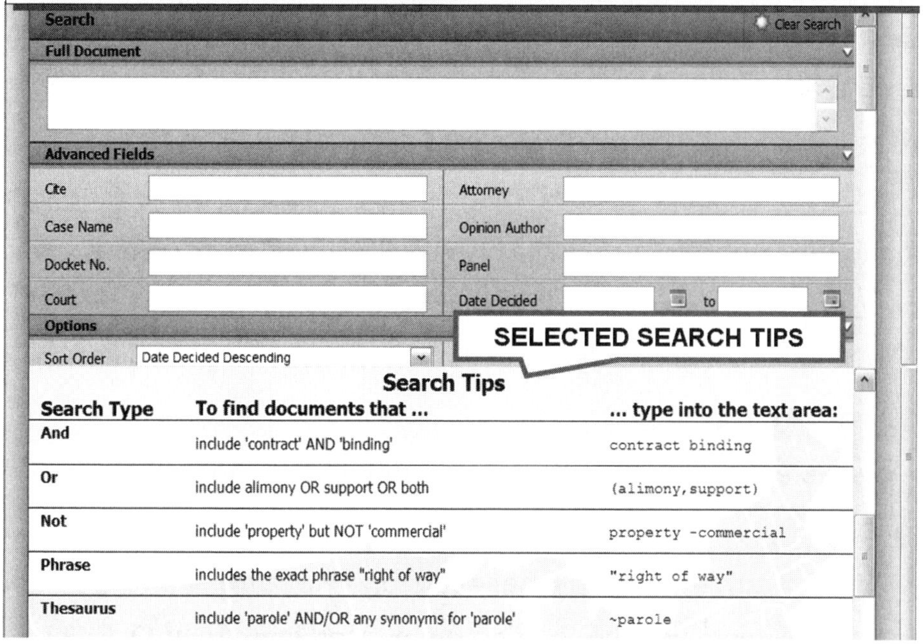

Search				Clear Search
Full Document				

Advanced Fields

Cite		Attorney	
Case Name		Opinion Author	
Docket No.		Panel	
Court		Date Decided	to

Options

Sort Order — Date Decided Descending

SELECTED SEARCH TIPS

Search Tips

Search Type	To find documents that ...	... type into the text area:
And	include 'contract' AND 'binding'	contract binding
Or	include alimony OR support OR both	(alimony,support)
Not	include 'property' but NOT 'commercial'	property -commercial
Phrase	includes the exact phrase "right of way"	"right of way"
Thesaurus	include 'parole' AND/OR any synonyms for 'parole'	~parole

Casemaker can be keyword searched, field searched, or browsed. The illustration above shows the state case law database *Search* menu (the search menu for federal case law research is similar). Field searching for cases is by *Docket Number*, *Date*, *Cite*, *Opinion Author*, *Panel*, *Case Name*, *Court*, and *Attorney*.

For keyword searching, we recommend that you read the *Search Tips* at the bottom of the *Search* page because some of their Boolean and proximity connectors may be unfamiliar to lawyers who are used to **Lexis** and **Westlaw** (and search engines, such as **Google**). For example, placing keywords in parentheses and putting a comma in between each keyword will be treated as an *OR* Boolean connector (which is completely different from searching at **Google** which requires you to merely type the word *OR* in between your keywords).

From **Casemaker's** *Search* page, you can choose to have results sorted by *Date Decided Descending*, *Date Decided Ascending*, or *Rank* (relevancy).

If you choose the *Browse* tab, it allows you to browse cases by volume and page number or to browse statutes by Title, Chapter, or Section. (The statutory databases include a *Supercode* feature to display any pending legislative changes in the law. (Note: this *Supercode* feature will disappear in the version 2.2 upgrade.)

If there are relevant articles (from ABA, ALI-ABA, or state bar association publications), they'll be displayed in a separate column, labeled *Caseknowledge*, to the right of the results list. Access to these items is fee-based and can be purchased online with a credit card.

After you select a specific result from the results list (e.g., a case), a column to the right displays **CASEcheck,** which is **Casemaker's** citator service. A list of citing cases is displayed (if there are any). When you click on one of those citing cases, you are taken to the exact page, in that case, where your cited case is mentioned.

As we are writing this book, **Casemaker** is in the midst of two major changes. First, it is rolling out a new subscription citator product (one state at a time), **CASEcheck Plus**. Like **Shepard's** and **KeyCite**, it offers editorial treatment to indicate whether a case is still good law. As of October1, 2010 the following states are included in **CASEcheck Plus**: Hawaii, Indiana, Michigan, Ohio, and Texas. A monthly subscription is $19.95 (discounted by 17% if subscribed to annually), while a twenty-four hour subscription is $4.95. Second, **Casemaker** is upgrading from its version 2.1 interface to a version 2.2 interface. Some of the new features of the version 2.2 upgrade include:

- Continuously updated Codes throughout the year (instead of the *Supercode* feature noted earlier in this section that displays any pending legislative changes in the law). Each section will display a date.
- *History* links at the end of each Code section so you can read the act.
- *Archive* links to prior Codes (In one of our searches, the section of the Code we were searching went back to 2001. Archive dates may vary.)
- You can view and print multiple sections of a Code together. (For instance, you can choose to view and print *Article 3*, which may include sections 3.1 through 3.20, instead of viewing and printing one section at a time.)
- Expanded case law database
- Dual citation (official and unofficial) and dual columns for state and regional reporters
- Linked footnotes within case law

Smartphone users can also access their (existing) **Casemaker** accounts from their Blackberry, iPhone, and Droid mobile devices. You will need to create your **Casemaker** account in advance of your first mobile use, but it is free to any **Casemaker** customer.

Casemaker also offer a separate subscription to its **CASEMAKERdigest** database (although some states, such as Texas, offer it free as a member benefit). **CASEMAKERdigest** summarizes new cases within forty-eight hours of being decided. (Note: **Casemaker** adds new cases to its main database as soon as a case is released by the courts.) **CASEMAKERdigest** can be customized to your needs by filtering results by one or more of the following: practice area (there are fifty-seven), courts, judges, and keywords. You can receive the entire **CASEMAKERdigest** as an RSS feed or you can receive a filtered **CASEMAKERdigest** (with the filters you select).

By January 2011, **Casemaker** plans on another upgrade, dubbed **CASEMAKERelite**. Here is a preview of some of its features:

- Field search boxes will be only be accessible from the *Advanced Search* page.

- Natural language searching will be added.

- More **Google**-type searches, such as *Related searches* will be added.

- For those who have a **CASEMAKERdigest** subscription, when you perform a **Casemaker** search, you will be able to read the **digest** before reading the full case

- *CASEcite* will display cases that others have clicked on (when searching the same keywords as you).

- *Copy with Reference* will allow you to highlight portions of text and print only that portion.

- *My Casemaker* will allow you to customize your page and save searches.

- *CASEtime* will allow you to track billable time.

- *CASElibra* will allow you to purchase entire practice area *Libraries* instead of just one article.

Fastcase: Free Member Benefit Database of Case Law (Plus Other Legal Materials)

As of October 2010, eighteen state-level bar associations (as well as some local and specialty bars, and a few libraries) have subscribed to **Fastcase's** free case law, statutory, and regulatory research database and offer it for free as a benefit to their members. This represents 400,000 lawyers with access to **Fastcase** as a member benefit. The following is a list of the eighteen subscribing state bar associations: Arizona, Arkansas, Florida, Illinois, Iowa, Louisiana, Maryland, Minnesota, Missouri, Nevada, New Jersey, Oklahoma, Oregon, South Dakota, Tennessee, Wisconsin, Virginia, and West Virginia. Visit your bar association's Web site or visit the list of state, local, and specialty bars (and a few libraries) at http://www.fastcase.com/barmembers/ to see if any of the associations to which you belong have contracted with **Fastcase** on your behalf.

Fastcase began as a full-text case law only database. The site later integrated statutes and regulations into its database. Because of copyright concerns, however, they only include the statutes of forty-five states and the District of Columbia. Cases and statutes must be searched separately (unlike **Casemaker** which offers its *Multi-Book Search,* where you can search cases, statutes, and other materials together, one state at a time though). **Fastcase** provides links to the official (free) statutory databases of the other five states and also to other types of free material (regulations, constitutions, and court rules). The site also provides links to other pay databases (e.g., newspaper articles, legal forms, and public records), but before paying for information from any of these resources be sure to look in this book's index to learn if there are any comparable free resources and review pages 145-146 to learn if your public library offers access to free newspaper articles.

Fastcase users can search federal and state case law together (something that **Casemaker** just began offering in 2010 with its 2.2 version) by entering their query into the *Quick Caselaw Search* box and clicking into the *All Jurisdictions* radio button. To search case law in multiple jurisdictions simultaneously, users must select the *Switch to Advanced Caselaw Search* link.

Fastcase automatically saves your last ten searches and displays them on your *Welcome* page. It also allows you to save specific cases in your *Fastcase Favorites* folder.

FASTCASE HOME PAGE

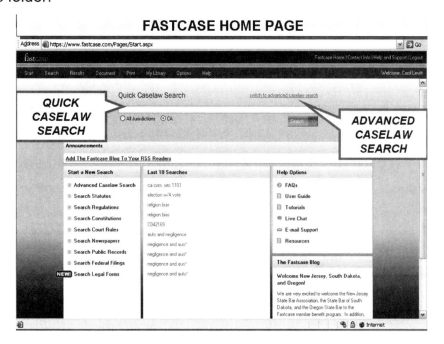

Fastcase's Federal court database contains cases from the following courts:

- United States Supreme, 1754 to present
- Circuit Courts of Appeal, 1924 to present
- Various specialized federal courts (such as the U.S. Tax Court), Dates vary

Fastcase's State court database contains cases from the following courts:

- Supreme Court, 1950 (or earlier) to present
- Courts of Appeal, 1950 (or earlier) to present

Note that some bar associations offer their members free access to **Fastcase's** Federal District Courts (1912 to present) and Federal Bankruptcy Courts (1979 to present) databases, while others leave their attorney-members to pay **Fastcase** an additonal $195 annual fee for this "Premium service." (These same courts are included as a free member benefit for all **Casemaker** participating bar associations.)

If your bar association does not offer free access to **Casemaker** or **Fastcase** (or another database), you can purchase an individual **Fastcase** subscription (https://www.fastcase.com/Corporate/Home.aspx) at the following costs:

- National Premium: $95 per month or $995 annually
- National Appellate: $65 per month or $695 annually
- There is also a twenty-four hour free trial to search through all the databases

(**Casemaker** will begin offering a similar individual subscription plan sometime in late 2010 or early 2011.)

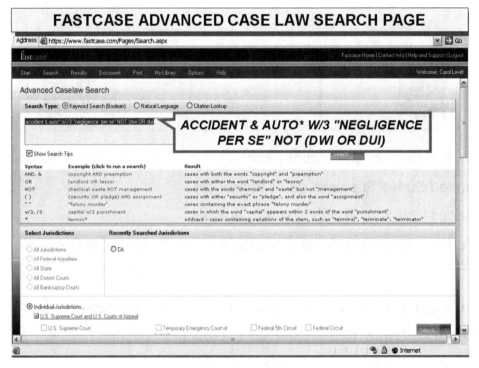

On **Fastcase's** *Advanced Caselaw Search* page, three radio buttons located above the search box allow you to select a search option: *Keyword Search (Boolean)*, *Natural Language*, and *Citation Lookup*. **Fastcase's** search interface is quite user-friendly and most attorneys will be familiar with **Fastcase's** Boolean and proximity connectors if they are **Google**, **Lexis**, or **Westlaw** searchers (although there are some slight variations). **Fastcase** does not have distinct search fields for judge, attorney, or party names, but it does have a date field.

Results can be displayed by title (case name), most relevant paragraph, or first paragraph. There are useful sorting features, such as the ability to sort results by jurisdiction. For those who prefer a visual representation of their results, there is also an interactive timeline and a citation summary.

Fastcase offers an *Authority* feature, which lists all cases that cite to the case being displayed. However, like **Casemaker**, it does not include editorial treatment (as **KeyCite** and **Shepard's** both do). On the other hand, unlike **Casemaker**, **Fastcase** offers links to **KeyCite** and **Shepard's** (for case law only), but users must pay for these services. (See the **Casemaker** section earlier in this chapter for information about its new subscription-based citator product, **CASEcheck Plus**.)

In the past year, **Fastcase** has added some useful features such as:

- *Forecite* (currently in beta) – If **Fastcase** identifies decisions that do not contain one or more of your search terms, but ascertains that they may, nonetheless, be relevant to your research topic, you will be alerted.

- *Fastcase for the iPhone/iPad* – This is a free application that allows you to search **Fastcase** for free (regardless of whether an organization to which you belong offers access as a member benefit), but you will need to register to use it.

- **Fastcase** allows for batch printing, so you can wait to print your results until after you have completed all of your searching. Whether using **Fastcase** (or **Casemaker**), you can choose to:

    - Print to Word, RTF, PDF (there is no WordPerfect choice but documents saved in RTF are viewable in Word Perfect, in addition to Word and WordPad)

    - Select dual column printing (**Fastcase** also has a single column printing option)

    - E-mail your case to yourself or someone else

Chapter Fourteen

INTERNET SITES FOR GOVERNMENTAL RESOURCES

Federal and State Government Internet Portals and Directories

The government, collectively from local to state to federal agencies, may be one of the most prolific Web publishers. To locate a government Web site, first try an educated guess by typing in an entity's full name or abbreviated name and then adding in the appropriate TLD (Top Level Domain) suffix, such as ".gov" (government entity). For example, if you need to conduct research about the White House, and you are interested only in a government site, typing "http://www.whitehouse.gov" into the browser address box will bring you to the relevant site. But don't spend too much time guessing a URL. What seems like the obvious URL may prove to be incorrect. For instance, although the URL "http://www.ussupremecourt.gov" seems to be the most obvious for the U.S. Supreme Court site, it does not lead to the court's site (the correct URL is: "http://www.supremecourt.gov").

For those who prefer not to use the "guessing game" to find governmental Web sites, you can keyword search or browse through agency names at **USA.gov** (http://www.USA.gov). It is the federal government's official portal for searching millions of federal, state, local, tribal, and territorial governmental documents on the Web. (See pages 276–279 for details.)

GPO (Government Printing Office) and GPO Access

The **GPO Government Printing Office** (http://www.gpo.gov), has been disseminating (in print), official federal governmental information from all three branches for nearly 150 years. It also offers some of its information online at **GPO Access** (http://www.gpoaccess.gov). Click on the *A–Z Resource List* at **GPO Access** for a comprehensive list of links to federal resources available on the Internet.

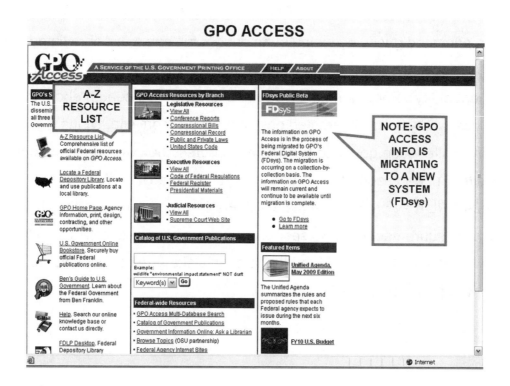

The *A–Z Resource* list (http://www.gpoaccess.gov/databases.html) is in alphabetical order, but you can also browse by branch of government by selecting the *Resources Grouped by Branch of Government* link located on the left-hand side of the page. Also on the left-hand side of the page you will find a link to *Search Across Multiple Databases*, such as the *U.S. Budget, Presidential Documents,* the *Congressional Record, Bills,* the *U.S. Code*, etc. To search multiple databases (or a single database) you can also use this direct URL: http://www.gpoaccess.gov/multidb.html. (Use the *control* key on your keyboard to select multiple databases from the list of sources.)

General **GPO Access** search tips can be found at http://www.gpoaccess.gov/help/searching.html. The following are a few of the major search tips that apply to almost all **GPO Access** databases:

- The Boolean operators *AND*, *OR*, *NOT*, and the proximity connector *ADJ* (adjacent) can be used to connect words and phrases.
- Phrases must be placed within quotation marks.
- Word roots can be searched using an asterisk (e.g., *safe** will retrieve *safe, safely,* and *safety*).

GPO ACCESS A-Z RESOURCE LIST

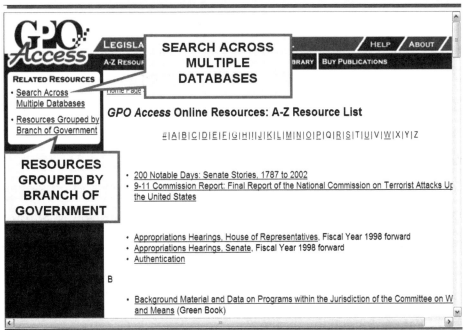

It's important to note that during 2009, **GPO Access** began migrating all of its government information to a new system: **FDsys** (Federal Digital System) at http://www.gpo.gov/fdsys/search/home.action.

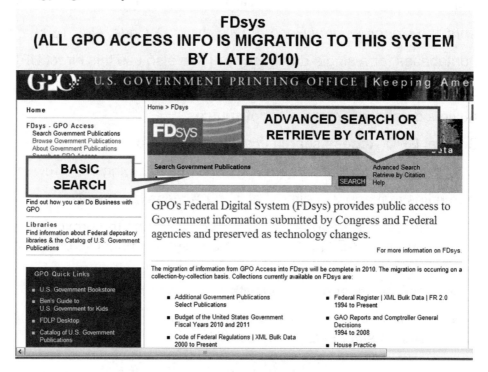

The migration is occurring on a collection-by-collection basis and was supposed to be completed by the end of 2009. This deadline was missed, but as of September 2010, the migration was nearly completed. During a transition period, the **GPO Access** system and the **FDsys** are both being maintained, so we will discuss both **FDsys** and **GPO Access** even though the only collections awaiting migration are the *9/11 Report* and the *Senate Art Book*.

FDsys's search protocol (e.g., its use of Boolean and proximity connectors and the way you can display and sort results) is the same throughout all of its collections; therefore, you only need to learn one search protocol to search any of the **FDsys** collections. Some of **FDsys's** *Proximity Search* options are more sophisticated than some of **GPO Access's**. The main difference between **FDsys** collections, however, is the *Search Criteria*. After you choose a specific collection and then click on the downward arrow to the right of *Full-Text*

Publications and Metadata, each collection will display a pop-up menu of *Search Criteria* appropriate to that collection. For example, if you choose the *U.S.C.* collection (see page 335), its *Search Criteria* would include a search by *U.S. Code Amendment* or *U.S. Code Future Amendments Title* (among others), while the *CFR* collection's search criteria (see page 353) includes different options. If you opt to search multiple collections, then you will only be able to use a limited number of search criteria (e.g. criteria that is not collection-specific).

FDsys offers a "simple" search from the home page (http://www.gpo.gov/fdsys/search/home.action) and also offers (on the home page) links to an *Advanced Search* and a *Retrieve by Citation* search. (See the preceding illustration.)

According to the documentation at **FDsys**, its simple search is similar to a "typical search engine such as Google." After you enter keywords (separated by spaces) into the search box, **FDsys** searches the metadata and full text of all collections contained in the **FDsys** database that include all of those keywords.

FDsys SIMPLE KEYWORD SEARCH

The next illustration shows how your search results are displayed, and how you can:

- re-sort results by *Collection, Date Published, Government Author, Organization, Person, Location,* or *keyword* (see the left-side column);

- search *Within Results* by clicking into the box to the right of the search box. This allows you to enter one or more keywords and re-run your search within your original search results to narrow down your search further;

- sort by: *Relevance, Date (New to Old* or *Old to New),* or *Alphabetically (Z to A or A to Z).*

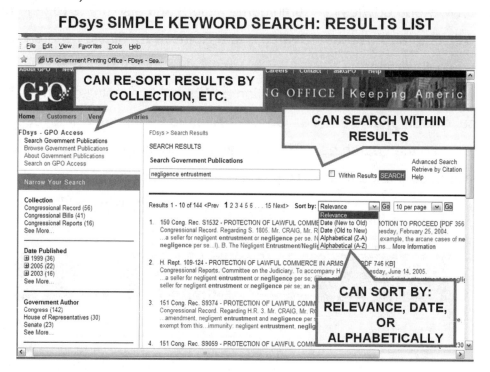

If you want to use Boolean searching (and other criteria), use the *Advanced Search* page (http://www.gpo.gov/fdsys/search/advanced/advsearchpage.action), as displayed in the next illustration. We will highlight some of the search features available at the *Advanced Search* page, but for even more detailed information and examples, see the **FDsys** *Help* page (http://www.gpo.gov/help/index.html#simple_search.htm).

FDsys uses the same Boolean connectors (*AND, OR, NOT*, -) as **Google** and most other major search engines. The *NOT* and minus sign (-) are interchangeable. Boolean connectors are case insensitive. While you can type the Boolean connector *AND* between each keyword, leaving a space between words will have the same effect.

In addition, **FDsys** allows for the following types of searches:

- *Phrase* (surround a phrase with quotation marks)
- *Proximity connectors* (*near/#, adj, before/#*).
  - *adj* specifies that one word is adjacent to another
  - *before/#* specifies that the first word is within the number of words, which you select, of the second word and the first word must precede the second word (e.g., *handgun before/3 protection*)
  - *near/#* specifies that the first word is within the number of words, which you select, of the second word and in any order (e.g., *handgun near/10 protection*)
- *Field operators*, which allow you to restrict your keywords to specific metadata fields (parts of a document), such as:
  - *Congress Member* Field. To search by this field, enter your search this way – *member:mcconnell*
  - *President* Field: To search by this field, enter your search this way — *president:clinton*
- *Wildcards*, which are indicated by:
  - the question mark symbol (?) to replace one character before, within, or, after a search term
  - the asterisk symbol (*) to replace one or more characters before, within, or, after a search term. Typing *int**city* into the search box indicates a search for any word that begins with *int*, is followed by any two characters, and then ends with *city*. The search results might include the words *intercity* or *intracity*, or both words.
    - *Parentheses,* which should be used when creating complex searches such as those where you use multiple proximity connectors and/or multiple field operators. The following is an example — *(congressional OR executive) AND hearing AND (member:mcconnell)*

FDsys ADVANCED SEARCH

```
File  Edit  View  Favorites  Tools  Help
☆  📄 US Government Printing Office - FDsys - Adv...
```

Publication Date:
If publication date is not available, search is performed on date of submission into FDsys.

[All Dates ▼]   **CAN LIMIT BY DATES**

SEARCH ALL COLLECTIONS OR ADD OR REMOVE ONE OR MORE

Collections:

Available Collections

Additional Government Publications
Budget of the United States Government
Code of Federal Regulations
Compilation of Presidential Documents
Congressional Bills
Congressional Calendars
Congressional Committee Prints
Congressional Directory
Congressional Documents
Congressional Hearings
Congressional Record
Congressional Record Bound
Congressional Record Index
Congressional Reports
Economic Indicators

[Add >>]
[<< Remove]

Selected Collections

All Collections

SEARCH IN: FULL-TEXT OR USE DROP-DOWN MENU FOR OTHER CRITERIA

ENTER KEYWORDS HERE

Search in:

[Full-Text of Publications and Metadata ▼] for [_____]

Add more search criteria (5 max)   **ADD MORE SEARCH CRITERIA**

On the *Advanced Search* page you can also:

- limit the *Publication Date* of documents retrieved in results

- broaden the *Publication Date* by selecting *All Dates*

- limit the search to one (or multiple) collections from the *Available Collection* drop-down menu

- broaden the search by selecting *All Collections* from the *Selected Collections* box

- conduct a broad keyword search by selecting *Full Text of Publications and Metadata* from the *Search In* drop-down menu

- conduct a narrower keyword search by selecting *Branch, Category, Citation, Government Author, Sudoc Class Number,* or *Title* from the *Search In* drop-down menu.

- narrow your search by selecting the *Add More Search Criteria* (up to five) listed at the bottom of the page

Those who prefer to search by a known citation should choose the *Retrieve by Citation* link from the **FDsys** home page (see the first illustration in this section; page 316). From the *Retrieve by Citation* page, you must first choose a collection. For example, in the next illustration, we chose the *Code of Federal Regulations* collection.

FDsys: RETRIEVE BY CITATION

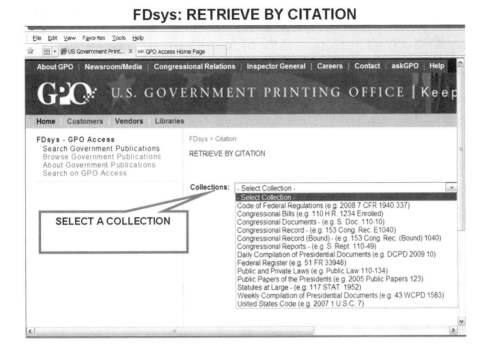

After we chose the *Code of Federal Regulations* collection, the search menu that is appropriate for searching that particular collection is displayed (see the next illustration).

FDsys: RETRIEVE BY CITATION FROM THE CODE OF FEDERAL REGULATIONS COLLECTION

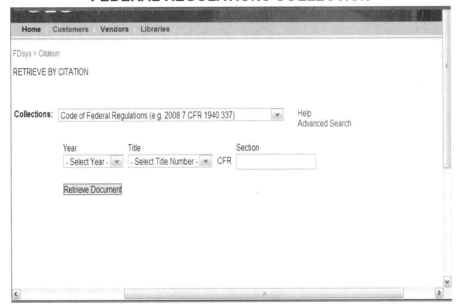

Academic Portals and Directories That Link to U.S. Federal and State Governmental Sites

There are many excellent academic portals and directories that link to U.S. government sites (and foreign government sites, and international organizations), such as the **University of Michigan (UM) Government Resources on the Web** site (http://www.lib.umich.edu/govdocs/govweb.html). For other academic portals and directories that link to governmental sites, see pages 281-285.

From newly introduced or recently signed bills, to bills that never made it out of committee, or a section of the *United States Code (U.S.C),* **GPO Access** (http://www.gpoaccess.gov/legislative.html*),* **FDsys** (http://www.gpo.gov/fdsys/search/advanced/advsearchpage.action), and the **Library of Congress's Thomas** site (http://thomas.loc.gov) all hold the key to tracking the federal legislative process.

FDsys FEDERAL STATUTORY RESEARCH

To access and keyword search the *U.S. Constitution* visit **GPO Access** (http://www.gpoaccess.gov/constitution/index.html; see page 315 for details). You can also use the preceding URL to read the *Declaration of Independence* by clicking on the *U.S. Constitution With the Declaration of Independence* link (to keyword search the *Declaration*, use your browser's *Find* function — *control f).*

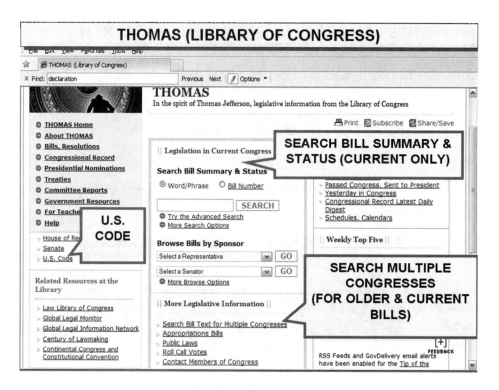

Another useful government site for statutory research is the **Library of Congress Thomas** site (http://thomas.loc.gov), with detailed information about bills and a bill's legislative history. It also has a link to The Office of the Law Revision Counsel of the U.S. House of Representatives' *U.S. Code* database. (See pages 329–330 for details.)

GPO Seal of Authenticity/Digital Signatures

Many **GPO** documents, such as *Bills*, *Public and Private Laws*, and the *Budget* (http://www.gpoaccess.gov/authentication/index.html) are now being authenticated by **GPO**. The **GPO** Web site states that, "To help meet the challenge of the digital age, **GPO** has begun implementing digital signatures to certain electronic documents on **GPO** Access that not only establish **GPO** as the trusted information disseminator, but also provide the assurance that an electronic document has not been altered since **GPO** disseminated it… A digital signature, viewed through the **GPO** Seal of Authenticity, verifies document integrity and authenticity on **GPO** online Federal documents…" (http://www.gpoaccess.gov/authentication/index.html).

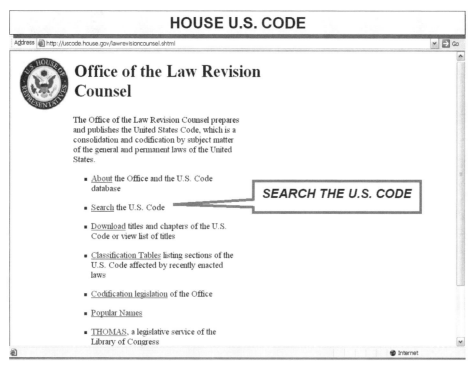

The **GPO Access** (http://www.gpoaccess.gov/uscode/index.html), **FDsys** (http://www.gpo.gov/fdsys/search/advanced/advsearchpage.action), and the **House of Representatives' Office of the Law Revision Counsel** sites (http://uscode.house.gov/search/criteria.shtml) all offer a free online version of the *U.S.C.* (in addition to other legislative material). While it lacks much of the legislative material that the three preceding sites contain, **Cornell Law School's LII** site (http://www.law.cornell.edu/), offers a searchable database of the *U.S.C.* at http://www4.law.cornell.edu/uscode (see pages 331–334 for details). **Cornell** also offers a searchable database of the *Constitution* (http://topics.law.cornell.edu/constitution) and provides links to state and foreign statutes and codes.

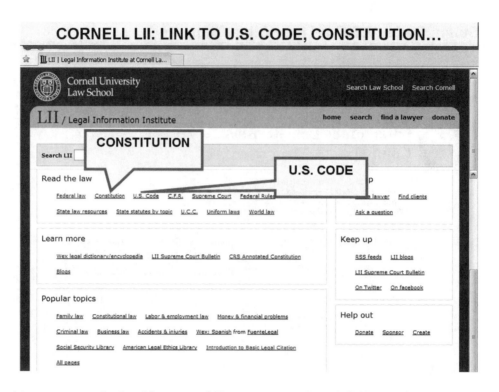

However, only the **House of Representatives' Office of the Law Revision Counsel** <u>print</u> version of the *U.S.C.* is the "official" version (published every six years). All three Web sites use the **House** version of the *U.S.C.* to create their online searchable databases and although it may seem redundant to have three databases, each is unique in terms of its search and updating features, and also dates of coverage. Thus, deciding which database to search will change from time to time, depending on your needs.

If a researcher wants to use the most up-to-date *U.S.C.*, the **FDsys** version is actually a better choice than the **House's**. In addition to being as current as the **House's**, (even though **FDsys** provides no documentation about the currency of its *U.S.C.* collection, our test searches show it is), it is easier to use (see pages 335-336).

According to the **House** *U.S.C.* site (http://uscode.house.gov/about/info.shtml), as of August 16, 2010, Titles 1 through 41 and the Table of Popular Names are based on Supplement III of the 2006 edition of the Code (published on February 1, 2010 and containing laws up to January 5, 2010). Titles 42 through 50 Appendix and tables I-VI are based on Supplement II of the 2006 edition (published on January 5, 2009). The Organic

Laws (e.g., the Constitution) are based on the 2006 edition (published on January 3, 2007) of the Code. In the top-right corner of every section of the **House's** version of the *U.S.C.* will be a date that shows when that section was enacted. Thus, there is a gap from January 5, 2010 until the current date (e.g., the date on which you're searching). To close this gap, you will need to search the *Public Laws and Private Laws*. We recommend using **FDsys's** version (see page 345 for details). **Cornell** has an update feature for their *U.S.C.* database (discussed on page 332).

The **Cornell** site states its *U.S.C.* is twenty-four hours behind the **House's** *U.S.C.* but does not make any guarantees about keeping that level of currency. The **GPO Access's** *U.S.C.* is the least current; it covers only laws in effect as of January 3, 2007.

For a researcher who wants to conduct a retrospective *U.S.C.* search, the **House** site is the answer because it goes back to the 1988 Edition. **Cornell** only has the current version of the *U.S.C.*, and **FDsys** and **GPO Access** both go back to 1994 (see pages 336 and 337, respectively).

For a researcher who prefers to jump back and forth between sections (offering the look and feel of a book), the **House** or **Cornell** versions will be the best choices.

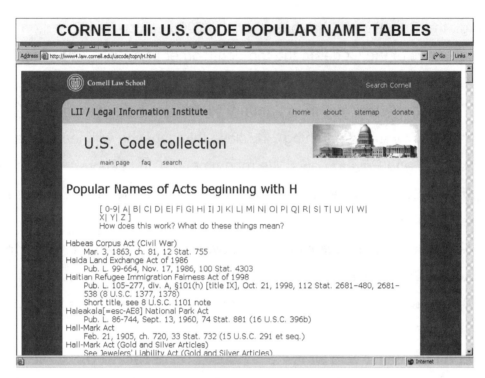

If a researcher only knew the "popular" name of an Act, the best choices for those who prefer to browse through lists would be **Cornell's** *Popular Names of Act* feature (http://www.law.cornell.edu/uscode/topn/) or the **House's** *Popular Name Tool* (http://uscode.house.gov/popularnames/popularnames.htm). For those who prefer to keyword search, the best choices would be **GPO Access**, which offers a *Popular Name* keyword search at its *U.S.C.* database (see http://www.gpoaccess.gov/uscode/tips.html for an example) and **FDsys** (choose the *Short Title* search).

HOUSE OF REPRESENTATIVES OFFICE OF THE LAW
REVISION COUNSEL'S U.S. CODE

The **House's** *U.S.C.* database
(http://uscode.house.gov/search/criteria.shtml) can be searched by *Search Word(s),* which includes phrases, placed in <u>single</u> quotation marks, and topics. Researchers can also search by *Title, Section*, etc., or a combination of any of the criteria displayed above. Boolean connectors (*AND, OR, NOT*) and proximity connectors (*near/, adjacent, w/*) may be employed to refine the search as illustrated above. Instead of conducting a keyword search of the entire *U.S.C.,* keywords can be limited to a specific portion of the *U.S.C.,* such as to a specific *Titlc* (as illustrated above where the number *6* was entered into the *Title* search box).

A "citation" search can be conducted by leaving the keyword search box empty and filling in any of the search boxes that relate to a portion of a *U.S.C.* citation (e.g., *Title, Section*, or *Part*).

The **House's** *U.S.C.* site offers various types of wildcard searches. A question mark, an asterisk, and a dollar sign symbol are used to indicate the various types of wildcard searches. For example, each question mark wildcard symbol represents one character. Typing *int??city* into the search box indicates a search for any word that begins with *int,* is followed by any two characters, and then ends with *city*. The search results might include the words *intercity* or *intracity*, or both words. An asterisk wildcard indicates an unlimited number of characters. For example, a search for *child** would return search results that include *child, child's, children, childish*, etc. A dollar sign represents one or zero characters. For example, searching mari$uana will retrieve both marijuana and marihuana.

A *Topic* search allows one to enter (into the keyword search box) a word, such as *grape,* to locate all code sections about grapes — even if the word *grape* is not used. For example, a topic search for *grape* might also find code sections about *wine.*

Some other useful features of the **House** site include:
(1) portions of the code that can be downloaded (by *Title*, *Section*, etc.); (2) various classification tables to help researchers find sections of the code that have been recently affected by newly enacted laws or to translate specific citations to *Public Laws* and *Statutes At Large* into their current *U.S.C.* citation; and (3) a search to find sections containing references to a specific title and section (although this is a very imprecise type of search). For more sample searches, see http://uscode.house.gov/search/help/uschelp.shtml).

At the **Cornell LII** *U.S.C.* home page, there are various searching and browsing options (http://www.law.cornell.edu/uscode/). The illustration below shows how a researcher can browse a numerical list of *Titles* or an alphabetical list of *Popular Names,* perform a citation search by *Title* and *Section,* or perform a *Keyword* search of all *Titles* of the *U.S.C.* Another search (not readily apparent) is a *Keyword* search of a specific *Title.* To perform this search, you would first click on the *Listing of all Titles* link, select a specific *Title*, and then enter keywords into the search box located on the left-hand side of the page.

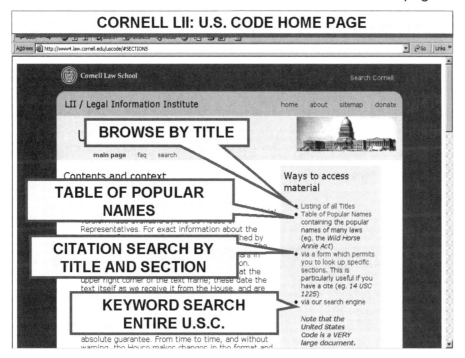

Cornell's *U.S.C.* database does not offer as sophisticated Boolean and proximity searching as the **House** or **FDsys** sites do. To keyword search Cornell's *U.S.C.* database, use the Boolean connectors *AND, OR, NOT* (*AND* is the default, so there is no need to type it in — simply leave spaces between words). Phrase searching is allowed (surround phrases by quotation marks). The asterisk (*) acts as a wildcard when placed at the end of a keyword to stem that root (e.g., a search for *safe** will return results that include *safe*, *safety*, and *safely*).

After you select a *Chapter* or *Section* of a *Title*, click the *How Current is This* link to update it (see the illustration below).

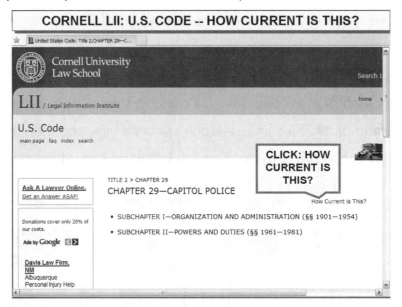

Clicking on the link displays the **House's** *Classification Tables* where you can learn about recent changes to the *Code* (see illustration below).

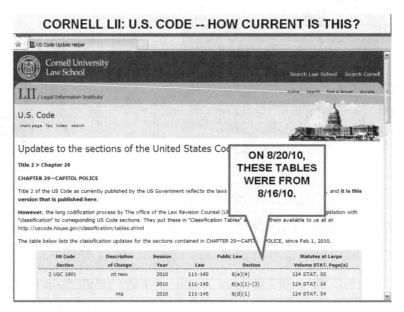

An empty *Classification Table* indicates that there is no relevant change to the *U.S.C.* section that is displayed. The *Classification Table* shown in the above illustration was taken from the most current (at the time) **House** *Classification Table.* (August 2010).

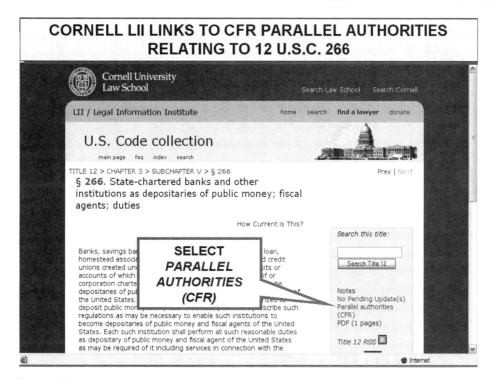

One of the most useful features of **Cornell's LII** *U.S.C.* database (http://www.law.cornell.edu/uscode/) is the ability to automatically link to the rules and regulations in the *CFR* that relate to the *U.S.C.* section being viewed. This feature is activated by clicking on the *Parallel Authorities* link on the right side of the screen (see preceding illustration). The next screen that appears (see the next illustration) shows whether there are *CFR Parallel Authorities*. If there are parallel authorities, clicking on their links takes you to the **e-CFR** database located on the **GPO Access** site (see page 352 for a complete discussion of the **e-CFR** database).

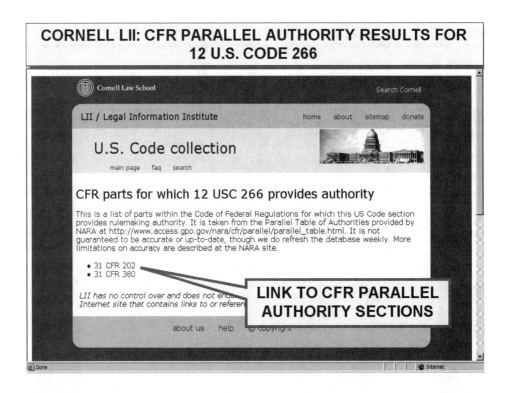

CORNELL LII: CFR PARALLEL AUTHORITY RESULTS FOR 12 U.S. CODE 266

At the **GPO Access** site, the relevant CFR sections are then displayed. In the illustration below, 31 CFR 202 is displayed (the parallel authority to Title 12, Section 266 of the **U.S. Code** shown above). Note that the **U.S. Code** and **CFR** parallel authority title and section numbers do not necessarily match up, as shown in the above illustration, but they are, nevertheless, related.

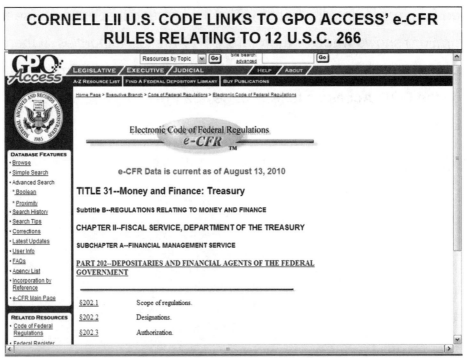

CORNELL LII U.S. CODE LINKS TO GPO ACCESS' e-CFR RULES RELATING TO 12 U.S.C. 266

The *U.S.C.* collection has recently migrated to **FDsys** (http://www.gpo.gov/fdsys/search/advanced/advsearchpage.action), but it still also exists on the **GPO Access** site (see page 337). As noted earlier, the main difference between various **FDsys** collections is their *Search Criteria*. For example, after you choose the *U.S.C.* collection and click the downward arrow to the right of *Full-Text Publications and Metadata,* you are offered *U.S.C.* collection-*specific Search Criteria*. Also, as noted earlier in this chapter, all **FDsys** collections follow the same search protocol, so be sure to review the search protocol discussed on pages 316-321.

FDsys U.S. CODE

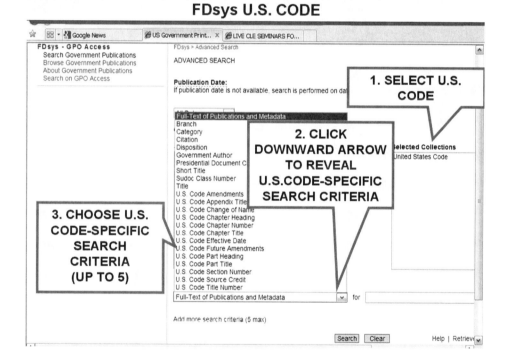

Down the middle of our search results page (see next illustration), there are links to several versions of the full-text of U.S. Code sections dealing with our search (*"water pollution"*) and a link to *Show only recent editions.* We can refine our search by clicking on links in the left-hand column, such as *Government Author, Organization*, and *Date Published* (which shows that the *U.S. Code* collection, at least for this section, goes back to 2006). To update the *U.S.C.,* see page 345. In our test searches of sections that should go back to 1995, sometimes the 1995 version appeared and sometimes it didn't. Since **FDsys** is still in beta, this is not a total surprise, but is disconcerting, nevertheless. It might be best to cross check your results at the **GPO Access** site.

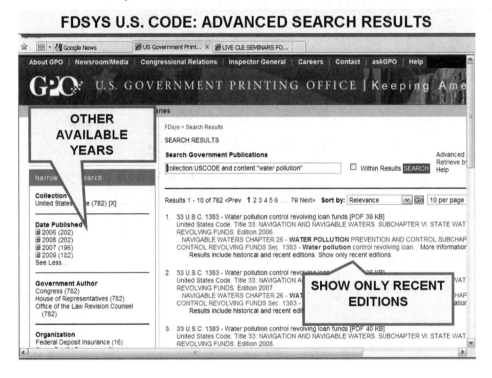

It is unclear whether this database will eventually disappear oncethe migration to **FDsys** is completed, so we will continue to include it in this edition, especially since its date coverage goes further back than **FDsys's** *U.S.C.* collection.

GPO ACCESS: U.S. CODE

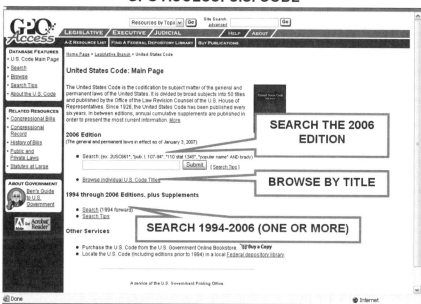

On the **GPO Access** *U.S.C.* site (http://www.gpoaccess.gov/uscode/index.html), a search box is provided for keyword and phrase searching the most current *U.S.C.* To search the 1994 or 2000 versions (and their supplements), visit http://www.gpoaccess.gov/uscode/search.html. To browse the *U.S.C.* in Title order, see http://www.gpoaccess.gov/uscode/browse.html.

For general **GPO Access** search tips, see page 314-315. However, to learn how to create *U.S.C.*-specific searches, click on the *Search Tips* link at the *U.S.C.* site (or visit http://www.gpoaccess.gov/uscode/tips.html). Illustrations on that page show how to search by: (1) *U.S. Code Citation* (e.g., to retrieve a section: *42USC1204,* or to retrieve a subsection: *2USC661**); (2) *Popular Name* (e.g., "*popular name*" AND *brady*); (3) *Public Law Number* (e.g., "*pub. l. 104–45*"); and (4) *Statutes at Large Citation* (e.g., "*110 stat 1345*").

Researching Legislative/Congressional Materials (Public Laws, Bills, Resolutions, Hearings, etc.)

Searchable databases of legislative/congressional materials (other than the U.S. Code discussed above), such as public laws, bills, resolutions, hearings, congressional reports, and committee reports can be found at three governmental sites (which we will describe individually in the upcoming sections).

Legislative/congressional materials are valuable to researchers for the following reasons:

- to track a current bill as it is going through the legislative process
- to discern the legislative intent of a bill
- to conduct historical research about a bill that was never passed (and, thus, would not be contained in a *Public Law* database or the *U.S.C.*)
- to read a public law in its entirety (instead of trying to piece it together once it has been scattered throughout various sections of the *U.S.C.*)

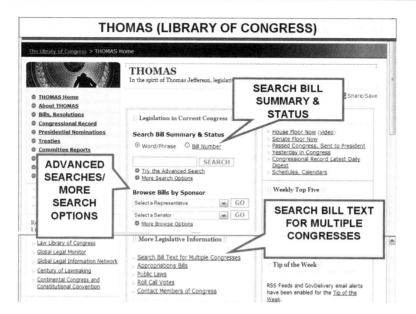

The **Library of Congress's Thomas** site (http://thomas.loc.gov) offers various databases, such as:

- *Bills, Resolutions:* This database (see the left-hand column of the preceding illustration) contains current and older bills back to 1989 and is full-text searchable by *Keywords and Phrases* (limited to *Exact Match Only* or expanded to *Include Variants*). It can also be browsed by *Bill Number, Popular and Short Titles, Public Laws, Private Laws, Vetoed Bills,* and *Sponsor Summaries.*

  - You can choose to search the bills and resolutions one Congress at a time (http://thomas.loc.gov/home/c111query.html; see below)

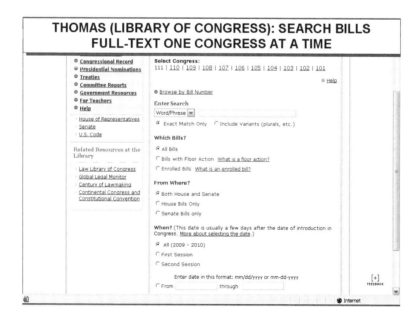

- Alternatively, you can also choose to search the bills and resolutions from multiple Congresses (http://thomas.loc.gov/home/multicongress/multicongress.html; see below)

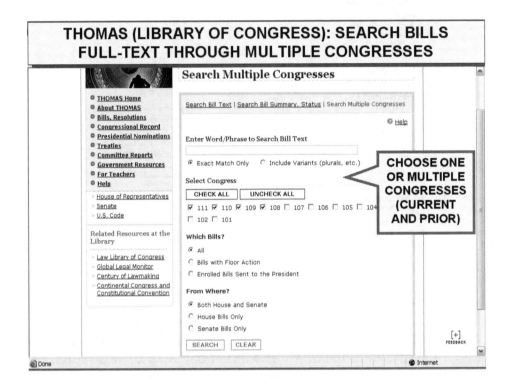

THOMAS (LIBRARY OF CONGRESS): SEARCH BILLS FULL-TEXT THROUGH MULTIPLE CONGRESSES

- *Bill Summary and Status* available from the home page of **Thomas** (http://thomas.loc.gov/; see below) goes back to 1973, while the full-text database noted above goes back only to 1989. It can be searched by *Keywords and Phrases* or by *Bill Number*. There is also an *Advanced Search* option at http://thomas.loc.gov/bss/, where one can search by *Keywords and Phrases* (which can be limited to *Exact Match Only* or expanded to *Include Variants*), *House or Senate Members, Committee, Stage in Legislative Process, Date of Introduction, Type of Legislation,* and *Standard Subject Term.*

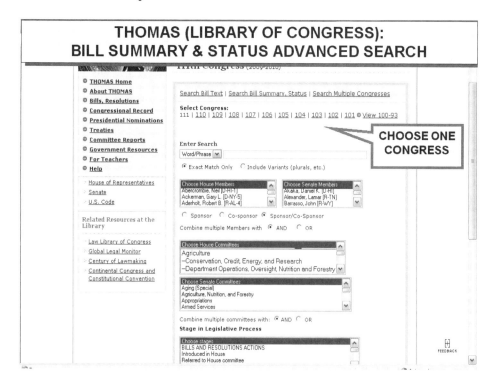

- *Congressional Record* (http://thomas.loc.gov/home/r111query.html) goes back to 1989 and is searchable by *Keywords, Phrases, Date Received or Session, Member of Congress,* and *Section of Congressional Record.*

- *Committee Reports* (http://thomas.loc.gov/cp111/cp111query.html) goes back to 1995, is searchable by *Keywords* and *Phrases, Report Number, Committees,* or *Date Available Online.* The reports can also be browsed by selecting *House, Senate, Conference,* or *Joint.*

- *Public Laws and Private Laws* (http://thomas.loc.gov/home/LegislativeData.php?&n=PublicLaws&c=111 and http://thomas.loc.gov/bss/d111/d111prlaws.html) cannot be keyword searched. Instead, the only option is to browse the laws in numeric order. However, the database goes back to 1973, which is much further back in time than the **GPO Access's** *Public and Private Laws* database (discussed later in this chapter).

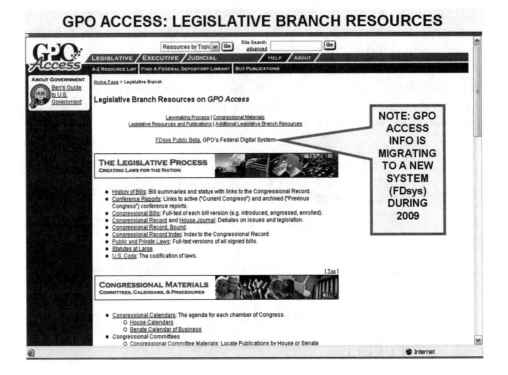

While legislative information has migrated from **GPO Access's Legislative** site (http://www.gpoaccess.gov/legislative.html) to the new **FDsys** site (http://www.gpo.gov/fdsys/search/home.action), as long as it is still available at both sites we will explain how to use both sites. As noted on pages 314-315, most of the **GPO Access Legislative** databases can be searched in a similar fashion so please review the search tips on those pages.

However, some of the **GPO Access** databases have additional search options specific only to their database, and we make note of those options as we discuss each one of the **GPO Access** databases that follow.

- *Public and Private Laws* (http://www.gpoaccess.gov/plaws/index.html: The *Laws* can be searched by *Keywords, Phrases, U.S.C. Citation, Statutes at Large Citation, Bill Number, or Public Law Number* back to 1995 (http://www.gpoaccess.gov/plaws/search.html). All of the above searches, except for the *Keyword* and *Subject* searches, must be placed in quotation marks, as illustrated on the *Public and Private Laws'* search page (http://www.gpoaccess.gov/plaws/search.html). For more detailed sample searches, see http://linkon.in/d2vKpN. *Laws* can also be browsed by number, one congress at a time (http://www.gpoaccess.gov/plaws/browse.html). Beginning with the 110th Congress, the *Public and Private Laws* on **GPO Access** have been digitally signed and certified (see page 324).

- *Congressional Bills*: Current bills can be searched at the home page (http://www.gpoaccess.gov/bills/index.html) and earlier bills (back to 1993) can be searched through one or <u>multiple</u> Congresses. at http://www.gpoaccess.gov/bills/search.html. Full-text search options are by *Bill Number, Subject*, and *Keywords* or *phrases*. (See search tips at http://linkon.in/bBUSqI for complete explanations of how to search and sample searches.) *Bills* can also be browsed (back to 1993) in numerical order (http://linkon.in/bjMSO0). Bills for the 111th and 110th Congress have been digitally signed and certified (see page 324).

- *History of Bills* (http://www.gpoaccess.gov/hob/search.html): This database differs from the above *Congressional Bills* database in three ways: (1) it only includes summaries of the bills (and their histories), (2) it goes back further in time (to 1983), and (3) it provides more search options. Like the *Congressional Bills* database, it can also be searched through multiple Congresses. See http://www.gpoaccess.gov/hob/tips.html for complete explanations of how to search and for sample searches.

- *Congressional Reports* (also referred to as *Committee Reports*): *Reports* can be searched back to 1995 either by *Keywords* and *Phrases* (see pages 314-315), *Congress, Type of Report, Subject, Report Number, Executive Report and Corresponding Treaty Document*, or *Bill Number* (http://www.gpoaccess.gov/serialset/creports/index.html). *Reports* can be searched through multiple Congresses at http://www.gpoaccess.gov/serialset/creports/search.html. For complete explanations of how to search and for sample searches, see http://www.gpoaccess.gov/serialset/creports/tips.html.

- *Conference Reports* for the current Congress can be browsed at http://www.conferencereport.gpoaccess.gov/ and archived *Reports* for two Congresses preceding the current Congress can be browsed at http://www.gpoaccess.gov/confrpts/browse.html.

- The current *Congressional Record* can be searched at its home page (http://www.gpoaccess.gov/crecord/index.html) by entering criteria into the *Quick Search* box. To search with *Keywords* and *Phrases*, pages 314-315. To conduct *Congressional Record*-specific searches, select the *Search Tips* link, (http://www.gpoaccess.gov/crecord/tips.html) to learn how to search by *Subject, Volume Number, Section, Issue, Issue Date, Page Number, Bill Number, Member of Congress,* and *Roll-call Vote Number.*

  - Earlier *Congressional Records* can be "simple" searched through multiple congresses back to 1994 at http://www.gpoaccess.gov/crecord/search.html. The same search tips and sample searches noted above for the current *CR Quick Search* also apply to the *Simple Search.*

  - Earlier *Congressional Records* can be *Advanced Searched* through multiple Congresses at http://www.gpoaccess.gov/crecord/advanced.html, but only back to 1995. The reason this is referred to as an *Advanced Search* is (probably) because the page offers multiple search boxes to enter information into, but these are the same choices one can enter into the single search box found at both the *Simple Search* page and the current *Congressional Record Quick Search* page. Our advice is to use the *Simple Search* only if one needs to search the 1994 *CR*.

  - The *Congressional Record* can be browsed (http://www.gpoaccess.gov/crecord/index.html) a variety of ways (e.g., *Page Number, Day of Session.*). The date coverage varies, depending on the browse feature chosen.

- *Statutes At Large* can be searched by *Statutes At Large Citation, Public Law Number, Subject, U.S. Code Citation, Proclamation Number, Concurrent Resolution Citation, Popular Name,* and *Bill Number* (http://www.gpoaccess.gov/statutes/index.html). See http://www.gpoaccess.gov/statutes/tips.html for search tips. *Statutes At Large* can also be browsed (http://www.gpoaccess.gov/statutes/browse.html).

  NOTE: As of September 2010, the most recent online edition of *Statutes At Large* is the 109th Congress, 2nd Session (2006) and the oldest edition goes back to 2003.

Each of **FDsys's** legislative/congressional collections can be accessed from the **FDsys** *Advanced Search* page (http://www.gpo.gov/fdsys/search/advanced/advsearchpage.action) by selecting the specific collection from the *Collection* drop-down menu. For the most part, the legislative/congressional collections at **FDsys** and **GPO Access** mirror each other, as far as the type of information available and the dates of coverage (unless noted otherwise below). One of the major differences, however, is that **FDsys** offers more ways to search (by selecting criteria from its *Search In* drop-down menu). If you prefer to retrieve a document by its citation, visit the *Retrieve By Citation* page (http://www.gpo.gov/fdsys/search/showcitation.action) and choose a collection from the *Collection* drop-down menu.

As noted on pages 316-322, **FDsys's** search protocol (e.g., its use of Boolean and proximity connectors and the way you can display and sort results) is the same throughout all of its collections; therefore, you should review this information before you search **FDsys's** legislative/congressional collections discussed in this section.

- *Public and Private Laws* collection goes back to 1995. You can also use this collection to update the text of a section of the *U.S.C.* For example, after reading the text of 22 U.S.C. 6208 at the **House** or **GPO Access** site, visit **FDsys** and select the *Public and Private Laws* collection, then select *United States Code Citation* criterion from the *Search In* box's drop-down menu and enter the U.S.C. citation (be sure to place periods in between each letter because "USC" will not work).

- *Congressional Bills* can be searched back to 1993 by eighteen different criteria and through one or multiple Congresses. To browse *Bills* in numerical order, choose the *Congress Number* criterion. To browse *Bills* by sponsor, you would select the *Sponsors and Co-sponsors* criterion. However, you would need to type in the sponsor's name. We prefer the **Library of Congress's Thomas** site for this type of search because there, we are offered a list of names from which to choose.

345

- *History of Bills* offers fourteen different criteria by which to search. While this collection is not available at the *Retrieve by Citation* page, a *Bill Number Citation* search criterion is one of the fourteen criteria that can searched. If you don't know which Congress a specific Bill number was introduced in, you can search all Congresses (back to 1983) by selecting the *Bill Number Citation* and entering the bill number (e.g., enter *s. 9* to search for the history of every Senate Bill number 9 in every Congress back to 1983).

- *Congressional Reports* (also referred to as *Committee Reports*) offers twenty-one different criteria by which to search.

- *Conference Reports* are not listed as a separate collection, but can be searched by choosing the *Conference Reports* search criterion within the *Congressional Reports* collection. Dates of coverage go back to 1995 (this is further back than **GPO Access's** collection).

- *Congressional Record* can be searched by thirty different criteria. While the information in this collection mirrors the **GPO Access** information, the date coverage might only go back to 1995 (whereas **GPO Access** can be searched back to 1994 using its *Simple Search*).

- *Statutes At Large* can be searched by twenty different criteria.

House and Senate Web Sites

For more information on the legislative process in general (or even just to find your Senator or Representative), use the **Senate** Web site at http://www.senate.gov and the **House** Web site at http://www.house.gov/.

You can use either **GPO Access** or **FDsys** as your starting points to conduct research about the executive branch of the federal government. We will discuss both systems in this section because, as noted on page 316, until **GPO Access** completes the process of migrating to **FDsys,** both systems are running concurrently.

The **GPO Access's** *Executive Branch Resources* page (http://www.gpoaccess.gov/executive.html) is divided between three major types of federal executive information: (1) *The Regulatory Process,* (2) *Presidential Documents*, and (3) *Executive Publications*. **FDsys** allows you to access all of its executive branch collections from the same page you would access any of its other collections (http://www.gpo.gov/fdsys/search/advanced/advsearchpage.action).

There are many federal agencies within the executive branch. There are two useful government sites and one university site to aid you in researching federal (and state, local, territorial, and tribal) agencies. The first government site is the **GPO Access's United States Government Manual** site (http://www.gpoaccess.gov/gmanual/index.html) and the second is **USA.gov**. The university site, which even **GPO Access** suggests that you use to research federal agencies, is **Louisiana State University Federal Agencies Directory** (http://www.lib.lsu.edu/gov/index.html). All of these sites will be discussed in this chapter.

Starting Points to Research the Federal Regulatory Process

The *Regulatory Process* section of **GPO Access's** *Executive Branch Resources* page (http://www.gpoaccess.gov/executive.html) links to various regulatory databases, such as current and historical (back to 1996 for most Titles) versions of the Code of Federal Regulations (*CFR*; http://www.gpoaccess.gov/cfr/index.html), the List of (CFR) Section Affected (*LSA*; http://www.gpoaccess.gov/lsa/about.html**)**, and the Federal

Register (*FR*; http://www.gpoaccess.gov/fr/index.html). The *CFR* represents the codification of the general and permanent rules of the executive departments and agencies of the Federal Government. The *CFR* is divided into fifty Titles — distinct areas that are subject to federal regulation (e.g., Title 1 is *Energy*, Title 26 is *Internal Revenue*). One-quarter of the Titles are updated at a time on a rolling quarterly basis, until the full *CFR* has been updated each year. The rules are first published in the *FR* as proposed rules, subject to public comment. The *FR* is issued daily, Monday–Friday; it also includes final rules and new presidential documents.

Searching the CFR via GPO Access

From the *CFR* home page (http://www.gpoaccess.gov/cfr/index.html) you can search the *Most Current 50 Titles* by *Keyword*, *Phrase*, *Subject*, *Agency Name*, or *Identification Code* or you can browse the current *CFR*. There are also links to browse, retrieve by citation, or search (by *Keyword*, *Phrase*, *Subject*, *Agency Name*, or *Identification Code*) the current <u>and</u> historical *CFRs* (separately or together) back to 1996.

GPO ACCESS CFR HOME PAGE

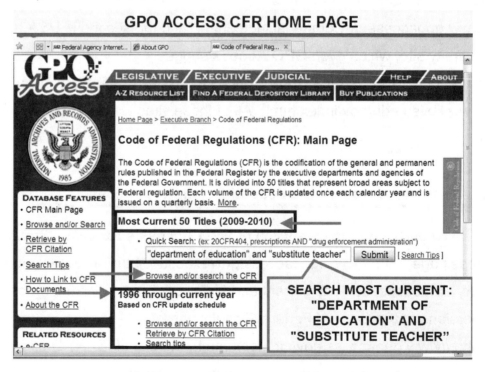

Word roots can be searched using an asterisk as a wildcard (e.g., *safe** will retrieve *safe, safely,* and *safety*). Boolean operators *AND, OR, NOT*, and the proximity connector *ADJ* (adjacent) can also be employed to connect words and phrases. Phrases must be placed within quotation marks. These various types of searches can be mixed and matched. For example, an *Agency Name* search can be combined with a *Keyword* or *Phrase* search and must be placed in parentheses (e.g., *"department of education" AND "metric system"*). Any of the sample searches at http://www.gpoaccess.gov/cfr/tips.html that show quotation marks surrounding the citations or words, such as an *Identification Code* search, should be entered into the search box surrounded by quotation marks and without any spaces (like this: *"7CFR246.11"*).

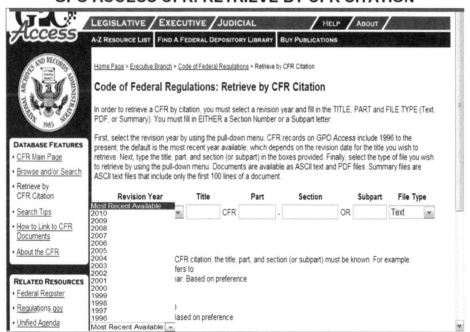

GPO ACCESS CFR: RETRIEVE BY CFR CITATION

The current and historical *CFRs* back to 1996 can be searched by exact citation, as noted above (http://www.gpoaccess.gov/cfr/retrieve.html). From the drop-down menu, select *Most Recent Available* or a specific year and then enter a citation.

GPO ACCESS CFR: BROWSE OR SEARCH BY REVISION DATES AND TITLES

- To search or browse a **single** CFR Title for a given year, click on the desired revision date for that Title in the table below.
  - or -
- To search or browse **one or more** CFR Titles, click the appropriate checkbox(es) in the table below, then click CONTINUE.

CONTINUE   CLEAR

CLICK INTO CHECKBOXES OR ON DATES BELOW, THEN CLICK *CONTINUE* TO SEARCH

Available CFR Titles on *GPO Access*

Title	Revision Date (Unless noted, all parts for a given Title are available)														
	2010	2009	2008	2007	2006	2005	2004	2003	2002	2001	2000	1999	1998	1997	1996
1 General Provisions	☑ Jan. 1, 2010	Jan. 1, 2009	☑ Jan. 1, 2008	☑ Jan. 1, 2007	Jan. 1, 2006	**CLICK INTO ONE OR MORE CHECKBOXES OR...**									
2 Grants and Agreements	☐ Jan. 1, 2010	☐ Jan. 1, 2009	☐ Jan. 1, 2008	☐ Jan. 1, 2007	☐ Jan. 1, 2006	☐ **CLICK ON A DATE**									
		☐	☐	☐	☐	☐	☐	☐	☐	☐	☐	☐	☐		

To search (by *Keyword, Phrase, Subject, Agency Name*, or *Identification Code*) or browse a single *CFR* Title for a particular year, click on the revision date for that Title and then click *CONTINUE* (as pictured in the table above; http://www.access.gpo.gov/nara/cfr/cfr-table-search.html#page1). To search (by *Keyword, Phrase, Subject, Agency Name*, or *Identification Code*) or browse one or more *CFR* Titles (in one or more years), click the appropriate checkbox(es) and then click *CONTINUE* (as pictured in the table above).

GPO ACCESS CFR: KEYWORD SEARCH A TITLE IN TWO DIFFERENT REVISION DATES

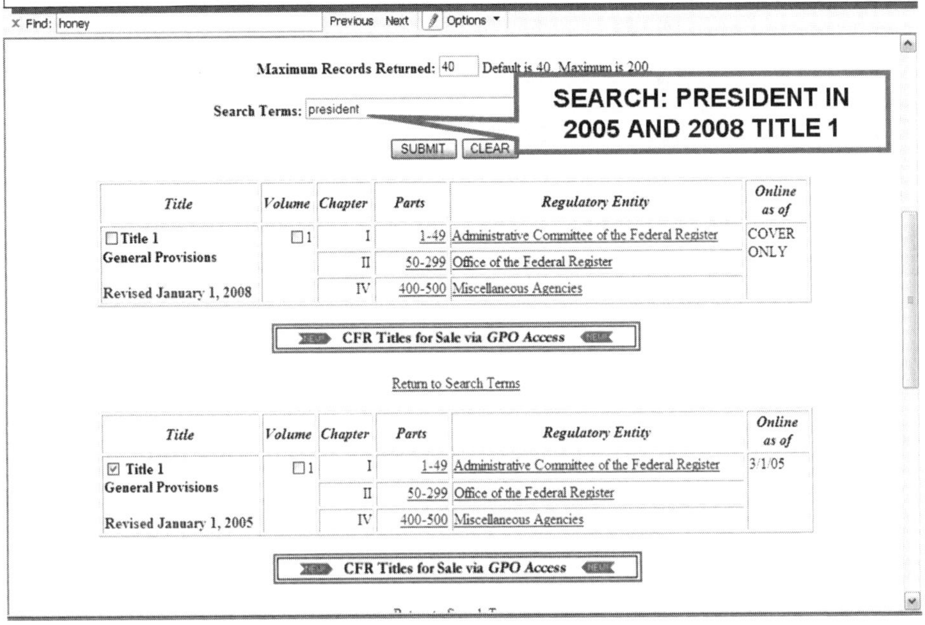

After we clicked on the 2005 and the 2008 revision dates for *Title 1* and then clicked *CONTINUE* a search box was presented where we entered our keyword (see above illustration). Clicking *Submit* brought back results for any document in Title 1 from 2005 and 2008.

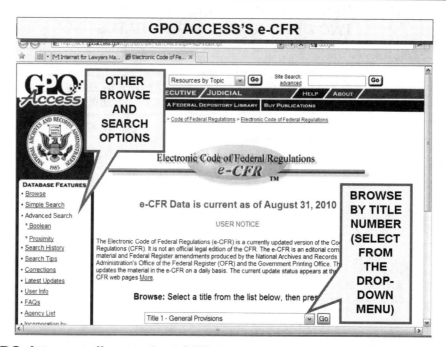

GPO ACCESS'S e-CFR

OTHER BROWSE AND SEARCH OPTIONS

BROWSE BY TITLE NUMBER (SELECT FROM THE DROP-DOWN MENU)

GPO Access offer another *CFR* database that you can use: the *e-CFR* (http://www.gpoaccess.gov/ecfr). It was in a beta test mode for many years but is now out of beta. However, it is still not deemed to be the "official" *CFR* and is described as an "editorial compilation of *CFR* material and *Federal Register* amendments produced by the National Archives and Records Administration's Office of the Federal Register (OFR) and the Government Printing Office." While the *CFR* database discussed in the previous section is updated only annually, the *e-CFR* is updated every day. As amendments become effective, the Office of the Federal Register adds the changes to the current *CFR* database so one can view the full text of the updated *CFR* in one place instead of having to run a search in both the *CFR* and *FR* (or in both the *CFR* and *LSA* discussed on pages 353-356). You can browse the *e-CFR* database numerically by *Title* or keyword search the database using the *Simple Search* option or the *Advanced Search* option (on the left-hand column). The *Simple Search* option allows you to search the entire *CFR* (current) or just one *CFR* Title (current). You can search for your term anywhere within the text or within a specific region, such as a *Part* or a *SubPart*. The *Advanced Search* option offers you a *Boolean* or a *Proximity* search. Detailed *Search Tips* can be found at http://tinyurl.com/ecfrsearchtips.

The *CFR* database at **FDsys** can be searched by first selecting the *CFR (Code of Federal Regulations)* collection from the drop-down menu on the *Advanced Search* page (http://www.gpo.gov/fdsys/search/advanced/advsearchpage.action).

FDSYS CFR: ADVANCED SEARCH

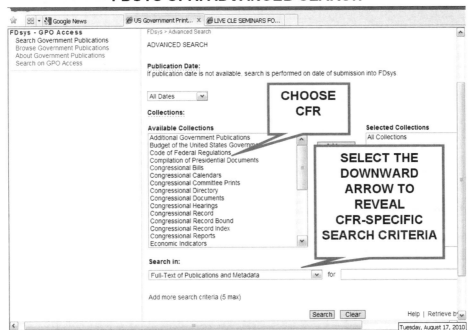

After you choose the collection, the search criteria appropriate to that collection will be available by clicking on the downward arrow on the right-hand side of the *Search in* box. We have chosen to search by the *Title* criteria and *Section criteria* (see next illustration). This search is different from a *Retrieve by Citation* search. A *Retrieve by Citation* limits you to one year while our search allows us to search through all years (from 2000 to current). *Retrieve by Citation* searches are discussed on pages 321-322.

You can also perform a keyword search. See pages 316-320 for instructions on **FDsys's** keyword search protocol.

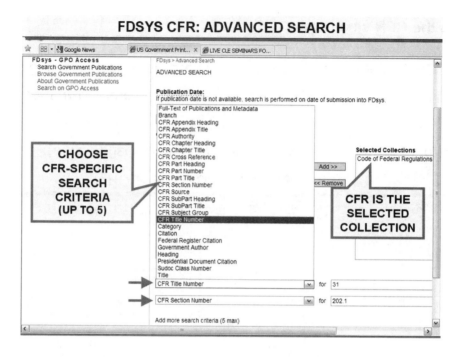

FDSYS CFR: ADVANCED SEARCH

Down the middle of our search results page (see next illustration), there are short annotations and links to several editions (years) of the full-text of our requested *CFR Title* and *Section*. There is also a link to *Show only recent editions*. We can refine our search by clicking on links in the left-hand column, such as *Government Author, Location*, and *Date Published*. If we click on the *See More* link under *Date Published,* we will be able to read versions of this *Title/Section* back to 2000.

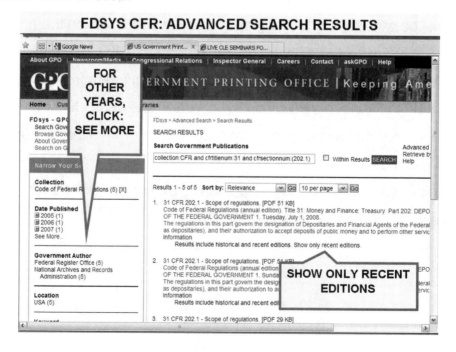

FDSYS CFR: ADVANCED SEARCH RESULTS

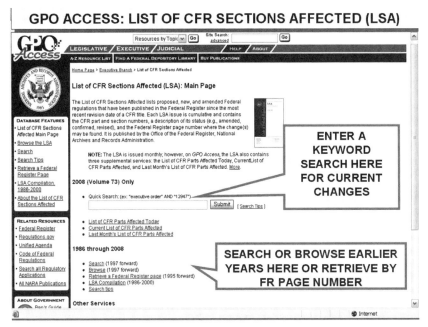

The *LSA* (http://www.gpoaccess.gov/lsa) updates the most recent annual revision of a *CFR* title with any new, proposed, or amended regulations published in the daily *FR*. You might wonder why you would use the *LSA* instead of simply using the *e-CFR* which incorporates all changes into the *e-CFR* database on a daily basis. The answer is this: There are searches at the *LSA* that cannot be accomplished at the *e-CFR* site, such as conducting historical research (by browsing the 1986–2000 *LSA Compilation*, searching older volumes back to 1997, or retrieving a specific *FR* page by its page number. From the home page, you can:

- search the current *LSA* by using the *Quick Search* box.
- view only the current day's changes (by clicking the *List of CFR Parts Affected Today* link)
- view only the *CFR* parts affected since the last monthly issue of the *LSA* (by clicking on the *Current List of CFR Parts Affected* link)
- view only the *CFR* parts affected during the last month (by clicking the *Last Month's List of CFR Parts Affected* link)
- search or browse older volumes (back to 1997 and through the current volume) individually or by multiple volumes, by selecting either the *Browse* or the *Search* links on the home page (browsing is by Year/Month/Title)

To refine your keyword searches of the current or older *LSA* volumes, you can use:

- Boolean connectors (*AND, OR* and *NOT*)
- Proximity connectors (*ADJ*, which stands for "Adjacent")
- Word stemming (to find variations on words) – to stem, add the asterisk wildcard to the root. For instance, *govern** will retrieve *govern, government*, and *governor*, among other words.)

You can also search *LSA* volumes by *Subject, Identification Codes* or *CFR Citation* (For detailed search tips, see http://www.gpoaccess.gov/lsa/tips.html).

Searching the LSA via FDsys

The *LSA* database has migrated to **FDsys** http://www.gpo.gov/fdsys/search/home.action, but only the data back to 1997 are available there. The 1986–2000 LSA Compilation available at the **GPO Access** site is not available at **FDsys**. To browse the *LSA* database at the **FDsys**, visit http://www.gpo.gov/fdsys/browse/collection.action?collectionCode=LSA. There you can click on *Monthly LSA* to browse by year and month back to 1997 or you can click on *Browse CFR Parts Affected from the Federal Register* where you can choose to browse by *Last 24 hours, Latest Week, Latest Month*, or *Create Date Range*. To search by keywords and other criteria, visit the *Advanced Search* page (http://www.gpo.gov/fdsys/search/advanced/advsearchpage.action), enter a date (or leave the *All Dates* default selection), choose the *List of CFR Sections Affected* from the *Available Collections* list, choose which part of the collection to search (from the *Search In* list), and enter keywords (or other criteria, such as *Branch, Citation*, or *Title*). Although you can conduct a *Citation* search from the *Advanced Search* page, *LSA* is not listed on the *Retrieve by Citation* search at http://www.gpo.gov/fdsys/search/showcitation.action. For more details on how to search the **FDsys**, see pages 316–322.

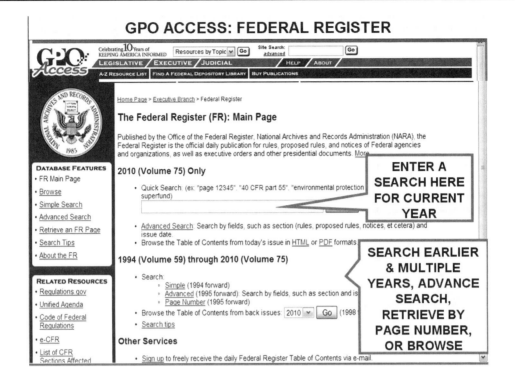

The *FR* online goes back to 1994 and can be accessed from the **GPO Access Executive Branch Resources** page (http://www.gpoaccess.gov/executive.html) or directly from this link: http://www.gpoaccess.gov/fr/index.html. The *FR* database offers a *Simple Search* (back to 1994) and an *Advanced Search* (but only back to 1995). Both the *Simple* and *Advanced Searches* offer:

- Boolean searching, using the *AND*, *OR* and *NOT* connectors

- Proximity searching, using the *ADJ* (adjacent) connector

- Word stemming searching, to find variations on words. (To stem, add the asterisk wildcard to the root. For instance, *govern** will retrieve *govern*, *government*, and *governor*, among other words).

- Multiple-year searching

The *FR's Simple Search* (http://www.gpoaccess.gov/fr/search.html) allows searching back to 1994 (single or multiple years) by:

- *Subject*
- *Citation* (*Volume and Page Number*)
- *Keywords* or *Phrases*
- *Page Number*
- *Search by Page Number in the 1994 Database* (Page numbers do not appear in the 1994 *FR* database, except in the table of contents and the *LSA*, so there is a two part process to search the 1994 *FR* by page number. For detailed instructions, see http://www.gpoaccess.gov/fr/tips.html.)
- *Code of Federal Regulations Part Number*
- *Dates* (specific or ranges)
- *Agency Name*
- *List of CFR Parts Affected*

Most of the above searches must be surrounded by quotation marks. For example a *Title* and *Part* search looks like this: *"40 CFR part 55."* The *Advanced Search* option (http://www.gpoaccess.gov/fr/advanced.html) allows you to search single or multiple years using the same search criteria noted above at the *Simple Search* and also by the following "fielded searches:"

- *Volume*
- *Section* (e.g., *Final Rules, Presidential Documents*, etc.)
- *Issue Date*

For more detailed information on how to construct a *Simple Search* and an *Advanced Search*, see http://www.gpoaccess.gov/fr/tips.html.

You can browse the *FR Table of Contents* back to 1998 (http://www.gpoaccess.gov/fr/browse.html) or subscribe to the free daily *FR Table of Contents* mailing list (or to any of the free topical *FR* mailing lists to receive only preliminary information from a specific agency). To subscribe to either type of list, go to http://listserv.access.gpo.gov/, click the *Online Mailing List Archives* link, select *FEDREGTOC-L*, click the *Join or leave the list* link, enter your name and e-mail address, and then select *FEDREGTOC-L FR Table of Contents* (or one of the topical mailing lists) from the drop-down menu.

In addition to accessing federal regulations at the *FR* database, *Presidential Documents* can be accessed there by using the *Advanced Search* (http://www.gpoaccess.gov/fr/advanced.html) and restricting the search to *Presidential Documents* under *Select a Section.*

Searching the FR via FDsys

While still available on the **GPO Access** site, the *FR* database (from 1994 to present) has migrated to the **FDsys**. To browse the **FDsys** *FR* database by Year/Month/Date/Agency, visit http://www.gpo.gov/fdsys/browse/collection.action?collectionCode=FR. In the left hand column, there is also a link to a new feature which allows you to download multiple issues (from 2000 to current) in XML. According to a story in the Washington Post (http://www.washingtonpost.com/wp-dyn/content/article/2009/10/04/AR2009100402533.html?hpid=sec-politics), "The technology [XML] will allow users, including website designers, to quickly gather data and manipulate the information with tools such as mapping software, word clouds, spreadsheets and e-mail alert systems..."

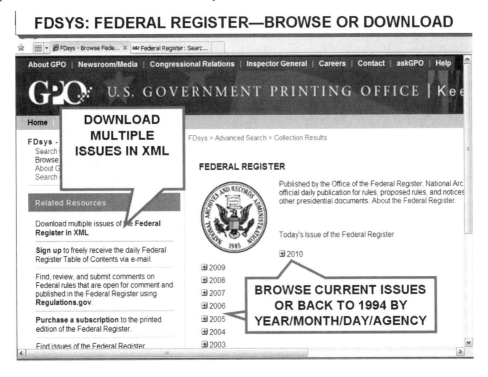

FDSYS: FEDERAL REGISTER—BROWSE OR DOWNLOAD

To search by keywords and other criteria (such as *Citation*, *Action,* etc.), visit the *Advanced Search* page (http://www.gpo.gov/fdsys/search/home.action) and enter a date (or leave the *All Dates* default selection); choose the *Federal Register* from the *Available Collections* list; choose how to search (such as by *Citation, Action*, etc.) from the *Search In* list; and then enter keywords or citations into the search box. To see more details on how to search the **FDsys**, see pages 316–322.

Although you can search the *FR* collection back to 1994, you can only *Retrieve by Citation* (http://www.gpo.gov/fdsys/search/submitcitation.action?publication=FR) back to 1995 because, as noted earlier, page numbers do not appear in the 1994 *FR* database, except in the table of contents and the *LSA.*

The **GPO Access's** *Executive Branch Resources* page

(http://www.gpoaccess.gov/executive.html) links to Presidential materials such as

- *Public Papers of the Presidents of the United States* (http://www.gpoaccess.gov/pubpapers/index.html), which include papers and speeches of the current and former administrations back to 1991. Tips for searching by keywords/phrases (with Boolean connectors) and for viewing either the Table of Contents or appendix are displayed at the bottom of the main search page (http://www.gpoaccess.gov/pubpapers/search.html). Tips for searching by subject, name, country, or document type are found at http://www.gpoaccess.gov/pubpapers/tips.html. The papers can also be browsed by President, in chronological order (http://www.gpoaccess.gov/pubpapers/browse.html). Tips for searching individual years or multiple years can be found at http://www.gpoaccess.gov/help/optionboxes.html.

- The *State of the Union Addresses* can be viewed as *Text* or *PDF* files dating back to 1992 (http://www.gpoaccess.gov/sou/index.html).

- *Weekly Compilation of Presidential Documents* (http://www.gpoaccess.gov/wcomp/index.html), from 1993 through January 20, 2009, includes Presidential statements, messages, remarks, executive orders, etc., released by the White House Press Secretary. The documents can be searched by keyword, phrases, subject, Executive Order number, issue date, and page number, by a single or multiple years; or browsed (only 2001-2009) in chronological order.

As of January 2, 2009, the *Weekly Compilation* became a *Daily Compilation* and can be browsed at http://www.gpoaccess.gov/presdocs/index.html. However, to search the *Daily Compilation*, you will need to visit the **FDsys** site noted in the next section.

FDsys and Presidential Materials

FDsys offers several collections relating to the President, including the *Compilation of Presidential Documents,* which is comprised of the *Daily Compilation* (January 2, 2009 to date) and its predecessor, the *Weekly Compilation* (February 1992 through its change to a daily on January 2, 2009). At

FDsys, the *Weekly* and the *Daily Compilation* can be browsed (http://www.gpo.gov/fdsys/browse/collection.action?collectionCode=CPD) and also *Advanced Searched* (http://www.gpo.gov/fdsys/search/advanced/advsearchpage.action). As noted in the previous section, the *Daily Compilation* can be browsed at the **GPO** site (http://www.gpoaccess.gov/presdocs/index.html) but cannot be searched there.

The *Public Papers of the Presidents of the United States* collection can be browsed at **FDsys** back to 1991 (http://www.gpo.gov/fdsys/browse/collection.action?collectionCode=PPP) and searched by choosing it from the drop-down menu at http://www.gpo.gov/fdsys/search/advanced/advsearchpage.action.

You can conduct a *Retrieve by Citation* search for the *Public Papers of the Presidents of the United States* and the *Weekly* and *Daily Compilations* (http://www.gpo.gov/fdsys/search/submitcitation.action?publication=CPD)

There does not seem to be a separate *State of the Union Addresses* collection at **FDsys**, but they can be searched by selecting the *Compilation of Presidential Documents*, choosing *Title* from the *Search in* box and searching the phrase *State of the Union* (if you wanted to narrow down your search to a specific year, you could also add a date).

For details on how to search these various Presidential collections at **FDsys**, see pages 316–322.

The White House

The **White House's** site is at http://www.whitehouse.gov. There you can take a tour of the White House, get biographical information about the current and past presidents and vice-presidents (and first ladies), e-mail the current ones, read press briefings, and more. You can even view the President's speeches at **YouTube** (http://www.youtube.com/whitehouse) and follow the White House (along with nearly two million followers) on **Twitter** (http://www.twitter.com/whitehouse), and a host of other social media sites. All documents on the White House site are searchable by keyword.

The Executive branch also includes numerous federal agencies. Their Web sites can include a wide range of information, from directories of staff, rules, regulations, and reports to administrative decisions, laws, and forms. Sometimes it is easier to pinpoint a rule, regulation, or law at an agency's Web site instead of searching through the *CFR*, *FR,* or **U.S. Code**. For an example, see the **Social Security Online** site below (http://www.ssa.gov).

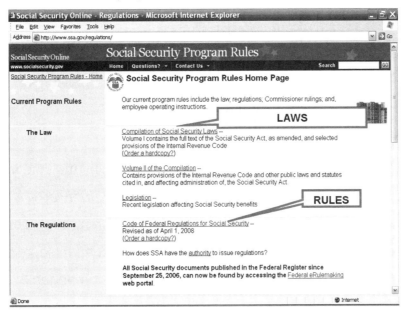

Finding Federal (and State, Local, Territorial, and Tribal) Agency Web Sites

GPO Access's *United States Government Manual* (http://www.gpoaccess.gov/gmanual/index.html), which is the official handbook of the Federal Government, is useful for locating agency Web sites. In addition to providing comprehensive information about executive branch agencies and staff, it also includes comprehensive information about legislative, judicial, and quasi-official agencies; international organizations (in which the United States participates); boards; commissions; and committees. It also provides links to these entities.

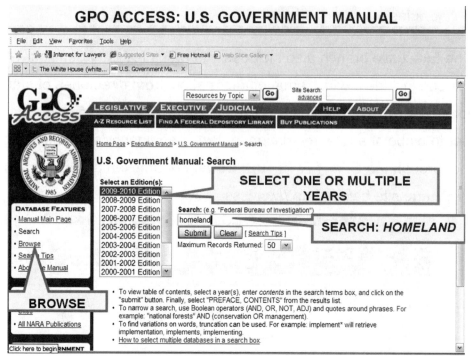

The *Manual* can be searched by a single year or by multiple years (from 1995 to the present) using *Keywords*, *Phrases*, *Subject*, *Individual's Name*, or *Agency Name* (http://www.gpoaccess.gov/gmanual/search.html). There are instructions on the search page explaining how to select multiple years. The same options available for searching the *FR*, discussed on pages 357-358, apply to the *United States Government Manual*. The results list offers a *Summary* or a full-text view in either *PDF* or *HTML* format. The HTML version of the *Manual* provides clickable hyperlinks to the agency's Web site while the *PDF* version's URLs are only clickable if viewed with a copy of the free Adobe Reader newer than version 7.

The *United States Government Manual* can also be browsed (http://www.gpoaccess.gov/gmanual/browse.html) by year and then by Title (back only to 1997 to the present), in contrast to the search function that goes back to 1995. The results list offers a full-text view in either the *PDF* or *Text* format.

The *United States Government Manual*, from 1995 to present, has migrated to **FDsys.** It can be browsed by year at http://www.gpo.gov/fdsys/search/home.action, where you can view or download the entire year's *Manual* (or a specific section) as a *PDF* or *TEXT* file. The *Manual* can also be searched (by *Keyword*, *Citation*, etc.) by choosing *Government Manual* from the *Available Collections* drop-down menu on the *Advanced Search* page (http://www.gpo.gov/fdsys/search/advanced/advsearchpage.action). For details on how to search the *Government Manual* collection at **FDsys**, see pages 316–322.

USA.gov is the second government site useful for locating agencies. In addition to linking to federal agencies (which the **United States Government Manual** allows you to do), **USA.gov** also provides links to *Local*, *State*, and *Tribal* agencies. You can browse an alphabetical list of all federal government departments and agencies (by name) at **USA.gov's** *A–Z Index of U.S. Government Departments and Agencies* (http://www.usa.gov/Agencies/Federal/All_Agencies/index.shtml). From that same page, you can also browse by jurisdiction by selecting the *Federal*, *State*, *Local*, or *Tribal* links located on the right-hand side of the page.

The **Louisiana State University's Federal Agencies Directory** (http://www.lib.lsu.edu/gov/index.html) is useful for locating federal agencies' Web sites. They include *Boards*, *Commissions*, and *Committees* (see below). On the right-hand side of the page (which this site refers to as the *tool box*), you can browse an alphabetical list of all agencies by clicking *Expand All* or you can keyword search the directory (if you are unsure of the exact agency name).

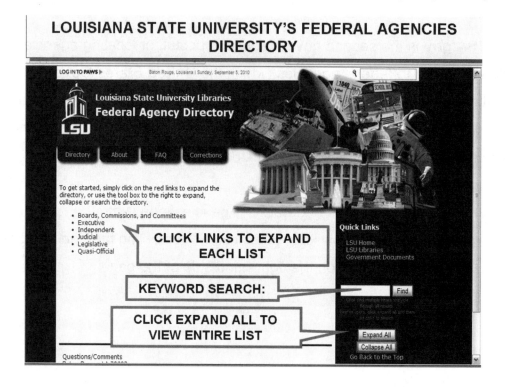

Finding Defunct Federal Agencies' and Commissions' Web Sites

The **CyberCemetery** Web site (http://govinfo.library.unt.edu/default.htm) offers permanent access to defunct federal government agencies' and commissions' Web sites and publications. It is a partnership between the **University of North Texas Libraries** and the **GPO**.

FOREIGN COUNTRIES' EXECUTIVE BRANCHES

To access information about foreign countries' executive branches, see the *Foreign and International Law* resources section on pages 413–414.

Almost all federal courts have "gone virtual," from putting their opinions, rules, and forms online to e-filing. The **GPO Access's** *Judicial Branch Resources* page (http://www.gpoaccess.gov/judicial.html) offers links to judicial resources hosted by **GPO**, such as the **U.S. House Committee on the Judiciary** site (http://www.gpoaccess.gov/congress/house/judiciary/index.html) but only links to its two *U.S. Supreme Court decisions* databases:

- *Supreme Court Decisions* from 1937–1975 (http://www.gpoaccess.gov/supcrt/index.html), which is full-text searchable.
- *U.S. Supreme Court Opinions Archive*, from 1992–2000, which is not full-text searchable; it can only be browsed in docket number order (http://fedbbs.access.gpo.gov/court01.html)

There are a variety of other free (and better) sites you can use to search U.S. Supreme Court decisions, from the **U.S. Supreme Court's** site (http://www.supremecourtus.gov) and sites discussed earlier in *Chapter Twelve* (such as **Justia**, **FindLaw**, and **LexisONE**, among several others) to bar association member benefit databases discussed in *Chapter Thirteen*. We would recommend these over the **GPO** site because they generally have more sophisticated search features and better date coverage (and not because of **GPO's** warning: "This application was created by the Air Force and is not an official version of the Supreme Court's opinions. Since the GPO has not performed costly validation processes, we cannot guarantee the authenticity or completeness of the data.") This warning could also pertain to the other online U.S. Supreme Court case law databases (even the one at the court's own site), because only the government's printed version (*United States Reports*) is considered official.

The Administrative Office of the U.S. Courts, maintains the Federal Judiciary's **U.S. Courts** site (http://www.uscourts.gov). It provides information about the entire federal court system (choose the *Federal Courts* tab seen in the illustration below) and links to all federal courts (use the *Court Locator* seen in the illustration below to either enter a location or select the *Court Map* tab).

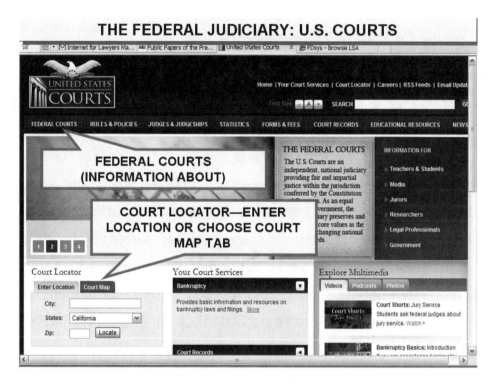

The *Court Map* tab brings you to a page where you can click on any state (or territory or district) to view a list of all the federal courts in that jurisdiction (pictured in the next illustration). There is then a multi-step process by which you can link to a specific federal court. First, you select a court. Second, you are shown a page with the court's address and phone number and an *Internet Web Site* link and an *ECF* (Electronic Court Filing) link. Third, you would then click on the *Internet Web Site* link to visit the court's Web site. (The *ECF* link brings you to a page where you can file electronically [see page 387] or log in to search **PACER** [see page 383]).

THE FEDERAL JUDICIARY: U.S. COURT LOCATOR MAP

Clicking *Judiciary Links* (seen in the illustration above) displays links to many courts (seen in the next illustration), such as (the *U.S. Supreme Court* and specialized federal courts (e.g., the *Tax Court* and the *U.S. Court of International Trade*). It also links to court-related sites, such as the **Federal Judicial Center**, which is the education, history, and research arm of the courts (http://www.fjc.gov), and also includes judicial biographies. Clicking *Judiciary Services* displays links to **PACER** and other services.

THE FEDERAL JUDICIARY: U.S. COURTS ADVANCED COURT LOCATOR SEARCH

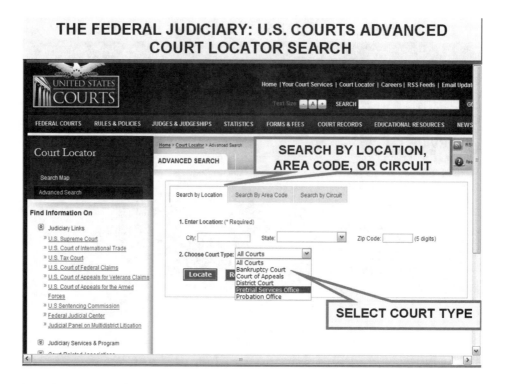

The *Court Locator Advanced Search* (above) offers you three types of searches: *Location* (by one or more of these choices: *Zip Code*, *City*, or *State)*, *Area Code*, or *Circuit*. All three searches also allow you to narrow down by *Court Type*, or search for a federal court Web site by, *Area Code*, etc.

U.S. Supreme Court: Official and Unofficial Sites

The **United States Supreme Court** was probably one of the last federal courts to create a Web site (http://www.supremecourt.gov/). It appeared in May 2000, after many state and even local courts had already created their Web sites. Many unofficial sites, however, had already stepped up and created full-text searchable databases for the U.S. Supreme Court decisions (and other documents such as dockets and briefs). We'll discuss both the official and unofficial sites below.

U.S. Supreme Court: Official Site

Since the last edition of this book (2009), the **Supreme Court of the United States'** official site has undergone a number of changes, from its URL (http://www.supremecourt.gov) and its design, to some of the search protocols.

The **Supreme Court's** site includes:

- *Court Rules*
- *Case Handling Information*
- *Calendar* (current term)
- PDFs of the bound volumes of the official *U.S. Reports,* from Volume 502 (1991) through Volume 549 (2006) (http://www.supremecourt.gov/opinions/boundvolumes.html). Viewing an opinion from the bound volumes of the *U.S. Reports* is useful for pinpoint citation. Each volume includes an alphabetical *Table of Cases* and a *Topical Index*. Only one volume at a time can be searched full-text (by using the Adobe Acrobat "Find" function on the PDF toolbar; as described on page 72)
- *Current Slip Opinions*
- *Sliplists* from 2006-2009
- *Oral Argument Transcripts* from 2000-present (browsed by the *Date Argued* at; http://linkon.in/bKKJy6)
- *Docket Files*
- and more

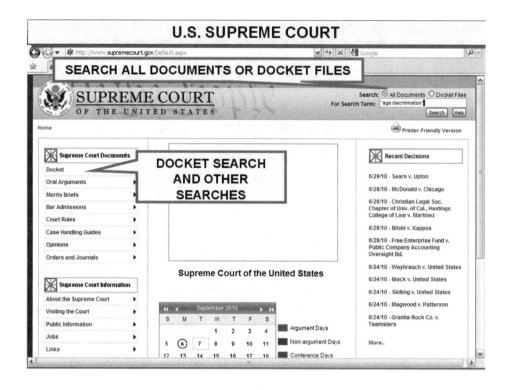

The main design change we noticed at the U.S. Supreme Court Web site was on the home page, where a *Docket Files* search and an *All Documents* search are now listed in the upper right-hand corner. (*All Documents* seems to be the new label for what had been the *Supreme Court Files* search.) An *All Documents* search will bring back results from a variety of document types (see next illustration) such as *Speeches*, *Slip Opinions*, *Opinions* (from *Bound Volumes*), *Questions Presented*, *Transcripts of Oral Arguments*, and *Court Rules*. Coverage dates will vary from database to database.

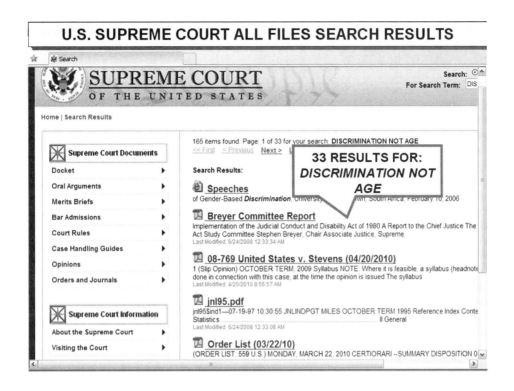

The *Docket* database contains information about pending and decided cases for the current and prior terms. Although you can enter your search into a search box located on the top right-hand side of the home page (and clicking into the *Docket Files* radio button), we recommend that you instead click the *Docket* tab located on the left-hand column of the home page and then select *Docket Search* from the drop-down menu (or use this direct URL: http://www.supremecourt.gov/docket/docket.aspx). We prefer using this search option because various search tips are offered on this page to help you conduct a more effective search. For instance, you are informed that you can search by a *Supreme Court docket number* (e.g. by term year/number: such as: 06-123), a *lower court docket number*, or a *case name*. Keyword searches can also be performed, but no examples are given on this page. You will need to visit the *Search Tips* page at http://www.supremecourt.gov/search_help.aspx. On this page we learned that some of the search protocols had recently changed. One of the major changes is that phrases must now be placed within quotation marks. Another change relates to the Boolean connector used to exclude keywords (or phrases) from your search: instead of using *AND NOT* you are now instructed to use *NOT*. Keywords and phrases can be strung together with the Boolean connectors: *AND* (or just leave a space between keywords and phrases) or *OR*. The proximity connector *NEAR* (which is defined by this site as *within 50 words*) can also be employed. Although not stated on the *Search Tips* page, keep in mind that keyword and phrase searching can also include a name search (such as a party, attorney, or expert's name).

Missing from this official site are: opinions before 1991, dockets and calendars older than the past term, briefs, and any audio recordings of oral arguments and oral opinions. This missing information can be found (for free) at one or both of the two sites discussed in the next sections (**FindLaw** and **Oyez**). (Earlier Supreme Court opinions are also available at numerous other sites discussed on pages 244, 250, 255, 291-295, and in *Chapter Thirteen*).

U.S. Supreme Court: Unofficial Sites for Case Law and More

To search full-text (and by other criteria, such as citation, party name, etc.) through multiple volumes of U.S. Supreme Court opinions, there are a multitude of databases freely available (see pages on pages 244, 250, 255, 291-295, and *Chapter Thirteen* for details). However, in this section of the book, we'll highlight the two free sites that offer Supreme Court case law databases, among other information.

Visit the recently re-designed **Oyez Project U.S. Supreme Court Media** Web site (http://www.oyez.org/) to access U.S. Supreme Court written opinions back to 1792, the Court's calendar, over 5,000 hours of any audio (oral arguments and oral opinions) recorded in the Court since 1981, and selective audio from 1955 to 1981 (in the MP3 or Real Audio format). **Oyez's** goal is to provide access to a complete audio archive back to October 1955. There is also a "virtual tour" of the Court (http://www.oyez.org/tour).

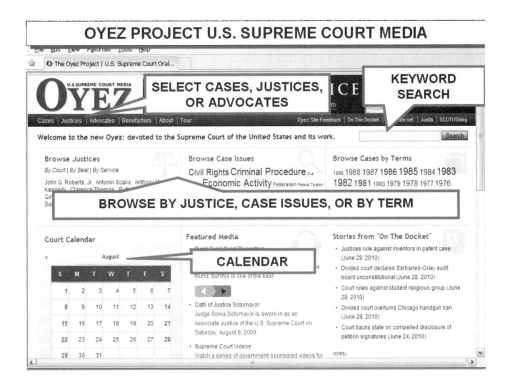

OYEZ PROJECT U.S. SUPREME COURT MEDIA

On the home page are three options to view cases: *Browse Justices* (*By Court*, *By Seat*, or *By Service*), *Browse Case Issues* (e.g., *Civil Rights*) or *Browse Cases By Term* (choose a range of years or a single year). The *Browse Case Issues* and the *Browse Cases By Term* results will be displayed in a table that can be re-sorted by (1) *Case* (alphabetically by plaintiff's name), (2) *Docket No.*, (3) *Argued* (date), or (4) *Decided* (date). You can choose to display the last three re-sorting options in ascending or descending order. The results table also displays the *Majority Author* and the *Vote*.

Any information (including cases) on the site can also be keyword searched but instead of using the *Search this site* box on the top, right-hand side

of the home page for searching, visit
http://www.oyez.org/search/apachesolr_search/ for an advanced search menu
(see below) to narrow down a search by *Content Type* (*Transcript, Case*, etc.) or
by *Speaker.* (The *Speaker* designation refers to the name of the attorney arguing
the case or the name of the justice asking a question. However, while viewing
some of the transcripts, we find the identifier *Unknown Speaker* is displayed often.)

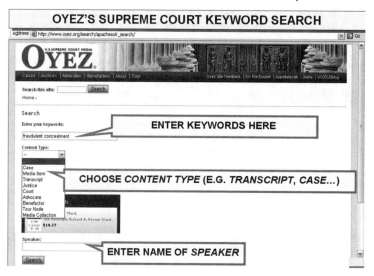

After selecting an opinion from the results list, the following information will
be displayed (if available — it can vary per opinion; see below): links to *Media
Items* (audio files of the *Oral Argument* and the *Opinion Announcement*), written
transcripts of arguments (hidden behind the *Expanded View* link), the *Facts of
the Case*, *Question* [Presented], and the *Conclusion*.

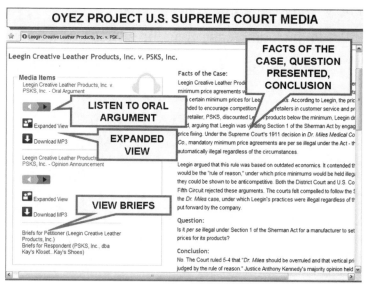

As you scroll down the page (see below), also displayed will be some docket information such as the name of the *Advocates*, *Case Basics*, including a link to the opinion (click the citation listed to the right of the word *Opinion* to read the opinion, which is supplied by **Justia**), and *Decisions* (how each justice voted). **Oyez** uses color coding to show how each judge voted, but we did not see a key to the color coding. It's easier to click the citation and read the text of the opinion to learn how each justice voted.

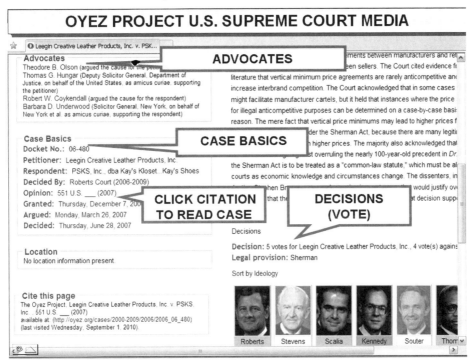

FindLaw also hosts a *Supreme Court Center* (http://supreme.lp.findlaw.com/supreme_court/resources.html) with free access to Supreme Court documents (in addition to **FindLaw's** *U.S. Supreme Court Opinions* database, discussed on page 244). However, **FindLaw's** *Supreme Court Center* is more useful for historical research because most of its documents (except for *Dockets*) are no longer being updated (as noted below). **FindLaw** offers *Dockets*, *Orders*, and *Calendar* information that goes back further in time than the offerings at the Court's official site.

- *Dockets* (1999 to present; http://linkon.in/aWDAO3) Despite the fact that the selection of coverage years listed on the home page only goes back to 2007 (see the next illustration), if you click on *Dockets* (or visit the direct URL above), you will see that the *Dockets* database is current. Each docket displays the *Question Presented*, links to the Supreme Court briefs, the lower court decisions, and, when available, to a written transcript or audio of the oral arguments. Because **FindLaw's** docket database is actually a summary of the official docket sheet, there are links to the official Supreme Court's full docket sheet. However, links to dockets older than the current and past terms do not work because the Court has taken them down and links to the current and immediate past term's dockets do not work because the Court changed its URL and **FindLaw** has not kept up with the change.

- *Briefs* (1999 to 2007; http://linkon.in/bZla9e) It does not appear as if this database is being kept up to date.

- *Decisions* (2003 to 2008; http://linkon.in/dB8idk) Decisions are listed in reverse chronological order.

- *Orders* (1999 to 2008; http://linkon.in/d7OAHY)

- *Calendar* (1999 to 2007; http://linkon.in/anGWI0)

- *Case Index by Topic* (2000 to 2007; http://linkon.in/9YuaMZ) Cases are listed by year/topic.

- *Rules* (2003 version; http://linkon.in/aHcJYh)

- *Guides* (2000 versions; http://linkon.in/afLN9v)

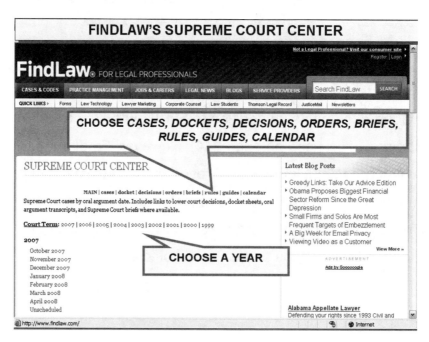

U.S. Courts of Appeal: Official "Court Locator"

For general information regarding the Courts of Appeal, visit the **Federal Judiciary U.S. Courts** site (http://www.uscourts.gov/courtsofappeals.html).

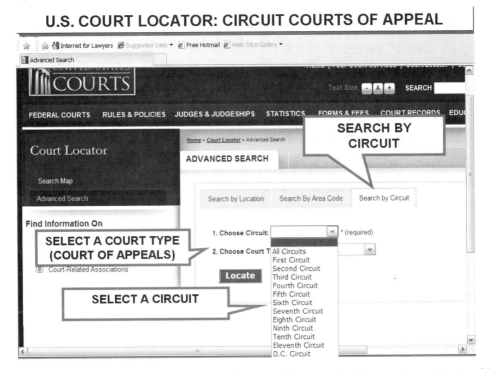

To link to an individual circuit's Court of Appeal's Web site, visit the **U.S. Courts** *Court Locator* page (http://www.uscourts.gov/Court_Locator/CourtLocatorSearch.aspx) and select *Search by Circuit*, choose a specific circuit (or *All Circuits*) from the drop-down menu; then choose the *Court Type* (*Court of Appeals*). You can also search by *Area Code* or *Location.* You could also use the *Court Locator* map (http://www.uscourts.gov/Court_Locator.aspx) to view a list of all the federal courts in a jurisdiction by clicking any state (or territory or district; pictured on page 369).

U.S. Courts of Appeal: Individual Circuit's Official Sites

The type of information available at each U.S. Courts of Appeal Web site varies from circuit to circuit. Most is free, with the exception of dockets (see **PACER** on page 383). The types of information that might be found include the following:

- Opinions (sometimes full-text searchable, but usually searchable by party name or docket number only)
- Forms
- Court Calendars
- Rules
- Guides
- Pattern Jury Instructions
- Slip opinions
- Links to **PACER** and **ECF**

At some Circuits, we have found audio recordings of oral arguments (e.g., at the Ninth Circuit; http://www.ca9.uscourts.gov/media/), RSS Feeds (e.g., at the Ninth Circuit; http://www.ca9.uscourts.gov/rss), or a list of admitted attorneys (e.g., at the Second Circuit; http://www.ca2.uscourts.gov/attyadmissions.htm).

U.S. Courts of Appeal: Unofficial Sites for Case Law Searching

For free full-text keyword, docket number, and case title searching (and other search criteria), see pages 291–299, 244, 251, and 255.

U.S. Courts of Appeal: Dockets

To access the U.S. Courts of Appeal's civil and criminal dockets (and the underlying documents), you will need to obtain a subscription to **PACER** (see page 386 for details), **Westlaw CourtExpress.com** (http://courtexpress.westlaw.com/), or **LexisNexis CourtLink.com** (http://www.lexisnexis.com/courtlink/). See page 392, to learn about **Justia's** recent addition of U.S. Courts of Appeal dockets to its *U.S. District Courts' Civil Case Filings*.

Although it is not a full docket database, **Courthouse News** (http://www.courthousenews.com) is a pay site that will alert you when new complaints are filed (from over 1,600 federal, state, and local courts).

U.S. District Courts and U.S. Bankruptcy Courts: Official "Court Locator"

The **Federal Judiciary U.S. Courts'** site offers general information about the federal district court system (http://www.uscourts.gov/districtcourts.html) and the federal bankruptcy court system (http://www.uscourts.gov/bankruptcycourts.html).

To link to any federal district or federal bankruptcy courts' Web site, visit the **U.S. Courts** *Court Locator* page (http://www.uscourts.gov/Court_Locator/CourtLocatorSearch.aspx). Using the *Court Locator* (pictured on page 369), select *Search by Circuit*, choose a specific circuit (or *All Circuits*) from the drop-down menu, and then choose the *Court Type* (*Bankruptcy Court* or *District Court*). On this same page, you can also search by *Area Code* or *Location* if you are uncertain in which circuit the district or bankruptcy court is located. In the alternative, you could also use the *Court Locator's* map (http://www.uscourts.gov/Court_Locator.aspx) to view a list of all the federal courts in a jurisdiction by clicking any state, territory, or district (pictured on page 369).

U.S. District Courts and U.S. Bankruptcy Courts: Individual Court's Official Sites

Information found at each district or bankruptcy court's site varies, but may include opinions, court fees, filing procedures, court forms, general orders, judge's requirements, or local rules.

U.S. District Courts and U.S. Bankruptcy Courts: Unofficial Sites for Case Law Searching

For many years, most free case law sites did not provide a searchable database of U.S. District or Bankruptcy cases. **Justia** was the first site to offer a FREE full-text keyword searchable database of District Court opinions and orders (civil and criminal), from 2004 to present (but not Bankruptcy cases). However,

Justia's *Federal District Court Opinions and Orders* database is currently undergoing an upgrade, so it is offline as we go to press with this book.

More recently, **Google Scholar** began offering a free full-text searchable database of U.S. District and Bankruptcy cases (and other federal and state cases). See pages 295–299 for details. Prior to that, **FindACase.com** had introduced a free database of U.S. District (but not Bankruptcy) cases (see page 293). **Casemaker** (a member benefit case law database discussed on page 302) also offers a full-text searchable database of U.S. District and Bankruptcy cases.

U.S. District Courts and U.S. Bankruptcy Courts: Dockets

To access District and Bankruptcy Courts' docket sheets (and underlying documents and opinions), you will usually need to have subscriptions to **PACER** (see page 386), **Westlaw CourtExpress.com** (http://courtexpress.westlaw.com/), or **LexisNexis CourtLink.com** (http://www.lexisnexis.com/courtlink/). You can use one of the three free options: (1) **RECAP** (partial Federal District and Bankruptcy Court dockets only; see page 388), (2) **Justia** (Federal District Court <u>civil</u> dockets; see page 391), and (3) **Freecourtdockets.com** (Federal District and Bankruptcy Court dockets; see page 391).

Directory of Federal, State, and Local Dockets

In addition to almost all federal courts placing dockets online, some state and local courts have also placed dockets online. For a useful directory that links to federal, state, and local court dockets, use **LLRX.com** (http://www.llrx.com/courtrules). To browse the list, scroll down to *Type of Resource (Federal & State)* and then click *Dockets.* This database can also be browsed by type of court (e.g., bankruptcy), by jurisdiction (e.g., federal or state), or searched with keywords.

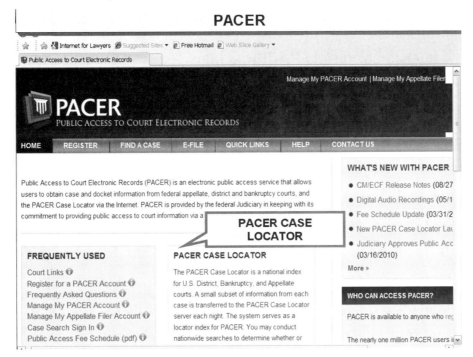

PACER (http://www.pacer.gov/) is the federal government's court docket database, covering over 33 million cases from the Circuit Courts of Appeal, District Courts, and Bankruptcy Courts. See page 169 for more details about **PACER** bankruptcy court searching and an illustration of the Bankruptcy Court search page. **PACER** includes the case's docket sheet, its underlying documents (but not necessarily for all cases), transcripts, and the written opinions. You can access **PACER** from each court's Web site (using the Federal Judiciary's **U.S. Courts'** *Court Locator* discussed on page 369) or from the *Individual Court Pacer Sites'* page at **PACER** (http://www.pacer.gov/psco/cgi-bin/links.pl). Dates of coverage vary for each court and will be indicated at each court's site.

Docket searching is useful for many reasons, such as learning: (1) how litigious someone is (by searching a person or company's name); (2) whether someone has declared bankruptcy (by searching for a name or Social Security Number); (3) which practice areas are heating up (by searching by the NOS, which stands for "Nature of [the] Suit"); or (4) to track a known case (by searching by docket number). Some attorneys use **PACER** to find sample pleadings either by searching for a similar case they know of or by conducting a NOS search.

Aside from searching an individual court's **PACER** docket database, you can use **PACER's** *Case Locator* (formerly *U.S. Party/Case Index*; https://pcl.uscourts.gov/search) to search one or more courts together. To begin a *Case Locator* search, log into **PACER** at https://pacer.login.uscourts.gov/cgi-bin/login.pl?court_id=00pcl and then choose *All Courts* to conduct a nearly national search. (Because the Federal Circuit Court is not yet participating in the *Case Locator,* you are unable to conduct a true "national" search. You will need to conduct a separate search at the Federal Circuit's **PACER** page after conducting your *All Courts Case Locator* search.)

At the *Case Locator* page, you can, in addition to conducting an *All Courts* search, choose to search a specific court type (*Appellate, Bankruptcy, Civil* or *Criminal*). Once you choose *All Courts* or a specific court type, then you can choose to conduct a *Basic Search* or an *Advanced Search.* Depending on which court type you select to search, you will see that some offer more search options than others. For example, the search displayed in the next illustration is a *Basic Search* of *All Courts*, where you can search by *Party Name, Case Number,* or *Region.*

A *Region* search allows you to conduct a broad search (*All Courts*) or a narrower search by a specific Circuit or State. Selecting a particular Circuit will search all the Federal Courts within that Circuit (District, Bankruptcy, and the Circuit Courts of Appeal). For example, a search of the Third Circuit will include all Federal District and Bankruptcy courts within Delaware, New Jersey, Pennsylvania, and the Virgin Islands, in addition to the Third Circuit Courts of Appeal. If you choose a specific state, its corresponding Circuit Courts of Appeal will also be searched. For example, if searching Colorado, all federal District and Bankruptcy courts in Colorado plus the Tenth Circuit Courts of Appeal will be searched. You can also choose to search a specific court, such as the Northern District of California.

If you choose the *Appellate* tab or the *Civil* tab (see illustration below), one additional search option is offered: *NOS* (see page 383). And, if you choose the *Bankruptcy* tab, two additional search options are offered: (1) a combination *Four-Digit SSN* (Social Security Number)/*Party Name* search or (2) a full *SSN* or *TIN* (Taxpayer Identification Number) search.

PACER CASE LOCATOR SEARCH

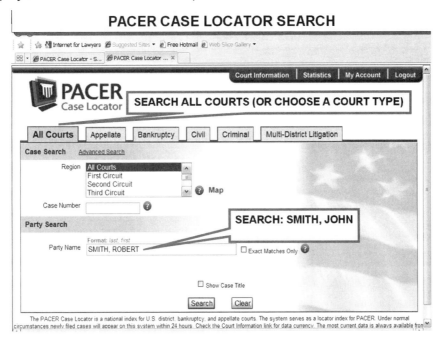

The *Case Locator* (pictured below) also offers an *Advanced Search* to limit or expand your search by *Case Title, Date Filed*, and *Date Closed*.

PACER CASE LOCATOR ADVANCED SEARCH

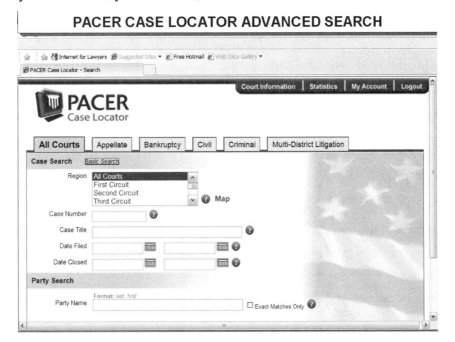

Once a docket is found, you can click on the docket number link to access the full docket sheet. If a court also offers immediate downloading of the underlying documents, you will see an underlined number to the left of the document description (see below). (Note: We have redacted the debtor's name in the docket displayed below. When you search **PACER**, names are displayed.)

Filing Date	#	Docket Text
03/19/2007	1	Chapter 7 Voluntary Petition. Filed by _____ (Attachments: # 1 Signature Page Signature Page _____ (Entered: 03/19/2007)
03/19/2007		
03/19/2007	2	**UNDERLINED NUMBERS INDICATE THE DOCUMENT IS AVAILABLE FOR IMMEDIATE VIEWING/DOWNLOADING**
03/19/2007	3	Debtor has received a briefing from an approved credit counseling agency and does have a certificate from the agency describing the services provided. _____ (Entered: 03/19/2007)
03/19/2007	4	Statement of Social Security Number (image restricted) _____ (Entered: 03/19/2007)
03/19/2007	5	Statement pursuant to NM LBR 1002-1 certifying that individual debtor has no spouse. Filed by Debtor _____ (Entered: 03/19/2007)
03/19/2007	6	Statement of Intention. Filed by _____ (Entered: 03/19/2007)
03/19/2007	7	Disclosure of Compensation. Filed by _____ (Entered: 03/19/2007)
03/22/2007	8	BNC Certificate of Mailing - Meeting of Creditors. (RE: related document(s)2 Meeting (Chapter 7), Meeting (Chapter 7)). No. of Notices: 20. Service Date 03/22/2007. (Admin.) (Entered: 03/22/2007)
03/29/2007	9	Request for Notice Filed by Creditor Navistar Financial Corporation. (Wolske, Janet) (Entered: 03/29/2007)
04/10/2007	10	Amended Schedule(s) J. (No Fee is required) Filed by Debtor _____ (Entered:

Speaking of redaction, in an April 5, 2010 Federal Judicial Study, 2,899 documents with unredacted Social Security numbers were found in **PACER** documents (approximately one out of every 3,400 court documents), with a greater number found in bankruptcy documents (http://www.fjc.gov/public/pdf.nsf/lookup/ssnctdoc.pdf/$file/ssnctdoc.pdf), despite the Federal Rules of Procedure (Civil, Criminal, and Bankruptcy) requiring redaction (or truncation) of full Social Security numbers.

To open a **PACER** account you must register at https://www.pacer.gov/psco/cgi-bin/regform.pl. For same day registration, you must provide a credit card. No annual fee is imposed; you pay only for actual use. At eight cents per page, with a $2.40 cap for most documents and free access to written opinions for **PACER** subscribers, it's very affordable. However, there is no cap on the cost of transcripts or docket sheets, so the fee could rise above $2.40 if the document is over 30 pages long. Previously, users were allowed $10 worth of free documents per year, but now are allowed $10 worth per quarter.

In other new **PACER** developments, audio recordings of court proceedings are being made available at a few federal district and bankruptcy courts (http://www.pacer.gov/announcements/general/audio_pilot.html), with the fee dropping from $26 for a CD to $2.40 to access the audio online. A pilot program was also instituted in twelve courts to publish federal district and bankruptcy court opinions via **FDsys** (http://tinyurl.com/newpacerinfo).

In January 2007, **PACER** offered free access at seventeen federal depository libraries in fourteen states in a joint, two-year project by the Administrative Office of the U.S. Courts and the Government Printing Office. The libraries included court, county law, and law school libraries. In September 2008, the project was suspended so it could be evaluated (http://www.fdlp.gov/home/45-partnerships/88-pacer-access). As of June 2009, **PACER** was no longer available free at federal depository libraries. However, **PACER** public access terminals are provided free at federal courthouses (but only for filings in the courthouse where the terminal is located), with printouts priced at ten cents per page. (The charge for copies from paper case file at the clerk's office is fifty cents per page.)

Federal Docket Database for Electronic Filing and E-Alerts: CM/ECF (Case Management/Electronic Case Files)

As of October 2010, nearly all of the federal courts (http://www.pacer.gov/cmecf/ecfinfo.html) have switched over to **CM/ECF** (**Case Management/Electronic Case Files**), an electronic case management and filing system that began to roll out in 2001. **CM/ECF** is explained by the Administrative Office of the U.S. Courts as, "a comprehensive case management system that allows courts to maintain electronic case files and offer electronic filing over the Internet. Think **PACER** for searching and **CM/ECF** for filing. **PACER** searches can find **CM/ECF** documents but you need a separate account to use **CM/ECF** to file documents" (http://www.pacer.gov). Using **CM/ECF**, each attorney of record, including pro se litigants, receives free e-mail docket alerts, with hyperlinks back to the court documents (http://www.pacer.gov/psc/efaq.html#CMECF). To obtain this service, you would log into your **CM/ECF** account with your court-issued filing log-in (the **PACER** log-in does not work for this e-mail notice service) and supply your e-mail address and the docket number of your case. You can also supply additional e-mail addresses for others to also receive alerts. You can choose to receive an e-mail alert for each new event relating to a filing or a daily summary notice of all filings. One free copy of each document is made available to each attorney of record and to any secondary addressee listed under the e-mail information screen. Non-parties can also receive notices for cases they are interested in, but they must register for a **PACER** ID and password, a **CM/ECF** filer ID and password, and be an approved registrant in a Federal court (for more details, see http://www.pacer.gov/psc/efaq.html#CMECF). See pages 390–391 for information about other docket alert vendors.

RECAP (PACER Spelled Backwards): Free (Partial) Federal District and Bankruptcy Court Dockets Database

RECAP (at https://www.recapthelaw.org/) is a project of the **Center for Information Technology Policy** at **Princeton University** that allows free access to millions of U.S. Federal District and Bankruptcy Court documents (http://archive.recapthelaw.org/about/). Note: there is no access to Courts of Appeal dockets. According to the founders of **RECAP**, "We created **RECAP** in hopes of hastening the day when court records would be freely available to the general public via the Internet" (https://www.recapthelaw.org/why-it-matters/). By downloading an "add on" to your **Firefox** Web browser (at https://www.recapthelaw.org/), **PACER** users can automatically donate **PACER** documents each time they purchase one from **PACER**. The document is uploaded to a public repository hosted by the **Internet Archive** where it becomes available for free to other **RECAP** users. **RECAP** explains this "saves users money by alerting them when a document they are searching for is already available from this repository" (https://www.recapthelaw.org/about). **RECAP** also creates more user-friendly file names for its **PACER** users by including the **PACER** court, case number, and the docket entry number as the file name (https://www.recapthelaw.org/features/).

You can search the **RECAP** *Archive* at http://archive.recapthelaw.org or conduct an *Advanced Search* by clicking the *Advanced Search* link (see the next illustration). When searching the **RECAP** *Archive*, it is important to understand that the docket is unofficial and may be incomplete or out-of-date, so it is advisable to use the **RECAP** *Archive* only when searching for a known document.

Although the **RECAP** *Archive* offers access to millions of PDFs, the search interface does not permit you to search through the full text of these PDFs. Instead, you are searching through short descriptions of each document that are part of the docket sheet. (This is also the case at **PACER**.). **RECAP** hopes to offer a full-text search in the future.

Notice the *Search Tips* link in the next illustration below. Some of the tips explain that you can use the asterisk (*) character as a wildcard to extend the root of a word and you can exclude a word (just as you can in **Google**) by using the minus sign.

RECAP ARCHIVE ADVANCED SEARCH

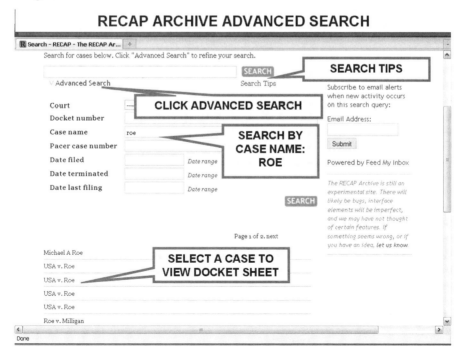

The **RECAP** docket sheet (pictured below) indicates if a document is available for free (click *Download*) or whether it must be purchased (click *Buy from PACER*). You can also subscribe to an e-mail alert for new case activity.

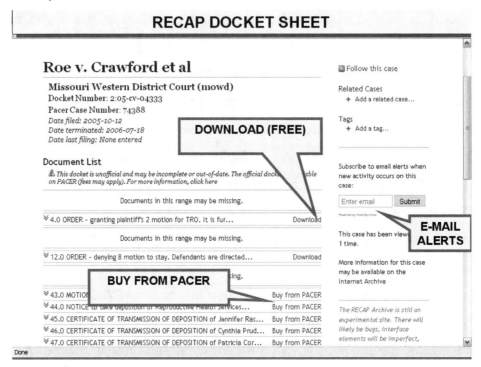

U.S. Supreme Court Dockets Not Available on PACER or CM/ECF

The U.S. Supreme Court is not part of the **PACER** system or **CM/ECF**. As noted on pages 372–374, the Court offers free access to the current Term's and the most immediate prior Term's dockets while **FindLaw** and **Oyez** offer abbreviated docket information for the current Term and past Terms (offering older date coverage than the ones at the Court's own site). **Freecourtdockets.com** also offers free U.S. Supreme Court dockets (see page 391).

Docket and E-Alert Databases With More Sophisticated Searching and More Jurisdictions Than PACER

To access more sophisticated docket searching and e-mail alerts than **PACER** offers (and of more jurisdictions), you will need to subscribe to a pay

docket database such as: **Westlaw CourtExpress.com**
(http://courtexpress.westlaw.com/) or **LexisNexis CourtLink.com**
(http://www.lexisnexis.com/courtlink/). Based on your search criteria, these
databases can alert you whenever a new docket is filed in a particular court or
when a new document is added to a particular docket sheet. Both services also
include many state and local court dockets, in addition to federal courts.

Free Federal Dockets from Justia and Freecourtdockets.com

Freecourtdockets.com (http://www.freecourtdockets.com) provides access
to the dockets (not just the summaries) of approximately 33 million cases going
back twenty years, from the following courts: U.S. Supreme, U.S. District Civil and
Criminal, U.S. Bankruptcy, U.S. Federal Claims, and U.S. International Trade (the
U.S. Appellate is not yet available). To access **Freecourtdockets.com**, you must
first request an invitation code (which is free). To retrieve a docket from
Freecourtdockets.com:

- select the court type and then a court
- enter the case/docket number
- enter the invitation code
- click the *Retrieve Docket* button

On the bottom of the last page of every docket is a notation as to when the
docket was last updated and an option to update it. Tracking a docket is not yet
available. The underlying documents are not provided; however, there are links
to the appropriate **PACER/CM/ECF** databases, where you would then enter your
PACER password to retrieve opinions (free) and other documents (for a fee).
One drawback to **Freecourtdockets.com** is that docket retrieval is by
case/docket number only.

Justia offers a free database to retrieve federal dockets back to 2004. On
Justia's home page (lower right-hand corner), the database is called *U.S.
District Courts' Civil Case Filings* (http://www.justia.com), but when you link to the
page it is simply called *Dockets and Filings* (http://dockets.justia.com). The

database used to include only U.S. District Court civil dockets, but now (despite its name, as listed on the home page), also includes U.S. Circuit Courts of Appeal dockets (see the first illustration on the next page). The database is poorly documented (possibly because it is still in beta mode), but we have run many test searches to assist you in using this database.

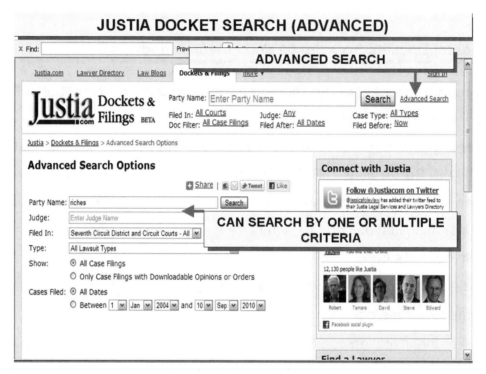

At the *Advanced Search* page (pictured above), you can search by one or more of the following criteria: *Party Name*; *Judge Name*, *Filed In* (select *All Federal District Courts*, *Circuit Courts of Appeal—All*, or all of one state's federal district courts or just a specific one); *Type* (this refers to **PACER's** Nature of Suit (NOS) designation, *e.g., patent law*); *Show* (choose either *All Case Filings* or *Only Case Filings with Downloadable Opinions or Orders*), or *Cases Filed* (select *All Dates* or enter a date range).

While many of **Justia's** docket results provide just a summary of the docket sheet, some include the full docket sheet. Also, if you see a gavel icon (see the next illustration), this indicates the opinion and orders are available.

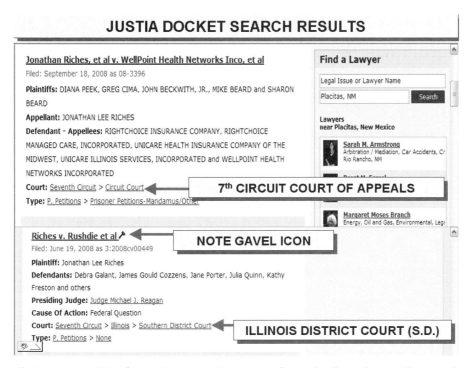

JUSTIA DOCKET SEARCH RESULTS

If you click a case title from the results page (e.g. in the above illustration, we clicked on *Riches* v. *Rushdie*), the full docket sheet and a link to available documents will be displayed (see illustration below). To download a document, such as the order noted in the next illustration, click its docket entry number (e.g. 3). You can also opt to receive free RSS feeds of filings that meet your search criteria.

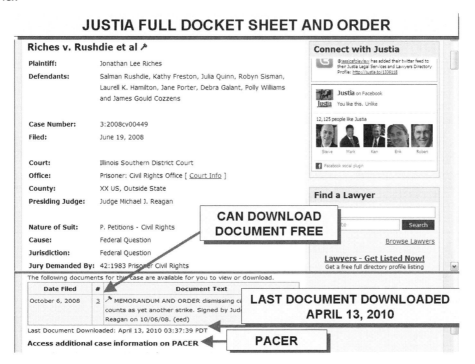

JUSTIA FULL DOCKET SHEET AND ORDER

Some dockets include all of the e-Filing (underlying) documents. This would be indicated by a yellow star icon. If **Justia** does not have the full docket sheet or any (or less than all) of the underlying documents, **Justia** points users to **PACER** (see previous illustration). See page 383 for details about **PACER**.

The database can be browsed in a variety of ways, such as *By Type of Lawsuit* (Nature of Suit). To conduct that search, you would click an option from the *Type of Lawsuit* list (e.g., *Contracts*), and then select an option from the list (e.g., *Marine*). The database can also be browsed by *Circuit*, *State*, or *Most Recently Filed.*

Justia and **Freecourtdockets.com** both have pros and cons, and the savvy searcher should use both. Some of **Justia's** strengths over **Freecourtdockets.com** are its party name and NOS (Nature of Suit) searching, the option of searching all District Courts together, and retrieving (in some instances) the full docket with underlying documents, opinions, and orders. **Freecourtdockets.com's** strengths over **Justia** are access to more courts (with more years of coverage and a full docket for every case.

State Courts' Online Dockets (and Documents) and State E-Filing

For information about which State courts offer online public access to court dockets and documents, visit the **National Center for State Courts (NCSC)** site (http://tinyurl.com/statedockets). To review the status of State e-filing, see **NCSC's** 2009 survey (http://tinyurl.com/stateefilingsurvey).

STARTING POINTS FOR STATE, LOCAL, U.S. TERRITORIAL, AND TRIBAL GOVERNMENT INTERNET RESEARCH

There are several useful directory sites for linking to each state, local, territorial, and tribal government's home page to determine if their statutes, ordinances, courts, opinions, and other resources are on the Internet.

USA.gov is a useful site not only for federal government links (as discussed earlier on pages 276–279), but also for links to state and territorial

(http://www.usa.gov/Agencies/State_and_Territories.shtml),
local (http://www.usa.gov/Agencies/Local.shtml), and
tribal (http://www.usa.gov/Government/Tribal_Sites/index.shtml) government
Web sites. The territories include: American Samoa, Federated States of
Micronesia, Guam, Midway Islands, Puerto Rico, and the U.S. Virgin Islands.

State and Local Government on the Net (http://www.statelocalgov.net)
provides three drop-down menus to link to any state or local government Web
site or to link by topic (such as *Legislation* or *Education*). The drop-down menus
are labeled: (1) *Select State* (which also includes territorial and tribal choices), (2)
Select Topic, and (3) *Local Govt.* After selecting from the drop-down menus, you
must click on the *Go* button. You cannot select more than one drop-down menu
at a time. Select the **Search** link underneath the *Local Govt.* drop-down menu to
search by keywords (e.g., *marriage records*).

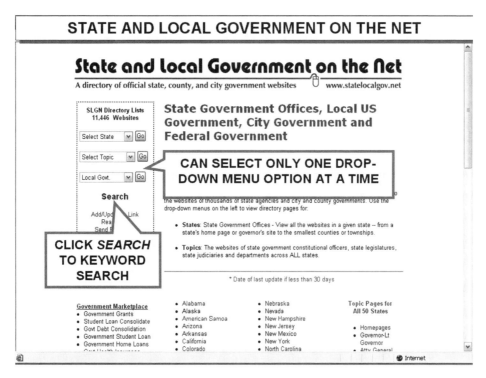

The **Library of Congress's** *State Government Information* page
(http://www.loc.gov/rr/news/stategov/stategov.html) provides links to all fifty
states' home pages and to some local government pages.

State, Local, Territorial, and Tribal Statutory and Regulatory Law

The **Full-text State Statutes and Legislation on the Internet** site (http://www.whpgs.org/f.htm) provides access to all states' and U.S. territories' statutory codes, administrative codes, regulations, bills, constitutions, and local ordinances. **FindLaw** (http://www.findlaw.com/casecode/) offers similar state links, but only links to one territory, Guam (scroll down to *State Resources* and select a state or Guam). By using these two sites' directories, you don't have to remember the title of any state's (or territory's) statutory or regulatory material (e.g., *New York Consolidated Laws, Arizona Revised Statutes*) because the directories make it easy for you to browse through each state's list.

For links to local codes (county and city), see page 399. For links to tribal statutory and regulatory law (and treaties) see (http://linkon.in/9YPHS8 and http://linkon.in/901CYw)

State, Local, Territorial, and Tribal Executive Branches, Agencies, Boards, and Commissions(U.S.)(U.S.)

The **State and Local Government on the Net** site (noted earlier in this chapter; http://www.statelocalgov.net/), can be used to link to state, local, and territorial executive branches, agencies, etc. From the home page, click on the *Select State* drop-down menu on the left and choose a state or territory. Then, scroll down to *Executive Branch* (which will list agencies) or scroll down to *Boards and Commissions.* Browse through the list to link to the appropriate entity's Web site. For links to local executive branches and agencies, use the *Local Govt* link. For links to tribal agencies and organizations, see **USA.gov** (http://www.usa.gov/Government/Tribal_Sites/index.shtml).

Directory of Official State, Local, Territorial, and Tribal Courts

FindLaw.com offers links to a directory of official state and territorial court Web sites (http://www.findlaw.com/11stategov). Select a state from the *Browse U.S. States* list or select a territory from the *Browse Territories* list and then click on *Courts* to link to that state's court sites or that territory's court sites. **FindLaw's** territory court links are somewhat sparse, so it may be a better idea to visit **USA.gov** (http://www.usa.gov/) and search with keywords (e.g., *Guam court*). **Justia** also has a directory of state court links (http://www.justia.com/courts/state-courts). For tribal court links, see **USA.gov** (http://www.usa.gov/Government/Tribal_Sites/index.shtml). To find local (county or city) court links, a keyword search at **USA.gov** (http://www.usa.gov/) is the easiest method (e.g., *Bernalillo "New Mexico" court*).

Directory of State Case Law Databases

FindLaw.com provides a directory to state case law databases (visit http://www.findlaw.com/casecode and scroll down to *State Resources*). Most of the links are to case law databases created by **FindLaw**. See pages 243 for complete information on **FindLaw**.

State Case Law Databases

For information about free (and free "member benefit") state case law databases, see *Chapter Twelve*, *Free Online Case Law Databases* and *Chapter Thirteen*, *Free "Member Benefit To Lawyers" Online Legal Research Databases: Case Law And More.*

Some state and local courts have placed dockets online. To find links to those courts, use **LLRX's** database (http://www.llrx.com/courtrules; see page 382) State court dockets are also available on pay sites, such as **West CourtExpress** (http://www.courtexpress.westlaw.com) and **LexisNexis CourtLink** (http://www.lexisnexis.com/courtlink).

Local Government Web Sites: County and City Level

The **State and Local Government on the Net** site (mentioned on page 395) provides links to both county and city Web sites, in addition to the states' sites. The **NACO** (**National Association of Counties**) Web site (http://www.naco.org/) is devoted strictly to counties. Basic information for each county, such as demographics and government contact information is provided, along with links to each county's site (click *About Counties* and choose *Find County*). Various examples of county ordinances and codes by topic are provided at http://www.naco.org/research/solutions/Pages/CodesandOrdiances.aspx.

Many local jurisdictions' codes can be found online for free either at the jurisdiction's Web site or at one of the three Code publishers' sites (noted below). Most of the local Codes are full-text keyword/phrase searchable, although some only offer the ability to browse by *Title* or *Chapter*.

- **American Legal Publishing** offers hundreds of keyword/phrase-searchable local codes in thirty-two states (http://www.amlegal.com/library/). It is the only vendor that offers a free search of all of its state codes together. The option is listed in the middle of the home page (click *View and search ALL the codes in our Online Library*) or it can be selected from the drop-down menu on the home page labeled *Select a State*. To begin a search, select a state from the map or from the *Select a State* drop-down menu and then choose a city or county. You can also opt to search all the local codes in one state. The *Advanced Search* page allows you to enter keywords and phases into various pre-set Boolean and phrase search boxes. In addition, you can check the *Find alternate word forms (stemming)* box or the *Find synonyms* box. The *Boolean Search* page allows you to enter keywords and phrases into a single search box and connect them with Boolean and proximity connectors. Be sure to study the *Search Syntax Summary* listed at the bottom of the *Boolean Search* page because some of the syntax may be unfamiliar to you. You can create slightly more complex searches than you can at the other municipal code sites listed on the vnext page. You can search the entire Code or just a specific chapter. The Codes can also be browsed.

- **MuniCode** offers keyword/phrase-searchable codes for over 1,600 local governments in 50 states (http://www.municode.com). Individual codes can be searched for free, but to search multiple codes, there is an annual fee. To begin a search, click on the *MuniCode Library* tab at the top of the home page. You can then choose a state from the map or from the drop-down menu, and then choose a city or county. The *Boolean Search* page allows you to enter keywords and phrases into a single search box and connect them with Boolean connectors (use quotation marks to enclose phrases, the plus [+] sign to require words, and the minus [-] sign to exclude words). In addition, you can add an asterisk to the end of a word root to expand the word (e.g., a search for *child** would return *child, children, childish*) or add an asterisk within a word to find variations of words (e.g., a search for *a*n* will bring back results that include *addition, assign*). You can search an entire Code or just a specific chapter. The *Advanced Search* page allows you to enter keywords and phases into various pre-set Boolean and phrase search boxes. In addition, the *Advanced Search* page allows you to deploy the OR Boolean connector (by adding words into the search box labeled *and containing any of these words*) and to expand your search by choosing the *Find alternate word forms (stemming)* option. Codes can also be browsed. In 2009 **MuniCode** acquired more than 500 customers from **LexisNexis**. When we attempted to visit **LexisNexis's** formerly free **Municipal Codes** site at http://municipalcodes.lexisnexis.com/, we were re-directed to **MuniCode's** site.

- **General Code** upgraded its **E-Codes** interface and re-launched as **eCode360** (http://www.generalcode.com/webcode2.html). **General Code** provides Codes for twenty-four states and one city in Canada. Individual codes can be searched for free, but to search multiple codes, there is an annual fee. In addition to offering keyword/phrase-searching of local codes (connected by Boolean connectors), you can now open an entire chapter or just portions of one and also search by a specific section number. To begin a search, choose a state from the *State Index* and then choose a city or county. Only one code can be searched at a time. Codes can also be browsed by their Table of Contents or Index.

Two other sites where you can find links to local codes were discussed on page 396 (**Full-text State Statutes and Legislation on the Internet** at http://www.whpgs.org/f.htm and **FindLaw** at http://www.findlaw.com/casecode).

STATISTICAL INFORMATION AND DATABASES: U.S. FEDERAL, STATE, AND LOCAL (AND ALSO FOREIGN COUNTRIES)

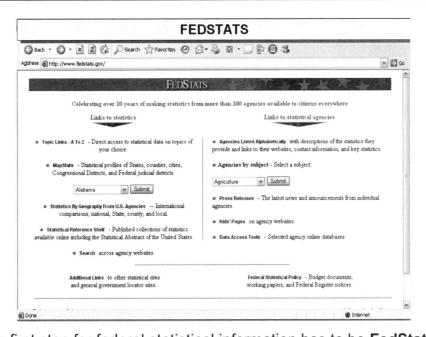

The first stop for federal statistical information has to be **FedStats** (http://www.fedstats.gov), where you can search the statistical databases of more than 100 federal agencies in a variety of ways. From the left-hand side of the site's home page, you can click on (1) *Topic Links A to Z* (for an alphabetical list by topic of agencies' statistical databases); (2) *MapStats* (for statistical profiles of states, counties, cities, congressional districts, and federal judicial districts; click on the link or use the drop-down menu to select a state); (3) *Statistics by Geography from U.S. Agencies;* (4) *Statistical Reference Shelf* (to link to other statistical resources, such as the **Statistical Abstract of the United States** site; see pages 402-403 for details); (5) *Search across agency Web sites* (to search through all 100 agencies' statistical resources simultaneously); and (6) *Additional links to other statistical sites* (including other federal, non-federal, and non-U.S. statistical sites).

On the right-hand side of the home page, you can click on (1) *Agencies Listed Alphabetically* (access an alphabetical list of agencies that provide statistics), (2) *Agencies by Subject* (select a subject from the drop-down menu to retrieve a list of agencies that provide statistics on that subject), (3) *Press Releases*, or (4) *Data Access Tools* (select statistical information interactively to create customized reports), among other options.

Two of the more commonly used individual governmental statistical sites are the **U.S. Census Bureau** at http://www.census.gov/ (along with its **Statistical Abstract of the United States** at http://www.census.gov/compendia/statab) and the **U.S. Department of Labor Bureau of Labor Statistics** at http://www.bls.gov/.

The 2000 census is available online at the Census Bureau site (http://www.census.gov/main/www/cen2000.html), but according to the site the, "1990 Census Lookup data access tool is no longer available, due to resource limitations." However, some of the 1990 data are available at http://www.census.gov/main/www/cen1990.html. Some census data back to 1790 are available at http://www.census.gov/population/www/censusdata/hiscendata.html. Statistics from the 2010 Census are not yet available online. In addition to these government sites, many public libraries have full census information available through the **Ancestry** database. An in-person visit to the library is usually required to access this database.

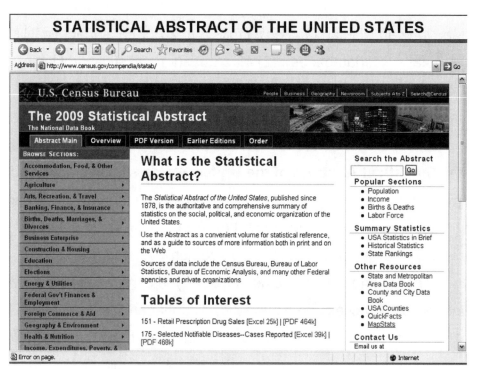

The current edition of the **Statistical Abstract of the United States** is available full-text (by section) as a PDF (http://www.census.gov/compendia/statab/2010edition.html) and can also be keyword searched (http://www.census.gov/compendia/statab/index.html) by entering keywords into the *Search the Abstract* search box located on the upper right-hand side of the page. The site also includes links to earlier editions of the **Statistical Abstract** back to 1878 (http://www.census.gov/compendia/statab/past_years.html) and to other statistical books that relate to state, county, and city statistics.

The **University of Virginia County and City Data Books** site (http://www2.lib.virginia.edu/ccdb) is a compilation of all the statistical data from the *County and City Data Books* for the entire U.S. covering the years 1944 through 2000. Search by selecting one or multiple states, cities, or counties. You can create customized reports based on seventy-five different topics. Topics range from *Population* (by race, age, etc.) to *Number of Banks*.

Need to know the number of female state legislators or the addresses of all central banks in the world? In addition to links to governmental federal statistical sources, the **University of Michigan Documents Center's Statistical Resources on the Web** (http://www.lib.umich.edu/government-records-center/explore) links to state, local, and foreign governmental statistical databases; as well as also non-governmental statistical databases, such as private non-profits and universities. Click on any topic for a list of links to statistical databases covering that topic (e.g., *State Government*). You can also narrow the list of displayed results down using the *Filter by Sub-Topic* option on the right-hand side of the results page. The databases are maintained by various entities and have varying currency/coverage dates.

Need worldwide facts? Check out the **CIA's World Factbook** (https://www.cia.gov/library/publications/the-world-factbook/index.html). The 2010 edition is available as either a text file that can be easily viewed online or as a downloadable PDF (the links are underneath the *Select a Country or Location* drop-down menu on the top right of the page; note that the PDF is very large). The online version is continually updated, with a *Page Last Updated* notation on the top left-hand side of the page when reading a country's entry. For example, when we viewed the Afghanistan country profile on October 1, 2010, a notation showed that it was last updated on September 15, 2010. Previous editions of the Factbook, back to 2000, are available for download at https://www.cia.gov/library/publications/download/.

GOVERNMENT PRINT AND WEB PUBLICATIONS

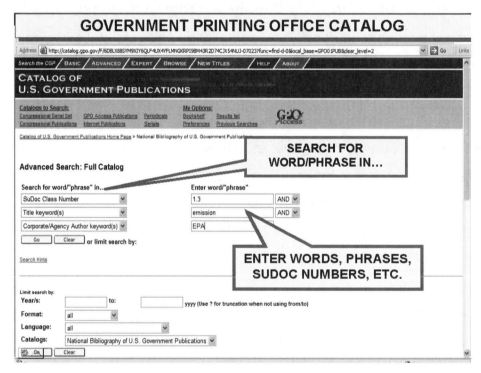

The next time someone asks you if a specific government publication is available on the Web or if you need to find a government document referred to by the opposition's expert, try using the **Government Printing Office's Catalog** at http://catalog.gpo.gov/F. Be sure to click on the *Advanced Search* link in the middle of the page and then make note of the *Advanced Search* page's drop-down menus. Click on the arrow labeled *Search for word/"phrase" in* to limit the search to *Title Keywords*, *SuDoc* (Superintendent of Documents) *Class Number* (which is like a library call number), *Corporate/Agency Author Keywords*, etc. Documents that are available online will include a link to the online version in the

Internet Access column on the right-hand side of the results list. For documents not directly available online, if you click on the publication title link (in the results list), the next page will display the full record for that title, including a *Locate in a Library* link (towards the bottom of the page), which takes you to another page where you can enter a city or state name or an area code to discover if the title is available form a nearby regional depository library. To find other government documents online, see pages 276–279 for information about **USA.gov**.

Chapter Fifteen

FINDING LEGAL WEB SITES THAT ARE TOPIC-, JURISDICTION-, OR FORMAT-SPECIFIC

Most legal Web sites are topic-, jurisdiction-, or format-specific. A topic-specific legal site focuses on one area of law (such as advertising law). A jurisdiction-specific site focuses on one (or more) counties, states, countries, etc. A format-specific site focuses on one or a few related types of information, such as all court forms available free on the Web. These topic-, jurisdiction-, or format-specific Web sites might provide content at their site and/or might link to various other sites that focus on that specific topic, jurisdiction, or format. With the proliferation of blogs, there are now even more avenues for finding topic-, jurisdiction-, or format-specific sites. For an annotated, topically arranged index of legal blogs, see **TheBlogsofLaw** (http://www.theblogsoflaw.com) and **Justia's Blawgsearch** (http://blawgsearch.justia.com/), which can also be keyword searched.

The following pages provide some samples of topic-, jurisdiction-, and format-specific Web sites.

Advertising Law

The law firm of **Reed Smith** originally created an advertising and marketing law Web site. It used to be updated bi-weekly, but it has now morphed into a blog, **Adlaw by Request** (http://www.adlawbyrequest.com), which is updated more frequently. Tabs in the left-hand column labeled *In the Courts, Legislation, Regulators, International,* and *Industry* (among others), allow visitors to focus on specific types of advertising law and topics like *Green Corner* or *KidAdLaw*. The site provides a search engine to search by keyword for any document in the site. The firm also has other topical blogs.

The law firm of **Arnold & Porter** sponsors the **Consumer Advertising Law Blog** (http://www.consumeradvertisinglawblog.com/). Posts are listed in categories ranging from *Children/Kids* and *Financial Services* to *Green Claims* and *Weight Loss*. Clicking on any of these categories listed on the lower right-hand side of the blog (scroll down past the *Recent Posts* to see them) lists only the posts that have been assigned to the category you clicked. The site also provides a search engine to search by keyword for any post in the site.

Bankruptcy Law

The **American Bankruptcy Institute** (**ABI**), which was founded in 1982 to provide Congress and the public with unbiased analysis of bankruptcy issues, has a site at http://www.abiworld.org. Naturally, the information is U.S.-centric. The more useful information can be found by clicking on the *Online Resources* (some resources require **ABI** membership) and the *Consumer Bankruptcy Center* (available to non-members) links located at the top of each of the site's pages.

For links to international and foreign bankruptcy law sites, in addition to U.S., see **HG.org** at http://www.hg.org/bankrpt.html. It provides links to bankruptcy laws, cases, publications, and organizations.

Timothy E. Eble, a contributing author to a leading treatise on class actions (*Newberg on Class Actions*), is the site owner of **Class Action Litigation Information** (http://www.classactionlitigation.com). The site contains the full text of the *Federal Class Action Practice Manual—Internet Edition* (http://www.classactionlitigation.com/fcapmanual/) and links to class action articles, legislation, and more.

Despite focusing mostly on their own firm's cases, the sites of two big players in the class action arena — **Robbins Geller Rudman & Dowd LLP** (http://www.rgrdlaw.com/) and **Milberg** (http://www.milberg.com) — provide some useful research information. For example, those who want to research the Enron case can visit the **Robbins Geller** site to link to various Enron court documents and press releases. The *Enron Fraud* link is on the left-hand side of the home page. (See the section on *Securities Law* on page 423 for a Securities class action site.)

Copyright Law

The **U.S. Copyright Office** (http://www.copyright.gov), a department of the Library of Congress, provides online access to forms, regulations, and laws relating to copyright; it also posts a primer about copyright. In addition, there is a user-friendly, Web searchable database of copyright records dating back to 1978 (http://www.copyright.gov/records/). To access 1870–1977 records, a researcher would need to use the copyright card catalog at the Copyright Office in Washington, D.C., or fill out a form (http://www.copyright.gov/forms/search_estimate.html) to request a search for $165 per hour. (Also see page 164.)

Stanford University Libraries are the name sponsor of the **Copyright & Fair Use** site (http://fairuse.stanford.edu). Tabs in the site's *What's New* section link to copyright-related *Featured Cases*, *Dockets*, *Legislation*, *Regulation*, *Articles*, *Blogs*, and more. The university also hosts it's own **Fairly Used** blog featuring posts on copyright-related issues (http://fairuse.stanford.edu/blog).

Corporate Law

Since many corporations are incorporated in Delaware, attorneys researching corporate law may find it useful to visit the **Delaware State Court** site (http://courts.delaware.gov/). It contains a keyword searchable database of opinions back to 2000 (the Superior court database inexplicably jumps back to also include opinions from 1996; 1997-1999 are not included) — click on the *Opinions* link (in the horizontal blue bar at the top of any of the site's pages). You can limit your search to the Chancery Court, which hears corporate issues, or expand your search to all courts. (Note that when choosing the *All Opinions* option, 1996 is listed on the *Year* drop-down menu. Only the Superior Court opinions from 1996 are included, as noted above.) To find the search box, scroll all the way over to the right.

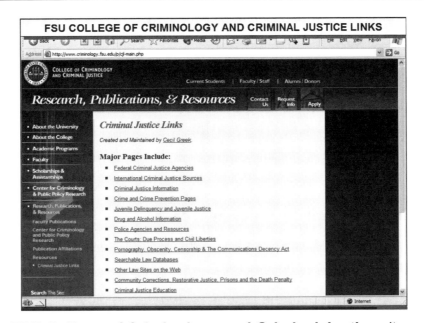

The **FSU College of Criminology and Criminal Justice** site (http://www.criminology.fsu.edu/p/cjl-main.php) provides links to federal and international criminal justice agencies, as well as information about drugs, alcohol, juvenile delinquency, and more.

The Association of Federal Defense Attorneys (http://www.afda.org) provides access to a brief bank of documents uploaded by the site's users, news, blogs, a chat room, discussion fora, and online video seminars, among other content. In the past, the site was available to members and non-members of the association for a fee. We were recently able to access the site for free (after registration) as part of a no-fee promotional period offered on the site.

The **National Association of Criminal Defense Lawyers'** (**NACDL**) site (http://www.criminaljustice.org) has information about criminal law in general, but mostly from the defense point of view.

For prosecutors and researchers interested in the prosecutorial point of view, see **The National District Attorneys Association (NDAA)** site (http://www.ndaa.org). While most of the site is for members only, there are interesting newsletters, information about new and pending criminal legislation, and state-by-state compilations of child abuse-related statutes, all available to non-members.

Employment Law Information Network (ELIN)

(http://www.elinfonet.com) includes articles, sample personnel policies and forms, links to employment laws, a discussion forum, a job board, and an attorney directory. The site is aimed at employment lawyers, in-house employment lawyers, and human resource staffs. The content is supplied by affiliates of **ELIN** (various law firms and the University of Pennsylvania's Wharton School of Business).

FindLaw's Labor and Employment page

(http://www.FindLaw.com/01topics/27labor/index.html) links to articles, blogs, databases, Web sites, laws, and government agencies dealing with employment/labor law for both the employer and the employee.

HG's Employment page (http://www.hg.org/employ.html) links to similar types of information to that of **FindLaw**, and in addition, is strong in international and foreign labor law links. This page also includes links to the Web sites of the Departments of Labor in all fifty states and the District of Columbia.

For links to hundreds of U.S. and foreign labor unions' sites, see the **Yahoo! Labor Union** page (http://linkon.in/cTWYAf).

Family Law

DivorceNet (http://www.divorcenet.com) has family law information for all fifty states, fora for posing family law questions, blogs, articles, and referrals to attorneys and experts.

Also useful is **Cornell's Divorce Law Overview** with links to all fifty states' divorce laws and also links to uniform laws and recent federal cases about divorce and related family law issues (http://topics.law.cornell.edu/wex/divorce).

Illinoisdivorce.com (http://illinoisdivorce.com/) has over 100 articles about divorce available for free on its site. This site is an example of e-lawyering. Everything is handled over the Web. For $500 they will handle an uncontested divorce (from filing the papers to representing clients in court), and for $185 they will fill out paper work and coach clients to file their own papers and represent themselves.

Foreign and International Law

The **University of Chicago's Law Library Foreign & International Law** page (http://www.lib.uchicago.edu/e/law/intl/) offers links to the laws, constitutions, and constitutional courts of foreign countries, the European Union, the United Nations, and more. The page also links to *Treaties and Other International Agreements*, *International Law Journals*, and practice-area-specific information such as *Intellectual Property* and *International Trade*.

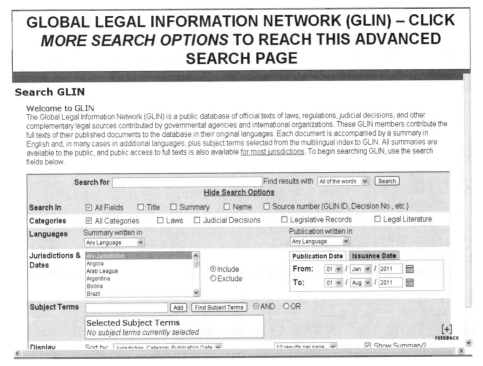

The **Law Library of Congress** offers the **Global Legal Information Network (GLIN),** a database of laws, judicial opinions, and regulations of foreign countries and international organizations (http://www.glin.gov/). Each country or organization contributes documents in the original language to the Library of Congress. The home page only displays one search box for keyword searching; for more sophisticated searching, click on the *More Search Options* link to focus the search by *Jurisdiction* (one or multiple jurisdictions), *Subject Terms* (by using the thesaurus), *Date*, *Languages*, *Category* (*Laws*, *Judicial Decisions*, etc.), or by any combination of the above criteria. Boolean and proximity searching are allowed. The results list displays the citation of the document and a summary in English. Searching and viewing the summary and citation of a document is free. Some of the summaries also provide a link to the full text of the document (in its original language), but some countries limit access to subscribers.

The **A.B.A. Legal Technology Resource Center** includes several foreign and international law journals in its free full-text legal publication search (http://www.abanet.org/tech/ltrc/lawreviewsearch.html). Coverage dates and online availability of the full text of articles varies from publication to publication.

Forms

Downloadable government electronic forms that are requested by the public on a regular basis are offered at **Uncle Sam—Forms from the Feds** (http://www.memphis.edu/govpub/forms.php). The forms are listed alphabetically by agency name.

Numerous federal agency forms can also be found at **Forms.gov** (http://www.forms.gov). There are three ways to search: (1) by keywords (including form number), (2) by selecting *Forms by Agency* to browse through forms (or once the list is brought up, you can narrow down the list by clicking the *Search within results* link and entering a full or partial agency name), or (3) by selecting *Forms by Name* to browse through an alphabetical list of forms (or once the list is brought up, you can narrow down the list by clicking the *Search within results* link to perform a keyword search through the list).

For access to over 2,000 transactional forms, from quitclaim deeds to employment agreements, for free (unless you want to pay for their *Professional MS Word and PDF formatting* forms at $9.99 each), see **The Internet Legal Resources Guide (ILRG)** (http://www.ilrg.com/forms). **The 'Lectric Law Library's Forms Room** (http://www.lectlaw.com/form.html) also offers free law practice, business, and general forms.

For court and transactional forms (free and pay), click on the *Forms* tab at **LexisONE** (http://law.lexisnexis.com/webcenters/lexisone/). You can search for forms by keyword and limit the forms by jurisdiction. Beneath the jurisdiction list there is a link for *Pay Forms* and another for *Free Forms* that will provide lists of each.

To search a database by state and practice area for over 104,000 free forms (court and transactional) and contracts, see **LawInfo,** (http://resources.lawinfo.com) and select a practice area from the *Forms* drop-down menu. Another drop-down menu will then appear to select a jurisdiction.

See **LLRX** for links to federal, state, and local court forms (http://www.llrx.com/courtrules). You can keyword search the collection of more than 1,400 forms using the *Find* box at the top of the page. You can use the three *Browse by one or more fields* search menus: (1) *Select Jurisdiction* (choose *Federal* or *State*), (2) *Select Type* (choose *Forms*)*,* and (3) *Select State*. You can also browse the forms by *Court Type (Federal & State)*, *Type of Resource (Federal & State)*, *Jurisdiction (Federal* or *State)*, or *States*.

Many state and local court forms are also accessible at each court's official Web site and sometimes at state and local bar association sites.

To access Federal tax forms and tax publications back to 1980, visit the **IRS** Web site (http://www.irs.gov/formspubs/index.html). The site can be browsed by *Form and Instruction number, Topical index*, and *Previous years*. There is an *Advanced Search* link (http://search.irs.gov/web/advanced-search.htm), located under the search box in the upper right-hand corner of the page, where you can enter keywords into various search boxes. You can search the *Entire Site*, limit the search to *Forms and Instructions* or to *Publications* (among other choices), limit results to a specific *File Format* (e.g., *PDF*), or choose a time range from the *Date Last Updated* drop-down menu. Forms from 1998 through the current tax year can be filled in online and saved to your hard drive. Those who own the full professional version of Adobe Acrobat can "typewriter enable" the 1980–1997 forms to fill them in and save to their hard drive. (See page 443.)

For links to states that have tax forms online free, see the **Federation of Tax Administrators'** site (http://www.taxadmin.org/fta/link/forms.html).

For links to every state insurance department and to insurance news for each state, see **Insure.com** (http://www.insure.com/articles/statesinsurance/). **Insure.com's** mission "is dedicated to providing impartial insurance information to consumers." Aside from the useful links, the site has a commercial side; it provides instant quotes from more than 200 insurers and insurance brokerage and policy placement services for site visitors.

Intellectual Property

See the **U.S. Patent and Trademark Office** (**USPTO**) site (http://www.uspto.gov) to search patent and trademark text and image databases. Although there is an *Interested in Copyrights* link (see at the bottom of the right-hand, *IP Law & Policy* column in the illustration below), the **USPTO** does not handle copyrights (see pages 409–410); the link takes you to information about the Office of the Administrator for External Affairs - Copyrights and provides a link to the **U.S. Copyright Office** site. The **USPTO** site also links to international and other countries' IP offices (http://www.uspto.gov/faq/other.jsp).

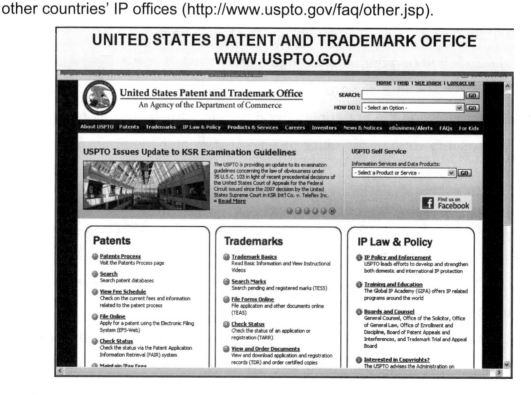

Google's Patent Search (http://www.google.com/patents) uses Google's familiar search interface to provide access to over seven million patents dating back to 1790.

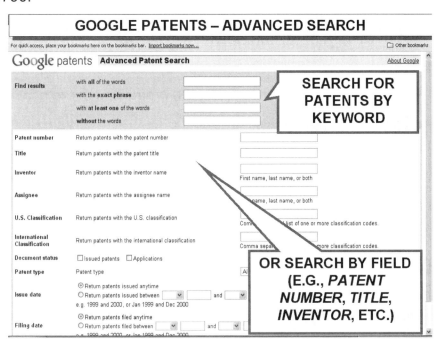

Google Patents' *Advanced Search* page allows for keyword and phrase searches similar to those on the **Google** Web search *Advanced Search* page. Additionally, you can search for information in specific areas of the patent document, such as *Patent number*, *Title*, *Inventor*, *Assignee*, and more.

Google also hosts downloadable versions of Patent data (grants, published applications, assignments, classification information, and maintenance fee events) and Trademark data (registrations, applications, assignments, and TTAB proceedings) (http://www.google.com/googlebooks/uspto.html).

Patent information can also be retrieved via **Google Scholar** (http://scholar.google.com) searches, but **Google Patents** offers more options to create a targeted search for this information.

The **American Intellectual Property Law Association's** (**AIPLA**) Web site (http://www.aipla.org/) is a legal association of 17,000 attorneys who deal with national and international intellectual property issues. Portions of the Web site are member-only. The *IP Issues and Advocacy* tab provides the full text of current IP legislation, **AIPLA's** Amicus briefs, and its Congressional testimony.

Journals and Magazines (General)

Before using any pay sites, visit your public library's Web site to see if they provide remote access to pay databases (and their articles) for free (for details, see pages 145–146). **IngentaConnect.com** (http://www.ingentaconnect.com) allows visitors to search and view (free of charge) abstracts of over four million articles, chapters, and reports from over 13,000 professional and academic publications. Visitors can purchase the full text of any article by credit card (prices vary). **BNET FindArticles** (http://www.findarticles.com/) is a keyword searchable archive of millions of published articles back to 1984 from thousands of academic, industry, and general interest magazines. Searching and reading the article annotations is free, but not all articles are free to view in full text. You can keyword search for articles using the search box on the home page or you can browse for publication by category (such as *Business* or *Reference*) from the links to the right of the *Find Articles In* label near the top of the page. Sometimes you can find a free article by simply entering the title, as a phrase, into a general search engine's search box (e.g., **Google** or **Yahoo!**).

Journals and Magazines (Legal)

The **University of Texas's Tarlton Law Library's Contents Pages from Law Reviews and Other Scholarly Journals** site (http://linkon.in/aPlfD5) offers a keyword searchable database to tables of contents for 750 U.S. and foreign law reviews (most recent three months only). The site is updated daily. If you can't find a free copy of the article you need, it can be ordered online for a fee from the Tarlton Law Library.

Washington and Lee Law School's Current Law Journal Content site (http://linkon.in/b2SGVV) takes **Tarlton's** database a few steps further by adding tables of contents from more journals (almost 1,600) and by going back further in time (to the year 2000 for most journals and 2005 for others). You can search articles and abstracts by author, title, journal name, or keywords. Wildcard searching and Boolean searching are available (for search tips, see http://linkon.in/a3xGvR). Links to the full text of articles may be provided, but not always from a free source.

The **A.B.A. Legal Technology Resource Center** (http://linkon.in/9HMlVi) has created a free full-text law review/law journal search engine with over 350 online law reviews and law journals. It also searches select online document repositories hosting academic papers and related publications such as Congressional Research Service reports. The search includes several foreign and international law journals. Coverage dates and online availability of the full text of articles varies from publication to publication.

The **University of Southern California (USC) Law Library** provides lists of law journals by category (e.g., *Subject Specific, Commercial, General, Foreign*) and indicates whether the articles are available as a paid subscription only or online for free in these formats: (1) in full text, (2) as abstracts only, or (3) in a table of contents format (http://linkon.in/alkIEk). Before using any pay sites, visit your public library's Web site to see if they provide remote access to any legal pay databases that contain articles (such as **LegalTrac**), for free (for details, see pages 145–146).

In the Fall of 2009, **Google** added *Legal Opinions and Journals* to its existing *Scholar* search of scholarly journals. See pages 295–299 for more information on searching this resource.

Legal Ethics

Cornell's American Legal Ethics Library
(http://www.law.cornell.edu/ethics) links to each state's code of professional responsibility, ethics opinions, disciplinary procedures, code of judicial conduct, and bar admissions rules (click on *Listing by Jurisdiction* to select a state). Commentary (referred to as *Narratives)* is also offered for twenty-two states and may include references to case law. In addition, there is a topical database (*Listing by Topic*) that shows which jurisdictions' rules are based on the A.B.A.'s Model Rules or its Model Code (or neither — e.g., California). Each rule from

each of the twenty-two jurisdictions for which the site has *Narratives* is compared to the Model Rule and Model Code.

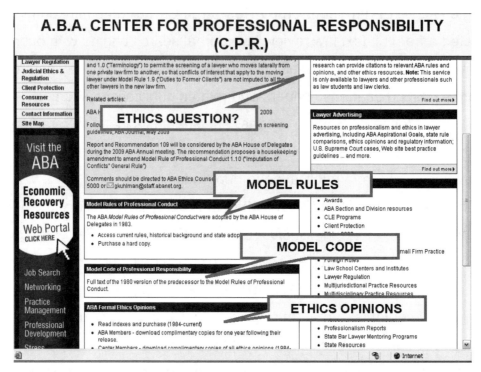

The **American Bar Association Center for Professional Responsibility** (**C.P.R.**) site (http://www.abanet.org/cpr/) posts the *Model Rules* online for free, with comments (http://linkon.in/cshkzE). The site offers free access to summaries of recent *Formal Opinions* (http://linkon.in/d6kqER). **C.P.R.** members have full-text access to all opinions from all years (back to 1984), while A.B.A. members can access opinions for free for one year from their date of release. Archived opinions can be purchased online for $7.50 each. *ETHICSearch* is another service offered on the A.B.A. site; it provides free initial consultations to ethics inquiries (http://linkon.in/bxX9Tt). Use this URL for links to all of the above-mentioned A.B.A. resources from one place: http://linkon.in/aJvYt8.

The **LegalEthics.com** (http://www.legalethics.com) blog, offered by Internet Legal Services (and updated by Professor David Hricik of Mercer University School of Law and Peter Krakaur), contains brief annotations about ethics issues, including new ethics opinions and court cases involving attorney ethical issues. The site can be keyword searched or browsed by topic (listed on the right side of the home page). Topics include *Advertising, Ethics Opinions,* and *Confidentiality.* There is also a *States* link that, when clicked, lists state-specific ethics material from the blog. Archived material is available back to 1995. There are a few longer ethics-related articles available by clicking the *Articles* link in the right-hand column, but they are not current.

Litigation/Practice Tools

Every litigator must assess a case's worth before agreeing to take that case. Researching verdicts and settlements of similar cases can help litigators with the assessment process. For details on free and pay jury verdict databases, see page 194.

Finding expert witnesses is another important litigation task. For details on free and pay expert witness databases, see pages 187–189.

Other litigation tasks include drafting pleadings, researching, and writing briefs. Finding samples of pleadings and briefs can speed these tasks along. They can serve as writing samples and also as research guides to the leading cases and statutes on the topic. Many government agencies, professional associations, law firms, and vendors offer sample litigation documents — some free and some for a fee. For example, (1) the professional association **AIPLA** posts its intellectual property-related amicus briefs online for free (see page 417; http://www.aipla.org); (2) the U.S. government's **PACER** site includes various federal court briefs at a low cost of $2.40, which can be searched topically using the NOS code (see page 383; http://www.pacer.gov); and (3) the commercial portal **FindLaw** posts U.S. Supreme Court briefs for free (see page 244; http://linkon.in/bZla9e).

Access to jury instructions, court rules, court dockets, and court forms are other needs of every litigator. Links to publicly available electronic versions of state jury instructions can be found at **LLRX.com** (http://www.llrx.com/columns/reference53.htm). Links to over 1,400 court dockets, forms, or rules online are also found at **LLRX.com's** *Court Rules, Forms and Dockets* database discussed on page 382 (http://www.llrx.com/courtrules/).

The **American Medical Association** (**AMA**) site (http://www.ama-assn.org/) is a good starting point to find information about nearly every one of the 814,000 licensed physicians in the United States. Unfortunately, it takes about five click-throughs to actually reach the search page where we can search the information we want. First, select the *DoctorFinder* link located on the right side of the site's home page. Second, enter the words or numbers you see in the Captcha image (Captcha is used to determine whether the user is human or just automated software). Third, scroll down and click on the image labeled *For Patients.* Fourth, click on the *DoctorFinder* link. Fifth, read the disclaimer and click *Accept.* You can search by *Last Name* or by *Speciality* (a *ZIP code* or *State* is required for both searches). Adding a *First Name* or a *City* is optional. Basic background and contact information is provided. You won't find any discipline information at the **AMA** database, but you might find some if you visit the **Association of State Medical Board Executive Directors DocFinder** site (http://www.docboard.org/docfinder.html). This site simultaneously searches twenty states' physician license databases and five osteopathic license databases. Discipline information is sometimes included. There are also links to the other states' licensing boards, and there you might find discipline information.

To conduct medical-related research, you can search several **National Library of Medicine** (NLM) databases simultaneously, using **NLM's Gateway** site (http://gateway.nlm.nih.gov/gw/Cmd). Some results are citations only, while others could be full text, audio, video, or images. Some of the more popular databases are **Clinical Trials** and **MedLine/PubMed. MedLine/PubMed** provides millions of abstracts to medical, toxicological, and forensic medicine literature back to 1950. Some results have links to the full text of the article (free) while others must be ordered for a fee. Before paying for any articles, check your library's remote databases (see pages 145–146) to see if they offer the full text for free. The site was redesigned in 2008; detailed search tips for the site are at http://www.nlm.nih.gov/pubs/techbull/jf08/jf08_gateway_redesign.html.

See **Cornell LII's Real Property Resources** page
(http://topics.law.cornell.edu/wex/real_property) for links to statutes and cases
relating to real property law. See pages 156–159 for information regarding
Property Assessor's records, and see **Zillow** on page 158 for information about
"zestimates" of real property values.

Securities Law

The **U.S. Securities and Exchange Commission's (S.E.C.)** site
(http://www.sec.gov/) has reams of information about securities law, litigation,
and regulations, and also provides access to **S.E.C.** company filings. (For
detailed information about searching **S.E.C.** filings — full text or by company
name — see page 167.) To obtain dockets for over 3,000 class action securities
fraud matters filed since 1996, with the full text of nearly 40,000 complaints,
briefs, and orders, see **Stanford's Securities Class Action Clearinghouse**
(http://securities.stanford.edu). The site also contains opinions, articles,
settlement news, reports, and charts about securities litigation. The

Clearinghouse offers two types of searches to retrieve documents from this collection. Both are accessed by clicking the *Search* link in the left-hand column. The *Database Records Search* allows you to search the filings by *Litigation Name, Ticker, Date, Industry Classification (Sector)*, *Securities Market,* and *Court*, among other criteria. According to the site, it will, "retrieve a list of filings that match the search criteria." The *Google Text Search* allows for keyword, Boolean, and natural language searching. According to the site, it will, "locate Webpages, including news articles and court filings, on our site that match the search keywords." The collection can also be browsed in a variety of ways at http://securities.stanford.edu/companies.html#All: (1) by their sub-indexes: *Chronological Index* (year), *First Character Index* (party name*, Alphabetical and Numerical Index*); (2) by choosing a year or a type of lawsuit from the *Chart: Filings By Type Of Lawsuit*; (3) by choosing a circuit from the *U.S. Court of Appeals* map; or (4) by using the search page which allows you to search by up to twelve criteria, in addition to keywords and phrases.

Check out your broker's background at the **Financial Industry Regulatory Authority** (**FINRA**) site (http://www.finra.org/Industry/index.htm) by clicking on the *FINRA BrokerCheck* link (the first link on the far right-hand column) or go directly to http://brokercheck.finra.org/Support/TermsAndConditions.aspx. Note: **FINRA** was formerly known as the **National Association of Securities Dealers** (**NASD**).

Tax Law

Besides the **IRS** site (http://www.irs.gov) noted earlier in the *Forms* section of this chapter (page 414), see **TAXSites.com**, which has divided its list of tax links into three categories: *Tax, Accounting*, and *Payroll/HR* (http://www.taxsites.com).

The **U.S. Tax Court's** *TC and Memorandum Decisions* (1995–present) and its *Summary Decisions* (2001–present) are available online in a searchable database (http://www.ustaxcourt.gov/UstcInOp/asp/HistoricOptions.asp). The search can be by one or more of the following criteria: *Text Search* (keywords), *Date Search, Case Name Keyword, Judge,* and *Opinion Type* (choose *All Types, TC, Memorandum,* or *Summary*). Use the *Sort by* drop-down menu to view your results by *Case Name* or *Release Date*. Dockets are also online and can be searched by *Docket Number, Individual Party Name,* or *Corporate Name Keyword* (http://www.ustaxcourt.gov/docket.htm).

Chapter Sixteen

HOW TO CITE RESOURCES ON THE INTERNET

For insight into how to cite to a site (Web site), the 19th edition of *The Bluebook: A Uniform System of Citation* provides more solutions than previous editions. The rules about citing to material on the Internet (Rules 18.2 through 18.7.3) have now been revised and expanded to acknowledge the increasing reliance people have placed on information found on the Internet. Examples of the expanded rules vary from how to cite to blogs and a rule that one should cite to PDFs rather than HTML documents (because the document's page numbers are more likely to be preserved in a PDF version over an HTML version of the document), to a rule allowing the use of timestamps to identify frequently updated sources, to guidance for citing podcast and online video recordings. Yet, the *Bluebook* still discourages citing to Web sites unless the materials are unavailable in printed form because sites can be so transient and can disappear from the Web. If no one is able to find and verify your citation to a Web site, you will not be allowed to rely upon it any longer for your argument. See pages 5–6 to learn how to save an Internet page to your computer.

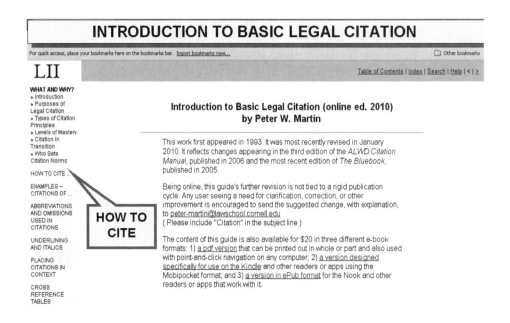

The *Bluebook* is now online (for a fee) at http://www.legalbluebook.com. Note that free PDF versions of editions 1-15 are available at http://www.legalbluebook.com/Public/Introduction.aspx. For those who are looking for a more current free alternative, visit **Cornell's** Web site and browse through its *Introduction to Basic Legal Citation* (http://www.law.cornell.edu/citation), which provides excellent examples of *Bluebook* citations. The information was last updated in 2005 to correlate to the 18th edition of the *Bluebook,* and it was updated again in 2010 to correlate to a newer legal citation manual, the *ALWD Citation Manual*, published by the Association of Legal Writing Directors (whose 3rd edition was published in 2006). To read about citing to Internet and other electronic resources in particular, look on the left side of the **Cornell** Web page and click *How to Cite* and then click *Electronic Sources*.

An Internet citation is required if the source is only found on the Internet. However, an Internet citation may be added as a parallel citation to a print version of a document, if it makes the source more accessible. The Internet citation should consist of all the same elements required by the *Bluebook* for any of the basic document types found in print. If the Internet citation is added as a parallel citation to the print source, indicate this by adding the explanatory phrase *available at* (in italics as shown below) prior to the Internet source citation.

For example, you would cite to a print version of a U.S. Supreme Court case that is also found on the **Cornell** site in this manner:

> *Hill v. Colorado*, 200 U.S. 404 (2000), *available at*
> http://supct.law.cornell.edu/supct/html/98-1856.ZS.html.

If the electronic source is the only known source, such as an e-mail, then no explanatory phrase is used, according to Rule 17.2.4. The following is an example of how to cite to an e-mail:

> E-mail from Beverly Loder, Director of Publications, ABA LPM, to Carole Levitt, Internet For Lawyers, Inc. (Oct. 31, 2005 06:15:01 CST) (on file with recipient).

If a journal appears only on the Internet, include (1) the author's name, (2) the volume number, (3) the title of the journal, (4) the sequential article number, (5) the paragraph number (if pinpoint citing), (6) the publication date if available (or the most recent modification date of the site, or the date you visited the site), and (7) the URL (with no explanatory phrase). For example:

> Carole Levitt, *How to Use the Internet for Legal Research*, 3 Net For Lawyers L. J. 1, par.8 (July 20, 1999),
> http://www.netforlawyers.com/levitt.html.

For blog posts, include (1) the author's name; (2) Title; (3) Main page title; (4) Titles for pages other than the main page, if relevant; (5) URL; and (6) Date and time of researchers last visit [if no clear dates are available referring to the material being cited]. For example:

> Mark Rosch, *Google Voice Now Open and Free to All - in the United States,* Internet For Lawyers,
> http://www.netforlawyers.com/content/google-voice-now-open-and-free-all-united-states, (Oct. 13, 2010 10:12:01 PST).

There are two schools of thought regarding the use of angle brackets ("< >") to set off URLs in citations. The first camp believes in following *The Chicago Manual of Style*, which does not favor using angle brackets because they can cause confusion (Web site designers also use angle brackets as part of Web page mark-up languages, such as HTML or XML).

The other camp thinks angle brackets are useful to show where a URL begins and ends. Starting with the 18th edition, the *Bluebook* no longer appears to use the angle brackets. In this book we often place URLs in parentheses to indicate where the URL begins and ends and to avoid the mark-up language confusion over angle brackets.

In 1996, the American Bar Association (A.B.A.) approved a resolution recommending that courts adopt a uniform public domain citation system "equally effective for printed case reports and for case reports electronically published on computer disks or network services." For a full copy of this report, go to http://www.abanet.org/tech/ltrc/research/citation/report.html. In February 2003, the A.B.A. House of Delegates passed the Universal Citation Facilitation Recommendation to supplement the 1996 resolution (http://www.abanet.org/tech/ltrc/research/citation/2003report.html). The following example is offered by the A.B.A. for citation to a Federal Court of Appeals decision found on an electronic site:

Smith v. Jones, 1996 5Cir 15, ¶ 18, 22 F.3d 955

The A.B.A. instructs that if a case is only available on the Internet, print it out for opposing counsel and the court.

The American Association of Law Libraries (AALL) published the *AALL Universal Citation Guide* to implement the A.B.A.'s resolution. The *Guide* is now in its second edition (version 2.1). It was placed online for public comment (http://www.aallnet.org/committee/citation/ucg/index.html) and is still available for free at that URL, but we are not certain if it represents the final version. The print version can be ordered at http://www.aallnet.org/products/pub_universal.asp. About seventeen states, two territories, one state trial court, and the 6th Circuit Court of Appeals have adopted a uniform citation standard (http://www.abanet.org/tech/ltrc/research/citation/uscourts.html).

Finally, if you don't find a specific rule or example in any of these sources, provide as much information as you can in your citation. Also, print out a copy of the material (as the A.B.A. instructs you to do for cases on the Internet) or use citation examples from either of the two nationally recognized general citation style manuals: the **A.P.A. (American Psychological Association)** *Electronic Sources Formats* at http://www.apastyle.org/learn or the *Chicago Manual of Style Online* at http://www.chicagomanualofstyle.org/home.html. The *Chicago Manual of Style* has a link on its home page to the *Chicago Style Q + A*, which offers helpful Internet citation tips. For example, the *Q + A* instructs us to use "Web site" (and not "website" or "web site"). The editors of the manual also welcome questions from readers. The answer may come as an individual response or may appear on the *Q + A* page. The *Q + A* can be browsed or keyword searched (there is a *Search* box at the top of the page on the right-hand side). After you conduct a search, the results page displays results in three categories: *The Chicago Manual of Style*, *Chicago Style Q + A* only, or *Forum*.

Chapter Seventeen

TECHNOLOGY TIPS

USING A "SEARCH ENGINE" FOR THE FILES ON YOUR OWN COMPUTER

The **Google Desktop Search** (http://desktop.google.com) makes it easy to find information on your own hard drive. This free application offers full-text searching through almost everything on your hard drive simultaneously — from Word documents and e-mail messages to Web history, chats, and Web pages you've visited previously (even when you're not online). It can even locate documents you've deleted (if they are still in your computer's "Trash" bin). The **Google Desktop Search**, like the **Google** search engine, creates an index of documents on your hard drive and maintains cached versions of the documents as you make changes.

To run the **Desktop Search**, your computer must have Windows® XP Service Pack 2 or newer (including Vista and Windows 7) and you must be using Microsoft Internet Explorer version 5 or newer, or Firefox 1.5 or newer. Versions of the Desktop Search are also available to Linux users running glibc 2.3.2+ or gtk+ 2.2.0+. For Mac users with operating system 10.5 or newer, the **Desktop Search** has been replaced by a similar product – **Google Quicksearch Box**.

Once the download is complete, you'll have an icon on your desktop labeled, aptly enough, *Desktop Setup.exe*. Double click on this to begin the installation process. During the installation process you are given the opportunity to opt out of providing **Google** with non-identifying search usage information. Opting out of providing this information to **Google** is one way to insure that your computer is not communicating externally "on its own."

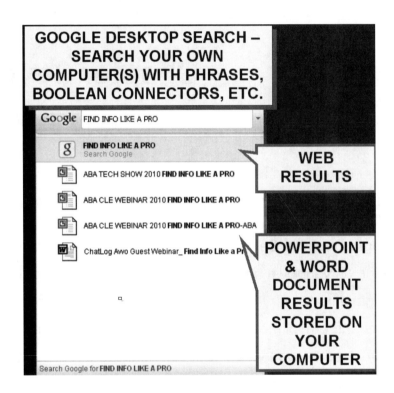

After the installation process is complete, double click the *Google Desktop Search* icon that appears on your desktop (or in the "System Tray" in the lower right-hand corner of your screen) and a *Google Desktop Search* box will appear on your desktop (pictured above).

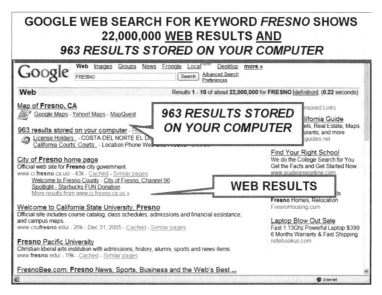

Once installed, the **Desktop Search** can be configured to simultaneously run a **Google** *Web search* and a *Desktop Search* in your Web browser. The items at the top of the results list will show documents available on your hard drive (*Google Integration*). Regular Web search results follow below (see illustration above). (Note, the *Desktop Search* box that appears on your computer's desktop [see the illustration on the previous page] also follows these same preferences.)

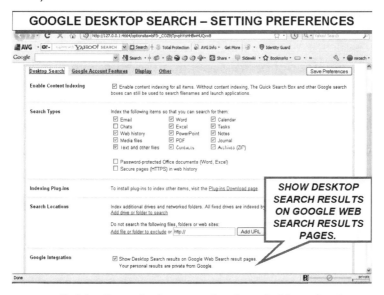

You can turn off this *Google Integration* by clicking *Options* on the **Google Desktop Search** box at the bottom of your computer's desktop (or the *Desktop Preferences* link on the **Google** *Desktop Search* home page when you're viewing it in your Web browser) and unchecking the *Google Integration* box (found by clicking on the *Desktop Search* tab). There are also a variety of other customization options available on the *Desktop Preferences* screens. For example, you can select the type of files to be indexed (*Word*, *Excel*, *Chats*, *Web History*, etc.) as seen in the previous illustration. You can also locate and install *Indexing Plug-ins* to index file types not included on the list, such as WordPerfect.

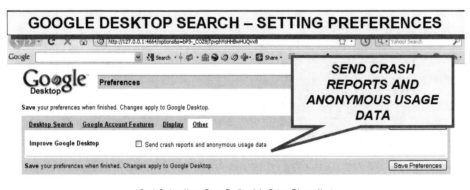

Also, if you did not opt out of providing **Google** with non-identifying search usage information during the installation process, you can do so afterwards by clicking the *Other* preference tab and unchecking the *Send crash reports and anonymous usage data* box.

The **Desktop Search** is useful, but still has a number of quirks to be worked out. For example, like **Google's** Web search, the **Desktop Search** creates cached copies of previous versions of your documents throughout the editing process (see pages 109–110). So, occasionally, documents may turn up in the **Desktop Search** results list because your keyword or phrase appears in one or more of the cached versions of the document even though you've edited it out of the current version. Also, when viewing a current document from the **Desktop Search** result list, search terms are not highlighted, but if you view a cached version, they are. We'd prefer to see the words highlighted in the current version.

The **Google Desktop Search** is available as part of the **Google Pack** free suite of utilities (http://pack.google.com). The **Google Pack** includes: Google's Chrome Web browser, Firefox Web browser (with Google Toolbar), Google Toolbar for Internet Explorer, Spyware Doctor (with Anti-Virus), Adobe Reader, Skype, Google Earth, and others. Using a simple checklist, you can select which of the utilities you want to download and install onto your computer.

The free **Windows Search 4.0** (http://www.microsoft.com/windows/desktopsearch/) offers a more robust Desktop search option for computers running Windows XP. Similar free options are also available for Windows Vista (Business, Ultimate, and Enterprise editions) and Windows 7 (Enterprise or Professional editions). **Copernic** (http://www.copernic.com) also offers a free **Desktop search** for personal use on Windows computers. In addition, there are several pay Desktop search applications, including **Copernic's** *Professional* and *Corporate* editions, **X1** (http://www.x1.com), and **ISYS** (http://www.isys-search.com/technology/isysworkgroup/index.html), among others.

The paid version of Adobe Acrobat (http://linkon.in/d4kEsC) is an excellent resource for attorneys to create, share, and manage documents to which Adobe is continually adding new features. As this book went to press, Adobe announced a new Version X. The most current version in wide use is Version 9. Acrobat 9 Professional Extended has a number of tools lawyers will find useful — the least of which is creating PDF documents. One advantage to creating or distributing documents in the Portable Document Format (PDF) is that you don't have to worry about whether the recipients have the proper software (or version) to open a WordPerfect or Word document that you send them. As long as the recipients have the free Adobe Reader software (http://get.adobe.com/reader/), they can read and in some instances collaborate with you on the document. With over a half-billion copies of the free Reader software in circulation, there's a good chance that the individual you send a PDF to will have the ability to read it.

An excellent resource for any attorney using Acrobat in their practice is the ABA's *The Lawyer's Guide to Adobe Acrobat* (http://linkon.in/b660L8). Additionally, Adobe has created a series of pages highlighting the features of the new Version X at http://www.adobe.com/products/acrobatpro/features.html.

Version 9 of Acrobat Pro Extended allows you as the creator of PDF documents to give more power to recipients reviewing documents in the free Adobe Reader. Acrobat Pro users can give document recipients with newer versions of the free Reader program the ability to suggest edits, add annotations, and add comments to PDF documents they receive.

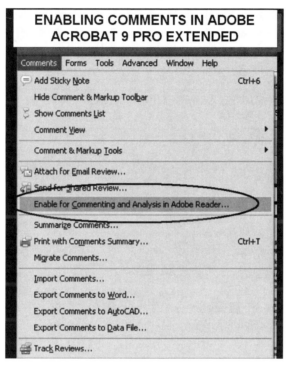

This is accomplished by clicking on *Comments* in the Acrobat Pro Extended Menu bar at the top of the document and then *Enable for Commenting and Analysis in Adobe Reader* on the subsequent drop-down menu prior to sending the document. All of the recipient's "mark-up" is added on top of the original document, so their changes do not permanently alter the original document and can be undone.

Until the release of version 8 of Acrobat Pro, it was necessary to purchase a third party add-on program if you wanted to add sequential numbering to a collection of documents ("Bates" numbering). While in earlier versions it was possible to add a running "header" at the top of a collection of documents that could serve as Bates numbers, there wasn't a dedicated feature until version 8. Version 9 of Acrobat Pro Extended has added greater flexibility in adding Bates numbers to collections of documents. In version 9 you can create "portfolios" of PDF and non-PDF documents and apply Bates numbers to all of them in a batch.

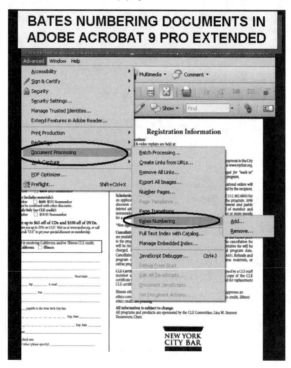

To begin Bates Numbering a document, click on *Advanced* in the Acrobat Pro Extended Menu bar at the top of the document and then *Document Processing*, *Bates Numbering* and then *Add* on the subsequent drop-down menus. The Bates numbers can be removed at a later time by selecting *Remove* on the last drop-down menu.

Version 8 of Acrobat Pro added the ability to completely remove blocks of text from a PDF document so that they cannot subsequently be recovered or discovered. Some previous methods of redacting information from documents did cover the text from view, but left the text intact "underneath." In many cases, recipients of these documents were able to extract the information the document's creator thought they had redacted—much to the chagrin and occasional embarrassment of the sender. Governments, large law firms, and courts have all been caught using this ineffectual form of redaction.

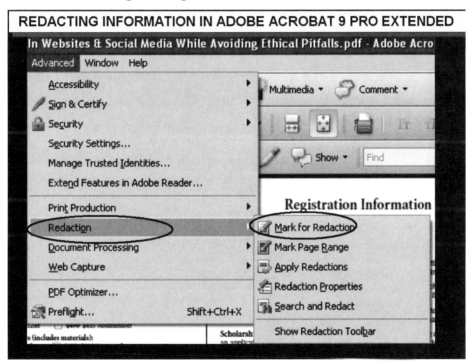

Acrobat Professional's redaction tool allows you to permanently remove all traces of the information the document's creator marks for removal, replacing it with a black box. Adobe *tells* us that once the information is removed, it cannot be recovered — even by the redactor. So, if you will need an un-redacted version of the document, be sure to make a copy prior to redaction.

This redaction tool can be found by clicking *Advanced* on the Menu bar and then *Redaction* and then *Mark for Redaction* on the subsequent drop-down menus (see above).

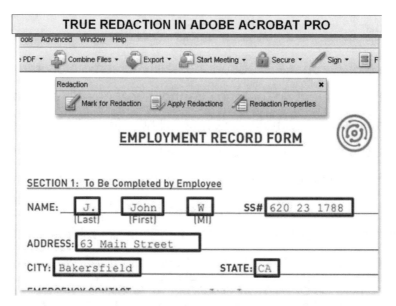

Once you've marked all of the information in the PDF that you want to redact (as shown above), clicking *Advanced* on the Menu bar and then *Redaction* and then *Apply Redaction* on the subsequent drop-down menus deletes the content you marked and replaces it with black boxes (as seen below).

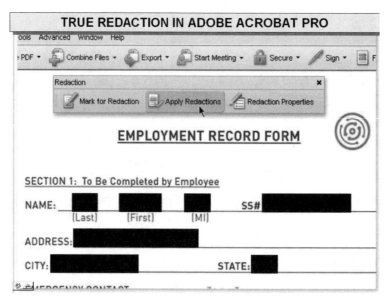

Adobe has also added a *Search and Redact* feature to Version 9 of Acrobat Pro Extended. This allows you to search for a *Single Word or Phrase*, *Multiple Words or Phrases*, or *Patterns* (e.g., Social Security Numbers, or phone numbers) and automatically redact them. This feature can be found by clicking *Advanced* on the Menu bar and then *Redaction* and then *Search and Redact* on the subsequent drop-down menus.

More and more, government agencies, courts, and other entities are posting their forms online as PDF files. Unfortunately, not every organization has the time or budget to make those forms interactive—giving you the ability to fill in the blanks electronically. With Acrobat Pro Extended's *Typewriter* feature, you can easily turn just about any PDF form you find online into a fill-in-able document. For documents that you need to fill in only once or twice, the *Typewriter* feature in Acrobat Pro Extended is the easiest way to enter information directly into the electronic form if the creator didn't already enable that feature.

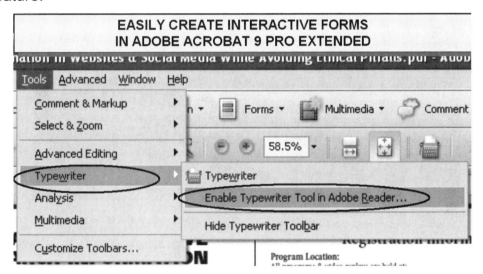

By clicking on *Tools* in the Menu bar at the top of the document, then *Typewriter* on the subsequent drop-down menu, and then *Enable Typewriter in Adobe Reader*, you (or anyone you send that document to who is using a newer version of the free Reader) will be able to place your cursor anywhere in the document and type in the requested information.

For forms that you might use repeatedly or want to post as interactive documents on your Web site, Acrobat Pro Extended has more sophisticated form recognition and creation tools that can be accessed by clicking on *Forms* in the Menu bar.

Some search engines (e.g., **Google**, **AltaVista**, **Yahoo!**, **Bing**) have created specialized tool bars to enhance your Web browsing by allowing you to perform a search no matter what Web page you're looking at. Generally free, toolbars seamlessly integrate with your Web browser and are easily downloaded and installed.

To install the **AltaVista Toolbar**, go to http://www.altavista.com/toolbar. The highlight of its toolbar is the *Translate* tab, which you can click to immediately translate a Web page into one of ten languages. The **Yahoo! Toolbar** can be downloaded at http://toolbar.yahoo.com/. It includes automatic notification of incoming mail to your free Yahoo! Mail account. **Bing** also offers a feature-laden **Toolbar** that gives instant access to its search features and other Microsoft services like **Hotmail** at http://www.discoverbing.com/toolbar. To install the **Google Toolbar**, go to http://toolbar.google.com/.

The **Google Toolbar** includes the following features:

- *Web* — allows you to access **Google** search from any Web page

- *Search Site* — searches only the pages of the site being viewed

- *PageRank* — see Shows **Google's** ranking of any page on the Web

- *Highlight all* — highlights search terms as they appear on the page — each word in its own color

- *Google Patents* — gives you one-click access to **Google's** search interface of U.S. Patent and Trademark Office (USPTO) patents back to 1790

- *Web History* — allows you to view searches conducted while logged into your free **Google** account and to keyword search through the list to locate specific searches

- *AutoFill* — completes Web forms with information that's saved securely on your own computer

- *New Tab Page* — gives you quick access to your most-frequently visited pages, recently-visited pages, or bookmarks

The newest version of the **Google Toolbar** requires Microsoft Windows XP, Vista, or 7 operating system and Microsoft Internet Explorer version 6.0 or newer. A version of the **Toolbar** is also available for the Firefox browser (version 2 or newer) running on Windows XP SP 2+/Vista/7 or Mac OS X 10.4 and above. Users of older Windows or Mac operating systems (or older browsers) can still download some previous versions of the **Toolbar** for their use via the *Previous version* link (when available).

KEEPING UP WITH YOUR PRACTICE AREA AND WITH TECHNOLOGY

There are so many ways to keep up with technology and your practice area, from mailing lists and e-newsletters to blogs, podcasts, RSS feeds, and even social networking sites like **LinkedIn**, **Twitter**, and **Facebook**, that it can become overwhelming. Select a few resources that cover the areas you are most interested in and set aside some time on a regular basis so you can keep up with your practice area and also with technology.

Mailing Lists — Your Online Community

Mailing lists (which are also referred to as "listservers," "listserves," or "discussion groups") are online communities typically devoted to one area of interest, such as an area of law or a technology issue. ("Listserv" refers to a specific type of mailing list software.) Mailing lists are similar to a roundtable discussion. When you join a mailing list, you become a subscriber who can post questions, answers, and comments to the list (via e-mail), and the postings will automatically be distributed to all of the other subscribers. You can also view other subscribers' questions, answers, and comments. It's a useful way of sharing information and keeping current. The messages appear in your e-mail in-box automatically, in contrast to newsgroups or bulletin boards, which require you to log onto a specific Internet location in order to view postings. Membership in some lists is by invitation only or restricted to individuals with specific credentials (e.g., family lawyers or private investigators), but many are open to anyone. Some lists are moderated by a gatekeeper who monitors the e-mails to insure they are appropriate, while others are un-moderated.

Visit **CataList** (http://www.lsoft.com/catalist.html) to keyword search any of the 53,227 public LISTSERV lists on the Internet or browse by country or host country. For a directory of A.B.A. law-related mailing lists, see http://mail.abanet.org/archives/index.html.

Some excellent mailing lists to join to keep up with the Internet or with technology as it affects the legal field are (1) **A.B.A.'s LawTech** and **Site-tation** (http://www.abanet.org/tech/ltrc/lists.html), (2) **A.B.A.'s SOLOSEZ** (http://mail.abanet.org/scripts/wa.exe?A0=SOLOSEZ), and (3) **TechnoLawyer**, with over 13,000 members, (http://www.technolawyer.com/).

Free E-Newsletters and Slip Opinion Alerts

You can visit **ZD Net News** (http://news.zdnet.com/) to read about the latest technology and Internet news. Searching the archive and viewing abstracts of articles is free, but to view the full-text of an article, you will need to register (for free).

You can keep up-to-date with your practice area and your jurisdiction's recent opinions by subscribing to **FindLaw's** free *Daily Case Summaries* (by court or by practice area) or *Weekly Case Summaries* (by practice area) (http://newsletters.findlaw.com/). Some of **FindLaw's** e-newsletters cover general *Legal News Headlines* and others cover specific legal topics. For instance, to receive an e-newsletter on entertainment law, choose *E Legal News* from the list of e-newsletters.

The authors of this book also publish a free e-mail newsletter and blog covering new developments in Internet research, search engine features, and technology useful to attorneys. The newsletter is available free via their **Internet for Lawyers** Web site at http://www.netforlawyers.com/blog.

RSS Feeds Bring Information to You

RSS (which stands for "rich site summary" or "really simple syndication") feed technology allows you to automatically receive new information as it's posted to a blog or other Web site. RSS feeds are, essentially, an electronic update service that allows a Web site to automatically deliver information directly to your desktop on a continual basis. Unlike a newsletter or other traditional online update service you may be familiar with, RSS feeds are not delivered via e-mail.

In order to receive a site's RSS feed, it is necessary to use an "aggregator" or "reader." These readers translate the XML programming language used to create RSS feeds into a list of headlines and abstracts for each of the most recent articles added to a site. Using an RSS reader you can easily keep up with new information from multiple sites by just checking one location (the RSS reader) without having to continually revisit each site individually. There are many different types of RSS aggregators. Most of them are available for download online (and must then be installed after they're downloaded). Some require a monthly service fee or flat usage fee but some are free. **Yahoo!** and **Google** have incorporated RSS reader features into their (free) *My Yahoo!* (http://my.yahoo.com) and *Google* (http://reader.google.com) accounts respectively. Other popular free RSS readers include **Feed Demon** (http://www.feeddemon.com) and **RSSReader** (http://www.rssreader.com).

merlin™
INFORMATION SERVICES

800-367-6646
www.merlindata.com

Free Trial!

Merlin Information Services supports continuing education for attorneys. In appreciation of Internet for Lawyers and the ongoing training they provide, we are pleased to offer a free trial of our online services for legitimate commercial business usage.

Please complete this certificate and fax it to us at 406-755-8568. A representative will contact you to discuss your specific needs. During the free trial, we will show you products and services best suited for your business, including sample searches for your review.

Please note that additional business documentation will be required prior to activating the free trial.

Name: _____

Company: _____ Department: _____

Address: _____

City: _____ State: _____ Zip: _____

Phone Number: _____ E-mail _____ Fax Number: _____

AVVO™ Marketing Solutions

"Avvo has ushered in a new era in lawyer marketing, one where both consumers and lawyers matter. I am proud to be affiliated t with such a visionary and responsible organization."

— Robert Hirshon, President, American Bar Association -- 2001-2002

Free Solutions

Avvo is revolutionizing lawyer marketing with free solutions that make online marketing easy.

Avvo Profile

Your Gateway to New Clients

Your basic profile is already listed on Avvo, all you have to do is "claim" it — it's free!

Search for your profile, go to:
http://www.avvo.com/claim-your-profile

Ask a Lawyer

Cultivate Clients by Answering Questions

Get in front of potential clients by answering their questions in our popular legal Q&A forum.

Avvo Legal Guides

Showcase Your Expertises

Publishing informative and insightful Legal Guides helps to increase your exposure to new clients who are looking for the kind of help you offer.

Advertising Solutions

We also offer smart, low-cost advertising solutions that put you on the fast track to get results.

Avvo Advertising

Smart, Affordable and Targeted

Our eye-catching sponsored listings and display ads get you noticed. When consumers are ready to call, your number is right there.

Avvo Pro

Take Your Profile to the Next Level

With Avvo Pro, convert more Avvo viewers into paying clients. Customize components of your profile, generate more leads through enhanced contact options and track performance with detailed reporting.

Generate more leads. Contact sales.   📱 **800-441-3596**   ✉ ads@avvo.com

SEARCH ENGINE FEATURES COMPARISON CHART
http://linkon.in/8XULKZ

INTERNET FOR LAWYERS

Search

Home > Search Engine Features Compared

Search Engine Features Compared
in Boolean connectors   search engines

Search Engine	Default Boolean Connector	Other Boolean Connectors Recognized	Proximity Connector	Search Term Limit	Cached Pages	Field Searches	Search Limiters
Google	AND	OR, +, -	" ", *	32 (previously had been 10 terms)	Yes	domain, intitle, inurl, link, site, et al	date, filetype, language, site, usage rights
Yahoo!	AND	AND, OR, NOT, -	" ", *	unreported (may be unlimited)	Yes	domain, intitle, inurl, link, site, et al	Creative Commons license, language, file type, date, site
Bing (Formerly Microsoft's Live Search)	AND	AND, OR, NOT, ( ), &, |, -	" ", NEAR	150 characters (previously had been 10 terms)	Yes	domain, inbody, intitle, site	feed, hasfeed, language, locaton, site
Ask	AND	OR, +, -	" "	unreported	No	inlink, intitle, inurl, site	country, date, language, site